FINANCIAL ACCOUNTING REPORTING AND ANALYSIS

At Pearson, we have a simple mission: to help people make more of their lives through learning.

We combine innovative learning technology with trusted content and educational expertise to provide engaging and effective learning experience that serve people wherever and whenever they are learning.

We enable our customers to access a wide and expanding range of market-leading content from world-renowned authors and develop their own tailor-made book. From classroom to boardroom, our curriculum materials, digital learning tools and testing programmes help to educate millions of people worldwide — more than any other private enterprise.

Every day our work helps learning flourish, and wherever learning flourishes, so do people.

To learn more, please visit us at: www.pearson.com/uk

FINANCIAL ACCOUNTING REPORTING AND ANALYSIS

SELECTED CHAPTERS FROM:

FINANCIAL ACCOUNTING FOR DECISION MAKERS
NINTH EDITION
PETER ATRILL & EDDIE MCLANEY

ACCOUNTING AND FINANCE FOR NON-SPECIALISTS
ELEVENTH EDITION
PETER ATRILL & EDDIE MCLANEY

Harlow, England • London • New York • Boston • San Francisco • Toronto • Sydney • Dubai • Singapore • Hong Kong
Tokyo • Seoul • Taipei • New Dehli • Cape Town • São Paulo • Mexico City • Madrid • Amsterdam • Munich • Paris • Milan

Pearson
KAO Two
KAO Park
Harlow
Essex CM17 9NA

And associated companies throughout the world

Visit us on the World Wide Web at:
www.pearson.com/uk

© Pearson Education Limited 2020

Compiled from:

Financial Accounting for Decision Makers
Ninth Edition
Peter Atrill & Eddie McLaney
ISBN 978-1-292-25125-7
© Prentice Hall Europe 1996, 1999 (print)
© Pearson Education Limited 2002, 2005, 2008, 2011 (print)
© Pearson Education Limited 2013, 2016, 2019 (print and electronic)

Accounting and Finance for Non-Specialists
Eleventh Edition
Peter Atrill & Eddie McLaney
ISBN 978-1-292-24401-3
© Prentice Hall Europe 1995, 1997 (print)
© Pearson Education Limited 2001, 2004, 2006, 2008, 2011 (print)
© Pearson Education Limited 2013, 2015, 2017, 2019 (print and electronic)

All rights reserved. No part of this publication may be reproduced, stored in a retrieval system, or transmitted in any form or by any means, electronic, mechanical, photocopying, recording or otherwise, without either the prior written permission of the publisher or a licence permitting restricted copying in the United Kingdom issued by the Copyright Licensing Agency Ltd, Barnard's Inn, 86 Fetter Lane, London, EC4A 1EN.

ISBN 978-1-78764-779-4

Printed and bound in Great Britain by Ashford Colour Press, Gosport, Hampshire.

CONTENTS

Chapter 1 Introduction to accounting   1
Originally chapter 1 in *Financial Accounting for Decision Makers* Ninth Edition
Peter Atrill & Eddie McLaney

Chapter 2 Measuring and reporting financial position   33
Originally chapter 2 in *Financial Accounting for Decision Makers* Ninth Edition
Peter Atrill & Eddie McLaney

Chapter 3 Measuring and reporting financial performance   73
Originally chapter 3 in *Financial Accounting for Decision Makers* Ninth Edition
Peter Atrill & Eddie McLaney

Chapter 4 Accounting for limited companies (1)   116
Originally chapter 4 in *Financial Accounting for Decision Makers* Ninth Edition
Peter Atrill & Eddie McLaney

Chapter 5 Accounting for limited companies (2)   160
Originally chapter 5 in *Financial Accounting for Decision Makers* Ninth Edition
Peter Atrill & Eddie McLaney

Chapter 6 Analysing and interpreting financial statements   202
Originally chapter 6 in *Accounting and Finance for Non-Specialists* Eleventh Edition
Peter Atrill & Eddie McLaney

Chapter 7 Governing a company   253
Originally chapter 12 in *Financial Accounting for Decision Makers* Ninth Edition
Peter Atrill & Eddie McLaney

Appendix A Solutions to self-assessment questions   305

Appendix B Solutions to critical review questions   312

Appendix C Solutions to selected exercises   319

Chapter 1
INTRODUCTION TO ACCOUNTING

INTRODUCTION

We begin this opening chapter of the book by considering the role of accounting. We shall see how accounting can be a valuable tool for decision making. We shall also identify the main users of accounting information and the qualities, or characteristics, needed for accounting information to be useful for decision-making purposes. We shall then go on to consider the two main strands of accounting: financial accounting and management accounting. We shall discuss the differences between them and why these differences arise.

Since this book is mainly concerned with accounting and financial decision making for private-sector businesses, we shall devote some time to examining the business environment. We shall consider the purpose of a private-sector business, the main forms of business enterprise that exist and the ways in which businesses may be structured. We also consider what the key financial objective of a business is likely to be. These are all important factors that help to shape the accounting and financial information produced.

Learning outcomes

When you have completed this chapter, you should be able to:

- explain the nature and role of accounting;
- identify the main users of financial information and discuss their needs;
- identify and discuss the qualities that make accounting information useful; and
- explain the purpose of a business and describe how businesses are organised and structured.

WHAT IS ACCOUNTING?

Accounting is concerned with *collecting*, *analysing* and *communicating* financial information. The ultimate aim is to help those using this information to make more informed decisions. Unless the financial information being communicated can improve the quality of decisions that users make, there is really no point in producing it.

Sometimes the impression is given that the purpose of accounting is simply to prepare financial (accounting) reports on a regular basis. While it is true that accountants undertake this kind of work, it does not represent an end in itself. As already mentioned, the ultimate aim of the accountant's work is to give users better financial information on which to base their decisions. This decision-making perspective of accounting fits in with the theme of the book and shapes the way in which we deal with each topic.

A useful starting point in exploring the subject is to ask who uses financial information and for what kind of decisions it is useful. It is to these issues that we now turn.

WHO ARE THE USERS OF ACCOUNTING INFORMATION?

For accounting information to be useful, the accountant must be clear *for whom* the information is being prepared and *for what purpose* the information will be used. There are likely to be various groups of people (known as 'user groups') with an interest in a particular organisation, in the sense of needing to make decisions about it. For a typical private-sector business, the more important of these groups are shown in Figure 1.1. Take a look at this figure and then try Activity 1.1.

Several user groups have an interest in accounting information relating to a business. The majority of these are outside the business but, nevertheless, have a stake in it. This is not meant to be an exhaustive list of potential users; however, the groups identified are normally the most important.

Figure 1.1 Main users of financial information relating to a business

Activity 1.1

Ptarmigan Insurance plc (PI) is a large motor insurance business. Taking the user groups identified in Figure 1.1, suggest, for each group, the sorts of decisions likely to be made about PI and the factors to be taken into account when making these decisions.

Your answer may be along the following lines:

User group	Decisions likely to be made
Customers	Whether to take further motor policies with PI. This might involve an assessment of PI's ability to continue in business and to meet customers' needs, particularly concerning any insurance claims made.
Competitors	How best to compete against PI or, perhaps, whether to leave the market on the grounds that it is not possible to compete profitably with PI. This might involve competitors using PI's performance in various respects as a 'benchmark' when evaluating their own performance. They might also try to assess PI's financial strength and to identify significant changes that may signal PI's future intentions (for example, raising funds as a prelude to market expansion).
Employees	Whether to continue working for PI and, if so, whether to demand higher rewards for doing so. The future plans, profits and financial strength of the business are likely to be of particular interest when making these decisions.
Government	Whether PI should pay tax and, if so, how much, whether it complies with agreed pricing policies, whether financial support is needed and so on. In making these decisions, an assessment of PI's profits, sales revenues and financial strength would be made.
Community representatives	Whether to allow PI to expand its premises and/or whether to provide economic support for the business. When making such decisions, PI's ability to continue to provide employment for the community, its use of community resources and its willingness to fund environmental improvements are likely to be important considerations.
Investment analysts	Whether to advise clients to invest in PI. This would involve an assessment of the likely risks and future returns associated with PI.
Suppliers	Whether to continue to supply PI with goods or services and, if so, whether to supply these on credit. This would require an assessment of PI's ability to pay for any goods or services supplied at the due dates.
Lenders	Whether to lend money to PI and/or whether to require repayment of any existing loans. PI's ability to pay the interest and to repay the principal sum on time would be important factors in such decisions.
Managers	Whether the performance of the business needs to be improved. Performance to date may be compared with earlier plans or some other 'benchmark' to decide whether action needs to be taken. Managers may also wish to consider a change in PI's future direction. This may involve determining whether the business has the financial flexibility and resources to take on new challenges
Owners	Whether to invest more in PI or to sell all, or part, of the investment currently held. This would involve an assessment of the likely risks and returns associated with PI. Owners may also be involved with decisions on the rewards offered to senior managers. When doing so, the financial performance and position of the business would normally be taken into account.

Although this answer covers many of the key points, you may have identified other decisions and/or other factors to be taken into account by each group.

THE CONFLICTING INTERESTS OF USERS

We have just seen that each user group will have its own particular interests. There is always a risk, however, that the interests of the various user groups will collide. The distribution of business wealth provides the most likely area for collisions to take place. Take, for example, the position of owners and managers. Although managers are appointed to act in the best interests of the owners, they may not always do so. Instead, they may use the wealth of the business to award themselves large pay rises, to furnish large offices or to buy expensive cars for their own use. Accounting can play an important role in monitoring and reporting how various groups benefit from the business. Owners may, therefore, rely on accounting information to see whether pay and benefits received by managers are appropriate and are in line with agreed policies.

There is also a potential collision of interest between lenders and owners. Funds loaned to a business, for example, may not be used for their intended purpose. They may be withdrawn by the owners for their own use rather than used to expand the business as agreed. Thus, lenders may rely on accounting information to see whether the owners have kept to the terms of the loan agreement.

Activity 1.2

Can you think of *two* other examples where accounting information may be relied upon by a user group to check whether the distribution of business wealth is appropriate and/or in accordance with particular agreements?

Two possible examples that spring to mind are:

- employees wishing to check that they are receiving a 'fair share' of the wealth created by the business and that managers are complying with agreed profit-sharing schemes;
- governments wishing to check that the owners of a monopoly do not benefit from excessive profits and that any pricing rules relating to the monopoly's goods or services have not been broken.

You may have thought of other examples.

HOW USEFUL IS ACCOUNTING INFORMATION?

No one would seriously claim that accounting information fully meets all of the needs of each of the various user groups. Accounting is a developing subject and we still have much to learn about user needs and the ways in which these needs should be met. Nevertheless, the information contained in accounting reports should help users make decisions relating to the business. The information should reduce uncertainty about the financial position and performance of the business. It should help to answer questions concerning the availability of funds to pay owners a return, to repay loans, to reward employees and so on.

Typically, there is no close substitute for the information provided by the financial statements. Thus, if users cannot glean the required information from the financial statements, it is often unavailable to them. Other sources of information concerning the financial health of a business are normally much less useful.

Activity 1.3

What other sources of information might, say, an investment analyst use in an attempt to gain an impression of the financial position and performance of a business? (Try to think of at least four.) What kind of information might be gleaned from these sources?

Other sources of information available include:

- meetings with managers of the business;
- public announcements made by the business;
- newspaper and magazine articles;
- websites, including the website of the business;
- radio and TV reports;
- information-gathering agencies (for example, agencies that assess the creditworthiness or credit ratings of the business);
- industry reports; and
- economy-wide reports.

These sources can provide information on various aspects of the business, such as new products or services being offered, management changes, new contracts offered or awarded, the competitive environment within which the business operates, the impact of new technology, changes in legislation, changes in interest rates and future levels of inflation.

The kind of information identified above is not really a substitute for accounting information. Rather, it is best used in conjunction with accounting information to provide a clearer picture of the financial health of a business.

Evidence on the usefulness of accounting

There are arguments, and convincing evidence, that accounting information is at least *perceived* as being useful to users. Numerous research surveys have asked users to rank the importance of accounting information, in relation to other sources of information, for decision-making purposes. Generally, these studies have found that users rank accounting information very highly. There is also considerable evidence that businesses choose to produce accounting information that exceeds the minimum requirements imposed by accounting regulations. For example, businesses often produce a considerable amount of accounting information for managers that is not required by any regulations. Presumably, the cost of producing this additional accounting information is justified on the grounds that users find it useful. Such arguments and evidence, however, leave unanswered the question of whether the information produced is actually used for decision-making purposes, that is: does it affect behaviour?

It is normally very difficult to assess the impact of accounting on decision-making behaviour. One situation arises, however, where the impact of accounting information can be observed and measured. This is where the shares (portions of ownership of a business) are traded on a stock exchange. The evidence shows that, when a business makes an announcement concerning its accounting profits, the prices at which shares are traded and the volume of shares traded often change significantly. This suggests that investors are changing their views about the future prospects of the business as a result of this new information becoming available to them. This, in turn, leads them to make a decision either to buy or to sell shares in the business.

While there is evidence that accounting reports are seen as useful and are used for decision-making purposes, it is impossible to measure just how useful they really are to users.

Activity 1.4

Can you figure out why it is impossible to measure this?

Accounting reports will usually represent only one input to a particular decision. The weight attached to them by the decision maker, and the resulting benefits, cannot normally be accurately assessed.

We cannot say with certainty, therefore, whether the cost of producing these reports represents value for money.

It is possible, however, to identify the kinds of qualities which accounting information must possess in order to be useful. Where these qualities are lacking, the usefulness of the information will be diminished. This point is now considered in some detail.

PROVIDING A SERVICE

One way of viewing accounting is as a form of service. The user groups identified in Figure 1.1 can be seen as the 'clients' and the accounting (financial) information produced can be seen as the service provided. The value of this service to the various 'clients' can be judged according to whether the accounting information meets their needs.

To be useful to users, particularly investors and lenders, the information provided should possess certain qualities, or characteristics. In particular, it must be relevant and it must faithfully represent what it is meant to represent. These two qualities, **relevance** and **faithful representation**, are regarded as fundamental qualities and require further explanation.

- *Relevance.* Accounting information should make a difference. That is, it should be capable of influencing user decisions. To do this, it should help to *predict future events* (such as predicting next year's profit), or help to *confirm past events* (such as establishing last year's profit), or do both. By confirming past events, users can check on the accuracy of their earlier predictions. This can, in turn, help them to improve the ways in which they make predictions in the future.

  To be relevant, accounting information must cross a threshold of **materiality**. An item of information is considered material, or significant, only if its omission or misstatement would change the decisions that users make.

Activity 1.5

Do you think that what is material for one business will also be material for all other businesses?

No, it will normally vary from one business to the next. What is material will depend on factors such as the size of the business, the nature of the information and the amounts involved.

Ultimately, what is considered material is a matter of judgement. When making this kind of judgement, managers should consider how this information is likely to be used by users. If a piece of information is not considered material, it should not be included within the accounting reports. It will merely clutter them up and, perhaps, interfere with the users' ability to interpret them.

- *Faithful representation.* Accounting information should represent what it is meant to represent. To do so, the information provided must reflect the *substance* of what has occurred rather than simply its *legal form*. Take for example a manufacturer that provides goods to a retailer on a sale-or-return basis. The manufacturer may wish to treat this arrangement as two separate transactions. Thus, a contract may be agreed for the sale of the goods and a separate contract agreed for the return of the goods if unsold by the retailer. This may result in a sale being reported when the goods are delivered to the retailer even though they are returned at a later date. The economic substance, however, is that the manufacturer made no sale as the goods were subsequently returned. They were simply moved from the manufacturer's business to the retailer's business and then back again. Accounting reports should reflect this economic substance. To do otherwise would be misleading.

To provide a perfectly faithful representation, the information should be *complete.* In other words, it should incorporate everything needed to understand what is being portrayed. Thus, information relating to a particular item would normally contain a description of its nature, some suitable numerical measurement and, where necessary, explanations of important facts. Information should also be *neutral,* which means that it should be presented and selected without bias. No attempt should be made to manipulate the information in such a way as to influence user attitudes and behaviour. Finally, it should be *free from error.* This is not the same as saying that it must be perfectly accurate. Accounting information often contains estimates, such as future sales or costs, which may turn out to be inaccurate. Nevertheless, estimates may still be faithfully represented providing they are accurately described and properly prepared.

Activity 1.6

In practice, do you think that each piece of accounting information produced will be perfectly complete, neutral and free from error?

Probably not – however, each piece of information should be produced with these aims in mind.

Accounting information should contain *both* of these fundamental qualities - relevance and faithful representation – if it is to be useful. There is usually little point in producing information that is relevant, but which lacks faithful representation, or producing information that is irrelevant, even if it is faithfully represented. Nevertheless, a trade-off between relevance and faithful representation may sometimes have to be made. Where, for example, an estimate of some future financial commitment is highly uncertain, it may not reflect a totally faithful portrayal of the item. This estimate may, however, be the most relevant information available. In such a situation, it may be better for users to receive the estimate, along with a description of the uncertainties that surround it, rather than receive no estimate at all.

Further qualities

Where accounting information is both relevant and faithfully represented, there are other qualities that, if present, can enhance its usefulness. These are comparability, verifiability, timeliness and understandability. Each of these qualities is now considered.

- *Comparability.* When choosing between alternatives, users of accounting information seek to make comparisons. They may want to compare performance of the business over time (for example, the profit for this year compared to that for last year). They may also want to compare certain aspects of business performance (such as the level of sales achieved during the year) to those of similar businesses. To help users make comparisons, items that are alike should be treated in the same way – both over time and between businesses. Items that are not alike, on the other hand, should not be treated as though they are. Users must be able to detect both similarities and differences in items being compared.
- *Verifiability.* This quality provides assurance to users that the accounting information provided faithfully portrays what it is supposed to portray. Accounting information is verifiable where different, independent experts can reach broad agreement, that it provides a faithful portrayal. Verification can be direct, such as checking a bank account balance, or indirect, such as checking the underlying assumptions and methods used to derive an estimate of a future cost.
- *Timeliness.* Accounting information should be made available in time for users to make their decisions. A lack of timeliness undermines the usefulness of the information. Broadly speaking, the later accounting information is produced, the less useful it becomes.
- *Understandability.* Accounting information should be presented in as clear and as concise a form as possible. Nevertheless, some accounting information may be too complex to be presented in an easily digestible form. This does not mean, however, that it should be ignored. To do so would result in reporting only a partial view of financial matters. (See Reference 1 at the end of the chapter.)

Activity 1.7

Accounting reports are aimed at users with a reasonable knowledge of accounting and business and who are prepared to invest time in studying them. Do you think, however, that accounting reports should be understandable to users without any knowledge of accounting or business?

It would be very helpful if everyone could understand accounting reports. This, however, is unrealistic as complex financial events and transactions cannot normally be expressed in simple terms. Any attempts to do so are likely to produce a very distorted picture of reality.

It is probably best that we regard accounting reports in the same way that we regard a report written in a foreign language. To understand either of these, we need to have had some preparation. When producing accounting reports, it is normally assumed that the user not only has a reasonable knowledge of business and accounting but is also prepared to invest some time in studying the reports. Nevertheless, the onus is clearly on accountants to provide information in a way that makes it as understandable as possible to non-accountants.

It is worth emphasising that the four additional qualities just discussed cannot make accounting information useful. They can only enhance the usefulness of information that is already relevant and faithfully represented.

WEIGHING UP THE COSTS AND BENEFITS

Even when an item of accounting information may have all the qualities described, this does not automatically mean that it should be collected and reported to users. There is still one more hurdle to jump. Consider Activity 1.8.

Activity 1.8

Suppose an item of information is capable of being provided. It is relevant to a particular decision and can be faithfully represented. It is also comparable, verifiable and timely, and can be understood by the decision maker.
  Can you think of the reason why, in practice, you might choose not to produce the information?

The reason is that you judge the cost of doing so to be greater than the potential benefit of having the information. This cost–benefit issue will limit the amount of accounting information provided.

In theory, a particular item of accounting information should only be produced if the costs of providing it are less than the benefits, or value, to be derived from its use. Figure 1.2 shows the relationship between the costs and value of providing additional accounting information.

The figure shows how the value of information received by the decision maker eventually begins to decline. This is, perhaps, because additional information becomes less relevant, or because of the problems that a decision maker may have in processing the sheer quantity of

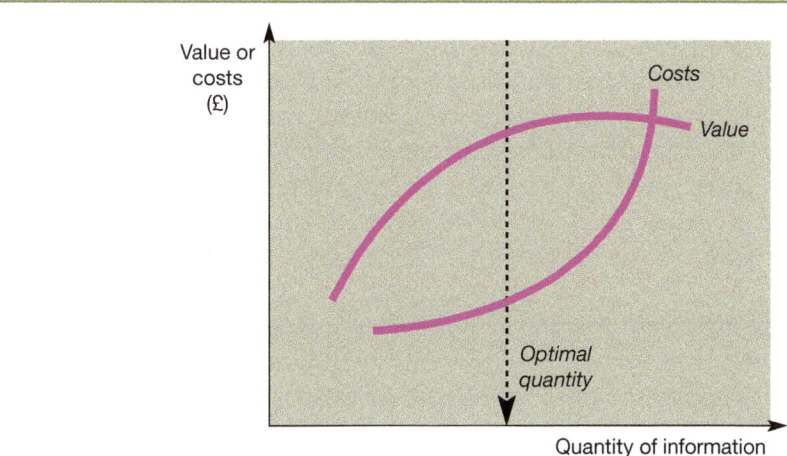

The benefits of accounting information eventually decline. The cost of providing information, however, will rise with each additional piece of information. The optimal level of information provision is where the gap between the value of the information and the cost of providing it is at its greatest.

Figure 1.2 Relationship between costs and the value of providing additional accounting information

information provided. The costs of providing the information, however, will increase with each additional piece of information. The broken line indicates the point at which the gap between the value of information and the cost of providing that information is at its greatest. This represents the optimal amount of information that can be provided. This theoretical model, however, poses a number of problems in practice.

To illustrate the practical problems of establishing the value of information, let us assume that we accidentally reversed our car into a wall in a car park. This resulted in a dented boot and scraped paintwork. We want to have the dent taken out and the paintwork re-sprayed at a local garage. We know that the nearest garage would charge £450 but we believe that other local garages may offer to do the job for a lower price. The only way of finding out the prices at other garages is to visit them, so that they can see the extent of the damage. Visiting the garages will involve using some fuel and will take up some of our time. Is it worth the cost of finding out the price for the job at the various local garages? The answer, as we have seen, is that if the cost of discovering the price is less than the potential benefit, it is worth having that information.

To identify the various prices for the job, there are several points to be considered, including:

- How many garages shall we visit?
- What is the cost of fuel to visit each garage?
- How long will it take to make all the garage visits?
- At what price do we value our time?

The economic benefit of having the information on the price of the job is probably even harder to assess. The following points need to be considered:

- What is the cheapest price that we might be quoted for the job?
- How likely is it that we shall be quoted a price cheaper than £450?

As we can imagine, the answers to these questions may be far from clear – remember that we have only contacted the local garage so far. When assessing the value of accounting information, we are confronted with similar problems.

Producing accounting information can incur significant costs. Furthermore, these costs can be difficult to identify. Although direct, out-of-pocket costs, such as salaries of accounting staff, can usually be identified without too much problem, these are only part of the total costs involved. There are other costs such as the cost of users' time spent on analysing and interpreting the information provided. These costs are much more difficult to identify and may vary between users.

Activity 1.9

What about the economic benefits of producing accounting information? Do you think it is easier, or harder, to identify the economic benefits of accounting information than the associated costs?

It is normally even harder to identify the benefits. We saw earlier that, even if we could accurately measure the economic benefits arising from a particular decision, accounting information will be only one factor influencing that decision. Furthermore, the benefits of accounting information, like the associated costs, can vary between users.

There are no easy answers to the problem of weighing costs and benefits. Although it is possible to apply some 'science' to the problem, a lot of subjective judgement is normally involved.

The qualities, or characteristics, influencing the usefulness of accounting information, which have been discussed above, are summarised in Figure 1.3.

There are two fundamental qualities that determine the usefulness of accounting information. In addition, there are four qualities that enhance the usefulness of accounting information. **The benefits of providing the information, however, should outweigh the costs.**

Figure 1.3 The qualities that influence the usefulness of accounting information

ACCOUNTING AS AN INFORMATION SYSTEM

We have already seen that accounting can be seen as the provision of a service to 'clients'. Another way of viewing accounting is as a part of the business's total information system. Users, both inside and outside the business, have to make decisions concerning the allocation of scarce resources. To ensure that these resources are efficiently allocated, users often need financial information on which to base decisions. It is the role of the accounting system to provide this information.

The **accounting information system** should have certain features that are common to all information systems within a business. These are:

- identifying and capturing relevant information (in this case, financial information);
- recording, in a systematic way, the information collected;
- analysing and interpreting the information collected; and
- reporting the information in a manner that suits the needs of users.

The relationship between these features is set out in Figure 1.4.

There are four sequential stages of an accounting information system. The first two stages are concerned with preparation, whereas the last two stages are concerned with using the information collected.

Figure 1.4 The accounting information system

Given the decision-making emphasis of this book, we shall be concerned primarily with the final two elements of the process: the analysis and reporting of financial information. We shall consider the way in which information is used by, and is useful to, users rather than the way in which it is identified and recorded.

Efficient accounting information systems are an essential ingredient of an efficient business. Where they contain errors, it can be both costly and disruptive. **Real World 1.1** describes how spreadsheets, which are widely used to prepare accounting and financial information, may introduce errors. This, in turn, can lead to poor financial decisions.

Real World 1.1

Systems error!

Almost one in five large businesses have suffered financial losses as a result of errors in spreadsheets, according to F1F9, which provides financial modelling and business forecasting to large businesses. It warns of looming financial disasters as 71 per cent of large British businesses always use spreadsheets for key financial decisions.

The company's new white paper entitled *Capitalism's Dirty Secret* showed that the abuse of the humble spreadsheet could have far-reaching consequences. Spreadsheets are used in the preparation of British company accounts worth up to £1.9 trillion and the UK manufacturing sector uses spreadsheets to make pricing decisions for up to £170 billion worth of business.

In total, spreadsheet calculations represent up to £38 billion of British private sector investment decisions per year, data harvested through YouGov found. Yet 16 per cent of large companies have admitted finding inaccurate information in spreadsheets more than 10 times in 2014.

Grenville Croll, a spreadsheet risk expert, said of the findings: 'Spreadsheets have been shown to be fallible yet they underpin the operation of the financial system. If the uncontrolled use of spreadsheets continues to occur in highly leveraged markets and companies, it is only a matter of time before another "Black Swan" event (an event that is highly unusual and difficult to predict) occurs causing catastrophic loss.'

The report warns that while 33 per cent of large businesses report poor decision-making as a result of spreadsheet problems, a third of the financial decision-makers using spreadsheets in large UK businesses are still given zero training.

Source: Adapted extract from: Burn-Callander, R. (2015) Stupid errors in spreadsheets could lead to Britain's next corporate disaster, *Daily Telegraph*, 7 April, www.telegraph.co.uk.

MANAGEMENT ACCOUNTING AND FINANCIAL ACCOUNTING

Accounting is usually seen as having two distinct strands. These are:

- **management accounting**, which seeks to meet the accounting needs of managers; and
- **financial accounting**, which seeks to meet the needs of owners and lenders. It should also, however, be useful to other users, identified earlier in the chapter , excluding the managers (see Figure 1.1).

The difference in their targeted user groups has led to each strand of accounting developing along different lines. The main areas of difference are as follows:

- *Nature of the reports produced.* Financial accounting reports tend to be general-purpose. As mentioned above, they are aimed primarily at providers of finance (owners and lenders) but contain financial information that should also be useful for a broad range of external users. Management accounting reports, on the other hand, are often specific-purpose reports. They are designed with a particular decision in mind and/or for a particular manager.
- *Level of detail.* Financial accounting reports provide users with a broad overview of the performance and position of the business for a period. As a result, information is aggregated (that is, added together) and detail is often lost. Management accounting reports, however, often provide managers with considerable detail to help them with a particular operational decision.
- *Regulations.* Financial accounting reports, for many businesses, are subject to accounting regulations imposed by the law and accounting rule makers. These regulations often require a standard content and, perhaps, a standard format to be adopted. Management accounting reports, on the other hand, are not subject to regulation and can be designed to meet the needs of particular managers.

Activity 1.10

Why do you think financial accounting reports are subject to regulation, whereas management accounting reports are not?

Financial accounting reports are for external publication. To protect external users, who depend on the quality of information provided by managers, they are subject to regulation. Management accounting reports, on the other hand, are produced exclusively for managers and so are for internal use only.

- *Reporting interval.* For most businesses, financial accounting reports are produced on an annual basis, although some large businesses produce half-yearly reports and a few produce quarterly ones. Management accounting reports will be produced as frequently as needed by managers. A sales manager, for example, may require routine sales reports on a daily, weekly or monthly basis, so as to monitor performance closely. Special-purpose reports can also be prepared when the occasion demands: for example, where an evaluation is required of a proposed investment in new equipment.
- *Time orientation.* Financial accounting reports reflect the performance and position of the business for the past period. In essence, they are backward looking. Management accounting reports, on the other hand, often provide information concerning future performance as well as past performance. It is an oversimplification, however, to suggest that financial accounting reports never incorporate expectations concerning the future. Occasionally, businesses will release projected information to other users in an attempt to raise funds or to fight off unwanted takeover bids. Even preparation of the routine financial accounting reports typically requires making some judgements about the future, as we shall see in Chapter 3.
- *Range and quality of information.* Two key points are worth mentioning. First, financial accounting reports concentrate on information that can be quantified in monetary terms. Management accounting also produces such reports, but is also more likely to produce reports that contain information of a non-financial nature, such as physical volume of inventories, number of sales orders received, number of new products launched, physical output per employee and so on. Second, financial accounting places greater emphasis on the use of objective, verifiable evidence when preparing reports. Management accounting reports may use information that is less objective and verifiable, but nevertheless provides managers with the information they need.

We can see from this that management accounting is less constrained than financial accounting. It may draw from a variety of sources and use information that has varying degrees of reliability. The only real test to be applied when assessing the value of the information produced for managers is whether or not it improves the quality of the decisions made.

The main differences between financial accounting and management accounting are summarised in Figure 1.5.

The differences between management accounting and financial accounting suggest that there are differences in the information needs of managers and those of other users. While differences undoubtedly exist, there is also a good deal of overlap between the needs of both.

Activity 1.11

Can you think of *two* areas of overlap between the information needs of managers and those of other users? (*Hint*: Think about the time orientation and the level of detail of accounting information.)

Two areas that spring to mind are:

- Managers will, at times, be interested in receiving a historical overview of business operations of the sort provided to other users.
- Other users would be interested in receiving detailed information relating to the future, such as the planned level of profits, and non-financial information, such as the state of the sales order book and the extent of product innovations.

Figure 1.5 Management and financial accounting compared

To some extent, differences between the two strands of accounting reflect differences in access to financial information. Managers have much more control over the form and content of the information that they receive. Other users have to rely on what managers are prepared to provide or what financial reporting regulations insist must be provided. Although the scope of financial accounting reports has increased over time, fears concerning loss of competitive advantage and user ignorance about the reliability of forecast data have resulted in other users not receiving the same detailed and wide-ranging information as that available to managers.

In the past, accounting systems tended to be primarily concerned with providing information for external users. Financial accounting requirements were the main priority and management accounting suffered as a result. Survey evidence suggests, however, that this is no longer the case. Modern management accounting systems usually provide managers with information that is relevant to their needs rather than that determined by external reporting requirements. External reporting cycles, however, retain some influence over management accounting. Managers tend to be aware of external users' expectations (see Reference 2 at the end of the chapter).

SCOPE OF THIS BOOK

This book is concerned with financial accounting rather than management accounting. In Chapter 2 we begin by introducing the three main financial statements:

- the statement of financial position;
- the income statement; and
- the statement of cash flows.

These statements are briefly reviewed before we go on to consider the statement of financial position in more detail. We shall see that the statement of financial position provides information concerning the wealth held by a business at a particular point in time and the claims against this wealth. Included in our consideration of the statement of financial position will be an introduction to the **conventions of accounting**. These are generally accepted rules that are followed when preparing financial statements.

Chapter 3 concentrates on the second of the major financial statements, the income statement. This statement provides information concerning the wealth (profit) created by a business during a period. We shall, therefore, be looking at such issues as how profit is measured, the point at which profit is recognised and the accounting conventions applied when preparing the income statement.

In the UK, and throughout much of the world, the limited company is the major form of business unit. In Chapter 4 we consider the accounting aspects of limited companies. Although these are, in essence, the same as for other types of business, some points of detail need to be considered. We shall continue our examination of limited companies in Chapter 5 and, in particular, consider the framework of rules governing the presentation of accounting reports to owners and external users.

The three major financial statements, the statement of cash flows. This financial statement is important in identifying the financing and investing activities of the business over a period. It sets out how cash was generated and how cash was used during a period.

How financial reporting rules have developed to try to provide clear definitions and recognition criteria for key items appearing in the financial statements. The ultimate purpose of these rules is to enhance the comparability of financial statements between businesses. In an increasingly complex world, there is a need for rules to help both preparers and users of financial statements.

The various techniques for analysing financial statements. To gain a deeper understanding about the financial health of a business, financial statements may be analysed using financial ratios and other techniques. Expressing two figures in the financial statements in the form of a ratio and then comparing it with a similar ratio for, say, another business, can often tell us much more than just reading the figures alone.

The typical large business in the UK operates as a group of companies rather than a single company. A group of companies exists where one company controls one or more other companies. The reasons why groups exist and explore the accounting issues raised by combining companies into groups.

The focus of financial reporting has changed over time to become more decision-oriented. We shall also look at possible ways in which the scope of financial reporting may be increased in order to meet the needs of users.

Finally, in Chapter 7, we consider the way in which larger businesses are managed. We examine the reasons why conflicts of interests may arise between owners and managers and how the behaviour of managers may be monitored and controlled.

THE CHANGING FACE OF ACCOUNTING

Over the past fifty years or so, the environment within which businesses operate has become increasingly turbulent and competitive. Various reasons have been identified to explain these changes, including:

- the increasing sophistication of customers;
- greatly improved speed and sophistication of communication (particularly with the Internet);
- the development of a global economy where national frontiers become less important;
- rapid changes in technology;
- the deregulation of domestic markets (for example, electricity, water and gas);
- increasing pressure from owners (shareholders) for competitive economic returns; and
- greater volatility of financial markets.

This new, more complex, environment has brought new challenges for managers and other users of accounting information. Their needs have changed and both financial accounting and management accounting have had to respond. To meet the changing needs of users, there has been a radical review of the kind of information to be reported.

The changed environment has given added impetus to the search for a clear conceptual framework, or framework of principles, upon which to base financial accounting reports. Various attempts have been made to clarify their purpose and to provide a more solid foundation for the development of accounting rules. Work on developing a conceptual framework tries to address fundamental questions such as:

- Who are the users of financial accounting information?
- What kinds of financial accounting reports should be prepared and what should they contain?
- How should items such as profit and assets be identified and measured?

The internationalisation of businesses has created a need for accounting rules to have an international reach. It can no longer be assumed that users of accounting information relating to a business are based in the country in which the business operates. Neither can it be assumed that the users are familiar with the accounting rules of that country. Thus, there has been increasing harmonisation of accounting rules across national frontiers.

Activity 1.12

How should the harmonisation of accounting rules benefit:

(a) an international investor?
(b) an international business?

(a) An international investor should benefit because the accounting definitions and policies used in preparing financial accounting reports will not vary across countries. This should make the comparison of performance between businesses operating in different countries much easier.
(b) An international business should benefit because the cost of producing accounting reports in order to comply with the rules of different countries can be expensive. Harmonisation can, therefore, lead to significant cost savings. It may also broaden the appeal of the business among international investors. Where there are common accounting rules, they may have greater confidence to invest.

In response to criticisms that the financial reports of some businesses are opaque and difficult for users to interpret, great efforts have been made to improve reporting rules. Accounting rule makers have tried to ensure that the accounting policies of businesses are more comparable and transparent and that the financial reports provide a more faithful portrayal of economic reality.

Management accounting has also changed by becoming more outward looking in its focus. In the past, information provided to managers has been largely restricted to that collected within the business. However, the attitude and behaviour of customers and rival businesses have now become the object of much information gathering. Increasingly, successful businesses are those that are able to secure and maintain competitive advantage over their rivals.

To obtain this advantage, businesses have become more 'customer driven' (that is, concerned with satisfying customer needs). This has led to the production of management accounting information that provides details of customers and the market, such as customer evaluation of services provided and market share. In addition, information about the costs and profits of rival businesses, which can be used as 'benchmarks' by which to gauge competitiveness, is gathered and reported.

To compete successfully, businesses must also find ways of managing costs. The cost base of modern businesses is under continual review and this, in turn, has led to the development of more sophisticated methods of measuring and controlling costs.

ACCOUNTING FOR BUSINESS

We have seen that the needs of the various user groups will determine the kind of accounting information to be provided. Those needs, however, will partly be shaped by the forms of business ownership and the ways in which a business is organised and structured. In the sections that follow, we shall consider the business environment within which accounting information is produced. This should help our understanding of points that crop up in later chapters.

WHAT IS THE PURPOSE OF A BUSINESS?

Peter Drucker, an eminent management thinker, has argued that 'the purpose of business is to create and keep a customer' (see Reference 3 at the end of the chapter). Drucker defined the purpose of a business in this way in 1967, at a time when most businesses did not adopt this strong customer focus. His view, therefore, represented a radical challenge to the accepted view of what businesses should do. More than fifty years on, however, his approach has become part of the conventional wisdom. It is now widely recognised that, in order to succeed, businesses must focus on satisfying the needs of the customer.

Although the customer has always provided the main source of revenue for a business, this has often been taken for granted. In the past, too many businesses have assumed that the customer would readily accept whatever services or products were on offer. When competition was weak and customers were passive, businesses could operate under this assumption and still make a profit. However, the era of weak competition has passed. Now, customers have much greater choice and are much more assertive concerning their needs. They now demand higher quality services and goods at cheaper prices. They also require that services and goods be delivered faster with an increasing emphasis on the product being tailored to their individual needs. If a business cannot meet these needs, a competitor often can. Thus, the business mantra for the current era is '*the customer is king*'. Most businesses recognise this fact and organise themselves accordingly.

Real World 1.2 describes how the Internet and social media have given added weight to this mantra. It points out that dissatisfied customers now have a powerful medium for broadcasting their complaints.

> **Real World 1.2**
>
> **The customer is king**
>
> The mantra that the 'customer is king' has gained even greater significance among businesses in recent years because of the rise of the Internet and social media. In the past, a dissatisfied customer might tell only a few friends about a bad buying experience. As a result, the damage to the reputation of the business concerned would normally be fairly limited. However, nowadays, through the magic of the Internet, several hundred people, or more, can be very speedily informed of a bad buying experience.
>
> Businesses are understandably concerned about the potential of the Internet to damage reputations, but are their concerns justified? Do customer complaints, which wing their way through cyberspace, have any real effect on the businesses concerned? A Harris Poll survey of 2,000 adults in the UK and US suggests they do and so businesses should be concerned. It seems that social media can exert a big influence on customer buying decisions.
>
> The Harris Poll survey, which was conducted online, found that around 20 per cent of those surveyed use social media when making buying decisions. For those in the 18 to 34 age range, the figure rises to almost 40 per cent. Furthermore, 60 per cent of those surveyed indicated that they would avoid buying from a business that receives poor customer reviews for its products or services.
>
> The moral of this tale appears to be that, in this Internet age, businesses must work even harder to keep their customers happy if they are to survive and prosper.
>
> *Source*: Based on information in Miesbach, A. (2015) Yes, the customer is still king, 30 October, www.icmi.com.

WHAT KINDS OF BUSINESS OWNERSHIP EXIST?

The particular form of business ownership has certain implications for financial accounting and so it is useful to be clear about the main forms of ownership that can arise. There are basically three arrangements for private-sector businesses:

- sole proprietorship;
- partnership; and
- limited company.

We shall now consider these.

Sole proprietorship

Sole proprietorship, as the name suggests, is where an individual is the sole owner of a business. This type of business is often quite small in terms of size (as measured, for example, by sales revenue generated or number of staff employed); however, the number of such businesses is very large indeed. Examples of sole-proprietor businesses can be found in most industrial sectors but particularly within the service sector. Hence, services such as electrical repairs, picture framing, photography, driving instruction, retail shops and hotels have a large proportion of sole-proprietor businesses.

The sole-proprietor business is easy to set up. No formal procedures are required and operations can often commence immediately (unless special permission is required because of the nature of the trade or service, such as running licensed premises (a pub)). The owner can decide the way in which the business is to be conducted and has the flexibility to restructure or dissolve the business whenever it suits. The law does not recognise the sole-proprietor business as being separate from the owner, so the business will cease on the death of the owner.

Although the owner must produce accounting information about the business to satisfy the taxation authorities, there is no legal requirement to provide it to other user groups. Some user groups, however, may demand accounting information about the business and may be in a position to enforce their demands (for example, a bank requiring accounting information on a regular basis as a condition of a loan). A sole proprietor has unlimited liability which means that no distinction is made between the proprietor's personal wealth and that of the business if there are business debts to be paid.

Partnership

A **partnership** exists where two or more individuals carry on a business together with the intention of making a profit. Partnerships have much in common with sole-proprietor businesses. They are usually quite small in size (although some, such as partnerships of accountants and solicitors, can be large). They are also easy to set up, as no formal procedures are required (and it is not even necessary to have a written agreement between the partners). The partners can agree whatever arrangements suit them concerning the financial and management aspects of the business. Similarly, the partnership can be restructured or dissolved by agreement between the partners.

Partnerships are not recognised in law as separate entities and so contracts with third parties must be entered into in the name of individual partners. The partners of a business usually have unlimited liability.

Activity 1.13

What do you think are the main advantages and disadvantages of a partnership compared to a sole-proprietor business?

The main advantages of a partnership over a sole-proprietor business are:

- sharing the burden of ownership;
- the opportunity to specialise rather than cover the whole range of services (for example, in a solicitors' practice each partner may specialise in a different aspect of the law); and
- the ability to raise capital where this is beyond the capacity of a single individual.

The main disadvantages of a partnership compared with a sole proprietorship are:

- the risks of sharing ownership of a business with unsuitable individuals; and
- the limits placed on individual decision making that a partnership will impose.

Limited company

A **limited company** can range in size from quite small to very large. There is no limit on the number of individuals who can subscribe capital and become the owners, which provides the opportunity to create a very large-scale business. The liability of owners, however, is limited (hence 'limited' company), which means that those individuals subscribing capital to the company are liable only for debts incurred by the company up to the amount that they have invested, or agreed to invest. This cap on the liability of the owners is designed to limit risk and to produce greater confidence to invest. Without such limits on owner liability, it is difficult to see how a modern capitalist economy could operate. In many cases, the owners of a limited company are not involved in the day-to-day running of the business and will, therefore, invest in a business only if there is a clear limit set on the level of investment risk.

Note that this 'limited liability' does not apply to sole proprietors and partners. These individuals have a legal obligation to meet all of their business debts, if necessary using, what they may have thought of as, private assets (for example, their private houses). The ability of the owners of limited companies to limit their liability can often make this type of type of business more attractive than either sole proprietorships or partnerships.

The benefit of limited liability, however, imposes certain obligations on such companies. To start up a limited company, documents of incorporation must be prepared that set out, among other things, the objectives of the business. Furthermore, a framework of regulations exists that places obligations on limited companies concerning the way in which they conduct their affairs. Part of this regulatory framework requires annual financial reports to be made available to owners and lenders and, usually, an annual general meeting of the owners has to be held to approve the reports. In addition, a copy of the annual financial reports must be lodged with the Registrar of Companies for public inspection. In this way, the financial affairs of a limited company enter the public domain.

With the exception of small companies, there is also a requirement for the annual financial reports to be subject to an audit. This involves an independent firm of accountants examining the annual reports and underlying records to see whether the reports provide a true and fair view of the financial health of the company and whether they comply with the relevant accounting rules established by law and by accounting rule makers. Limited companies are considered in more detail in Chapters 4 and 5.

All of the large household-name UK businesses (Marks and Spencer, Tesco, Shell, Sky, Rolls-Royce, BT, easyJet and so on) are limited companies.

Activity 1.14

What are the main advantages of forming a partnership business rather than a limited liability company? Try to think of at least three.

The main advantages are:

- the ease of setting up the business;
- the degree of flexibility concerning the way in which the business is conducted;
- the degree of flexibility concerning restructuring and dissolution of the business; and
- freedom from administrative burdens imposed by law (for example, the annual general meeting and the need for an independent audit).

As we saw earlier, the main disadvantage of a partnership compared with a limited company is that it is not normally possible to limit the liability of all of the partners. There is, however, a hybrid form of business ownership that is referred to as a Limited Liability Partnership (LLP). This has many of the attributes of a normal partnership but is different insofar that the LLP, rather than the individual partners, is responsible for any debts incurred. Accountants and solicitors often use this type of partnership.

This book concentrates on the accounting aspects of limited liability companies because they are, by far, the most important in economic terms. The early chapters will introduce accounting concepts through examples that do not draw a distinction between the different types of business. Once we have dealt with the basic accounting principles, which are precisely the same for all three types of business, we go on to see how they are applied to limited companies.

HOW ARE BUSINESSES ORGANISED?

Most businesses involving more than a few owners and/or employees are set up as limited companies. Finance will come from the owners (shareholders) both in the form of a direct cash investment to buy shares (in the ownership of the business) and through the shareholders allowing past profits, which belong to them, to be reinvested in the business. Finance will also come from lenders (banks, for example), who earn interest on their loans. Further finance will be provided through suppliers of goods and services being prepared to supply on credit.

In larger limited companies, the owners (shareholders) tend not to be involved in the daily running of the business; instead they appoint a board of directors to manage the business on their behalf. The board is charged with three major tasks:

1. setting the overall direction and strategy for the business;
2. monitoring and controlling the activities of the business; and
3. communicating with shareholders and others connected with the business.

Each board has a chairman, elected by the directors, who is responsible for running the board in an efficient manner. In addition, each board has a chief executive officer (CEO) who is responsible for running the business on a day-to-day basis. Occasionally, the roles of chairman and CEO are combined, although it is usually considered to be a good idea to separate them to prevent a single individual having excessive power. We shall consider the relationship between directors and shareholders in more detail in Chapters 4 and 7.

The board of directors represents the most senior level of management. Below this level, managers are employed, with each manager being given responsibility for a particular part of the business's operations.

THE QUEST FOR WEALTH CREATION

A business is normally created to enhance the wealth of its owners. This may come as a surprise, as there are other objectives that a business may pursue that would fulfil the needs of others with a stake in the business.

Activity 1.15

What other objectives might a business pursue? Try to think of at least two.

A business may seek:

- to provide well-paid jobs and good working conditions for its employees;
- to conserve the environment for the local community;
- to produce products or services that will benefit its customers; and/or
- to support local suppliers.

You may have thought of others.

Although a business may pursue other such objectives, it is normally set up primarily with a view to increasing the wealth of its owners. In practice, the behaviour of businesses over time appears to be consistent with this objective.

Within a market economy, there are strong competitive forces at work that ensure that failure to enhance owners' wealth will not be tolerated for long. Competition for the funds provided by the owners and competition for managers' jobs will normally mean that the owners' interests will prevail. If the managers do not provide the required increase in ownership wealth, the owners have the power to replace the existing management team with a new team that is more responsive to their needs.

MEETING THE NEEDS OF OTHER STAKEHOLDERS

The points made above do not mean that the needs of other groups with a stake in the business, such as employees, customers, suppliers, the community, are unimportant. In fact, the opposite is true, if the business wishes to survive and prosper over the longer term. For example, a business with disaffected customers may well find that they turn to another supplier, resulting in a loss of shareholder wealth. **Real World 1.3** provides examples of businesses that acknowledge the vital link between satisfying customers' needs and creating wealth (value) for their owners (shareholders).

Real World 1.3

Expressing its position

National Express plc, a leading transport provider, states its approach as follows:

> At National Express we believe our business model should start with our customers. By serving our customers with operational excellence, we are able to create profit and cash, thereby generating shareholder value.

Source: www.nationalexpress.com [accessed 2 January 2019].

> ### Adopting a customer focus
>
> John Menzies plc, a distribution and aviation logistics business, states:
>
> > We believe that the passion of our people, and their commitment to delivering great customer experiences, are crucial to delivering shareholder value – and this belief informs our entire approach to doing business.
>
> Source: www.johnmenziesplc.com [accessed 2 January 2019].

Other stakeholders that contribute towards the wealth-creation process must also be considered. A dissatisfied workforce can result in low productivity and strikes while dissatisfied suppliers can withhold vital supplies or give lower priority to orders received. A discontented local community can withdraw access to community resources. In each case, the owners' wealth will suffer.

Real World 1.4 describes how one well-known business came to recognise that future success depended on the support of key stakeholder groups.

> ### Real World 1.4
>
> ### The price of clothes
>
> Nike is a highly successful business with a globally-recognised brand. However, it was not so long ago that the business was mired in controversy. It had become a focal point for protesters who regarded the business as a byword for 'sweatshop' labour practices. In 1992, an article was published that exposed the low wages and poor working conditions of those producing Nike products in Indonesia. Subsequent protests and further revelations resulted in unwanted media attention to which the business was, at first, slow to properly respond. However, by 1998, weakening demand for its products meant that the issue could no longer be lightly dismissed. Nike publicly acknowledged the reputation it had gained for 'sweatshop' labour practices and the adverse effect this was having on customer attitudes.
>
> Its management realised that, if nothing else, it was good business to improve the working lives of those producing Nike products in third world countries. This resulted in a commitment to better working conditions, higher wages and a minimum working age. A code of conduct for Nike suppliers concerning the treatment of their workforce was established and independent audits were implemented to monitor adherence to the code. The business also committed to greater transparency: it now publishes reports on its responsibilities and the ways in which these have been fulfilled.
>
> Although Nike was not the only large business engaged in sweatshop practices, it took a lead in trying to eradicate them and, by doing so, removed the stain from its reputation. This has been rewarded by a continuing demand for its products.
>
> Source: Based on information in Nisen, M. (2013) *How Nike Solved it Sweatshop Problem* Business Insider 9 May and Allarey, R. (2015) *This Is How Nike Managed to Clean Up Its Sweatshop Reputation* 8 June http://www.complex.com.

It is clear from the above that creating wealth for the owners is not the same as seeking to maximise the current year's profit. Wealth creation is concerned with the longer term. It relates not only to this year's profit but to that of future years as well. In the short term, corners can be cut and risks taken that improve current profit at the expense of future profit. **Real World 1.5** provides some examples of how emphasis on short-term profit can be very damaging.

Real World 1.5

Short-term gains, long-term problems

For many years, under the guise of defending capitalism, we have been allowing ourselves to degrade it. We have been poisoning the well from which we have drawn wealth. We have misunderstood the importance of values to capitalism. We have surrendered to the idea that success is pursued by making as much money as the law allowed without regard to how it was made.

Thirty years ago, retailers would be quite content to source the shoes they wanted to sell as cheaply as possible. The working conditions of those who produced them was not their concern. Then headlines and protests developed. Society started to hold them responsible for previously invisible working conditions. Companies like Nike went through a transformation. They realised they were polluting their brand. Global sourcing became visible. It was no longer viable to define success simply in terms of buying at the lowest price and selling at the highest.

Financial services and investment are today where footwear was thirty years ago. Public anger at the crisis will make visible what was previously hidden. Take the building up of huge portfolios of loans to poor people on US trailer parks. These loans were authorised without proper scrutiny of the circumstances of the borrowers. Somebody else then deemed them fit to be securitised and so on through credit default swaps and the rest without anyone seeing the transaction in terms of its ultimate human origin.

Each of the decision makers thought it okay to act like the thoughtless footwear buyer of the 1970s. The price was attractive. There was money to make on the deal. Was it responsible? Irrelevant. It was legal, and others were making money that way. And the consequences for the banking system if everybody did it? Not our problem.

The consumer has had a profound shock. Surely we could have expected the clever and wise people who invested our money to be better at risk management than they have shown themselves to be in the present crisis? How could they have been so gullible in not challenging the bankers whose lending proved so flaky? How could they have believed that the levels of bonuses that were, at least in part, coming out of their savings could have been justified in 'incentivising' a better performance? How could they have believed that a 'better' performance would be one that is achieved for one bank without regard to its effect on the whole banking system? Where was the stewardship from those exercising investment on their behalf?

The answer has been that very few of them do exercise that stewardship. Most have stood back and said it doesn't really pay them to do so. The failure of stewardship comes from the same mindset that created the irresponsible lending in the first place. We are back to the mindset that has allowed us to poison the well: never mind the health of the system as a whole, I'm making money out of it at the moment. Responsibility means awareness for the system consequences of our actions. It is not a luxury. It is the cornerstone of prudence.

Source: Goyder, M. (2009) How we've poisoned the well of wealth, *Financial Times*, ft.com, 15 February. © The Financial Times Limited 2017. All rights reserved.

BALANCING RISK AND RETURN

All decision making concerns the future and financial decision making is no exception. The only thing certain about the future, however, is that we cannot be sure what will happen. Things may not turn out as planned and this risk should be taken into account when making financial decisions.

As in other aspects of life, risk and return tend to be related. Evidence shows that returns relate to risk in something like the way shown in Figure 1.6.

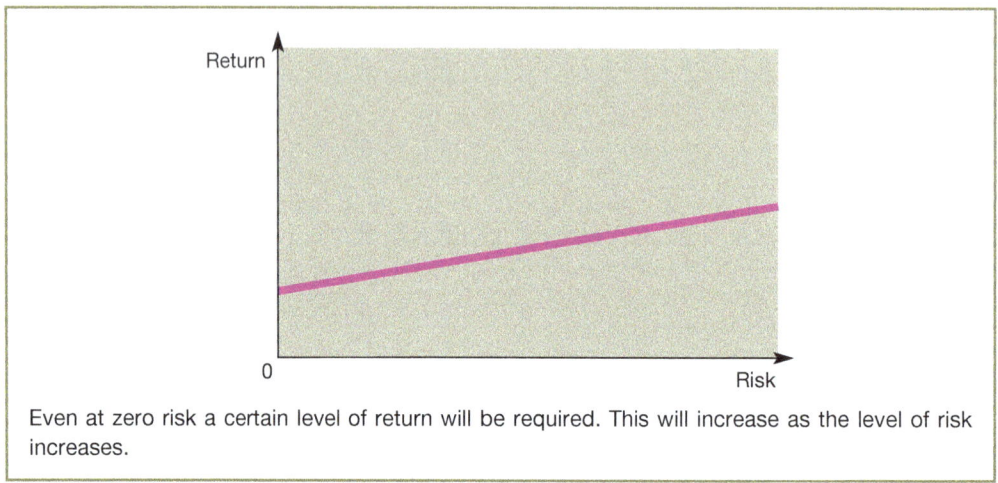

Even at zero risk a certain level of return will be required. This will increase as the level of risk increases.

Figure 1.6 Relationship between risk and return

Activity 1.16

Look at Figure 1.6 and state, in broad terms, where an investment in:

(a) UK government savings account; and
(b) shares in an oil business

should be placed on the risk–return line.

A UK government savings account is normally a very safe investment. Even if the government were in financial difficulties, it may well be able to print more money to repay investors. Returns from this form of investment, however, are normally very low.

Investing in shares in a commercial business runs a risk of losing part or, possibly, the entire amount invested. On the other hand, such an investment can produce very high positive returns. Thus, the government savings account should be placed towards the far left of the risk–return line and the oil business shares towards the far right.

This relationship between risk and return has important implications for setting financial objectives for a business. The owners will require a minimum return to induce them to invest at all, but will require an additional return to compensate for taking risks; the higher the risk, the higher the required return. Managers must be aware of this and must strike the appropriate balance between risk and return when setting objectives and pursuing particular courses of action.

The turmoil in the banking sector, earlier this century, has shown, however, that the right balance is not always struck. Some banks took on excessive risks in pursuit of higher returns and, as a consequence, incurred massive losses. They are now being kept afloat with taxpayers' money. **Real World 1.6** discusses the collapse of one leading bank, in which the UK government took a majority stake, and argues that the risk appetite of banks must now change.

Real World 1.6

Banking on change

The taxpayer has become the majority shareholder in the Royal Bank of Scotland (RBS). This change in ownership, resulting from the huge losses sustained by the bank, will shape the future decisions made by its managers. This does not simply mean that it will affect the amount that the bank lends to homeowners and businesses. Rather it is about the amount of risk that it will be prepared to take in pursuit of higher returns.

In the past, those managing banks such as RBS saw themselves as producers of financial products that enabled banks to grow faster than the economy as a whole. They did not want to be seen as simply part of the infrastructure of the economy. It was too dull. It was far more exciting to be seen as creators of financial products that created huge profits and, at the same time, benefited us all through unlimited credit at low rates of interest. These financial products, with exotic names such as 'collateralised debt obligations' and 'credit default swaps', ultimately led to huge losses that taxpayers had to absorb in order to prevent the banks from collapse.

Now that many banks throughout the world are in taxpayers' hands, they are destined to lead a much quieter life. They will have to focus more on the basics such as taking deposits, transferring funds and making simple loans to customers. Is that such a bad thing?

The history of banking has reflected a tension between carrying out their core functions and the quest for high returns through high risk strategies. It seems, however, that for some time to come they will have to concentrate on the former and will be unable to speculate with depositors' cash.

Source: Based on information in Peston, R. (2008) We own Royal Bank, BBC News, 28 November, www.bbc.co.uk.

REASONS TO BE ETHICAL

The way in which individual businesses operate in terms of the honesty, fairness and transparency with which they treat their stakeholders (customers, employees, suppliers, the community, the shareholders and so on) has become a key issue. There have been many examples of businesses, some of them very well known, acting in ways that most people would regard as unethical and unacceptable. Examples of such actions include:

- paying bribes to encourage employees of other businesses to reveal information about the employee's business that could be useful;
- oppressive treatment of suppliers, for example, making suppliers wait excessive periods before payment; and
- manipulating the financial statements to mislead users of them, for example, to overstate profit so that senior managers become eligible for performance bonuses (known as 'creative accounting').

Despite the many examples of unethical acts that have attracted publicity over recent years, it would be very unfair to conclude that most businesses are involved in unethical activities. Nevertheless, revelations of unethical practice can be damaging to the entire business community. Lying, stealing and fraudulent behaviour can lead to a loss of confidence in business and the imposition of tighter regulatory burdens. In response to this threat, businesses often seek to demonstrate their commitment to acting in an honest and ethical way. One way of doing this is to develop, and adhere to, a code of ethics concerning business behaviour.

Accountants are likely to find themselves at the forefront with issues relating to business ethics. In the three examples of unethical business activity listed above, an accountant would probably have to be involved either in helping to commit the unethical act or in covering it up. Accountants are, therefore, particularly vulnerable to being put under pressure to engage in unethical acts. Some businesses acknowledge this risk and produce an ethical code for their accounting staff. **Real World 1.7** provides an example of one such code.

Real World 1.7

The only way is ethics

Vodafone plc, the telecommunications business, has a code of ethics for its chief executive and senior finance and accounting staff. The code states that they to have a duty to:

. . . act with integrity. Integrity requires, among other things, being honest and candid. Deceit, dishonesty and subordination of principle are inconsistent with integrity. Service to the Company should never be subordinated to personal gain and advantage.

The code specifically states that they must:

- act with integrity, including being honest and candid while still maintaining the confidentiality of Company information where required or in the Company's interests;
- observe, fully, applicable governmental laws, rules and regulations;
- comply with the requirements of applicable accounting and auditing standards and Company policies in the maintenance of a high standard of accuracy and completeness in the Company's financial records;
- adhere to a high standard of business ethics and not seek competitive advantage through unlawful or unethical business practices; and
- avoid conflicts of interest wherever possible. Anything that would be a conflict for a Relevant Officer will also be a conflict if it is related to a member of his or her family or a close relative.

Source: Code of Ethics Vodafone plc Accessed 13 February 2019 www.vodafone.com.

NOT-FOR-PROFIT ORGANISATIONS

Although the focus of this book is accounting as it relates to private-sector businesses, there are many organisations that do not exist mainly for the pursuit of profit.

All of these organisations need to produce accounting information for decision-making purposes. Once again, various user groups need this information to help them to make decisions. These user groups are often the same as, or similar to, those identified for private-sector businesses. They often have a stake in the future viability of the organisation and may use accounting information to check that the wealth of the organisation is being properly controlled and is used in a way that conforms to its objectives.

Activity 1.17

Can you think of at least four types of organisation that are not primarily concerned with making profits?

We thought of the following:

- charities
- clubs and associations
- universities
- local government authorities
- national government departments
- churches
- trade unions.

Nevertheless, certain types of not-for-profit organisation, such as charities, often suffer from inadequate accounting systems and a lack of financial skills among its managers. This can have disastrous consequences. **Real World 1.8** describes how one high-profile UK charity collapsed amid claims of weak accounting controls and financial mismanagement.

Real World 1.8

No kidding?

Senior directors at the charity Kids Company repeatedly warned trustees of the need to build up financial reserves or face going to the wall, the *Guardian* can reveal, as an analysis of the accounts show that its funding increased by more than 75% in five years.

Two finance directors at Kids Company left in less than three years because of their frustrations that no one – from the board of trustees, led by the BBC's Alan Yentob, to the chief executive, Camila Batmanghelidjh – heeded warnings of the need to build a financial cushion to protect the charity from catastrophe, the *Guardian* understands.

'If you keep building an organisation without building reserves, then it's a house of cards and it will fall down,' said one source who worked in a senior role at the charity for several years.

A *Guardian* analysis of five years of accounts show how the charity got itself into dire financial straits. Despite receiving millions of pounds in government funding, it lived hand to mouth, never built up any reserves, and spent almost all its income each year.

Analysis of the charity's accounts from 2009 to 2013 shows the organisation was receiving huge injections of funding, which included millions of pounds in government grants. Between 2009 and 2013, its income increased by 77% from £13m to £23m, but the charity was spending almost every penny it brought in. In the same period, its outgoings increased by 72%.

Despite repeated warnings on the accounts seen by trustees and presented to the Charity Commission, no consistent reserve was built up.

In March 2014, an audit of the charity was commissioned by the Cabinet Office and carried out by accountancy firm PKF Littlejohn. It noted that the charity was facing a 'serious cashflow' issue.

Historical note: The charity collapsed in August 2015.

Source: Laville S., Barr C. and Slawson, N. (2015) *Kids Company trustees accused of ignoring finance warnings*, www.theguardian.com, 6 August.

SUMMARY

The main points of this chapter may be summarised as follows:

What is accounting?
- Accounting provides financial information to help various user groups make better judgements and decisions.

Accounting and user needs
- For accounting to be useful, it must be clear *for whom* and *for what purpose* the information will be used.
- Owners, managers and lenders are important user groups, but there are several others.
- Conflicts of interest between users may arise over the ways in which business wealth is generated or distributed.
- The evidence suggests that accounting is both used and useful for decision-making purposes.

Providing a service
- Accounting can be viewed as a form of service as it involves providing financial information to various users.
- To provide a useful service, accounting information must possess certain qualities, or characteristics. The fundamental qualities are relevance and faithful representation. Other qualities that enhance the usefulness of accounting information are comparability, verifiability, timeliness and understandability.
- Providing a service to users can be costly and financial information should be produced only if the cost of providing the information is less than the benefits gained.

Accounting information
- Accounting is part of the total information system within a business. It shares the features that are common to all information systems within a business, which are the identification, recording, analysis and reporting of information.

Management accounting and financial accounting
- Accounting has two main strands – management accounting and financial accounting.
- Management accounting seeks to meet the needs of the business's managers, and financial accounting seeks to meet the needs of owners and lenders, but should also be of use to other user groups.
- These two strands differ in terms of the types of reports produced, the level of reporting detail, the time orientation, the degree of regulation and the range and quality of information provided.

The changing face of accounting
- Changes in the economic environment have led to changes in the nature and scope of accounting.

- Financial accounting has improved its framework of rules and there has been greater international harmonisation of accounting rules.
- Management accounting has become more outward looking, and new methods for managing costs have been developed to help a business gain competitive advantage.

What is the purpose of a business?
- The purpose of a business is to create and keep customers.

What kinds of business ownership exist?
There are three main forms of business unit:
- sole proprietorship – easy to set up and flexible to operate, but the owner has unlimited liability;
- partnership – easy to set up and spreads the burdens of ownership, but partners usually have unlimited liability and there are ownership risks if the partners are unsuitable;
- limited company – limited liability for owners, but obligations are imposed on how a company conducts its affairs.

How are businesses organised and managed?
- Most businesses of any size are set up as limited companies.
- A board of directors is appointed by owners (shareholders) to oversee the running of the business.

The quest for wealth creation
- The key financial objective of a business is to enhance the wealth of the owners.
- To achieve this objective, the needs of other groups connected with the business, such as employees, suppliers and the local community, cannot be ignored.
- When setting financial objectives, the right balance must be struck between risk and return.

Ethical behaviour
- Accounting staff may be put under pressure to commit unethical acts.
- Many businesses produce a code of ethical conduct to help protect accounting staff from this risk.

Not-for-profit organisations
- These organisations also produce accounting information for decision-making purposes.
- They have user groups that are similar to, or the same as, those of private-sector businesses.

KEY TERMS

- accounting
- shares
- relevance
- faithful representation
- materiality
- comparability
- verifiability
- timeliness
- understandability
- accounting information system
- management accounting
- financial accounting
- conventions of accounting
- sole proprietorship
- partnership
- limited company

REFERENCES

1. International Accounting Standards Board (2018) *Conceptual Framework for Financial Reporting*, pp. 14–20.
2. Dugdale, D., Jones, C. and Green, S. (2006) *Contemporary Management Accounting Practices in UK Manufacturing*, CIMA/Elsevier.
3. Drucker, P. (1967) *The Effective Executive*, Heinemann.

FURTHER READING

If you would like to explore the topics covered in this chapter in more depth, we recommend the following:

Alexander, D. and Nobes, C. (2016) *Financial Accounting: An International Introduction*, 6th edn, Pearson, Chapters 1 and 3.

Drury, C. (2018) *Management and Cost Accounting*, 10th edn, Cengage Learning EMEA, Chapter 1.

Elliott, B. and Elliott, J. (2017) *Financial Accounting and Reporting*, 18th edn, Pearson, Chapters 6 and 7.

Scott W. (2014) *Financial Accounting Theory*, 7th edn, Pearson, Chapters 1 and 3.

CRITICAL REVIEW QUESTIONS

Solutions to these questions can be found at the back of the book, starting on page 312.

1.1 Accounting is sometimes described as 'the language of business'. Why do you think this is the case? Is this an apt description of accounting?

1.2 Identify the main users of accounting information for a university. For what purposes would different user groups need information? Is there a major difference in the ways in which accounting information for a university would be used compared with that of a private-sector business?

1.3 'Not-for-profit organisations are not interested in making a profit.' Is this statement true? Does accounting and finance have a less important role to play in not-for-profit organisations than for businesses?

1.4 Financial accounting statements tend to reflect past events. In view of this, how can they be of any assistance to a user in making a decision when decisions, by their very nature, can only be made about future actions?

Chapter 2

MEASURING AND REPORTING FINANCIAL POSITION

INTRODUCTION

We saw in Chapter 1 that accounting has two distinct strands: financial accounting and management accounting. This chapter, along with Chapters 3 to 5, examines the three major financial statements that form the core of financial accounting. We start by taking an overview of these statements to see how each contributes towards an assessment of the overall financial position and performance of a business.

Following this overview, we begin a more detailed examination by turning our attention towards one of these financial statements: the statement of financial position. We identify the key elements of this statement and consider the interrelationships between them. We also consider the main accounting conventions, or rules, to be followed when preparing the statement of financial position.

Learning outcomes

When you have completed this chapter, you should be able to:

- explain the nature and purpose of the three major financial statements;
- prepare a simple statement of financial position and interpret the information that it contains;
- discuss the accounting conventions underpinning the statement of financial position; and
- discuss the uses and limitations of the statement of financial position for decision-making purposes.

THE MAJOR FINANCIAL STATEMENTS – AN OVERVIEW

The major financial accounting statements aim to provide a picture of the financial position and performance of a business. To achieve this, a business's accounting system will normally produce three financial statements on a regular, recurring basis. These three statements are concerned with answering the following questions relating to a particular period:

- What cash movements took place?
- How much wealth was generated?
- What is the accumulated wealth of the business at the end of the period and what form does it take?

To address each of these questions, there is a separate financial statement. The financial statements are:

- the **statement of cash flows**;
- the **income statement** (also known as the profit and loss account); and
- the **statement of financial position** (also known as the balance sheet).

Together they provide an overall picture of the financial health of the business.

Perhaps the best way to introduce these financial statements is to look at an example of a very simple business. From this we shall be able to see the sort of information that each of the statements can usefully provide. It is, however, worth pointing out that, while a simple business is our starting point, the principles for preparing the financial statements apply equally to the largest and most complex businesses. This means that we shall continually encounter these principles again in later chapters.

Example 2.1

Paul was unemployed and unable to find a job. He therefore decided to embark on a business venture. With Christmas approaching, he decided to buy gift wrapping paper from a local supplier and to sell it on the corner of his local high street. He felt that the price of wrapping paper in the high street shops was unreasonably high. This provided him with a useful business opportunity.

He began the venture with £40 of his own money, in cash. On Monday, Paul's first day of trading, he bought wrapping paper for £40 and sold three-quarters of it for £45 cash.

What cash movements took place in Paul's business during Monday?

For Monday, a *statement of cash flows* showing the cash movements (that is, cash in and cash out) for the day can be prepared as follows:

Statement of cash flows for Monday

	£
Cash introduced (by Paul)	40
Cash from sales of wrapping paper	45
Cash paid to buy wrapping paper	(40)
Closing balance of cash	**45**

The statement shows that Paul placed £40 cash into the business. The business received £45 cash from customers, but paid £40 cash to buy the wrapping paper. This left £45 of cash by Monday evening. Note that we are taking the standard approach found in financial statements of showing figures to be deducted (in this case the £40 paid out) in brackets. We shall take this approach consistently throughout the chapters dealing with financial statements.

How much wealth (that is, profit) was generated by the business during Monday?

An *income statement* can be prepared to show the wealth generated (profit) on Monday. The wealth generated arises from trading and will be the difference between the value of the sales made and the cost of the goods (that is, wrapping paper) sold.

Income statement for Monday

	£
Sales revenue	45
Cost of goods sold ($3/4$ of £40)	(30)
Profit	**15**

Note that it is only the cost of the wrapping paper *sold* that is matched against (and deducted from) the sales revenue in order to find the profit, not the whole of the cost of wrapping paper acquired. Any unsold inventories (also known as *stock*) will be charged against any future sales revenue that it generates. In this case the cost of the unsold inventories is $1/4$ of £40 = £10.

What is the accumulated wealth on Monday evening and what form does it take?

To establish the accumulated wealth at the end of Monday's trading, we can draw up a *statement of financial position* for Paul's business. This statement will also list the forms of wealth held at the end of that day.

Statement of financial position as at Monday evening

	£
Cash (closing balance)	45
Inventories of goods for resale ($1/4$ of 40)	10
Total assets	**55**
Equity	**55**

Note the terms 'assets' and 'equity' that appear in this statement. 'Assets' are business resources (things of value to the business) and include cash and inventories. 'Equity' is the word used in accounting to describe the investment, or stake, of the owner(s) – in this case Paul – in the business. Both of these terms will be discussed in some detail a little later in this chapter. Note that the equity on Monday evening was £55. This represented the £40 that Paul put in to start the business, plus Monday's profit (£15) – profits belong to the owner(s).

Let us now continue by looking at what happens on the following day.

On Tuesday, Paul bought more wrapping paper for £20 cash. He managed to sell all of the new inventories and all of the earlier inventories, for a total of £48.

The statement of cash flows for Tuesday will be as follows:

Statement of cash flows for Tuesday

	£
Opening balance (from Monday evening)	45
Cash from sales of wrapping paper	48
Cash paid to buy wrapping paper	(20)
Closing balance	73

The income statement for Tuesday will be as follows:

Income statement for Tuesday

	£
Sales revenue	48
Cost of goods sold (£20 + £10)	(30)
Profit	18

The statement of financial position as at Tuesday evening will be:

Statement of financial position as at Tuesday evening

	£
Cash (closing balance)	73
Inventories	–
Total assets	73
Equity	73

We can see that the total business wealth had increased to £73 by Tuesday evening. This represents an increase of £18 (that is, £73 − £55) over Monday's figure – which, of course, is the amount of profit made during Tuesday as shown on the income statement.

We can see from the financial statements in Example 2.1 that each statement provides part of a picture of the financial performance and position of the business. We begin by showing the cash movements. Cash is a vital resource that is needed for any business to function effectively. It is used to meet debts that become due and to acquire other resources (such as inventories). Cash has been described as the 'lifeblood' of a business.

Reporting cash movements alone, however, is not enough to portray the financial health of the business. To find out how much profit was generated, we need an income statement. It is important to recognise that cash and profits rarely move in unison. During Monday, for example, the cash balance increased by £5, but the profit generated, as shown in the income statement, was £15. The cash balance did not increase in line with profit because part of the wealth (£10) was held in the form of inventories.

The statement of financial position that was drawn up as at the end of Monday's trading provides an insight into the total wealth of the business. This wealth can be held in various forms. For Paul's business, wealth is held in the form of cash and inventories. This means that, when drawing up the statement of financial position, both forms will be listed. For a large business, many other forms of wealth may be held, such as property, equipment, motor vehicles and so on.

> ### Activity 2.1
>
> On Wednesday, Paul bought more wrapping paper for £46 cash. However, it was raining hard for much of the day and sales were slow. After Paul had sold half of his total inventories for £32, he decided to stop trading until Thursday morning.
>
> Have a go at drawing up the three financial statements for Paul's business for Wednesday.
>
> **Statement of cash flows for Wednesday**
>
> | | £ |
> |---|---|
> | Opening balance (from Tuesday evening) | 73 |
> | Cash from sales of wrapping paper | 32 |
> | Cash paid to buy wrapping paper | (46) |
> | **Closing balance** | **59** |
>
> **Income statement for Wednesday**
>
> | | £ |
> |---|---|
> | Sales revenue | 32 |
> | Cost of goods sold ($\frac{1}{2}$ of £46) | (23) |
> | **Profit** | **9** |
>
> **Statement of financial position as at Wednesday evening**
>
> | | £ |
> |---|---|
> | Cash (closing balance) | 59 |
> | Inventories ($\frac{1}{2}$ of £46) | 23 |
> | **Total assets** | **82** |
> | **Equity** | **82** |

Note that the total business wealth has increased by £9 (that is, the amount of Wednesday's profit) even though the cash balance has declined. This is because the business is holding more of its wealth in the form of inventories rather than cash, compared with the position on Tuesday evening.

By Wednesday evening, the equity stood at £82. This arose from Paul's initial investment of £40, plus his profits for Monday (£15), Tuesday (£18) and Wednesday (£9). This represents Paul's total investment in his business at that time. The equity of most businesses will similarly be made up of injections of funds by the owner(s) plus any accumulated profits.

We can see that the income statement and statement of cash flows are both concerned with measuring flows (of wealth and cash respectively) during a particular period. The statement of financial position, however, is concerned with the financial position at a particular moment in time. Figure 2.1 illustrates this point.

The three financial statements discussed are often referred to as the **final accounts** of the business.

For external users (that is, virtually all users except the managers of the business concerned), these statements are normally backward-looking because they are based on information concerning past events and transactions. This can be useful in providing feedback on past performance and in identifying trends that provide clues to future performance. However, the statements can also be prepared using projected data to help assess likely future profits, cash flows and so on. Normally, this is done only for management decision-making purposes.

Now that we have an overview of the financial statements, we shall consider each one in detail. The remainder of this chapter is devoted to the statement of financial position.

> The income statement and statement of cash flows are concerned with measuring flows of wealth and cash (respectively) over time. The statement of financial position, however, is concerned with measuring the amount of wealth at a particular moment in time.

Figure 2.1 The relationship between the major financial statements

THE STATEMENT OF FINANCIAL POSITION

We saw a little earlier that this statement shows the forms in which the wealth of a business is held and how much wealth is held in each form. We can, however, be more specific about the nature of this statement by saying that it sets out the **assets** of a business, on the one hand, and the **claims** against the business, on the other. Before looking at the statement of financial position in more detail, we need to be clear about what these terms mean.

Assets

An asset is essentially a resource held by a business. To qualify as an asset for inclusion in the statement of financial position, however, a resource must possess the following characteristics:

- *It must be an economic resource.* This type of resource provides a right to potential economic benefits. These benefits must not, however, be equally available to others. Take, for example, what economists refer to as *public goods.* These include resources such as the road system, GPS satellites or official statistics. Although these may provide economic benefits to a business, others can receive the same benefits at no great cost. A public good cannot, therefore, be regarded as an asset of a business. Economic benefits flowing from a resource can take various forms depending on how it is used by a business. Note that an economic resource need only have the *potential* to generate benefits. They need not be certain or even probable.

Activity 2.2

What forms might economic benefits take? Try to think of at least two.

> These may include:
>
> - cash generated from producing goods or services;
> - cash received from the proceeds on selling the resource;
> - the value received when exchanged for another economic resource;
> - the value received when used to satisfy debts incurred by the business; and
> - cash generated from renting or leasing it.
>
> You may have thought of others.

- *The economic resource must be under the control of the business.* This gives a business the exclusive right to decide how the resource is used as well as the right to any benefits that flow. Control is usually acquired by a business through legal ownership or through a contractual agreement (for example, leasing equipment). The event, or transaction, leading to control of the resource must have occurred in the past. In other words, the business must already exercise control over it. (See Reference 1 at the end of the chapter.)

Activity 2.3

Assume a business owns a 40 per cent stake in a gold mine. As this ownership stake will not give control over the whole of the gold mine, can this resource be regarded as an asset of the business?

In this case, the asset of the business will be the 40 per cent share of the mine that is under its control, rather than the whole of the gold mine.

- *The economic resource must be capable of measurement in monetary terms.* Often, an economic resource cannot be measured with a great deal of certainty. Estimates may be used that ultimately prove to be inaccurate. Nevertheless, it can still be reported as an asset for inclusion in the statement of financial position as long as a sufficiently faithful representation of its measurement can be produced. There are cases, however, where uncertainty regarding measurement is so great that this cannot be done. Take for example, the title of a magazine (such as *Hello!* or *Vogue*) that has been created by its publisher. While it may be extremely valuable to the publishing business, any attempt to measure this resource would be extremely difficult: it would have to rely on arbitrary assumptions. As a result, any measurement produced is unlikely to be useful. The publishing title will not, therefore, appear as an asset in the statement of financial position.

Note that *all* the characteristics identified must exist if a resource is to qualify for recognition. This will strictly limit the resources that are regarded as an asset for inclusion in the statement of financial position. Once included, an asset will continue to be recognised until the economic benefits are exhausted, or the business disposes of it.

Figure 2.2 summarises the above discussion in the form of a decision chart.

Figure 2.2 Identifying an asset for inclusion in the statement of financial position

The characteristics identified are discussed in the chapter.

Activity 2.4

Indicate which of the following items could appear as an asset on the statement of financial position of a business. Explain your reasoning in each case.

1 £1,000 owed to the business by a credit customer who is unable to pay.
2 A patent, bought from an inventor, that gives the business the right to produce a new product. Production of the new product is expected to increase profits over the period during which the patent is held.
3 A recently hired new marketing director who is confidently expected to increase profits by over 30 per cent during the next three years.
4 A recently purchased machine that will save the business £10,000 each year. It is already being used by the business but it has been acquired on credit and is not yet paid for.

Your answer should be along the following lines:

1 Under normal circumstances, a business would expect a customer to pay the amount owed. Such an amount is therefore typically shown as an asset under the heading '**trade receivables**' (or 'debtors'). However, in this particular case, the customer is unable to pay. As a result, the item is not an economic resource and the £1,000 owing would not be regarded as an asset. Debts that are not paid are referred to as *bad debts*.
2 The patent would have all the characteristics identified and would, therefore, be regarded as an asset.

> 3 The new marketing director would not be considered as an asset. One argument in support of this position is that the business does not have rights of control over the director. Nevertheless, it may have control over the services that the director provides. Even if these services become the focus of attention, however, it is usually impossible to measure them in monetary terms with any degree of certainty.
> 4 The machine has the characteristics identified and so would be considered an asset even though it is not yet paid for. Once the business has contracted to buy the machine, and has accepted it, ownership will pass even though payment is still outstanding. (The amount outstanding would be shown as a claim, as we shall see shortly.)

The sorts of items that often appear as assets in the statement of financial position of a business include:

- property;
- plant and equipment;
- fixtures and fittings;
- patents and trademarks;
- trade receivables (debtors); and
- investments outside the business.

Activity 2.5

Can you think of two additional items that might appear as assets in the statement of financial position of a typical business?

You may be able to think of a number of other items. Two that we have met so far, because they were held by Paul's wrapping paper business (in Example 2.1), are inventories and cash.

Note that an asset does not have to be a physical item – it may be a non-physical one that gives a right to potential benefits. Assets that have a physical substance and can be touched (such as inventories) are referred to as **tangible assets**. Assets that have no physical substance but which, nevertheless, may provide future benefits (such as patents) are referred to as **intangible assets**.

Claims

A claim is an obligation of the business to provide cash, or some other form of benefit, to an outside party. It will normally arise as a result of the outside party providing assets for use by the business. There are essentially two types of claim against a business:

- **Equity**. This represents the claim of the owner(s) against the business. This claim is sometimes referred to as the *owner's capital.* Some find it hard to understand how the owner can have a claim against the business, particularly when we consider the example of a sole-proprietor-type business, like Paul's, where the owner *is,* in effect, the business. For accounting purposes, however, a clear distinction is made between the business and the owner(s). The business is viewed as being quite separate from the owner. It is seen as a separate entity with its own separate existence. This means that, when financial statements are prepared, they relate to the business rather than to the owner(s). Viewed from this perspective, any funds contributed by the owner will be seen as coming from outside the business and will appear as a claim against the business in its statement of financial position.

- **Liabilities**. Liabilities represent the claims of other parties, apart from the owner (s). They involve an obligation to transfer economic resources (usually cash) as a result of past transactions or events. A liability incurred by a business cannot be avoided and so will remain a liability until it is settled.

  Most liabilities arise for legal or contractual reasons, such as from acquiring goods or services or from borrowing funds. They can, however, arise from the policies and practices adopted by the business, such as 'no quibble' refunds.

Now that the meanings of the terms *assets*, *equity* and *liabilities* have been established, we can consider the relationship between them. This relationship is quite straightforward. If a business wishes to acquire assets, it must raise the necessary funds from somewhere. It may raise these funds from the owner(s), or from other outside parties, or from both. Example 2.2 illustrates this relationship.

Example 2.2

Jerry and Company is a new business that was created by depositing £20,000 in a bank account on 1 March. This amount was raised partly from the owner (£6,000) and partly from borrowing (£14,000). Raising funds in this way will give rise to a claim on the business by both the owner (equity) and the lender (liability). If a statement of financial position of Jerry and Company is prepared following these transactions, it will appear as follows:

Jerry and Company
Statement of financial position as at 1 March

	£
ASSETS	
Cash at bank	20,000
Total assets	20,000
EQUITY AND LIABILITIES	
Equity	6,000
Liabilities – borrowing	14,000
Total equity and liabilities	20,000

We can see from the statement of financial position that the total claims (equity and liabilities) are the same as the total assets. Thus:

$$\text{Assets} = \text{Equity} + \text{Liabilities}$$

This equation – which we shall refer to as the *accounting equation* – will always hold true. Whatever changes may occur to the assets of the business or the claims against it, there will be compensating changes elsewhere that will ensure that the statement of financial position always 'balances'. By way of illustration, consider the following transactions for Jerry and Company:

2 March	Bought a motor van for £5,000, paying by cheque.
3 March	Bought inventories (that is, goods to be sold) on one month's credit for £3,000. (This means that the inventories were bought on 3 March, but payment to the supplier will not be due until 3 April.)
4 March	Repaid £2,000 of the amount borrowed, to the lender, by cheque.
6 March	Owner introduced another £4,000 into the business bank account.

A statement of financial position may be drawn up after each day in which transactions have taken place. In this way, we can see the effect of each transaction on the assets and claims of the business. The statement of financial position as at 2 March will be:

Jerry and Company
Statement of financial position as at 2 March

	£
ASSETS	
Cash at bank (20,000 − 5,000)	15,000
Motor van	5,000
Total assets	20,000
EQUITY AND LIABILITIES	
Equity	6,000
Liabilities – borrowing	14,000
Total equity and liabilities	20,000

As we can see, the effect of buying the motor van is to decrease the balance at the bank by £5,000 and to introduce a new asset – a motor van – to the statement of financial position. The total assets remain unchanged. It is only the 'mix' of assets that has changed.

The claims against the business remain the same because there has been no change in the way in which the business has been funded.

The statement of financial position as at 3 March, following the purchase of inventories, will be:

Jerry and Company
Statement of financial position as at 3 March

	£
ASSETS	
Cash at bank	15,000
Motor van	5,000
Inventories	3,000
Total assets	23,000
EQUITY AND LIABILITIES	
Equity	6,000
Liabilities – borrowing	14,000
Liabilities – trade payable	3,000
Total equity and liabilities	23,000

The effect of buying inventories has been to introduce another new asset (inventories) to the statement of financial position. Furthermore, the fact that the goods have not yet been paid for means that the claims against the business will be increased by the £3,000 owed to the supplier, who is referred to as a **trade payable** (or trade creditor) on the statement of financial position.

Activity 2.6

Try drawing up a statement of financial position as at 4 March for Jerry and Company.

The statement of financial position as at 4 March, following the repayment of part of the borrowing, will be:

Jerry and Company
Statement of financial position as at 4 March

	£
ASSETS	
Cash at bank (15,000 − 2,000)	13,000
Motor van	5,000
Inventories	3,000
Total assets	**21,000**
EQUITY AND LIABILITIES	
Equity	6,000
Liabilities – borrowing (14,000 − 2,000)	12,000
Liabilities – trade payable	3,000
Total equity and liabilities	**21,000**

The repayment of £2,000 of the borrowing will result in a decrease in the balance at the bank of £2,000 and a decrease in the lender's claim against the business by the same amount.

Activity 2.7

Try drawing up a statement of financial position as at 6 March for Jerry and Company.

The statement of financial position as at 6 March, following the introduction of more funds, will be:

Jerry and Company
Statement of financial position as at 6 March

	£
ASSETS	
Cash at bank (13,000 + 4,000)	17,000
Motor van	5,000
Inventories	3,000
Total assets	**25,000**
EQUITY AND LIABILITIES	
Equity (6,000 + 4,000)	10,000
Liabilities – borrowing	12,000
Liabilities – trade payable	3,000
Total equity and liabilities	**25,000**

The introduction of more funds by the owner will result in an increase in the equity of £4,000 and an increase in the cash at bank by the same amount.

The example of Jerry and Company illustrates the point that the accounting equation (assets equals equity plus liabilities) will always hold true. It reflects the fact that, if a business wishes to acquire more assets, it must raise funds equal to the cost of those assets. The funds raised must be provided by the owners (equity), or by others (liabilities), or by a combination of the two. This means that the total cost of assets acquired should always equal the total equity plus liabilities. Similarly, if the business raises the funds by selling an existing asset, one asset replaces another, leaving the accounting equation holding true.

It is worth pointing out that businesses do not normally draw up a statement of financial position after each day, as shown in the example. We have done this to illustrate the effect on the statement of financial position of each transaction. In practice, a statement of financial position for a business is usually prepared at the end of a defined period. The period over which businesses measure their financial results is usually known as the *reporting period*, but it is sometimes called the 'accounting period' or 'financial period'.

Determining the length of the reporting period will involve weighing up the costs of producing the information against the perceived benefits of having that information for decision-making purposes. In practice, the reporting period will vary between businesses; it could be monthly, quarterly, half-yearly or annually. For external reporting purposes, an annual reporting period is the norm (although certain businesses, typically larger ones, report more frequently than this). For internal reporting purposes to managers, however, more frequent (perhaps monthly) financial statements are likely to be prepared.

THE EFFECT OF TRADING TRANSACTIONS

In the example (Jerry and Company), we showed how various types of transactions affected the statement of financial position. However, one very important type of transaction – trading transactions – has yet to be considered. To show how this type of transaction affects the statement of financial position, let us return to Jerry and Company.

Example 2.2 (continued)

The statement of financial position that we drew up for Jerry and Company as at 6 March was as follows:

Jerry and Company
Statement of financial position as at 6 March

	£
ASSETS	
Cash at bank	17,000
Motor van	5,000
Inventories	3,000
Total assets	25,000
EQUITY AND LIABILITIES	
Equity	10,000
Liabilities – borrowing	12,000
Liabilities – trade payable	3,000
Total equity and liabilities	25,000

On 7 March, the business managed to sell all of the inventories for £5,000 and received a cheque immediately from the customer for this amount. The statement of financial position on 7 March, after this transaction has taken place, will be:

Jerry and Company
Statement of financial position as at 7 March

	£
ASSETS	
Cash at bank (17,000 + 5,000)	22,000
Motor van	5,000
Inventories (3,000 − 3,000)	–
Total assets	**27,000**
EQUITY AND LIABILITIES	
Equity (10,000 + (5,000 − 3,000))	12,000
Liabilities – borrowing	12,000
Liabilities – trade payable	3,000
Total equity and liabilities	**27,000**

We can see that the inventories (£3,000) have now disappeared from the statement of financial position, but the cash at bank has increased by the selling price of the inventories (£5,000). The net effect has therefore been to increase assets by £2,000 (that is, £5,000 less £3,000). This increase represents the net increase in wealth (the profit) that has arisen from trading. Also note that the equity of the business has increased by £2,000, in line with the increase in assets. This increase in equity reflects the fact that wealth generated, as a result of trading or other operations, will be to the benefit of the owners and will increase their stake in the business.

Activity 2.8

What would have been the effect on the statement of financial position if the inventories had been sold on 7 March for £1,000 rather than £5,000?

The statement of financial position on 7 March would then have been:

Jerry and Company
Statement of financial position as at 7 March

	£
ASSETS	
Cash at bank (17,000 + 1,000)	18,000
Motor van	5,000
Inventories (3,000 − 3,000)	–
Total assets	**23,000**
EQUITY AND LIABILITIES	
Equity (10,000 + (1,000 − 3,000))	8,000
Liabilities – borrowing	12,000
Liabilities – trade payable	3,000
Total equity and liabilities	**23,000**

Measuring and Reporting Financial Position 47

> As we can see, the inventories (£3,000) will disappear from the statement of financial position, but the cash at bank will rise by only £1,000. This will mean a net reduction in assets of £2,000. This reduction represents a loss arising from trading and will be reflected in a reduction in the equity of the owners.

What we have just seen means that the accounting equation can be extended as follows:

> **Assets (at the end of the period)** = **Equity (amount at the start of the period)**
> **+ Profit (or Loss) for the period)**
> **+ Liabilities (at the end of the period)**

(This is assuming that the owner makes no injections or withdrawals of equity during the period.)

Any funds introduced or withdrawn by the owners also affect equity. If the owners withdrew £1,500 for their own use, the equity of the owners would be reduced by £1,500. If these drawings were in cash, the cash balance would decrease by £1,500 in the statement of financial position.

Like all items in the statement of financial position, the amount of equity is cumulative. This means that any profit not taken out as drawings by the owner(s) remains in the business. These retained (or 'ploughed-back') earnings have the effect of expanding the business.

CLASSIFYING ASSETS

In the statement of financial position, assets and claims are usually grouped into categories. This is designed to help users, as a haphazard listing of these items could be confusing. Assets are usually categorised as being either current or non-current.

Current assets

Current assets are basically assets that are held for the short term. To be more precise, they are assets that meet any of the following conditions:

- they are held for sale or consumption during the business's normal operating cycle;
- they are expected to be sold within a year after the date of the relevant statement of financial position;
- they are held principally for trading; and
- they are cash, or near cash such as easily marketable, short-term investments.

The operating cycle of a business, mentioned above, is the time between buying and/or creating a product or service and receiving the cash on its sale. For most businesses, this will be less than a year. (It is worth mentioning that sales made by most businesses are made on credit. The customer pays some time after the goods are received or the service is rendered.)

The most common current assets are inventories, trade receivables (amounts owed by customers for goods or services supplied to them on credit) and cash. For businesses that sell goods, rather than render a service, the current assets of inventories, trade receivables and cash are interrelated. They circulate within a business as shown in Figure 2.3. We can see that cash can be used to buy inventories, which are then sold on credit. When the credit customers (trade receivables) pay, the business receives an injection of cash and so on.

> Inventories (stock) → Trade receivables (trade debtors) → Cash → Inventories
>
> Inventories may be sold on credit to customers. When the customers pay, the trade receivables will be converted into cash, which can then be used to purchase more inventories. Then the cycle begins again.

Figure 2.3 The circulating nature of current assets

For purely service businesses, the situation is similar, except that inventories are not involved.

Non-current assets

Non-current assets (also called *fixed assets*) are simply assets that do not meet the definition of current assets. They tend to be held for long-term operations. Non-current assets may be either tangible or intangible. Tangible non-current assets normally consist of **property, plant and equipment**. We shall refer to them in this way from now on. This is a rather broad term that includes items such as land and buildings, machinery, motor vehicles and fixtures and fittings.

The distinction between those assets continuously circulating (current) and those used for long-term operations (non-current) may help readers of the statement of financial position when assessing the mix of assets held. Most businesses need a certain amount of both types of asset to operate effectively.

Activity 2.9

Can you think of two examples of assets that may be classified as non-current assets for an insurance business?

Examples of assets that may be defined as being non-current include:

- property;
- furniture;
- motor vehicles;
- computers;
- computer software; and
- reference books.

This is not an exhaustive list. You may have thought of others.

The way in which a particular asset is classified (that is, between current and non-current) may vary according to the nature of the business. This is because the *purpose* for which the asset is held may vary. For example, a motor van retailer will normally hold inventories of motor vans for sale; it would, therefore, classify them as part of the current assets. On the other hand, a business that buys one of these vans to use for delivering its goods to customers (that is, as part of its long-term operations) would classify it as a non-current asset.

Activity 2.10

The assets of Kunalun and Co., a large advertising agency, are as follows:

- cash at bank;
- fixtures and fittings;
- office equipment;
- motor vehicles;
- property;
- computers; and
- work in progress (that is, partly completed work for clients).

Which of these do you think should be defined as non-current assets and which should be defined as current assets?

Your answer should be as follows:

Non-current assets	*Current assets*
Fixtures and fittings	Cash at bank
Office equipment	Work in progress
Motor vehicles	
Property	
Computers	

CLASSIFYING CLAIMS

As we have already seen, claims are normally classified into equity (owner's claim) and liabilities (claims of outsiders). Liabilities are further classified as either current or non-current.

Current liabilities

Current liabilities are basically amounts due for settlement in the short term. To be more precise, they are liabilities that meet any of the following conditions:

- they are expected to be settled within the business's normal operating cycle;
- they arise principally as a result of trading;
- they are due to be settled within a year after the date of the relevant statement of financial position; and
- there is no right to defer settlement beyond a year after the date of the relevant statement of financial position.

Non-current liabilities

Non-current liabilities represent amounts due that do not meet the definition of current liabilities and so represent longer-term liabilities.

> **Activity 2.11**
>
> **Can you think of one example of a current liability and one of a non-current liability?**
>
> An example of a current liability would be amounts owing to suppliers for goods supplied on credit (**trade payables**) or a bank overdraft (a form of short-term bank borrowing that is repayable on demand). An example of a non-current liability would be long-term borrowings.

It is quite common for non-current liabilities to become current liabilities. For example, borrowings to be repaid 18 months after the date of a particular statement of financial position will normally appear as a non-current liability. Those same borrowings will, however, appear as a current liability in the statement of financial position as at the end of the following year, by which time they would be due for repayment after six months.

This classification of liabilities between current and non-current helps to highlight those financial obligations that must shortly be met. It may be useful to compare the amount of current liabilities with the amount of current assets (that is, the assets that either are cash or will turn into cash within the normal operating cycle). This should reveal whether the business can cover its maturing obligations.

The classification of liabilities between current and non-current also helps to highlight the proportion of total long-term finance that is raised through borrowings rather than equity. Where a business relies on borrowings, rather than relying solely on funds provided by the owner(s), the financial risks increase. This is because borrowing brings a commitment to make periodic interest payments and capital repayments. The business may be forced to stop trading if this commitment cannot be fulfilled. Thus, when raising finance, a reasonable balance must be struck between borrowings and owners' equity.

STATEMENT LAYOUTS

Having looked at the classification of assets and liabilities, we shall now consider the layout of the statement of financial position. Although there is an almost infinite number of ways in which the same information on assets and claims could be presented, we shall consider two basic layouts. The first of these follows the style that we adopted with Jerry and Company earlier (see pages 42 to 47). A more comprehensive example of this style is shown in Example 2.3.

Example 2.3

Brie Manufacturing
Statement of financial position as at 31 December 2018

	£000
ASSETS	
Non-current assets	
Property	45
Plant and equipment	30
Motor vans	19
	94
Current assets	
Inventories	23
Trade receivables	18
Cash at bank	12
	53
Total assets	147
EQUITY AND LIABILITIES	
Equity	60
Non-current liabilities	
Long-term borrowings	50
Current liabilities	
Trade payables	37
Total equity and liabilities	147

The non-current assets have a total of £94,000 which, together with the current assets total of £53,000, gives a total of £147,000 for assets. Similarly, the equity totals £60,000 which, together with the £50,000 for non-current liabilities and £37,000 for current liabilities, gives a total for equity and liabilities of £147,000.

Within each category of asset (non-current and current) shown in Example 2.3, the items are listed in reverse order of liquidity (nearness to cash). Thus, the assets that are furthest from cash come first and the assets that are closest to cash come last. In the case of Brie manufacturing's non-current assets, property is listed first as this asset is tends to be the most difficult to turn into cash and motor vans are listed last as there is usually a ready market for them. In the case of current assets, we have already seen that inventories are converted to trade receivables and then trade receivables are converted to cash. As a result, under the heading of current assets, inventories are listed first, followed by trade receivables and finally cash itself. This ordering of assets will occur irrespective of the layout used.

Note that, in addition to a grand total for assets held, subtotals for non-current assets and current assets are shown. Subtotals are also used for non-current liabilities and current liabilities when more than one item appears within these categories.

A slight variation from the layout illustrated in Example 2.3 is as shown in Example 2.4.

Example 2.4

Brie Manufacturing
Statement of financial position as at 31 December 2018

	£000
ASSETS	
Non-current assets	
Property	45
Plant and equipment	30
Motor vans	19
	94
Current assets	
Inventories	23
Trade receivables	18
Cash at bank	12
	53
Total assets	147
LIABILITIES	
Non-current liabilities	
Long-term borrowings	(50)
Current liabilities	
Trade payables	(37)
Total liabilities	(87)
Net assets	60
EQUITY	60

We can see that the total liabilities are deducted from the total assets. This derives a figure for net assets – which is equal to equity. Using this format, the basic accounting equation is rearranged so that:

$$\text{Assets} - \text{Liabilities} = \text{Equity}$$

This rearranged equation highlights the fact that equity represents the residual interest of the owner(s) after deducting all liabilities of the business.

Figure 2.4 summarises the two types of layout discussed in this section.

The layout shown in Example 2.3 seems to be much the most popular in practice and so will be used throughout the book.

CAPTURING A MOMENT IN TIME

As we have already seen, the statement of financial position reflects the assets, equity and liabilities of a business at *a specified point in time*. It has been compared to a photograph. A photograph 'freezes' a particular moment in time and will represent the situation only at that moment. Hence, events may be quite different immediately before and immediately after the photograph was taken. When examining a statement of financial position, therefore, it is important to establish the date for which it has been drawn up. This information should be prominently displayed in the heading to the statement, as shown above in Example 2.4.

> The standard layout reflects the accounting equation Assets = Equity + Liabilities, whereas the alternative layout reflects a re-arrangement of this equation: Assets − Liabilities = Equity.

Figure 2.4 Layouts for the statement of financial position

When we are trying to assess current financial position, the more recent the statement of financial position date, the more helpful it is likely to be.

A business will normally prepare a statement of financial position as at the close of business on the last day of its annual reporting period. In the UK, businesses are free to choose the date of the end of their reporting period and, once chosen, it will normally change only under exceptional circumstances. When making a decision on which year-end date to choose, commercial convenience can often be a deciding factor. For example, a business operating in the retail trade may choose to have a year-end date early in the calendar year (for example, 31 January) because trade tends to be slack during that period and more staff time is available to help with the tasks involved in the preparation of the annual financial statements (such as checking the amount of inventories held ('stocktaking')). Since trade is slack, the amount of inventories held by the retail business is likely to be unusually low compared with other times of the year.

Activity 2.12

Does this pose a problem for external users seeking to assess the business's financial health?

While the statement of financial position may provide a fair view of the inventories held at the time it was drawn up, it will not be typical of the position over the rest of the year.

THE ROLE OF ACCOUNTING CONVENTIONS

Accounting has a number of conventions, or rules, that have evolved over time. They have evolved as attempts to deal with practical problems experienced by preparers and users of financial statements, rather than to reflect some theoretical ideal. In preparing the statements of financial position earlier in this chapter, we have followed various **accounting conventions**, although they have not been explicitly mentioned. We shall now identify and discuss the major conventions that we have applied.

Business entity convention

For accounting purposes, the business and its owner(s) are treated as being quite separate and distinct. This is why owners are treated as being claimants against their own business in respect of their investment. The **business entity convention** must be distinguished from the legal position that may exist between businesses and their owners. For sole proprietorships and partnerships, the law does not make any distinction between the business and its owner(s). For limited companies, on the other hand, there is a clear legal distinction between the business and its owners. (As we shall see in Chapter 4, the limited company is regarded as having a separate legal existence.) For accounting purposes, these legal distinctions are irrelevant and the business entity convention applies to all businesses.

Historic cost convention

The **historic cost convention** holds that the value of assets shown on the statement of financial position should be based on their historic cost (that is, acquisition cost). The use of historic cost means that problems of measurement reliability are minimised, as the amount paid for a particular asset is often a matter of demonstrable fact. Reliance on opinion is avoided, or, at least reduced, which should enhance the credibility of the information in the eyes of users. A key problem, however, is that the information provided may not be relevant to user needs. Even quite early in the life of some assets, historic costs may become outdated compared to current market values. This can be misleading when assessing current financial position.

Many argue that recording assets at their current value would provide a more realistic view of financial position and would be relevant for a wide range of decisions. A system of measurement based on current value does, however, bring its own problems. The term 'current value' can be defined in different ways. It can be defined broadly, as either the current replacement cost or the current realisable value (selling price) of an asset. These two types of valuation may result in quite different figures being produced to represent the current value of an item. Furthermore, the broad terms 'replacement cost' and 'realisable value' can be defined in different ways. We must therefore be clear about what kind of current value accounting we wish to use.

Activity 2.13 illustrates some of the problems associated with current value accounting.

Activity 2.13

Plumber and Company has a fleet of motor vans that are used for making deliveries to customers. The owners want to show these vans on the statement of financial position at their current values rather than at their historic cost. They would like to use either current replacement cost (based on how much would have to be paid to buy vans of a similar type, age and condition) or current realisable value (based on how much a motor van dealer would pay for the vans, if the business sold them).

Why is the choice between the two current valuation methods important? Why would both current valuation methods present problems in establishing reliable values?

> The choice between the two current valuation methods is important because the values derived under each method are likely to be quite different. Normally, replacement cost values for the motor vans will be higher than their current realisable values.
>
> Establishing current values will usually rely on opinions, which may well vary from one dealer to another. Thus, instead of a single, unambiguous figure for, say, the current replacement cost for each van, a range of possible current replacement costs could be produced. The same problem will arise when trying to establish the current realisable value for each van.

We should bear in mind that the motor vans discussed in Activity 2.13 are less of a problem than are many other types of asset. There is a ready market for motor vans, which means that a value can be obtained by contacting a dealer. For a custom-built piece of equipment, however, identifying a replacement cost or, worse still, a selling price, could be very difficult.

Where the current values of assets are based on the opinion of managers of the business, there is a greater risk that they will lack credibility. Some form of independent valuation, or verification, may therefore be required to reassure users.

Despite the problems associated with current values, they are increasingly used when reporting assets in the statement of financial position. This has led to a steady erosion in the importance of the historic cost convention. Thus, many businesses now prepare financial statements on a modified historic cost basis. We shall consider the valuation of assets in more detail a little later in the chapter.

Prudence convention

In broad terms, the **prudence convention** holds that caution should be exercised when preparing financial statements. This may not seem to be a contentious issue: it would, after all, be difficult to argue that an incautious approach should be taken. Nevertheless, the prudence convention has excited much debate over the years. The root cause has been the way in which the convention is often applied. It can be used to support a bias towards the understatement of financial strength: that is, the understatement of assets and profit and the overstatement of liabilities.

Those who support this approach to prudence argue that it is better to understate than to overstate financial strength. They make the point that, by overstating financial strength, users of financial statements may be misled into making poor decisions.

Activity 2.14

What sort of poor decisions may be made as a result of overstating the financial strength of a business? Try to think of at least two.

Examples of poor decisions may include:

- excessive amounts being paid out of profit to the owners, thereby, depleting their equity and undermining the financial health of the business;
- excessive bonuses being paid to managers based on overstated profits;
- new owners paying more to acquire a part, or the whole, of a business than is justified; and
- lenders providing funds to a business based on a rosier picture of financial strength than is warranted by the facts.

You may have thought of others.

The bias towards the understatement of financial strength evolved in order to counteract the excessive optimism of managers. However, just as overstatement can lead to poor decisions, understatement can lead to the same. It may, for example, result in existing owners selling their business too cheaply, lenders refusing a loan application based on a distortedly pessimistic picture of financial strength and so on.

The systematic bias towards understatement just described clashes with the need for *neutrality* in preparing financial statements.

Activity 2.15

In Chapter 1 we discussed neutrality as a desirable element of one of the major qualitative characteristics of financial information. Can you remember which one?

Neutrality is one of three elements needed to ensure faithful representation. (The other two elements are completeness and freedom from error.)

Neutrality, by definition, requires that financial statements are not slanted or weighted so as to present either a favourable or unfavourable picture to users. To accommodate the concept of neutrality, therefore, prudence must be interpreted and applied in a different way than described above. Adopting a cautious approach to preparing financial statements should not result in the deliberate understatement of financial strength. In other words, assets and profit should not be understated and liabilities should not be overstated.

Going concern convention

Under the **going concern convention**, the financial statements should be prepared on the assumption that a business will continue operations for the foreseeable future, unless there is evidence to the contrary. In other words, it is assumed that there is no intention, or need, to sell off the non-current assets of the business.

Where a business is in financial difficulties, however, non-current assets may have to be sold to repay those with claims against the business. The realisable (sale) value of many non-current assets is often much lower than the values reported in the statement of financial position. In the event of a forced sale of assets, therefore, significant losses might arise. These losses must be anticipated and fully reported when, but only when, a business's going concern status is called into question.

Dual aspect convention

The **dual aspect convention** asserts that each transaction has two aspects, both of which will affect the statement of financial position. This means that, for example, the purchase of a computer for cash results in an increase in one asset (computer) and a decrease in another (cash). Similarly, the repayment of borrowings results in the decrease in a liability (borrowings) and the decrease in an asset (cash).

Activity 2.16

What are the two aspects of each of the following transactions?

1. Purchasing £1,000 of inventories on credit.
2. Owner withdrawing £2,000 in cash.
3. Paying a supplier £1,000 for inventories bought on credit a few weeks earlier.

Your answer should be as follows:

1. Inventories increase by £1,000, trade payables increase by £1,000.
2. Equity reduces by £2,000, cash reduces by £2,000.
3. Trade payables reduce by £1,000, cash reduces by £1,000.

Recording the dual aspect of each transaction ensures that the statement of financial position will continue to balance, that is the accounting equation will continue to be valid.

Figure 2.5 summarises the main accounting conventions that exert an influence on the construction of the statement of financial position.

These are the key accounting conventions relating to the statement of financial position.

Figure 2.5 Accounting conventions influencing the statement of financial position

MONEY MEASUREMENT

We saw earlier that a resource will only be regarded as an asset and included on the statement of financial position where it is capable of being measured in monetary terms with a reasonable degree of certainty. Unless a measure can faithfully portray the resource, it is unlikely to be useful.

Various resources of a business fail to meet this criterion and so are excluded from the statement of financial position.

> **Activity 2.17**
>
> Can you identify any of these resources? Try to think of at least two.
>
> They may include:
>
> - human resources;
> - business reputation;
> - business location; and
> - customer and supplier relationships.

From time to time, attempts are made to measure and report some of these resources in order to provide a more complete picture of financial position. However, these attempts usually attract little support. Measures with a high degree of uncertainty lead to inconsistency in reporting and create doubts in the minds of users. This, in turn, can undermine the integrity and credibility of the financial statement.

Let us now move on to discuss some key economic resources that normally pose measurement problems.

Goodwill and brands

Some intangible non-current assets are similar to tangible non-current assets: they have a clear and separate identity and the cost of acquiring the asset can be measured with a reasonable degree of certainty. Examples normally include patents, trademarks, copyrights and licences. Other intangible non-current assets, however, are quite different. They lack a clear and separate identity and reflect a hotch-potch of attributes, which are part of the essence of the business. Goodwill and product brands are often examples of assets that lack a clear and separate identity.

The term '**goodwill**' is often used to cover various attributes such as the quality of the products, the skill of employees and the relationship with customers. The term 'product brands' is also used to cover various attributes, such as the brand image, the quality of the product, the trademark and so on. Where goodwill and product brands have been generated internally by the business, it is often difficult to determine their cost or to measure their current market value or even to be clear that they really exist. They are, therefore, excluded from the statement of financial position.

When such assets are acquired through an 'arm's-length transaction', however, the problems of uncertainty about their existence and measurement are resolved. (An arm's-length transaction is one that is undertaken between two unconnected parties.) If goodwill is acquired, when taking over another business, or if a business acquires a particular product brand, from another business, these items will be separately identified and a price agreed for them. Under these circumstances, they can be regarded as assets (for accounting purposes) by the business that acquired them and included in the statement of financial position.

To agree a price for acquiring goodwill or product brands means that some form of valuation must take place and this raises the question as to how it is done. Usually, the valuation will be based on estimates of future earnings from holding the asset – a process that is fraught with difficulties. Nevertheless, a number of specialist businesses now exist that are prepared to take on this challenge.

Human resources

Attempts have been made to place a monetary measurement on the human resources of a business, but without any real success. There are, however, certain limited circumstances in which human resources are measured and reported in the statement of financial position. Professional football clubs provide an example of where these circumstances normally arise. While football clubs cannot own players, they can own the rights to the players' services. Where these rights are acquired by compensating other clubs for releasing the players from their contracts with those other clubs, an arm's-length transaction arises and the amounts paid provide a reliable basis for measurement. This means that the rights to services can be regarded as an asset of the club for accounting purposes (assuming, of course, the player will bring benefits to the club).

Real World 2.2 describes how one leading club reports its investment in players on the statement of financial position.

Real World 2.1

United players appear on the team sheet and on the statement of financial position

Manchester United Football Club has acquired several key players as a result of paying transfer fees to other clubs. In common with most UK football clubs. The club reports the cost of acquiring the rights to the players' services on its statement of financial position. The club's statement as at 30 June 2017 shows the total cost of registering its squad of players at more than £645 million. A total of 70 players were under contract at the year end, which included reserve team and youth team players. The club treats a proportion of each player's transfer fee as an expense each year. The exact proportion depends on the length of the particular player's contract.

The £645 million does not include 'home-grown' players such as Jesse Lingard, because United did not pay a transfer fee for them and so no clear-cut value can be placed on their services. During the year to 30 June 2017, the club was active in the transfer market and spent more than £205 million on acquiring new players, including Paul Pogba from Juventus, Henrikh Mkhitaryan from Borussia Dortmund and Anthony Martial from AS Monaco. Some players also left the club during the year, including Angel Di Maria and Morgan Schneiderlin.

The item of players' registrations is shown as an intangible asset in the statement of financial position as it is the rights to services, not the players, that are the assets. It is shown net of depreciation (or *amortisation* as it is usually termed for intangible non-current assets). The net amount at 30 June 2017 was more than £290 million and represented almost 19 per cent of Manchester United's total assets, as shown in the statement of financial position.

Source: Manchester United plc, Annual Report 2017.

Monetary stability

When using money as the unit of measurement, we normally fail to recognise the fact that it will change in value over time, despite the fact that in the UK, and throughout much of the world, inflation has been a persistent problem. This has meant that the value of money has declined in relation to other assets. In past years, high rates of inflation have resulted in statements of financial position, which were prepared on a historic cost basis, reflecting figures for assets that were much lower than if current values were employed. Rates of inflation have been relatively low in recent years and so the disparity between historic cost values and current values has been less pronounced. Nevertheless, it can still be significant. The problem of inflation has added fuel to the more general debate concerning how to measure asset values in the statement of financial position. It is to the issue of valuing assets that we now turn.

VALUING ASSETS

We saw earlier that, when preparing the statement of financial position, the historic cost convention is normally applied for the reporting of assets. This point requires further explanation as, in practice, things are a little more complex than this. Large businesses throughout much of the world adhere to asset valuation rules set out in International Financial Reporting Standards. We shall now consider the key valuation rules.

Non-current assets

Non-current assets have useful lives that are either *finite* or *indefinite*. Those with a finite life provide benefits to a business for a limited period of time, whereas those with an indefinite life provide benefits without a foreseeable time limit. This distinction between the two types of non-current assets applies equally to both tangible and intangible assets.

Initially, non-current assets are recorded at their historic cost, which will include any amounts spent on getting them ready for use.

Non-current assets with finite lives

Benefits from assets with finite useful lives will be used up over time as a result of market changes, wear and tear and so on. The amount used up, which is referred to as *depreciation* (or *amortisation,* in the case of intangible non-current assets), must be measured for each reporting period for which the assets are held. Although we shall leave a detailed examination of depreciation until Chapter 3, we need to know that when an asset has been depreciated, this must be reflected in the statement of financial position.

The total depreciation that has accumulated over the period since the asset was acquired must be deducted from its cost. This net figure (that is, the cost of the asset less the total depreciation to date) is referred to as the carrying amount. It is sometimes also known as *net book value* or *written-down value.* The procedure just described is not really a contravention of the historic cost convention. It is simply recognition of the fact that a proportion of the historic cost of the non-current asset has been consumed in the process of generating, or attempting to generate, benefits for the business.

Non-current assets with indefinite useful lives

Benefits from assets with indefinite lives may, or may not, be used up over time. Property, in the form of land, is usually an example of a tangible non-current asset with an indefinite life. Purchased goodwill could be an example of an intangible one, although this is not always the case. These assets are not subject to routine depreciation each reporting period.

Activity 2.18

Try to identify *two* non-current assets of a large manufacturing business that have a finite useful life and that can be classified as:

1. tangible and
2. intangible.

Tangible assets normally considered to have a finite life include:

- machinery and equipment;
- motor vehicles; and
- computers.

Intangible assets normally considered to have a finite life include:

- patents (many patents are granted for a period of 20 years);
- leases taken out on assets (such as a property); and
- licences (such as a royalty licence).

Fair values

Initially, non-current assets of all types (tangible and intangible) are recorded at cost. Subsequently, however, an alternative form of measurement may be allowed. Non-current assets may be recorded using **fair values** provided that these values can be measured with a reasonable degree of certainty. Fair values are market based. They represent the selling price that can be obtained in an orderly transaction under current market conditions. The use of fair values, rather than cost, provides users with more up-to-date information. This could well be more relevant to their needs. It may also place the business in a better light, as assets such as property may have increased significantly in value over time. Increasing the statement of financial position value of an asset does not, of course, make that asset more valuable. Perceptions of the business may, however, be altered by such a move.

One consequence of upwardly revaluing non-current assets with finite lives is that the depreciation charge will be increased. This is because the depreciation charge is based on the new (increased) value of the asset.

Real World 2.3 shows the effect of the revaluation of non-current assets on the financial position of one large business.

Real World 2.2

Rising asset levels

During the year to 31 March 2010, Veolia Water UK plc, which owns Thames Water, changed its policy on the valuation of certain types of non-current assets. These assets included land and buildings, infrastructure assets and vehicles, plant and machinery. The business switched from the use of historic cost to the use of fair values and a revaluation exercise was carried out by independent qualified valuers.

The effect of this policy change was to report a revaluation gain of more than £436 million during the year. There was a 40 per cent increase in owners' (shareholders') equity, which was largely due to this gain.

Source: Veolia Water UK plc, Annual Report 2009/10.

Activity 2.19

Refer to the statement of financial position of Brie Manufacturing shown earlier in Example 2.3 (page 51). What would be the effect of revaluing the property to a figure of £110,000 in the statement of financial position? Show the revised statement.

The effect on the statement of financial position would be to increase the figure for property to £110,000 and the gain on revaluation (that is, £110,000 − £45,000 = £65,000) would be added to equity, as it is the owner(s) who will have benefited from the gain. The revised statement of financial position would therefore be as follows:

Brie Manufacturing
Statement of financial position as at 31 December 2018

	£000
ASSETS	
Non-current assets	
Property	110
Plant and equipment	30
Motor vans	19
	159
Current assets	
Inventories	23
Trade receivables	18
Cash at bank	12
	53
Total assets	212
EQUITY AND LIABILITIES	
Equity (60 + 65)	125
Non-current liabilities	
Long-term borrowings	50
Current liabilities	
Trade payables	37
Total equity and liabilities	212

Once non-current assets are revalued, the frequency of revaluation becomes an important issue. Reporting assets on the statement of financial position at out-of-date revaluations is the worst of both worlds. It lacks the objectivity and verifiability of historic cost; it also lacks the realism of current values. Thus, where fair values are used, revaluations should be frequent enough to ensure that the carrying amount of the revalued asset does not differ materially from its fair value at the statement of financial position date.

When an item of property, plant or equipment (a tangible asset) is revalued on the basis of fair values, all assets within that particular group must be revalued. It is not therefore acceptable to revalue some items of property but not others. Although this rule provides some degree of consistency within a particular group of assets, it does not prevent the statement of financial position from containing a mixture of valuations.

Intangible assets are not usually revalued to fair values. This is because an active market is required to determine fair values. For most intangible assets, an active market does not exist. A few intangible assets, however, such as transferable taxi licences, fishing licences and production quotas, provide the exception.

It has been argued that recent emphasis on the use of fair values in accounting has resulted in the exercise of prudence becoming less important. **Real World 2.4** is an extract from an article by John Kay that explains why this change has taken place. The article, which is well worth reading in full, is highly critical of the change.

Real World 2.3

It's really not fair

Once upon a time, values were based on cost, unless assets were no longer worth their cost, in which case they had to be written down. A bird in the hand was worth more than any number in the bush: only when the bird emerged from the bush were you permitted to count it at all.

Like finance, however, accounting became cleverer, and worse. By the 1980s accounting had become the principal means by which UK graduates prepared for business. Many of these trainees found jobs in the finance sector; others took jobs in non-financial business – and, since they were smart, many rose to senior positions. Young accountants were smarter, greedier, less schooled in prudence and better schooled in economics. 'Fair value' increasingly replaced conservatism (prudence) as a guiding principle. But this route to the 'true and fair view' – the traditional holy grail of the accountant – often led to an outcome that was just the opposite of fair.

Source: Kay, J. (2015) Playing dice with your money, ft.com, 4 September. © The Financial Times Limited 2015. All rights reserved.

The impairment of non-current assets

All types of non-current asset are at risk of suffering a significant fall in value. This may be caused by changes in market conditions, technological obsolescence and so on. In some cases, this results in the carrying amount of the asset being higher than the amount that could be recovered from the asset; either through its continued use or through its sale. When this occurs, the asset value is said to be impaired and the general rule is to reduce the carrying amount on the statement of financial position to the recoverable amount. Unless this is done, the asset value will be overstated. The amount by which the asset value is reduced is known as an **impairment loss**. Note that this type of impairment in value should not be confused with routine depreciation of assets with finite lives. Routine depreciation arises from 'wear and tear' of the asset and/or the passage of time. Impairment results from a fundamental shift in market conditions or technological obsolescence.

Activity 2.20

With which one of the accounting conventions that we discussed earlier is this accounting treatment of impaired assets consistent?

The answer is prudence, which requires that we should adopt a cautious approach when preparing financial statements. The value of assets should not be overstated in the statement of financial position.

Real World 2.5 provides an example of where one large business incurred large impairment losses on the value of its assets.

> ### Real World 2.4
>
> # All going impaired shape
>
> More than £430 million was wiped off the market value of Daily Mail and General Trust (DMGT) on Monday as the company said revenues from its media division would fall in 2018 and warned of 'challenging' trading conditions. Shares in the group, which owns the Daily Mail and MailOnline website as well as an events business and a portfolio of business information companies, fell close to 24 per cent on concerns about 2018 trading and a £206 million impairment charge against several of its investments.
>
> 'I think they're in a real pickle,' said Alex DeGroote at Cenkos Securities. He pointed to the impairment charges taken against DMGT investments in Genscape, its energy information business, and Xceligent and SiteCompli, which provide property information, describing the charges as 'pretty devastating'. 'What does it say about the growth potential or scalability of these assets?' he added.
>
> In common with other UK newspaper groups, DMGT has been diversifying in recent years to reduce its reliance on a turbulent media sector – but in the process has created a complex web of investments and assets.
>
> **FT** *Source*: Extracts from Garrahan, M. (2017) Daily Mail and General Trust shares drop 24%, ft.com, 30 November. © The Financial Times Limited 2017. All rights reserved.

Intangible non-current assets with indefinite useful lives must be tested for impairment as at the end of each reporting period. Other non-current assets, however, must also be tested where events suggest that impairment has taken place.

> ### Activity 2.21
>
> **Why might it be a good idea to have impairment tests carried out by independent experts?**
>
> Impairment tests involve making judgements about the appropriate value to place on assets. Employing independent valuers to make these judgements will normally give users of the financial statements greater confidence in the information reported. There is always a risk that managers will manipulate impairment values to portray a picture that they would like users to see.

When a non-current asset with a finite useful life has its value impaired, the future, periodic, depreciation expense for that asset will be based on the new (lower) impaired value.

Inventories

It is not only non-current assets that run the risk of a significant fall in value. The inventories of a business could also suffer this fate as a result of changes in market taste, obsolescence, deterioration, damage and so on. Where a fall in value means that the amount likely to be recovered from the sale of the inventories will be lower than their cost, this loss must be reflected in the statement of financial position. Thus, if the net realisable value (that is, selling price less any selling costs) falls below the historic cost of inventories held, the former should be used as the basis of valuation. This reflects, once again, the influence of the prudence convention on the statement of financial position.

The published financial statements of large businesses will normally show the basis on which inventories are valued. **Real World 2.6** shows how one business reports this information.

Real World 2.5

Reporting inventories

The 2016/17 annual report of Ted Baker plc, a leading designer clothes brand, includes the following explanation concerning inventories:

> Inventories and work in progress are stated at the lower of cost and net realisable value. Cost includes materials, direct labour and inward transportation costs. Net realisable value is based on estimated selling price, less further costs expected to be incurred to completion and disposal. Provision is made for obsolete, slow moving or defective items where appropriate.

Source: Ted Baker plc, Annual Report and Accounts 2016/17, p. 90.

MEETING USER NEEDS

The statement of financial position is the oldest of the three main financial statements and may help users in the following ways:

- *It provides insights about how the business is financed and how its funds are deployed.* The statement of financial position shows how much finance the owners contribute and how much is contributed by outside lenders. It also shows the different kinds of assets acquired and how much is invested in each kind.
- *It can provide a basis for assessing the value of the business.* Since the statement of financial position lists, and places a value on, the various assets and claims, it can provide a starting point for assessing the value of the business. We have seen earlier, however, that accounting rules may result in assets being shown at their historic cost, which may vary quite considerably from the current valuation, and that the restrictive definition of assets may completely exclude certain business resources from the statement of financial position.
- *Relationships between assets and claims can be assessed.* It can be useful to look at relationships between various statement of financial position items, for example the relationship between how much wealth is tied up in current assets and how much is owed in the short term (current liabilities). From this relationship, we can see whether the business has sufficient short-term assets to cover its maturing obligations.

- *Performance can be assessed.* The effectiveness of a business in generating wealth can usefully be assessed against the amount of investment that was involved. Thus, the relationship between profit earned during a period and the value of the net assets invested can be helpful to many users, particularly owners and managers.

Once armed with the insights that a statement of financial position can provide, users are better placed to make investment and other decisions. **Real World 2.7** shows how a small business was able to obtain a loan because its bank was impressed by its strong statement of financial position.

Real World 2.6

A sound education

Sandeep Sud is a qualified solicitor who also runs a school uniform business based in Hounslow, in partnership with his parents. The business, which has four full-time employees, uses its statement of financial position to gauge how it is progressing. The statement has also been a key factor in securing a bank loan for the improvement and expansion of the business premises.

According to Sandeep,

> Having a strong statement of financial position helped when it came to borrowing. When we first applied for a refurbishment loan we couldn't provide up-to-date accounts to the bank manager. This could have been a problem, but we quickly got our accounts in order and the loan was approved straight away. Because our statement of financial position was strong, the bank thought we were a good risk. Although we decided not to draw down on the loan – because we used cashflow instead – it did open our eyes to the importance of a strong statement of financial position.

Source: Adapted from Balance sheets: the basics, www.businesslink.gov.uk [accessed 14 April 2010]. Available under the Open Government Licence v3.0, www.nationalarchives.gov.uk/doc/open-government-licence/version/3/.

Self-assessment question 2.1

The following information relates to Simonson Engineering as at 30 September 2018:

	£
Plant and equipment	25,000
Trade payables	18,000
Short-term borrowings	26,000
Inventories	45,000
Property	72,000

	£
Long-term borrowings	51,000
Trade receivables	48,000
Equity at 1 October 2017	117,500
Cash in hand	1,500
Motor vehicles	15,000
Fixtures and fittings	9,000
Profit for the year to 30 September 2018	18,000
Drawings for the year to 30 September 2018	15,000

Required:
(a) Prepare a statement of financial position for the business as at 30 September 2018 using the standard layout illustrated in Example 2.3.
(b) Comment on the financial position of the business based on the statement prepared in (a).
(c) Show the effect on the statement of financial position shown in (a) of a decision to revalue the property to £115,000 and to recognise that the net realisable value of inventories at the year end is £38,000.

The solution to this question can be found at the back of the book, on page 305.

SUMMARY

The main points of this chapter may be summarised as follows:

The major financial statements

- There are three major financial statements: the statement of cash flows, the income statement and the statement of financial position.
- The statement of cash flows shows the cash movements over a particular period.
- The income statement shows the wealth (profit) generated over a particular period.
- The statement of financial position shows the accumulated wealth at a particular point in time.

The statement of financial position

- The statement of financial position sets out the assets of the business, on the one hand, and the claims against those assets, on the other.
- Assets are resources of the business that have certain characteristics, such as the right to future economic benefits.
- Claims are obligations on the part of the business to provide cash, or some other benefit, to outside parties.
- Claims are of two types: equity and liabilities.
- Equity represents the claim(s) of the owner(s) and liabilities represent the claims of others.

- The statement of financial position reflects the accounting equation:

> **Assets = Equity + Liabilities**

Classification of assets and liabilities
- Assets are normally categorised as being current or non-current.
- Current assets are cash, or near cash, or are held for sale or consumption in the normal course of business, or for trading, or for the short term.
- Non-current assets are assets that are not current assets. They are normally held for the long-term operations of the business.
- Liabilities are normally categorised as being current or non-current liabilities.
- Current liabilities represent amounts due in the normal course of the business's operating cycle, or are held for trading, or are to be settled within a year of, or cannot be deferred for at least a year after, the end of the reporting period.
- Non-current liabilities represent amounts due that are not current liabilities.

Statement of financial position layouts
- The standard layout begins with assets at the top of the statement of financial position and places equity and liabilities underneath.
- A variation of the standard layout also begins with the assets at the top of the statement of financial position, but then the non-current and current liabilities are deducted from the total assets figure to arrive at a net assets figure. Equity is placed underneath.

Accounting conventions
- Accounting conventions are the rules of accounting that have evolved to deal with practical problems experienced by those preparing financial statements.
- The main conventions relating to the statement of financial position include the business entity, historic cost, prudence, going concern and dual aspect conventions.

Money measurement
- Using money as the unit of measurement limits the scope of the statement of financial position.
- Certain resources such as goodwill, product brands and human resources are difficult to measure. An 'arm's-length transaction' is normally required before such assets can be measured reasonable certainty and reported on the statement of financial position.
- Money is not a stable unit of measurement – it changes in value over time.

Asset valuation
- The initial treatment is to show non-current assets at historic cost.
- Fair values may be used rather than historic cost, provided that they can be reliably obtained. This is rarely possible, however, for intangible non-current assets.
- Non-current assets with finite useful lives should be shown at cost (or fair value) less any accumulated depreciation (amortisation).

- Where the value of a non-current asset is impaired, it should be written down to its recoverable amount.
- Inventories are shown at the lower of cost or net realisable value.

The usefulness of the statement of financial position

- The statement of financial position shows how finance has been raised and how it has been deployed.
- It provides a basis for valuing the business, although it can only be a starting point.
- Relationships between various statement of financial position items can usefully be explored.
- Relationships between wealth generated and wealth invested can be helpful indicators of business effectiveness.

KEY TERMS

statement of cash flows
income statement
statement of financial position
final accounts
asset
claim
trade receivable
tangible asset
intangible asset
equity
liability
trade payable
reporting period
current asset

non-current (fixed) asset
property, plant and equipment
current liability
non-current liability
accounting convention
business entity convention
historic cost convention
prudence convention
going concern convention
dual aspect convention
goodwill
fair value
impairment loss

REFERENCE

1. International Accounting Standards Board (2018) *Conceptual Framework for Financial Reporting*, pages 28 to 31.

FURTHER READING

If you would like to explore the topics covered in this chapter in more depth, we recommend the following:

Elliott, B. and Elliott, J. (2017) *Financial Accounting and Reporting*, 18th edn, Pearson, Chapters 17, 19 and 20.

International Accounting Standards Board (2016) *A Guide through IFRS Standards (Green Book)*, IAS 16 *Property, Plant and Equipment* and IAS 38 *Intangible Assets*.

The KPMG International Financial Reporting Group (2017) *Insights into IFRS*, 14th edn, Sweet and Maxwell, Sections 3.2, 3.3, 3.8 and 3.10 (a summarised version of this is available free at www.kpmg.com).

Melville, A. (2017) *International Financial Reporting: A Practical Guide*, 6th edn, Pearson, Chapters 5, 6, and 7.

CRITICAL REVIEW QUESTIONS

Solutions to these questions can be found at the back of the book, starting on page 312.

2.1 An accountant prepared a statement of financial position for a business. In this statement, the equity of the owner was shown next to the liabilities. This confused the owner, who argued 'My equity is my major asset and so should be shown as an asset on the statement of financial position.' How would you explain this misunderstanding to the owner?

2.2 'The statement of financial position shows how much a business is worth.' Do you agree with this statement? Explain the reasons for your response.

2.3 The statement of financial position is sometimes seen as the least important of the three major financial statements discussed in this chapter. Can you see why this might be the case?

2.4 From time to time, there have been attempts to place a value on the 'human assets' of a business in order to derive a figure that can be included on the statement of financial position. Do you think humans should be treated as assets? Would 'human assets' meet the conventional definition of an asset for inclusion on the statement of financial position?

EXERCISES

Solutions to exercises with coloured numbers can be found at the back of the book, starting on page 319.

Basic-level exercises

2.1 On Thursday, the fourth day of his business venture, Paul, the street trader in wrapping paper (see earlier in the chapter, pages 34 to 37), bought more inventories for £53 cash. During the day he sold inventories that had cost £33 for a total of £47.

Required:
Draw up the three financial statements for Paul's business venture for Thursday.

2.2 The equity of Paul's business belongs to him because he is the sole owner of the business. Can you explain how the figure for equity by Thursday evening has arisen? You will need to look back at the events of Monday, Tuesday and Wednesday (pages 34 to 37) to do this.

Intermediate-level exercises

2.3 While on holiday, Helen had her credit cards and purse stolen from the beach while she was swimming. She was left with only £40, which she had kept in her hotel room, but she had three days of her holiday remaining. She was determined to continue her holiday and decided to make some money to enable her to do so. She decided to sell orange juice to holiday-makers using the local beach. On the first day she bought 80 cartons of orange juice at £0.50 each for cash and sold 70 of these at £0.80 each. On the following day she bought 60 cartons at £0.50 each for cash and sold 65 at £0.80 each. On the third and final day she bought another 60 cartons at £0.50 each for cash. However, it rained and, as a result, business was poor. She managed to sell 20 at £0.80 each but sold off the rest of her inventories at £0.40 each.

Required:
Prepare an income statement and statement of cash flows for each day's trading and prepare a statement of financial position at the end of each day's trading.

2.4 On 1 March, Joe Conday started a new business. During March, he carried out the following transactions:

1 March Deposited £20,000 in a newly opened business bank account.
2 March Bought fixtures and fittings for £6,000 cash and inventories £8,000 on credit.
3 March Borrowed £5,000 from a relative and deposited it in the bank.
4 March Bought a motor car for £7,000 cash and withdrew £200 in cash for his own use.
5 March Bought a further motor car costing £9,000. The motor car bought on 4 March was given in part exchange at a value of £6,500. The balance of the purchase price for the new car was paid in cash.
6 March Conday won £2,000 in a lottery and paid the amount into the business bank account. He also repaid £1,000 of the borrowings.

Required:
Draw up a statement of financial position for the business at the end of each day.

2.5 The following is a list of assets and claims of a manufacturing business at a particular point in time:

	£
Short-term borrowings	22,000
Property	245,000
Inventories of raw materials	18,000
Trade payables	23,000
Plant and equipment	127,000
Loan from Manufacturing Finance Co. (long-term borrowing)	100,000
Inventories of finished goods	28,000
Delivery vans	54,000
Trade receivables	34,000

Required:
Write out a statement of financial position in the standard format incorporating these figures. (*Hint*: There is a missing item that needs to be deduced and inserted.)

2.6 You have been talking to someone who had read a few chapters of an accounting text some years ago. During your conversation, the person made the following statements:

(a) The income statement shows how much cash has come into and left the business during the accounting period and the resulting balance at the end of the period.
(b) In order to be included in the statement of financial position as an asset, an item must have a resale value – that is all.
(c) The accounting equation is:

Assets + Equity = Liabilities

(d) Non-current assets are things that cannot be moved.
(e) Goodwill has an indefinite life and so should not be amortised.

Required:
Comment critically on each of the above statements, going into as much detail as you can.

Advanced-level exercises

2.7 The following is a list of the assets and claims of Crafty Engineering as at 30 June last year:

	£000
Trade payables	86
Motor vehicles	38
Long-term borrowing (loan from Industrial Finance Company)	260
Equipment and tools	207
Short-term borrowings	116
Inventories	153
Property	320
Trade receivables	185

Required:

(a) Prepare the statement of financial position of the business as at 30 June last year from the information provided, using the standard layout. (*Hint*: There is a missing item that needs to be deduced and inserted.)
(b) Discuss the significant features revealed by this financial statement.

2.8 The statement of financial position of a business at the start of the week is as follows:

	£
ASSETS	
Property	145,000
Furniture and fittings	63,000
Inventories	28,000
Trade receivables	33,000
Total assets	**269,000**
EQUITY AND LIABILITIES	
Equity	203,000
Short-term borrowing (bank overdraft)	43,000
Trade payables	23,000
Total equity and liabilities	**269,000**

During the week, the following transactions took place:

(a) Sold inventories for £11,000 cash; these inventories had cost £8,000.
(b) Sold inventories for £23,000 on credit; these inventories had cost £17,000.
(c) Received cash from trade receivables totalling £18,000.
(d) The owners of the business introduced £100,000 of their own money, which was placed in the business bank account.
(e) The owners bought a motor van, valued at £10,000, into the business.
(f) Bought inventories on credit for £14,000.
(g) Paid trade payables £13,000.

Required:
Show the statement of financial position after all of these transactions have been reflected.

Chapter 3

MEASURING AND REPORTING FINANCIAL PERFORMANCE

INTRODUCTION

In this chapter, we shall continue our examination of the major financial statements by looking at the income statement. This statement was briefly considered in Chapter 2, but we shall now look at it in some detail. We shall see how it is prepared and how it links with the statement of financial position. We shall also consider some of the key measurement problems to be faced when preparing the income statement.

Learning outcomes

When you have completed this chapter, you should be able to:

- discuss the nature and purpose of the income statement;
- prepare an income statement from relevant financial information and interpret the information that it contains;
- discuss the main recognition and measurement issues to be considered when preparing the income statement; and
- explain the main accounting conventions underpinning the income statement.

THE INCOME STATEMENT

Businesses exist for the primary purpose of generating wealth, or **profit**. The income statement – or *profit and loss account*, as it is sometimes called – measures and reports how much profit a business has generated over a period. It is, therefore, an immensely important financial statement for many users.

To measure profit, the total **revenue** generated during a particular period must be identified. Revenue is simply a measure of the inflow of economic benefits arising from the ordinary operations of a business. These benefits will result in either an increase in assets (such as cash or amounts owed to the business by its customers) or a decrease in liabilities. Different forms of business enterprise will generate different forms of revenue. Some examples of the different forms that revenue can take include:

- sales of goods (for example, by a manufacturer);
- fees for services (for example, of a solicitor);
- subscriptions (for example, of a club); and
- interest received (for example, by an investment fund).

Real World 3.1 shows the various forms of revenue generated by a leading football club.

Real World 3.1

Gunning for revenue

Arsenal Football Club generated total revenue of £353 million for the year ended 31 May 2017. Like other leading clubs, it relies on various forms of revenue to sustain its success. Figure 3.1 shows the contribution of each form of revenue for the year.

Figure 3.1 Arsenal's revenue for the year ended 31 May 2017

Source: Based on information in Arsenal Holdings plc, Annual Report 2016/2017, p. 47.

- Property development 0.3%
- Player trading 1.6%
- Gate and other match day revenues 23.6%
- Commercial 21.4%
- Retail and licensing 6.2%
- Broadcasting 46.9%

The total **expenses** relating to each period must also be identified. Expense is really the opposite of revenue. It represents the outflow of economic benefits arising from the ordinary operations of a business. This outflow results in either a decrease in assets (such as cash) or an increase in liabilities (such as amounts owed to suppliers). Expenses are incurred in the process of generating revenue or, at least, in attempting to generate it. The nature of the business will again determine the type of expenses that will be incurred. Examples of some of the more common types of expense include:

- the cost of buying, or making, the goods sold during the period concerned – known as cost of sales or *cost of goods sold*;
- salaries and wages;
- rent;
- motor vehicle running expenses;
- insurance;
- printing and stationery;
- heat and light; and
- telephone and postage.

The income statement simply shows the total revenue generated during a particular reporting period and deducts from this the total expenses incurred in generating that revenue. The difference between the total revenue and total expenses will represent either profit (if revenue exceeds expenses) or loss (if expenses exceed revenue). Therefore:

> **Profit (or loss) for the period = Total revenue for the period**
> **− Total expenses incurred in generating that revenue**

DIFFERENT ROLES

The income statement and the statement of financial position are not substitutes for one another. Rather, they perform different roles. The statement of financial position sets out the wealth held by the business at a single moment in time, whereas the income statement is concerned with the *flow* of wealth (profit) over a period of time. The two statements are, however, closely related.

The income statement for a reporting period links the statements of financial position at the beginning and the end of that period. At the start of a new reporting period, the statement of financial position shows the opening wealth position of the business. At the end of that reporting period, an income statement is prepared to show the wealth generated over that period. A statement of financial position is then prepared to show the new wealth position at the end of the period. It will reflect changes in wealth that have occurred since the previous statement of financial position was drawn up.

We saw in Chapter 2 (page 46) that the effect on the statement of financial position of making a profit (or loss) means that the accounting equation can be extended as follows:

> **Assets (at the end of the period) = Equity (amount at the start of the period**
> **+ Profit (or − Loss) for the period)**
> **+ Liabilities (at the end of the period)**

(This is assuming that the owner makes no injections or withdrawals of equity during the period.)

Activity 3.1

Can you recall from Chapter 2 how a profit, or loss, for a period is shown in the statement of financial position?

It is shown as an adjustment to owners' equity. Profit is added and a loss is subtracted.

The accounting equation can be further extended to:

> Assets (at the end of the period) = Equity (amount at the start of the period)
> + (Sales revenue − Expenses) (for the period)
> + Liabilities (at the end of the period)

In theory, it is possible to calculate the profit (or loss) for the period by making all adjustments for revenue and expenses through the equity section of the statement of financial position. However, this would be rather cumbersome. A better solution is to have an 'appendix' to the equity section, in the form of an income statement. By deducting expenses from revenue for the period, the income statement derives the profit (or loss) by which the equity figure in the statement of financial position needs to be adjusted. This profit (or loss) figure represents the net effect of trading for the period. Through this 'appendix', users are presented with a detailed and more informative view of performance.

INCOME STATEMENT LAYOUT

The layout of the income statement will vary according to the type of business to which it relates. To illustrate an income statement, let us consider the case of a retail business (that is, a business that buys goods in their completed state and resells them).

Example 3.1 sets out a typical layout for the income statement of a retail business.

Example 3.1

Better-Price Stores
Income statement for the year ended 30 June 2018

	£
Sales revenue	232,000
Cost of sales	(154,000)
Gross profit	78,000
Salaries and wages	(24,500)
Rent	(14,200)
Heat and light	(7,500)
Telephone and postage	(1,200)
Insurance	(1,000)
Motor vehicle running expenses	(3,400)
Depreciation – fixtures and fittings	(1,000)
– motor van	(600)
Operating profit	24,600
Interest received from investments	2,000
Interest on borrowings	(1,100)
Profit for the period	25,500

Gross profit

The first part of the income statement is concerned with calculating the **gross profit** for the period. We can see that revenue, which arises from selling the goods, is the first item to appear. Deducted from this item is the cost of sales figure (also called cost of goods sold) during the period. This gives the gross profit, which represents the profit from buying and selling goods, without taking into account any other revenues or expenses associated with the business.

Operating profit

Operating expenses (overheads) incurred in running the business (salaries and wages, rent, insurance and so on) are deducted from the gross profit. The resulting figure is known as the **operating profit**. This represents the wealth generated during the period from the normal activities of the business. It does not take account of income from other activities. Better-Price Stores in Example 3.1 is a retailer, so interest received on some spare cash that the business has invested is not part of its operating profit. Costs of financing the business are also ignored in the calculation of the operating profit.

Profit for the period

Having established the operating profit, we add any non-operating income (such as interest receivable) and deduct any interest payable on borrowings to arrive at the **profit for the period** (or *net profit*). This final measure of wealth generated represents the amount attributable to the owner(s) and will be added to the equity figure in the statement of financial position. It is a residual: that is, the amount remaining after deducting all expenses incurred in generating the sales revenue and taking account of non-operating income and expenses.

Activity 3.2

Look back to Example 3.1 and assume that a trainee accountant had prepared the income statement. Subsequent checking by the chief financial officer revealed the following errors:

1. Sales performance bonuses payable to staff amounting to £12,500 had been charged to cost of sales.
2. The depreciation charge for fixtures and fittings should be £10,000 not £1,000.
3. Stationery costing £500 had been treated as interest on borrowings.

What will be the gross profit, operating profit and profit for the period after these errors have been corrected?

→

> Staff bonuses should be treated as part of the salaries and wages expense of the business. This means that cost of sales will decrease by £12,500 and gross profit will increase by a corresponding amount. The corrected gross profit is therefore £90,500 (that is, £78,000 + £12,500).
>
> The operating profit and profit for the period, however, will not be affected by this correction. Although the operating expense salaries and wages will increase, this is offset by a compensating increase in gross profit.
>
> The increase in the depreciation charge from £1,000 to £10,000 will decrease operating profit by £9,000. Furthermore, by treating stationery correctly, operating expenses will increase by £500, thereby decreasing operating profit by a corresponding amount. The corrected operating profit figure is, therefore, £15,100 (that is, £24,600 − £9,500).
>
> Finally, the corrected profit for the period is calculated by taking the corrected operating profit £15,100, adding the interest received from investments, £2,000, and deducting the correct amount of interest on borrowing £600 (that is, £1,100 − £500) = £16,500.

FURTHER ISSUES

Having set out the main principles involved in preparing an income statement, let us consider some further points.

Cost of sales

The **cost of sales** (or cost of goods sold) figure for a period can be identified in different ways. In some businesses, it is identified for each individual item at the time of sale. By so doing, each item sold is matched with the relevant cost of that sale. Many large retailers (for example, supermarkets) have point-of-sale (checkout) systems that not only record each sale but also simultaneously pick up the cost of the goods that are the subject of the particular sale. Businesses that sell a relatively small number of high-value items (for example, an engineering business producing custom-made equipment) also tend to match sales revenue for each individual item with the cost of the goods sold at the time of sale. However, many businesses (for example, small retailers) may not find it practical to do this. Instead, they identify the cost of sales after the end of the reporting period.

To understand how this is done, we must remember that the cost of sales represents the cost of goods that were *sold* during the reporting period rather than the cost of goods that were *bought* during the period. Part of the goods bought during the period may remain, as inventories, at the end of the period. These will normally be sold in the next period. To derive the cost of sales, we need to know the amount of opening and closing inventories for the period and the cost of goods bought during the period. Example 3.2 illustrates how the cost of sales is derived.

Example 3.2

> Better-Price Stores, which we considered in Example 3.1, began the year with unsold inventories of £40,000 and during that year bought inventories at a cost of £189,000. At the end of the year, unsold inventories of £75,000 were still held by the business.

The opening (beginning of the year) inventories *plus* the goods bought during the year represent the total goods available for resale, as follows:

	£
Opening inventories	40,000
Purchases (goods bought)	189,000
Goods available for resale	229,000

The closing inventories represent that portion of the total goods available for resale that remains unsold at the end of the year. This means that the cost of goods actually sold during the year must be the total goods available for resale *less* the inventories remaining at the end of the year. That is:

	£
Goods available for resale	229,000
Closing inventories	(75,000)
Cost of sales (or cost of goods sold)	154,000

These calculations are sometimes shown on the face of the income statement as in Example 3.3.

Example 3.3

	£	£
Sales revenue		232,000
Cost of sales:		
Opening inventories	40,000	
Purchases (goods bought)	189,000	
Closing inventories	(75,000)	(154,000)
Gross profit		78,000

This is just an expanded version of the first section of the income statement for Better-Price Stores, as set out in Example 3.1. We have simply included the additional information concerning inventories balances and purchases for the year, provided in Example 3.2.

Classifying expenses

The classification of expense items is often a matter of judgement. For example, the income statement set out in Example 3.1 could have included the insurance expense with the telephone and postage expense under a single heading – say, 'general expenses'. Such decisions are normally based on how useful a particular classification will be to users. This will usually mean that expense items of material size will be shown separately. For businesses that trade as limited companies, however, rules dictate the classification of expense items for external reporting purposes. These rules will be discussed in Chapter 5.

Activity 3.3

The following information relates to the activities of H & S Retailers for the year ended 30 April 2018:

	£
Motor vehicle running expenses	1,200
Closing inventories	3,000
Rent payable	5,000
Motor vans – cost less depreciation	6,300
Annual depreciation – motor vans	1,500
Heat and light	900
Telephone and postage	450
Sales revenue	97,400
Goods purchased	68,350
Insurance	750
Loan interest payable	620
Balance at bank	4,780
Salaries and wages	10,400
Opening inventories	4,000

Prepare an income statement for the year ended 30 April 2018. (*Hint*: Not all items listed should appear on this statement.)

Your answer should be as follows:

H & S Retailers
Income statement for the year ended 30 April 2018

	£	£
Sales revenue		97,400
Cost of sales:		
Opening inventories	4,000	
Purchases	68,350	
Closing inventories	(3,000)	(69,350)
Gross profit		28,050
Salaries and wages		(10,400)
Rent payable		(5,000)
Heat and light		(900)
Telephone and postage		(450)
Insurance		(750)
Motor vehicle running expenses		(1,200)
Depreciation – motor vans		(1,500)
Operating profit		7,850
Loan interest		(620)
Profit for the period		7,230

Note that neither the motor vans nor the bank balance are included in this statement. This is because they are both assets and so are neither revenues nor expenses.

Figure 3.2 shows the layout of the income statement.

```
Sales revenue
    │ less
    ▼
Cost of sales
    │ equals
    ▼
Gross profit
    │ less
    ▼
Operating expenses
    │ equals
    ▼
Operating profit
    │ less
    ▼
Non-operating expenses
(for example, interest payable)
    │ plus
    ▼
Non-operating income
(for example, interest receivable)
    │ equals
    ▼
Profit for the period
```

Figure 3.2 The layout of the income statement

RECOGNISING REVENUE

The financial amount to which a business is entitled for providing goods or services to a customer should be recognised as revenue. It should be recognised as soon as control of the goods or services is transferred to the customer. At this point, the business has satisfied its obligations towards the customer. To determine when control has passed, there are important indicators, such as when:

- physical possession passes to the customer;
- the business has the right to demand payment for the goods or services;
- the customer has accepted the goods or services;
- legal title passes to the customer; and
- significant risks and rewards of ownership passes to the customer.

If we take the example of a self-service store, where sales are for cash, the above indicators suggest that revenue can normally be recognised when the customer checks out. However, revenue recognition is not always so straightforward. Activity 3.4 provides the opportunity to apply the indicators to a slightly trickier situation.

Activity 3.4

A manufacturer produces and sells a standard product on credit, which is transported to customers using the manufacturer's delivery vans. Managers believe there are four different points in the production/selling cycle at which revenue *might* be recognised. These are:

1. when the goods are produced;
2. when an order is received from a customer;
3. when the goods are delivered to, and accepted by, the customer; or
4. when the cash is received from the customer.

At which of these points do you think the manufacturer should recognise revenue?

The indicators listed above point towards to point 3, that is when the goods are passed to, and accepted by, the customer. At this point, the customer acquires legal title, takes possession of the goods and so on.

The point at which revenue is recognised is not simply an academic issue. It can have a significant impact on reported revenues, and therefore profit, for a period. Where a credit sale transaction straddles the end of a reporting period, the point chosen for recognising revenue can determine whether it is included in an earlier reporting period or a later one.

Revenue recognition and cash receipts

We can see from Activity 3.4 above that a sale on credit is usually recognised *before* the cash is received. This means that the total sales revenue shown in the income statement may include sales transactions for which the cash has yet to be received. The total sales revenue will, therefore, often be different from the total cash received from sales during the period. For cash sales (that is, sales where cash is paid at the same time as the goods are transferred), there will be no difference in timing between reporting sales revenue and cash received.

Activity 3.5

Although revenue for providing services is often recognised before the cash is received, there are occasions when it is the other way around: a business will require payment before providing the service.
   Can you think of two examples? (*Hint:* Try to think of services that you may use.)

Examples of cash being received in advance of the service being provided may include:

- rent received from letting premises;
- telephone line rental charges;
- TV licence (BBC) or subscription fees (for example, Sky); and
- subscriptions received by health clubs or golf clubs.

You may have thought of others.

Recognising revenue over time

Control of goods or services may be transferred to a customer over time rather than as a single 'one-off' event. When this occurs, the total revenue must be recognised over time. This situation may arise where:

- *the customer enjoys the benefits as the business carries out its obligations*. This can occur with service contracts, such as where an accounting firm undertakes employee payroll services for a large business or when an Internet service is being provided.
- *the business creates, or improves, an asset held by the customer*. This can occur with building contracts, such as where a builder undertakes the refurbishment of a shop owned by a retailer or when a shipbuilder carries out extensive repairs to a large ship.
- *the business creates an asset with no alternative use and the customer has agreed to pay for work carried out*. This can apply to special orders, such as where an engineering business produces specially-designed equipment for a manufacturer or where a furniture manufacturer makes customised furniture for a hotel chain.

Where control is transferred over time, the total revenue will be spread across the reporting periods covered by the contract. In other words, part of the total contract price will be treated as revenue in each reporting period. This is providing, however, it is possible to measure progress towards complete fulfilment of the business's obligations towards the customer. Otherwise, the amount of progress made during a particular period cannot really be determined.

To determine the appropriate revenue for each period, some method of measuring progress towards transferring the goods or services is needed. Various methods are available. Some are based on outputs, or achievements, such as particular 'milestones' reached in completing the contract, the number of units delivered, the number of services provided. Others are based on inputs, or effort expended, such as costs incurred, materials consumed, or hours worked. There is no single correct method: it depends on the particular circumstances. Nevertheless, methods based on output usually provide a more direct measure of the value of goods or services transferred to customers than those based on inputs. Hence, output-based measures are often preferred.

Activity 3.6

Why might a business choose input-based methods to measure progress if they are generally considered to be inferior?

Where methods based on output are unreliable, or unavailable, methods based on input may be the only real choice.

To illustrate one approach to recognising revenue over time, let us take the example of a builder entering into a contract with a manufacturer to build a factory. The work will be carried out on land owned by the manufacturer and will take three years to complete. The contract recognises that building the factory can be broken down into the following stages:

- Stage 1 – clearing and levelling the land and putting in the foundations.
- Stage 2 – building the walls.
- Stage 3 – putting on the roof.
- Stage 4 – putting in the windows and completing all the interior work.

It is expected that Stage 1 of the contract will be completed by the end of Year 1, Stages 2 and 3 will be completed by the end of Year 2 and Stage 4 by the end of Year 3.

Once the performance obligations for a particular stage are satisfied, the builder can recognise the agreed proportion of the total contract price for that stage as revenue. Thus, the agreed proportion for completing Stage 1 will be reported as revenue in the income statement for Year 1 and so on. Normally the contract would specify that the client would be required to pay the builder the appropriate proportion of the total contract price, following successful completion of each stage.

RECOGNISING EXPENSES

Having considered the recognition of revenue, let us now turn to the recognition of expenses. The **matching convention** provides guidance on this. This convention states that expenses should be matched to the revenue that they helped to generate. In other words, the expenses associated with a particular item of revenue must be taken into account in the same reporting period as that in which the item of revenue is included. We saw how this convention is applied with the costs of sales for Better-Price Stores in Example 3.2. The appropriate expense was the cost of inventories actually sold, rather than the total cost of inventories available for sale, during the period.

Applying this convention often means that an expense reported in the income statement for a period may not be the same as the cash paid for that item during the period. The expense reported might be either more or less than the cash paid during the period. Let us consider two examples that illustrate this point.

When the expense for the period is more than the cash paid during the period

Example 3.4

Domestic Ltd, a retailer, sells household electrical appliances. It pays its sales staff a commission of 2 per cent of sales revenue generated. Total sales revenue for last year amounted to £300,000. This means that the commission to be paid on sales for the year will be £6,000. However, by the end of the year, the amount of sales commission actually paid was only £5,000. If the business reported this amount as the sales commission expense, it would mean that the income statement would not reflect the full expense for the year. This would contravene the matching convention because not all of the expenses associated with the revenue of the year would have been matched with it in the income statement. This will be remedied as follows:

- Sales commission expense in the income statement will include the amount paid plus the amount outstanding (that is, £6,000 = £5,000 + £1,000).
- The amount outstanding (£1,000) represents an outstanding liability at the end of the year and will be included under the heading **accrued expenses**, or 'accruals', in the statement of financial position. As this item will have to be paid within twelve months of the year end, it will be treated as a current liability.
- The cash will already have been reduced to reflect the commission paid (£5,000) during the period.

These points are illustrated in Figure 3.3.

Figure 3.3 Accounting for sales commission

This illustrates the main points of Example 3.4. We can see that the sales commission expense of £6,000 (which appears in the income statement) is made up of a cash element of £5,000 and an accrued element of £1,000. The cash element appears in the statement of cash flows and the accrued.

In principle, all expenses should be matched to the period in which the sales revenue to which they relate is reported. It is sometimes difficult, however, to match certain expenses to sales revenue in the same precise way that we have matched sales commission to sales revenue. For example, electricity charges incurred often cannot be linked directly to particular sales in this way. As a result, the electricity charges incurred by, say, a retailer would be matched to the *period* to which they relate. Example 3.5 illustrates this.

Example 3.5

Domestic Ltd has reached the end of its reporting period and has only paid for electricity for the first three quarters of the year (amounting to £1,900). This is simply because the electricity company has yet to send out bills for the quarter that ends on the same date as Domestic Ltd's year end. The amount of Domestic Ltd's bill for the last quarter of the year is £500. In this situation, the amount of the electricity expense outstanding is dealt with as follows:

- Electricity expense in the income statement will include the amount paid, plus the amount of the bill for the last quarter of the year (that is, £1,900 + £500 = £2,400) in order to cover the whole year.
- The amount of the outstanding bill (£500) represents a liability at the end of the year and will be included under the heading 'accrued expenses' in the statement of financial position. This item would normally have to be paid within twelve months of the year end and will, therefore, be treated as a current liability.
- The cash will already have been reduced to reflect the amount (£1,900) paid for electricity during the period.

This treatment will mean that the correct figure for the electricity expense for the year will be included in the income statement. It will also have the effect of showing that, at the end of the reporting period, Domestic Ltd owed the amount of the last quarter's electricity bill. Dealing with the outstanding amount in this way reflects the dual aspect of the item and will ensure that the accounting equation is maintained.

Domestic Ltd may wish to draw up its income statement before it is able to discover how much it owes for the last quarter's electricity. In this case it is quite normal to make an estimate of the amount of the bill and to use this amount as described above.

Activity 3.7

How will the eventual payment of the outstanding sales commission (Example 3.4) and the electricity bill for the last quarter (Example 3.5) be dealt with in the accounting records of Domestic Ltd?

When these amounts are eventually paid, they will be dealt with as follows:

- Reduce cash by the amounts paid.
- Reduce the amount of the accrued expense as shown on the statement of financial position by the same amounts.

Other expenses, apart from electricity charges, may also be matched to the period to which they relate.

Activity 3.8

Can you think of other expenses for a retailer that cannot be linked directly to sales revenue and for which matching will therefore be done on a time basis? Try to think of at least two examples.

You may have thought of the following:

- rent payable;
- insurance;
- interest payable; and
- licence fees payable.

This is not an exhaustive list. You may have thought of others.

When the amount paid during the period is more than the full expense for the period

It is not unusual for a business to be in a situation where it has paid more during the year than the full expense for that year. Example 3.6 illustrates how we deal with this.

Example 3.6

Images Ltd, an advertising agency, normally pays rent for its premises quarterly in advance (on 1 January, 1 April, 1 July and 1 October). On the last day of the last reporting period (31 December), it paid the next quarter's rent (£4,000) to the following 31 March, which was a day earlier than required. This would mean that a total of five quarters' rent was paid during the year. If Images Ltd reports all of the cash paid as an expense in the income statement, this would be more than the full expense for the year. This would contravene the matching convention because a higher figure than the expenses associated with the revenue of the year would appear in the income statement.

The problem is overcome by dealing with the rental payment as follows:

- Show the rent for four quarters as the appropriate expense in the income statement (that is, 4 × £4,000 = £16,000).
- The cash (that is, 5 × £4,000 = £20,000) would already have been paid during the year.
- Show the quarter's rent paid in advance (£4,000) as a prepaid expense under assets in the statement of financial position. (The rent paid in advance will appear as a current asset in the statement of financial position, under the heading **prepaid expenses** or 'prepayments'.)

In the next reporting period, this prepayment will cease to be an asset and will become an expense in the income statement of that period. This is because the rent prepaid relates to the next period during which it will be 'used up'.

These points are illustrated in Figure 3.4.

This illustrates the main points of Example 3.6. We can see that the rent expense of £16,000 (which appears in the income statement) is made up of four quarters' rent at £4,000 per quarter. This is the amount that relates to the period and is 'used up' during the period. The cash paid, £20,000 (which appears in the statement of cash flows), is made up of the cash paid during the period, which is five quarters at £4,000 per quarter. Finally, the prepayment of £4,000 (which appears on the statement of financial position) represents the payment made on 31 December and relates to the next reporting period.

Figure 3.4 Accounting for rent payable

In practice, the treatment of accruals and prepayments will be subject to the **materiality convention**. This convention states that, where the amounts involved are trivial, we should consider only what is expedient. This will usually mean treating an item as an expense in the period in which it is first recorded, rather than strictly matching it to the revenue to which it relates. For example, a large business may find that, at the end of a reporting period, it holds £20 worth of unused stationery. The time and effort taken to record this as a prepayment would outweigh the negligible effect on the measurement of profit or financial position. As a result, it would be treated as an expense of the current period and ignored in the following period.

PROFIT, CASH AND ACCRUALS ACCOUNTING

We have seen that, normally, for a particular reporting period, total revenue is not the same as total cash received and total expenses are not the same as total cash paid. As a result, the profit for the period (that is, total revenue minus total expenses) will not normally represent the net cash generated during that period. This reflects the difference between profit and liquidity. Profit is a measure of achievement, or productive effort, rather than a measure of cash generated. Although making a profit increases wealth, cash is only one possible form in which that wealth may be held.

These points are summarised in the **accruals convention**, which asserts that profit is the excess of revenue over expenses for a period, not the excess of cash receipts over cash payments. Leading on from this, the approach to accounting that is based on the accruals convention is frequently referred to as **accruals accounting**. The statement of financial position and the income statement are both prepared on the basis of accruals accounting.

Activity 3.9

What about the statement of cash flows? Is it prepared on an accruals accounting basis?

No. The statement of cash flows simply deals with cash receipts and payments.

The UK government has only fairly recently adopted accruals accounting for national income accounting. This is despite the fact that it has been standard practice in all private sector organisations, and many public sector ones, for very many years. **Real World 3.2** is based on a *Financial Times* article that discusses the change of approach.

Real World 3.2

Casting light on the UK economy

Only recently (2014) has the UK government started using accruals accounting principles in its assessment of national output, for example as measured by gross domestic product (GDP). Until then, it based its assessments of national economic effectiveness on a cash receipts and payments basis.

The main effect of the new, accruals, approach is that certain 'investments' will be recognised as such and not treated as 'expenses' as they tend to be with a cash-based approach.

Areas where a more logical approach to accounting for investments will have most effect are:

- research and development, that is the acquisition of economically valuable knowledge;
- expenditure on weapons systems; and
- cash invested in pension schemes.

It is estimated that the effect of introducing accrual accounting will raise the GDP value by between 3.5 per cent and 5 per cent. Similar changes in the accounting approach taken in the United States added 3.5 per cent to its GDP.

Source: Based on Giles, C. (2014) Accounting rules unravel the mysteries of Britain's economy, ft.com, 23 April. © The Financial Times Limited 2014. All Rights Reserved.

DEPRECIATION

The expense of **depreciation**, which we have already come across, requires further examination. Most non-current assets do not have a perpetual existence, but have finite, or limited, lives. They are eventually 'used up' in the process of generating revenue for the business. This 'using up' may relate to physical deterioration (as with a motor vehicle). It may however be linked to obsolescence (as with some IT software that is no longer useful) or the mere passage of time (as with a purchased patent, which has a limited period of validity).

In essence, depreciation is an attempt to measure that portion of the cost (or fair value) of a non-current asset that has been depleted in generating the revenue recognised during a particular period. In the case of intangibles, we usually refer to the expense as **amortisation**, rather than *depreciation*.

Calculating the depreciation expense

To calculate a depreciation expense for a period, four factors have to be considered:

- the cost (or fair value) of the asset;
- the useful life of the asset;
- the residual value of the asset; and
- the depreciation method.

The cost (or fair value) of the asset

The cost of an asset will include all costs incurred by the business to bring the asset to its required location and to make it ready for use. This means that, in addition to the cost of acquiring the asset, any delivery costs, installation costs (for example, setting up a new machine) and legal costs incurred in the transfer of legal title (for example, in purchasing a lease on property) will be included as part of the total cost of the asset. Similarly, any costs incurred in improving or altering an asset to make it suitable for use will also be included as part of the total cost.

Activity 3.10

Andrew Wu (Engineering) Ltd bought a new motor car for its marketing director. The invoice received from the motor car supplier showed the following:

	£
New BMW 325i	29,350
Delivery charge	280
Alloy wheels	860
Sun roof	800
Petrol	80
Number plates	60
Road fund licence	150
	31,580
Part exchange – Reliant Robin	(1,000)
Amount outstanding	30,580

What is the total cost of the new car to be treated as part of the business's property, plant and equipment?

The cost of the new car will be as follows:

	£
New BMW 325i	29,350
Delivery charge	280
Alloy wheels	860
Sun roof	800
Number plates	60
	31,350

This cost includes delivery charges, which are necessary to bring the asset into use, and it includes number plates, as they are a necessary and integral part of the asset. Improvements (alloy wheels and sun roof) are also regarded as part of the total cost of the motor car. The petrol and road fund licence, however, are costs of operating the asset. These amounts will, therefore, be treated as expenses in the period in which they were incurred (although part of the cost of the licence may be regarded as a prepaid expense in the period in which it was incurred).

The part-exchange figure shown is part payment of the total amount outstanding and so is not relevant to a consideration of the total cost.

The fair value of an asset was defined in Chapter 2 as the selling price that could be obtained in an orderly transaction under market conditions. As we saw, assets may be revalued to fair value only if this can be measured reliably. Where fair values have been applied, the depreciation expense should be based on those fair values, rather than on the historic costs.

The useful life of the asset

A non-current asset has both a *physical life* and an *economic life*. The physical life will be exhausted through the effects of wear and tear and/or the passage of time. The economic life will be decided by the effects of technological progress, by changes in demand for the business's output or by changes in the way that the business operates. The benefits provided by the asset are eventually outweighed by the costs as it becomes unable to compete with newer assets, or becomes irrelevant to the needs of the business. The economic life of an asset may be much shorter than its physical life. For example, a computer may have a physical life of eight years and an economic life of three years.

The economic life determines the expected useful life of an asset for depreciation purposes. It is often difficult to estimate, however, as technological progress and shifts in consumer tastes can be swift and unpredictable.

Residual value (disposal value)

When a business disposes of a non-current asset that may still be of value to others, some payment may be received. This payment will represent the **residual value**, or *disposal value*, of the asset. To calculate the total amount to be depreciated, the residual value must be deducted from the cost (or fair value) of the asset. The likely amount to be received on disposal can, once again, be difficult to predict. The best guide is often past experience of similar assets sold.

Depreciation methods

Once the amount to be depreciated (that is, the cost, or fair value, of the asset less any residual value) has been estimated, the business must select a method of allocating this depreciable amount between the reporting periods covering the asset's useful life. Although there are various ways in which this may be done, there are only two methods that are commonly used in practice.

The first of these is known as the **straight-line method**. This method simply allocates the amount to be depreciated evenly over the useful life of the asset. In other words, there is an equal depreciation expense for each year that the asset is held.

Example 3.7

To illustrate the straight-line method of depreciation, consider the following information:

Cost of machine	£78,124
Estimated residual value at the end of its useful life	£2,000
Estimated useful life	4 years

To calculate the depreciation expense for each year, the total amount to be depreciated must be calculated. This will be the total cost less the estimated residual value: that is, £78,124 − £2,000 = £76,124. The annual depreciation expense can then be derived by dividing the amount to be depreciated by the estimated useful life of the asset of four years. The calculation is therefore:

$$\frac{£76,124}{4} = £19,031$$

This means that the annual depreciation expense that appears in the income statement in relation to this asset will be £19,031 for each of the four years of the asset's life.

The amount of depreciation relating to the asset will be accumulated for as long as the asset continues to be owned by the business or until the accumulated depreciation amounts to the cost less residual value. This accumulated depreciation figure will increase each year as a result of the annual depreciation expense in the income statement. This accumulated amount will be deducted from the cost of the asset in the statement of financial position. At the end of the second year, for example, the accumulated depreciation will be £19,031 × 2 = £38,062. The asset details will appear on the statement of financial position as follows:

	£
Machine at cost	78,124
Accumulated depreciation	(38,062)
	40,062

As we saw in Chapter 2, this balance of £40,062 is referred to as the **carrying amount** (sometimes also known as the **written-down value** or **net book value**) of the asset. It represents that portion of the cost (or fair value) of the asset that has still to be treated as an expense (written off) in future years plus the residual value. This carrying-amount figure does not, except by coincidence, represent the current market value, which may be quite different. The only point at which the carrying amount is intended to represent the market value of the asset is at the time of its disposal. In Example 3.7, at the end of the four-year life of the machine, the carrying amount would be £2,000 – its estimated disposal value.

The straight-line method derives its name from the fact that the carrying amount of the asset at the end of each year, when plotted against time, will result in a straight line, as shown in Figure 3.5.

The carrying amount of the asset in Example 3.7 declines by a constant amount each year (£19,031). This is because the straight-line method provides a constant depreciation expense each year. The result, when plotted on a graph, is a straight line.

Figure 3.5 Graph of carrying amount against time using the straight-line method

The second approach to calculating the depreciation expense for a period is referred to as the **reducing-balance method**. This method applies a fixed percentage rate of depreciation to the carrying amount of the asset each year. The effect of this will be high annual depreciation expenses in the early years and lower expenses in the later years. To illustrate this method, let us take the same information that was used in Example 3.7. By using a fixed percentage of 60 per cent of the carrying amount to determine the annual depreciation expense, the effect will be to reduce the carrying amount to £2,000 after four years.

The calculations will be as follows:

	£
Cost of machine	78,124
Year 1 depreciation expense (60%* of cost)	(46,874)
Carrying amount	31,250
Year 2 depreciation expense (60% of carrying amount)	(18,750)
Carrying amount	12,500
Year 3 depreciation expense (60% of carrying amount)	(7,500)
Carrying amount	5,000
Year 4 depreciation expense (60% of carrying amount)	(3,000)
Residual value	2,000

* See the box below for an explanation of how to derive the fixed percentage.

Deriving the fixed percentage

Deriving the fixed percentage to be applied requires the use of the following formula:

$$P = (1 - \sqrt[n]{R/C} \times 100\%)$$

where:

P = the depreciation percentage
n = the useful life of the asset (in years)
R = the residual value of the asset
C = the cost, or fair value, of the asset.

The fixed percentage rate will, however, be given in all examples used in this book.

We can see that the pattern of depreciation is quite different between the two methods. If we plot against time the carrying amount of the asset, which has been derived using the reducing-balance method, the result will be as shown in Figure 3.6.

Under the reducing-balance method, the carrying amount of the asset in Example 3.7 falls by a larger amount in the earlier years than in the later years. This is because the depreciation expense is based on a fixed percentage of the carrying amount.

Figure 3.6 Graph of carrying amount against time using the reducing-balance method

Activity 3.11

Assume that the machine in Example 3.7 was owned by a business that made a profit before depreciation of £40,000 for each of the four years in which the asset was held.

Calculate the profit for the business for each year under each depreciation method, and comment on your findings.

Your answer should be as follows:

Straight-line method

	(a) Profit before depreciation £	(b) Depreciation £	(a − b) Profit £
Year 1	40,000	19,031	20,969
Year 2	40,000	19,031	20,969
Year 3	40,000	19,031	20,969
Year 4	40,000	19,031	20,969

Reducing-balance method

	(a) Profit before depreciation £	(b) Depreciation £	(a − b) Profit £
Year 1	40,000	46,874	(6,874)
Year 2	40,000	18,750	21,250
Year 3	40,000	7,500	32,500
Year 4	40,000	3,000	37,000

The straight-line method of depreciation results in the same profit figure for each year of the four-year period. This is because both the profit before depreciation and the depreciation expense are constant over the period. The reducing-balance method, however, results in very different profit figures for the four years, despite the fact that in this example the pre-depreciation profit is the same each year. In the first year a loss is reported and, thereafter, a rising profit.

Although the *pattern* of profit over the four-year period will be quite different, depending on the depreciation method used, the *total* profit for the period (£83,876) will remain the same. This is because both methods of depreciating will allocate the same amount of total depreciation (£76,124) over the four-year period. It is only the amount allocated *between years* that will differ.

In practice, the use of different depreciation methods may not have such a dramatic effect on profits as suggested in Activity 3.11. This is because businesses typically have more than one depreciating non-current asset. Where a business replaces some of its assets each year, the total depreciation expense calculated under the reducing-balance method will reflect a range of expenses (from high through to low), as assets will be at different points in their economic lives. This could mean that each year's total depreciation expense may not be significantly different from that which would have been derived under the straight-line method.

Selecting a depreciation method

The appropriate depreciation method to choose is the one that reflects the consumption of economic benefits provided by the asset. Where the economic benefits are consumed evenly over time (for example, with buildings), the straight-line method is usually appropriate. Where the economic benefits consumed decline over time (for example, with certain types of machinery that lose their efficiency), the reducing-balance method may be more appropriate.

There is an International Financial Reporting Standard (or International Accounting Standard) to deal with the depreciation of property, plant and equipment. As we shall see in Chapter 5, the purpose of financial reporting standards is to narrow areas of accounting difference and to ensure that information provided to users is transparent and comparable. The relevant standard endorses the view that the depreciation method chosen should reflect the pattern of consumption of economic benefits but does not specify particular methods to be used. It states that the useful life, depreciation method and residual values for property, plant and equipment should all be reviewed at least annually and adjustments made where appropriate. For intangible non-current assets with finite lives, there is a separate standard containing broadly similar rules. It does state, however, that the straight-line method must be chosen where the pattern of consumption of economic benefits is not clear.

Real World 3.3 sets out the depreciation policies of one large business.

Real World 3.3

Depreciating assets

Mothercare plc is a leading retailer that is focused on the needs of parents and young children. The annual report of the business for the 52 weeks ended 25 March 2017 set out the following depreciation policies.

Property, plant and equipment

Property, plant and equipment is carried at cost less accumulated depreciation and any recognised impairment losses. Depreciation is charged so as to write off the cost or valuation of assets, other than land and assets in the course of construction, over their estimated useful lives, using the straight-line method, on the following bases:

- Freehold buildings – 50 years
- Fixed equipment in freehold buildings – 20 years
- Leasehold improvements – the lease term
- Fixtures, fittings and equipment – 3 to 20 years

Intangible assets – software

Where computer software is not an integral part of a related item of computer hardware, the software is classified as an intangible asset. The capitalised costs of software for internal use include external direct costs of materials and services consumed in developing or obtaining the software and payroll and payroll-related costs for employees who are directly associated with and who devote substantial time to the project. These costs are amortised on a straight-line basis over their expected useful lives, which is normally five years.

Source: Extracts from Mothercare plc, Annual Report and Accounts 2017, p. 114, www.mothercare.com.

Mothercare plc is typical of most UK businesses in that it uses the straight-line method of depreciation. The reducing-balance method is very much less popular.

The approach taken to calculating depreciation is summarised in Figure 3.7.

Cost (or fair value)

less

Residual value

equals

Depreciable amount

| Year 1 Depreciation | Year 2 Depreciation | Year 3 Depreciation | Year 4 Depreciation |

Asset life (Number of years)

The cost (or fair value) of an asset less the residual value will represent the amount to be depreciated. This amount is depreciated over the useful life (four years in this particular case) of the asset using an appropriate depreciation method.

Figure 3.7 Calculating the annual depreciation expense

Impairment and depreciation

We saw in Chapter 2 that all non-current assets could be subjected to an impairment test. Where a non-current asset with a finite life has its carrying amount reduced following an impairment test, depreciation expenses for future reporting periods should be based on the impaired value.

Depreciation and asset replacement

Some appear to believe that the purpose of depreciation is to provide the funds for the replacement of a non-current asset when it reaches the end of its useful life. However, this is not the case. It was mentioned earlier that depreciation represents an attempt to allocate the cost or fair value (less any residual value) of a non-current asset over its expected useful life. The depreciation expense for a particular reporting period is used in calculating profit for that period. If a depreciation charge is excluded from the income statement, we shall not have a fair measure of financial performance. Whether or not the business intends to replace the asset in the future is irrelevant.

Where an asset is to be replaced, the depreciation expense in the income statement will not ensure that liquid funds are set aside specifically for this purpose. Although the depreciation expense will reduce profit, and therefore reduce the amount that the owners may decide to withdraw, the amounts retained within the business as a result may be invested in ways that are unrelated to the replacement of the asset.

Depreciation and judgement

From our discussions about depreciation, it is clear that accounting is not as precise and objective as it is sometimes portrayed as being. There are areas where subjective judgement is required.

Activity 3.12

What judgements must be made to calculate a depreciation expense for a period?

You may have thought of the following:

- the expected residual or disposal value of the asset;
- the expected useful life of the asset; and
- the choice of depreciation method.

Making different judgements on these matters would result in a different pattern of depreciation expenses over the life of the asset and, therefore, in a different pattern of reported profits. However, any underestimations or overestimations that are made will be adjusted for in the final year of an asset's life. As a result, the total depreciation expense (and total profit) over the asset's life will not be affected by estimation errors.

Real World 3.4 describes the effect on annual performance of extending the useful life of a non-current asset held by a well-known business.

Real World 3.4

Engineering an improvement?

BA reported a loss of £358 million for the 2008/09 financial year. This loss, however, would have been significantly higher had the business not changed its depreciation policies. The 2008/09 annual report of the business states:

> During the prior year, the Group changed the depreciation period for the RB211 engine, used on Boeing 747 and 767 fleets, from 54 months to 78 months. The change resulted in a £33 million decrease in the annual depreciation charge for this engine type.

Source: British Airways, Annual Report and Accounts 2008/09, Note 15, www.britishairways.com.

Activity 3.13

Sally Dalton (Packaging) Ltd bought a machine for £40,000. At the end of its useful life of four years, the amount received on sale was £4,000. When the asset was purchased the business received two estimates of the likely residual value of the asset. These were: (a) £8,000 and (b) zero.

Show the annual depreciation expenses over the four years and the total depreciation expenses for the asset under each of the two estimates. The straight-line method should be used to calculate the annual depreciation expenses.

The depreciation expense, assuming estimate (a), will be £8,000 a year (that is, (£40,000 − £8,000)/4)). The depreciation expense, assuming estimate (b), will be £10,000 a year (that is, £40,000/4). As the actual residual value is £4,000, estimate (a) will lead to under-depreciation of £4,000 (that is, £8,000 − £4,000) over the life of the asset and estimate (b) will lead to over-depreciation of £4,000 (that is, £0 − £4,000). These under- and overestimations will be dealt with in year 4.

The pattern of depreciation and total depreciation expenses will therefore be:

		Estimate (a) £	Estimate (b) £
Year			
1	Annual depreciation	8,000	10,000
2	Annual depreciation	8,000	10,000
3	Annual depreciation	8,000	10,000
4	Annual depreciation	8,000	10,000
		32,000	40,000
4	Under/(over)-depreciation	4,000	(4,000)
	Total depreciation	36,000	36,000

The final adjustment for under-depreciation of an asset is often referred to as 'loss (or deficit) on disposal of a non-current asset', as the amount actually received is less than the estimated residual value. Similarly, the adjustment for over-depreciation is often referred to as 'profit (or surplus) on disposal of a non-current asset'. These final adjustments are normally made as an addition to the expense (or a reduction in the expense) for depreciation in the reporting period during which the asset is disposed of.

Activity 3.14

In practice, would you expect it to be more likely that the amount of depreciation would be overestimated or underestimated? Why?

We might expect there to be systematic overestimations of the annual depreciation expense. Application of the prudence convention may lead to underestimating the lives and residual values of assets. Where this occurs, the result will be an overestimate for the annual depreciation charge.

COSTING INVENTORIES

The cost of inventories is important in determining financial performance and position. The cost of inventories sold during a reporting period will affect the calculation of profit and the cost of inventories held at the end of the reporting period will affect the portrayal of assets held.

To calculate the cost of inventories, an assumption must be made about the physical flow of inventories through the business. This assumption need not have anything to do with how inventories *actually* flow through the business. It is concerned only with identifying measures of performance and position that provide users of financial statements with useful information.

Three common assumptions used are:

- **first in, first out (FIFO)**, in which inventories are costed *as if* the earliest acquired inventories held are the first to be used;
- **last in, first out (LIFO)**, in which inventories are costed *as if* the latest acquired inventories held are the first to be used; and
- **weighted average cost (AVCO)**, in which inventories are costed *as if* inventories acquired lose their separate identity and go into a 'pool'. Any issues of inventories from this pool will reflect the weighted average cost of inventories held.

During a period of changing prices, the choice of assumption used in costing inventories can be important. Example 3.8 provides an illustration of how each assumption is applied and the effect of each on financial performance and position.

Example 3.8

A business that supplies grass seed to farmers and horticulturalists has the following transactions during a period:

		Tonnes	Cost/tonne £
1 May	Opening inventories	100	100
2 May	Bought	500	110
3 May	Bought	800	120
		1,400	
6 May	Sold	(900)	
	Closing inventories	500	

First in, first out (FIFO)

Using the FIFO approach, the first 900 tonnes of seed bought are treated *as if* these are the ones that are sold. This will consist of the opening inventories (100 tonnes), the purchases made on 2 May (500 tonnes) and some of the purchases made on 3 May (300 tonnes). The remainder of the 3 May purchases (500 tonnes) will comprise the closing inventories. This means that we have:

	Cost of sales			Closing inventories		
	Tonnes	Cost/tonne	Total	Tonnes	Cost/tonne	Total
		£	£000		£	£000
1 May	100	100	10.0			
2 May	500	110	55.0			
3 May	300	120	36.0	500	120	60.0
Cost of sales			101.0	Closing inventories		60.0

→

Last in, first out (LIFO)

Using the LIFO assumption, the later purchases will be treated *as if* these were the first to be sold. This is the 3 May purchases (800 tonnes) and some of the 2 May purchases (100 tonnes). The earlier purchases (the rest of the 2 May purchase and the opening inventories) will comprise the closing inventories. This can be set out as follows:

	Cost of sales			Closing inventories		
	Tonnes	Cost/tonne £	Total £000	Tonnes	Cost/tonne £	Total £000
3 May	800	120	96.0			
2 May	100	110	11.0	400	110	44.0
1 May			–	100	100	10.0
Cost of sales			107.0	Closing inventories		54.0

Figure 3.8 contrasts LIFO and FIFO.

Using FIFO, the oldest purchases of inventories are treated as the first to be used, leaving the later purchases in closing inventories. With LIFO, it is the opposite.

Figure 3.8 FIFO and LIFO treatment of the inventories in Example 3.8

Weighted average cost (AVCO)

Using the AVCO assumption, a weighted average cost will be determined that will be used to derive both the cost of goods sold and the cost of the remaining inventories held. This simply means that the total cost of the opening inventories and the total cost of the 2 May and 3 May purchases are added together and divided by the total number of tonnes to obtain the weighted average cost per tonne. Both the cost of sales and closing inventories values are based on that average cost per tonne. This means that we have:

	Tonnes	Cost/tonne £	Total £000
1 May	100	100	10.0
2 May	500	110	55.0
3 May	800	120	96.0
	1,400		161.0

The average cost is £161,000/1,400 = £115 per tonne.

Cost of sales			Closing inventories		
Tonnes	Cost/tonne £	Total £000	Tonnes	Cost/tonne £	Total £000
900	115	103.5	500	115	57.5

Activity 3.15

Suppose the 900 tonnes of inventories in Example 3.8 were sold for £150 per tonne.

(a) Calculate the gross profit for this sale under each of the three methods.
(b) What observations concerning the portrayal of financial position and performance can you make about each method when prices are rising?

Your answer should be along the following lines:

(a) Gross profit calculation:

	FIFO £000	LIFO £000	AVCO £000
Sales revenue (900 @ £150)	135.0	135.0	135.0
Cost of sales	(101.0)	(107.0)	(103.5)
Gross profit	34.0	28.0	31.5
Closing inventories	60.0	54.0	57.5

(b) These figures show that FIFO will give the highest gross profit during a period of rising prices. This is because sales revenue is matched with the earlier (and cheaper) purchases. LIFO will give the lowest gross profit because sales revenue is matched against the more recent (and dearer) purchases. The AVCO method will normally give a figure that is between these two extremes.

The closing inventories figure in the statement of financial position will be highest with the FIFO method. This is because the cost of goods still held will be based on the more recent (and dearer) purchases. LIFO will give the lowest closing inventories figure as the goods held will be based on the earlier (and cheaper) purchases. Once again, the AVCO method will normally give a figure that is between these two extremes.

Activity 3.16

Assume that prices are falling rather than rising. How would your observations concerning the portrayal of financial performance and position be different for the various costing methods?

When prices are falling, the positions of FIFO and LIFO are reversed. FIFO will give the lowest gross profit as sales revenue is matched against the earlier (and dearer) goods bought. LIFO will give the highest gross profit as sales revenue is matched against the more recent (and cheaper) goods bought. AVCO will give a cost of sales figure between these two extremes. The closing inventories figure in the statement of financial position will be lowest under FIFO as the cost of inventories will be based on the more recent (and cheaper) purchases. LIFO will provide the highest closing inventories figure and AVCO will provide a figure between the two extremes.

The different costing assumptions only have an effect on reported profit from one reporting period to the next. The figure derived for closing inventories will be carried forward and matched with sales revenue in a later period. If the cheaper purchases of inventories are matched to sales revenue in the current period, it will mean that the dearer purchases will be matched to sales revenue in a later period. Over the life of the business, therefore, total profit will be the same either way.

Inventories – some further issues

We saw in Chapter 2 that the convention of prudence requires that inventories be valued at the lower of cost and net realisable value. (The net realisable value of inventories is the estimated selling price less any further costs necessary to complete the goods and any costs involved in selling and distributing them.) In theory, this means that the valuation method applied to inventories could switch each year, depending on which of cost and net realisable value is the lower. In practice, however, the cost of the inventories held is usually below the current net realisable value – particularly during a period of rising prices. It is, therefore, the cost figure that will normally appear in the statement of financial position.

Activity 3.17

Can you think of any circumstances where the net realisable value will be lower than the cost of inventories held, even during a period of generally rising prices? Try to think of at least two.

The net realisable value may be lower where:

- goods have deteriorated or become obsolete;
- there has been a fall in the market price of the goods;
- the goods are being used as a 'loss leader', that is, they are deliberately going to be sold at a price lower than their cost; and/or
- bad buying decisions have been made.

There is also an International Financial Reporting Standard that deals with inventories. It states that, when preparing financial statements for external reporting, the cost of inventories should normally be determined using either FIFO or AVCO. The LIFO assumption is not acceptable for external reporting. (There is no reason, however, that a business should not apply LIFO when preparing financial statements for use by its own managers.) The standard also requires the 'lower of cost and net realisable value' rule to be used and so endorses the application of prudence.

> ### Activity 3.18
>
> Where inventories are written down (reduced) to their net realisable value, how do you think this should be treated in the financial statements?
>
> The amount written down should be treated as an expense in the income statement of the period in which the write down occurs. The value of inventories shown in the statement of financial position should then report the inventories at their net realisable value rather than their cost.

Real World 3.5 sets out the inventories' costing methods used by some of the UK's leading businesses.

> ### Real World 3.5
>
> #### Counting the cost
>
> Inventories costing methods used by some large UK businesses are as follows:
>
> | Name | Type of business | Costing method used |
> | --- | --- | --- |
> | J Sainsbury plc | Supermarket | AVCO |
> | Babcock International plc | Engineering support services | FIFO |
> | British American Tobacco plc | Tobacco manufacturer | AVCO |
> | Premier Foods plc | Food manufacturer | FIFO |
> | Marks and Spencer plc | Food and clothing retailer | AVCO |
> | Diageo plc | Alcoholic beverages | AVCO |
> | Tate and Lyle plc | Food ingredients | FIFO or AVCO |
> | AstraZeneca plc | Pharmaceuticals | FIFO or AVCO |
>
> Source: Annual reports of the relevant businesses for 2016 or 2017.
>
> Note that Tate and Lyle plc and AstraZeneca plc employ more than one inventories' costing method. Tate and Lyle plc state that the choice of costing method will depend on the materials and production processes used. AstraZeneca plc does not state what determines the choice of costing method. However, it will probably vary according to location, production processes or some other key factor.
>
> The table simply sets out a small, non-random sample of well-known businesses and so we cannot assess the relative popularity of the FIFO and LIFO methods in practice on the basis of this.

Costing inventories and depreciation provide two examples where the **consistency convention** should be applied. This convention holds that once a particular method of accounting is selected, it should be applied consistently over time. It would not be acceptable to switch from, say, FIFO to AVCO between periods (unless exceptional circumstances make it appropriate). The purpose of this convention is to help users make valid comparisons of performance and position from one period to the next. It, therefore, supports the qualitative characteristic of comparability that we considered in Chapter 1.

Activity 3.19

Reporting inventories in the financial statements provides a further example of the need to apply subjective judgement. For the inventories of a retail business, what are the main judgements that are required?

The main judgements are:

- the choice of costing method (FIFO, LIFO, AVCO); and
- deducing the net realisable value figure for inventories held.

One final point before leaving this topic. Costing inventories using FIFO, LIFO and AVCO applies to items that are interchangeable. Where they are not, as would be the case with custom-made items, the specific cost of the individual items must be used.

TRADE RECEIVABLES PROBLEMS

We have seen that, when businesses sell goods or services on credit, revenue will usually be recognised before the customer pays the amounts owing. Recording the dual aspect of a credit sale will involve increasing sales revenue and increasing trade receivables by the amount of the revenue from the credit sale.

With this type of sale there is always the risk that the customer will not pay the amount due. Where it becomes reasonably certain that the customer will not pay, the amount owed is considered to be a **bad debt**, which must be taken into account when preparing the financial statements.

Activity 3.20

What would be the effect on the income statement, and on the statement of financial position, of not taking into account the fact that a debt is bad?

The effect would be to overstate the assets (trade receivables) on the statement of financial position and to overstate profit in the income statement, as the revenue that has been recognised will not result in any future benefit.

To provide the users of the financial statements with a more realistic picture of financial performance and position, the bad debt must be 'written off'. This will involve reducing the trade receivables and increasing expenses (by creating an expense known as 'bad debts written off') by the amount of the bad debt. The matching convention requires that the bad debt is written off in the same period as the sale that gave rise to the debt is recognised.

Note that, when a debt is bad, the accounting response is not simply to cancel the original sale. If this were done, the income statement would not be so informative. Reporting the bad debts as an expense can be extremely useful in assessing management performance.

Real World 3.6 indicates the extent of the bad debts problem among small and medium size UK businesses.

Real World 3.6

Bad debts = Bad news

Questions are raging over the financial management behind the UK's SMEs (small and medium size enterprises), following revelations that they wrote off a total of £5.8 billion in bad debt during the last financial year.

According to a YouGov poll of senior SME decision-makers, carried out for insurer Direct Line, almost one in five (19%) had cancelled an average £31,330 of unpaid bills, while almost one in 10 (9%) had stopped pursuing debts in excess of £100,000.

Direct Line for Business head Nick Breton said: 'With more than one million SMEs based across the UK, these enterprises really do make up the backbone of the British economy.

'All of these debts add up – and with nearly 7,000 companies estimated to have entered liquidation in the first half of 2016 alone, the potentially disastrous knock-on effects of writing off monies owed are clear.'

The survey discovered that:

1. Overall, 82% of SMEs currently have outstanding balances, with each firm owed an average £62,957;
2. 40% of respondents do not even know the full value of monies owed them;
3. 29% said they were highly unlikely to receive monies owed because key trading partners had become insolvent;
4. 17% had given up on debts because they suspected the purchaser would not have sufficient funds to cover them; and
5. Almost two-thirds (65%) said that they were unsure about the function and purpose of an N1 Claim form – the standard document for beginning a civil claim in the UK court system. Only 16% know exactly what the N1 is for.

The poll's findings chime with other, recent research in the field, including a Bibby Financial Services (BFS) report of early August, which showed that 27% of UK SMEs had written off bad debt in the preceding 12 months.

According to BFS, that equates to 1.4 million SMEs suffering from bad-debt problems over the past year – with transport and construction emerging as the worst-affected sectors.

BFS Global chief executive David Postings said that bad debt was a 'chronic problem' for SMEs that could lead to 'staff cuts, delayed investment plans and – at worst – insolvency'.

Source: Extracts from *The Treasurer* (2016) UK SMEs write off £5.8bn of bad debt: Poll shows small firms are walking away from bad debt in droves, with almost one in 10 scrapping bills worth more than £100,000, Association of Corporate Treasurers, 15 September. www.treasurers.org/node/327677.

Doubtful debts

At the end of a reporting period, it may not be possible to identify, with certainty, all bad debts incurred during the period. Doubts may surround certain trade receivables, but it may only be at a later date that the true position will become clear. Nevertheless, the possibility that some trade receivables will not be paid should not be ignored. It would not be prudent, nor would it comply with the need to match expenses to the period in which the associated revenue is recognised.

The business must try to determine the amount of trade receivables that, at the end of the period, are doubtful (that is, there is a possibility that they may eventually prove to be bad). This amount may be derived by examining individual trade receivables accounts or by taking a proportion (usually based on past experience) of the total trade receivables outstanding.

Once a figure has been derived, an expense known as an **allowance for trade receivables** should be recognised. This will be shown as an expense in the income statement and deducted from the total trade receivables figure in the statement of financial position. In this way, full account is taken, in the appropriate reporting period, of those trade receivables where there is a risk of non-payment. This accounting treatment of these 'doubtful' trade receivables will be in addition to the treatment of the more certain bad debts described above.

Example 3.9 illustrates the reporting of bad debts and allowances for trade receivables.

Example 3.9

Desai Enterprises, which began trading on 1 July 2017, had trade receivables of £350,000 outstanding at the end of the reporting period to 30 June 2018. Investigation of these trade receivables revealed that £10,000 would probably be irrecoverable and that there was doubt concerning the recoverability of a further £30,000.

Relevant extracts from the income statement for that year would be as follows:

Income statement (extracts) for the year ended 30 June 2018

	£
Bad debts written off	10,000
Allowances for trade receivables	30,000

Statement of financial position (extracts) as at 30 June 2018

	£
Trade receivables	340,000*
Allowances for trade receivables	(30,000)
	310,000

*That is, £350,000 less £10,000 irrecoverable trade receivables.

The allowances for trade receivables figure is, of course, an estimate; it is quite likely that the actual amount of trade receivables that prove to be bad will be different from the estimate. Let us say that, during the next reporting period, it was discovered that, in fact, £26,000 of the trade receivables considered doubtful proved to be irrecoverable. These trade receivables must now be written off as follows:

- reduce trade receivables by £26,000; and
- reduce allowances for trade receivables by £26,000.

However, allowances for trade receivables of £4,000 will remain. This amount represents an overestimate made when creating the allowance as at 30 June 2018. As the allowance is no longer needed, it should be eliminated. Remember that the allowance was made by creating an expense in the income statement for the year to 30 June 2018. As the expense was too high, the amount of the overestimate should be 'written back' in the next reporting period. In other words, it will be treated as revenue for the year to 30 June 2019. This will mean:

- reducing the allowances for trade receivables by £4,000; and
- increasing revenue by £4,000.

Ideally, of course, the amount should be written back to the 2018 income statement; however, it is too late to do this. At the end of the year to 30 June 2019, not only will 2018's overestimate be written back, but a new allowance should be created to take account of the trade receivables arising from 2019's credit sales that are considered doubtful.

Activity 3.21

Clayton Conglomerates had trade receivables of £870,000 outstanding at the end of the reporting period to 31 March 2017. The chief financial officer believed £40,000 of those trade receivables to be irrecoverable and a further £60,000 to be doubtful. In the subsequent year, it was found that a pessimistic estimate of those trade receivables considered doubtful had been made and that only a further £45,000 of trade receivables had actually proved to be bad.

Show the relevant income statement extracts for both 2017 and 2018 to report the bad debts written off and the allowances for trade receivables. Also show the relevant statement of financial position extract as at 31 March 2017.

Your answer should be as follows:

Income statement (extract) for the year ended 31 March 2017

	£
Bad debts written off	40,000
Allowances for trade receivables	60,000

Income statement (extract) for the year ended 31 March 2018

	£
Allowances for trade receivables written back (revenue)	15,000

(*Note*: This figure will usually be netted off against any allowances for trade receivables created in respect of 2018.)

Statement of financial position (extract) as at 31 March 2017

	£
Trade receivables (870,000 − 40,000)	830,000
Allowances for trade receivables	(60,000)
	770,000

Activity 3.22

The accounting treatment of bad debts and allowances for trade receivables are two further examples where judgement is needed to derive an appropriate expense figure.

What will be the effect of different judgements concerning the appropriate amount of bad debts expense and allowances for trade receivables expense on the profit for a particular period and on the total profit reported over the life of the business?

The judgement concerning whether to write off a debt as bad will affect the expenses for the period and, therefore, the reported profit. Over the life of the business, however, total reported profit would not be affected, as incorrect judgements made in one period will be adjusted for in a later period.

Suppose that a debt of £100 was written off in a period and that, in a later period, the amount owing was actually received. The increase in expenses of £100 in the period in which the bad debt was written off would be compensated for by an increase in revenue of £100 when the amount outstanding was finally received (bad debt recovered). If, on the other hand, the amount owing of £100 was never written off in the first place, the profit for the two periods would not be affected by the bad debt adjustment and would, therefore, be different – but the total profit for the two periods would be the same.

A similar situation would apply where there are differences in judgements concerning allowances for trade receivables.

USES AND USEFULNESS OF THE INCOME STATEMENT

The income statement may help in providing information on:

- *How effective the business has been in generating wealth.* Since wealth generation is the primary reason for most businesses to exist, assessing how much wealth has been created is an important issue. The income statement reveals the profit for the period, or *bottom line* as it is sometimes called. This provides a measure of the wealth created for the owners. Gross profit and operating profit are also useful measures of wealth creation.
- *How profit was derived.* In addition to providing various measures of profit, the income statement provides other information needed for a proper understanding of business performance. It reveals the level of sales revenue and the nature and amount of expenses incurred, which can help in understanding how profit was derived.

Self-assessment question 3.1

TT and Co. is a new business that started trading on 1 January 2017. The following is a summary of transactions that occurred during the first year of trading:

1. The owners introduced £50,000 of equity, which was paid into a bank account opened in the name of the business.
2. Premises were rented from 1 January 2017 at an annual rental of £20,000. During the year, rent of £25,000 was paid to the owner of the premises.

3 Rates (a tax on business premises) were paid during the year as follows:

    For the period 1 January 2017 to 31 March 2017   £500
    For the period 1 April 2017 to 31 March 2018   £1,200

4 A delivery van was bought on 1 January 2017 for £12,000. This is expected to be used in the business for four years and then to be sold for £2,000.
5 Wages totalling £33,500 were paid during the year. At the end of the year, the business owed £630 of wages for the last week of the year.
6 Electricity bills for the first three quarters of the year were paid totalling £1,650. After 31 December 2017, but before the financial statements had been finalised for the year, the bill for the last quarter arrived showing a charge of £620.
7 Inventories totalling £143,000 were bought on credit.
8 Inventories totalling £12,000 were bought for cash.
9 Sales revenue on credit totalled £152,000 (cost of sales £74,000).
10 Cash sales revenue totalled £35,000 (cost of sales £16,000).
11 Receipts from trade receivables totalled £132,000.
12 Payments of trade payables totalled £121,000.
13 Van running expenses paid totalled £9,400.

At the end of the year it was clear that a credit customer who owed £400 would not be able to pay any part of the debt. All of the other trade receivables were expected to be settled in full.

The business uses the straight-line method for depreciating non-current assets.

Required:
Prepare a statement of financial position as at 31 December 2017 and an income statement for the year to that date.

The solution to this question can be found at the back of the book, starting on page 305.

SUMMARY

The main points of this chapter may be summarised as follows:

The income statement (profit and loss account)
- The income statement reveals how much profit (or loss) has been generated over a period and links the statements of financial position at the beginning and end of a reporting period.
- Profit (or loss) is the difference between total revenue and total expenses for a period.
- There are three main measures of profit:
    - gross profit – which is calculated by deducting the cost of sales from the sales revenue;
    - operating profit – which is calculated by deducting overheads from the gross profit;
    - profit for the period – which is calculated by adding non-operating income and deducting non-operating expenses (such as finance costs) from the operating profit.

Expenses and revenue

- Cost of sales may be identified by matching the cost of each sale to the particular sale or by adjusting the goods bought during a period by the opening and closing inventories.
- Classifying expenses is often a matter of judgement, although there are rules for businesses that trade as limited companies.
- Revenue is recognised when a business has performed its obligations, which is when control of the goods or services is passed to the customer.
- Revenue can be recognised over a period of time or at a particular point in time.
- The matching convention states that expenses should be matched to the revenue that they help generate.
- An expense reported in the income statement may not be the same as the cash paid. This can result in accruals or prepayments appearing in the statement of financial position.
- The materiality convention states that where the amounts are immaterial, we should consider only what is expedient.
- The accruals convention states that:

$$\text{profit} = \text{revenue} - \text{expenses (not cash receipts} - \text{cash payments)}.$$

Depreciation of non-current assets

- Depreciation requires a consideration of the cost (or fair value), useful life and residual value of an asset. It also requires a consideration of the method of depreciation.
- The straight-line method of depreciation allocates the amount to be depreciated evenly over the useful life of the asset.
- The reducing-balance method applies a fixed percentage rate of depreciation to the carrying amount of an asset each year.
- The depreciation method chosen should reflect the pattern of consumption of economic benefits of an asset.
- Depreciation allocates the cost (or fair value), less the residual value, of an asset over its useful life. It does not provide funds for replacement of the asset.

Costing inventories

- The way in which we derive the cost of inventories is important in the calculation of profit and the presentation of financial position.
- The first in, first out (FIFO) assumption is that the earliest inventories held are the first to be used.
- The last in, first out (LIFO) assumption is that the latest inventories are the first to be used.
- The weighted average cost (AVCO) assumption applies an average cost to all inventories used.
- When prices are rising, FIFO gives the lowest cost of sales figure and highest closing inventories figure and for LIFO it is the other way around. AVCO gives figures for cost of sales and closing inventories that lie between FIFO and LIFO.
- When prices are falling, the positions of FIFO and LIFO are reversed.
- Inventories are shown at the lower of cost and net realisable value.
- When a particular method of accounting, such as a depreciation method, is selected, it should be applied consistently over time.

> **Bad debts**
> - Where it is reasonably certain that a credit customer will not pay, the debt is regarded as 'bad' and written off.
> - Where it is doubtful that a credit customer will pay, an allowance for trade receivables expense should be created.
>
> **Uses of the income statement**
> - It provides measures of profit generated during a period.
> - It provides information on how the profit was derived.

KEY TERMS

profit	amortisation
revenue	residual value
expense	straight-line method
gross profit	carrying amount
operating profit	written-down value
profit for the period	net book value
cost of sales	reducing-balance method
matching convention	first in, first out (FIFO)
accrued expense	last in, first out (LIFO)
prepaid expense	weighted average cost (AVCO)
materiality convention	consistency convention
accruals convention	bad debt
accruals accounting	allowance for trade receivables
depreciation	

FURTHER READING

If you would like to explore the topics covered in this chapter in more depth, we recommend the following:

Alexander, D. and Nobes, C. (2016) *Financial Accounting: An International Introduction*, 6th edn, Pearson, Chapters 2, 3, 9 and 10.

Elliott, B. and Elliott, J. (2017) *Financial Accounting and Reporting*, 18th edn, Pearson, Chapters 2, 11, 20 and 21.

International Accounting Standards Board (2017) *2017 A Guide through IFRS Standards (Green Book)*, IAS 2 *Inventories* and IFRS 15 *Revenue from Contracts with Customers*.

KPMG (2017) *Insights into IFRS*, 14th edn, Sweet and Maxwell, Sections 3.2, 3.3, 3.8, 3.10 and 4.2A (a summarised version of this is available free at www.kpmg.com).

CRITICAL REVIEW QUESTIONS

Solutions to these questions can be found at the back of the book, starting on page 312.

3.1 'Although the income statement is a record of past achievement, the calculations required for certain expenses involve estimates of the future.' What does this statement mean? Can you think of examples where estimates of the future are used?

3.2 'Depreciation is a process of allocation and not valuation.' What do you think is meant by this statement?

3.3 What is the convention of consistency? Does this convention help users in making a more valid comparison between businesses?

3.4 'An asset is similar to an expense.' In what ways is this true or untrue?

EXERCISES

Solutions to exercises with coloured numbers can be found at the back of the book, starting on page 319.

Basic-level exercises

3.1 You have heard the following statements made. Comment critically on them.

(a) 'Equity only increases or decreases as a result of the owners putting more cash into the business or taking some out.'
(b) 'An accrued expense is one that relates to next year.'
(c) 'Unless we depreciate this asset we shall be unable to provide for its replacement.'
(d) 'There is no point in depreciating the factory building. It is appreciating in value each year.'

3.2 Singh Enterprises, which started business on 1 January 2016, has a reporting period to 31 December and uses the straight-line method of depreciation. On 1 January 2016, the business bought a machine for £10,000. The machine had an expected useful life of four years and an estimated residual value of £2,000. On 1 January 2017, the business bought another machine for £15,000. This machine had an expected useful life of five years and an estimated residual value of £2,500. On 31 December 2018, the business sold the first machine bought for £3,000.

Required:
Show the relevant income statement extracts and statement of financial position extracts for the years 2016, 2017 and 2018.

3.3 The owner of a business is confused and comes to you for help. The financial statements for the business, prepared by an accountant, for the last reporting period revealed a profit of £50,000. However, during the reporting period the bank balance declined by £30,000. What reasons might explain this apparent discrepancy?

Intermediate-level exercises

3.4 Fill in the values (a) to (f) in the following table on the assumption that there were no opening balances involved.

	Relating to period		At end of period	
	Paid/Received	Expense/revenue for period	Prepaid	Accruals/deferred revenues
	£	£	£	£
Rent payable	10,000	(a)	1,000	
Rates and insurance	5,000	(b)		1,000
General expenses	(c)	6,000	1,000	
Interest payable on borrowings	3,000	2,500	(d)	
Salaries	(e)	9,000		3,000
Rent receivable	(f)	1,500		1,500

3.5 Spratley Ltd is a builders' merchant. On 1 September the business had, as part of its inventories, 20 tonnes of sand at a cost of £18 per tonne and, therefore, at a total cost of £360. During the first week in September, the business bought the following amounts of sand:

	Tonnes	Cost per tonne £
2 September	48	20
4 September	15	24
6 September	10	25

On 7 September, the business sold 60 tonnes of sand to a local builder.

Required:
Calculate the cost of goods sold and of the remaining inventories using the following costing methods:

(a) first in, first out;
(b) last in, first out;
(c) weighted average cost.

Advanced-level exercises

3.6 The following is the statement of financial position of TT and Co. (see Self-Assessment Question 3.1 on page 108) at the end of its first year of trading:

Statement of financial position as at 31 December 2017

	£
ASSETS	
Non-current assets	
Property, plant and equipment	
Delivery van at cost	12,000
Depreciation	(2,500)
	9,500
Current assets	
Inventories	65,000
Trade receivables	19,600
Prepaid expenses*	5,300
Cash	750
	90,650
Total assets	100,150
EQUITY AND LIABILITIES	
Equity	
Original	50,000
Retained earnings	26,900
	76,900
Current liabilities	
Trade payables	22,000
Accrued expenses[†]	1,250
	23,250
Total equity and liabilities	100,150

* The prepaid expenses consisted of rates (£300) and rent (£5,000).
[†] The accrued expenses consisted of wages (£630) and electricity (£620).

During 2018, the following transactions took place:

1. The owners withdrew £20,000 of equity as cash.
2. Premises continued to be rented at an annual rental of £20,000. During the year, rent of £15,000 was paid to the owner of the premises.
3. Rates on the premises were paid during the year as follows: for the period 1 April 2018 to 31 March 2019, £1,300.
4. A second delivery van was bought on 1 January 2018 for £13,000. This is expected to be used in the business for four years and then to be sold for £3,000.
5. Wages totalling £36,700 were paid during the year. At the end of the year, the business owed £860 of wages for the last week of the year.
6. Electricity bills for the first three quarters of the year and £620 for the last quarter of the previous year were paid totalling £1,820. After 31 December 2018, but before the financial statements had been finalised for the year, the bill for the last quarter arrived showing a charge of £690.
7. Inventories totalling £67,000 were bought on credit.
8. Inventories totalling £8,000 were bought for cash.
9. Sales revenue on credit totalled £179,000 (cost £89,000).
10. Cash sales revenue totalled £54,000 (cost £25,000).
11. Receipts from trade receivables totalled £178,000.
12. Payments to trade payables totalled £71,000.
13. Van running expenses paid totalled £16,200.

The business uses the straight-line method for depreciating non-current assets.

Required:
Prepare a statement of financial position as at 31 December 2018 and an income statement for the year to that date.

3.7 The following is the statement of financial position of WW Associates as at 31 December 2017:

Statement of financial position as at 31 December 2017

	£
ASSETS	
Non-current assets	
Machinery	25,300
Current assets	
Inventories	12,200
Trade receivables	21,300
Prepaid expenses (rates)	400
Cash	8,300
	42,200
Total assets	67,500
EQUITY AND LIABILITIES	
Equity	
Original	25,000
Retained earnings	23,900
	48,900
Current liabilities	
Trade payables	16,900
Accrued expenses (wages)	1,700
	18,600
Total equity and liabilities	67,500

During 2018, the following transactions took place:

1. The owners withdrew £23,000 of equity in cash.
2. Premises were rented at an annual rental of £20,000. During the year, rent of £25,000 was paid to the owner of the premises.
3. Rates on the premises were paid during the year for the period 1 April 2018 to 31 March 2019 and amounted to £2,000.
4. Some machinery (a non-current asset), which was bought on 1 January 2017 for £13,000, has proved to be unsatisfactory. It was part-exchanged for some new machinery on 1 January 2018 and WW Associates paid a cash amount of £6,000. The new machinery would have cost £15,000 had the business bought it without the trade-in.
5. Wages totalling £23,800 were paid during the year. At the end of the year, the business owed £860 of wages.
6. Electricity bills for the four quarters of the year were paid totalling £2,700.
7. Inventories totalling £143,000 were bought on credit.
8. Inventories totalling £12,000 were bought for cash.
9. Sales revenue on credit totalled £211,000 (cost £127,000).
10. Cash sales revenue totalled £42,000 (cost £25,000).
11. Receipts from trade receivables totalled £198,000.
12. Payments to trade payables totalled £156,000.
13. Van running expenses paid totalled £17,500.

The business uses the reducing-balance method of depreciation for non-current assets at the rate of 30 per cent each year.

Required:
Prepare an income statement for the year ended 31 December 2018 and a statement of financial position as at that date.

3.8 The following is the income statement for Nikov and Co. for the year ended 31 December 2018, along with information relating to the preceding year.

Income statement for the year ended 31 December

	2018 £000	2017 £000
Sales revenue	420.2	382.5
Cost of sales	(126.1)	(114.8)
Gross profit	294.1	267.7
Salaries and wages	(92.6)	(86.4)
Selling and distribution costs	(98.9)	(75.4)
Rent and rates	(22.0)	(22.0)
Bad debts written off	(19.7)	(4.0)
Telephone and postage	(4.8)	(4.4)
Insurance	(2.9)	(2.8)
Motor vehicle expenses	(10.3)	(8.6)
Depreciation – delivery van	(3.1)	(3.3)
– fixtures and fittings	(4.3)	(4.5)
Operating profit	35.5	56.3
Loan interest	(4.6)	(5.4)
Profit for the year	30.9	50.9

Required:
Analyse the performance of the business for the year to 31 December 2018 in so far as the information allows.

Chapter 4

ACCOUNTING FOR LIMITED COMPANIES (1)

INTRODUCTION

Most businesses in the UK, from the very largest to some of the very smallest, operate in the form of limited companies. Nearly four million limited companies now exist, accounting for the majority of business activity and employment. The economic significance of the limited liability company is not confined to the UK; it can be seen in virtually all of the world's developed countries.

In this chapter we shall examine the main features of a limited company and how this form of business differs from sole-proprietorship and partnership businesses. This expands on the discussion of various business forms contained in Chapter 1. We shall see that the nature of limited companies makes it necessary to distinguish between different aspects of equity finance, based on how each arose. These different aspects will be considered, along with the restrictions that owners face when seeking to withdraw part of their equity.

The financial statements of limited companies reflect several key features of this type of business. We shall discuss how the financial statements discussed in the previous two chapters are adapted to accommodate these. We shall see that the adaptations relate to matters of detail rather than of underlying principle.

Learning outcomes

When you have completed this chapter, you should be able to:

- discuss the nature and financing of a limited company;
- describe the different aspects of equity for a limited company;
- explain the restrictions placed on owners seeking to withdraw part of their equity; and
- describe how the income statement and statement of financial position of a limited company differ in detail from those of sole proprietorships and partnerships.

THE MAIN FEATURES OF LIMITED COMPANIES

Legal nature

Let us begin our examination of limited companies by discussing their legal nature. A *limited company* has been described as an artificial person that has been created by law. This means that a company has many of the rights and obligations that 'real' people have. It can, for example, enter into contracts in its own name. It can also sue other people (real or corporate) and it can be sued by them. This contrasts sharply with unincorporated businesses, such as sole proprietorships and partnerships, where it is the owner(s) rather than the business that must enter into contracts, sue and so on. This is because those businesses have no separate legal identity.

With the rare exceptions of those that are created by Act of Parliament or by Royal Charter, all UK companies are created (or *incorporated*) by registration. To create a company the person or persons wishing to create it (usually known as *promoters*) fill in a few simple forms and pay a modest registration fee. After having ensured that the necessary formalities have been met, the Registrar of Companies, a UK government official, enters the name of the new company on the Registry of Companies. Thus, in the UK, companies can be formed very easily and cheaply (for about £100).

All of the shares of a limited company may be owned by just one person, but most have more than one owner and some have many owners. The owners are usually known as *members* or *shareholders*. The ownership of a company is normally divided into a number of shares, each of equal size. Each owner, or shareholder, owns one or more shares in the company. Large companies typically have a very large number of shareholders. For example, at 31 March 2017, BT Group plc, the telecommunications business, had 791,000 different shareholders. These shareholders owned nearly 10 billion shares between them.

Since a limited company has its own legal identity, it is regarded as being quite separate from those that own and manage it. It is worth emphasising that this legal separateness of owners and the company has no connection with the business entity convention discussed in Chapter 2. This accounting convention applies equally to all business types, including sole proprietorships and partnerships where there is no legal distinction between the owner(s) and the business.

The legal separateness of the limited company and its shareholders leads to two important features of the limited company: perpetual life and limited liability. These are now explained.

Perpetual life

A company is normally granted a perpetual existence and so will continue even where an owner of some, or even all, of the shares in the company dies. The shares of the deceased person will simply pass to the beneficiary of his or her estate. The granting of perpetual existence means that the life of a company is quite separate from the lives of those individuals who own or manage it. It is not, therefore, affected by changes in ownership that arise when individuals buy and sell shares in the company.

Although a company may be granted a perpetual existence when it is first formed, it is possible for either the shareholders or the courts to bring this existence to an end. When this is done, the assets of the company are usually sold to generate cash to meet the outstanding liabilities. Any amounts remaining after all liabilities have been met will then be distributed between the shareholders. Shareholders may agree to end the life of a company where it has achieved the purpose for which it was formed or where they feel that the company has no real future. The courts may bring the life of a company to an end where creditors (those owed money by the company) have applied to the courts for this to be done because they have not been paid.

Where shareholders agree to end the life of a company, it is referred to as a 'voluntary liquidation'. **Real World 4.1** describes the demise of one company by this method.

Real World 4.1

Monotub Industries in a spin as founder gets Titan for £1

Monotub Industries, maker of the Titan washing machine, yesterday passed into corporate history with very little ceremony and with only a whimper of protest from minority shareholders.

At an extraordinary meeting held in a basement room of the group's West End headquarters, shareholders voted to put the company into voluntary liquidation and sell its assets and intellectual property to founder Martin Myerscough for £1 [The shares in the company were at one time worth 650p each.]

The only significant opposition came from Giuliano Gnagnatti who, along with other shareholders, has seen his investment shrink faster than a wool twin-set on a boil wash.

The not-so-proud owner of 100,000 Monotub shares, Mr Gnagnatti, the managing director of an online retailer, described the sale of Monotub as a 'free gift' to Mr Myerscough. This assessment was denied by Ian Green, the chairman of Monotub, who said the closest the beleaguered company had come to a sale was an offer for £60,000 that gave no guarantees against liabilities, which are thought to amount to £750,000.

The quiet passing of the washing machine, eventually dubbed the Titanic, was in strong contrast to its performance in many kitchens.

Originally touted as the 'great white goods hope' of the washing machine industry with its larger capacity and removable drum, the Titan ran into problems when it kept stopping during the spin cycle, causing it to emit a loud bang and leap into the air.

Summing up the demise of the Titan, Mr Green said: 'Clearly the machine had some revolutionary aspects, but you can't get away from the fact that the machine was faulty and should not have been launched with those defects.'

The usually-vocal Mr Myerscough, who has promised to pump £250,000 into the company and give Monotub shareholders £4 for every machine sold, refused to comment on his plans for the Titan or reveal who his backers were. But . . . he did say that he intended to 'take the Titan forward'.

Source: Urquhart L. (2003) Monotub Industries in a spin as founder gets Titan for £1, *Financial Times*, 23 January. © The Financial Times Limited 2012. All rights reserved.

Limited liability

Since the company is a legal person in its own right, it must take responsibility for its own debts and losses. This means that, once the shareholders have paid what they have agreed to pay for the shares, their obligation to the company, and to the company's creditors, is satisfied. Thus shareholders can limit their losses to the amount that they have paid, or agreed to pay, for their shares. This is of great practical importance to potential shareholders since they know that what they can lose, as part owners of the business, is limited.

Contrast this with the position of sole proprietors or partners. They cannot 'ring-fence' assets that they do not want to put into the business. If a sole-proprietorship or partnership business finds itself in a position where liabilities exceed the business assets, the law gives unsatisfied creditors the right to demand payment out of what the sole proprietor or partner may have regarded as 'non-business' assets. Thus the sole proprietor or partner could lose everything – house, car, the lot. This is because the law sees Jill, the sole proprietor, as being the same as Jill the private individual.

Real World 4.2 gives an example of a well-known case where the shareholders of a particular company were able to avoid any liability to those that had lost money as a result of dealing with the company.

Real World 4.2

Carlton and Granada 1 – Nationwide Football League 0

Two television broadcasting companies, Carlton and Granada, each owned 50 per cent of a separate company, ITV Digital (formerly ON Digital). ITV Digital signed a contract to pay the Nationwide Football League (in effect the three divisions of English football below the Premiership) more than £89 million on both 1 August 2002 and 1 August 2003 for the rights to broadcast football matches over three seasons. ITV Digital failed to sell sufficient subscriptions for the broadcasts and so collapsed because it was unable to meet its liabilities. The Nationwide Football League tried to force Carlton and Granada (ITV Digital's only two shareholders) to meet ITV Digital's contractual obligations. It was unable to do so because the shareholders could not be held legally liable for the amounts owing.

Carlton and Granada subsequently merged into one business, but at the time of ITV Digital were two independent companies.

Activity 4.1

The fact that shareholders can limit their losses to that which they have paid, or have agreed to pay, for their shares is of great practical importance to potential shareholders.

Can you think of any practical benefit to a private-sector economy, in general, of this ability of shareholders to limit losses?

Business is a risky venture – in some cases very risky. People will usually be happier to invest money when they know the limit of their liability. If investors are given limited liability, new businesses are more likely to be formed and existing ones are likely to find it easier to raise more finance. This is good for the private-sector economy and may ultimately lead to the generation of greater wealth for society as a whole.

Although **limited liability** has this advantage to the providers of equity finance (the shareholders), it is not necessarily to the advantage of all of the others who have a stake in the business, as we saw in the case of the Nationwide Football League clubs in Real World 4.2. Limited liability is attractive to shareholders because they can, in effect, walk away from the unpaid debts of the company if their committed contribution is not enough to cover those debts. As a consequence, individuals, or businesses, may be wary of entering into a contract with a limited company. This can be a real problem for smaller, less established companies. Suppliers may insist on cash payment before delivery of goods or the rendering of a service.

Alternatively, they may require a personal guarantee from a major shareholder that the debt will be paid before allowing trade credit. In this way, the supplier circumvents the company's limited liability status by demanding the personal liability of an individual. Larger, more established companies, on the other hand, find it easier to gain the confidence of suppliers.

LEGAL SAFEGUARDS

Various safeguards exist to protect individuals and businesses contemplating dealing with a limited company. They include the requirement to indicate limited liability status in the name of the company. This should alert prospective suppliers and lenders to the potential risks involved.

A further safeguard is the restrictions placed on the ability of shareholders to withdraw their equity from the company.

Activity 4.2

Can you think how these restrictions on the withdrawal of equity can act as a safeguard?

They are designed to prevent shareholders from protecting their own investment and, as a result, leaving lenders and suppliers in an exposed position.

We shall consider this point in more detail later in the chapter.

In addition, and importantly, limited companies are required to produce annual financial statements (income statements, statements of financial position and statements of cash flows) and make these publicly available. This means that anyone interested can gain an impression of the financial performance and position of the company. The form and content of the first two of these statements are considered in some detail later in the chapter and in Chapter 5.

PUBLIC AND PRIVATE COMPANIES

When a company is registered with the Registrar of Companies, it must be registered either as a public or as a private company. The main practical difference between these is that a **public limited company** can offer its shares for sale to the general public, but a **private limited company** cannot. A public limited company must signal its status to all interested parties by having the words 'public limited company', or its abbreviation 'plc', in its name. For a private limited company, the word 'limited' or 'Ltd' must appear as part of its name.

Private limited companies tend to be smaller businesses where the ownership is divided among relatively few shareholders who are usually fairly close to one another – for example, a family company. There are vastly more private limited companies in the UK than public limited companies. Of the nearly four million UK limited companies now in existence, only around 6,900 (representing 0.19 per cent (that is, one in about 540) of the total) are public limited companies.

Real World 4.3 shows the trend in the numbers of public and private limited companies in recent years.

Real World 4.3

Company trends

Recent years have seen a steady decline in the number of public limited companies, yet at the same time the number of private ones has shown a steady increase. Figure 4.1 shows these trends.

There was a rise in the number of private limited companies over the period. Over the same period there has been a decline in the number of public limited companies.

Figure 4.1 Numbers of public and private limited companies in the UK, 2012/13 to 2016/17

Source: Based on information in Companies Registration Activities 2012/13 to 2016/17, Table 1, www.companieshouse.gov.uk.

Since individual public companies tend to be larger, they are often economically more important. In some industry sectors, such as banking, insurance, oil refining and grocery retailing, they are completely dominant. Although some private limited companies are large, many are little more than the vehicle through which one-person businesses operate.

Real World 4.4 shows the extent of the market dominance of public limited companies in one particular business sector.

Real World 4.4

A big slice of the market

The grocery sector is dominated by four large players: Tesco, Sainsbury, Morrison and Asda. The first three are public limited companies and the fourth, Asda, is owned by a large US public company, Wal-Mart Inc. Figure 4.2 shows the share of the grocery market of each during the twelve-week period to 22 April 2018.

- Tesco 27.6%
- Sainsbury 15.9%
- Asda 15.5%
- Morrisons 10.5%
- Others 30.5%

Tesco had by far the largest market share and the four largest grocery companies, when taken together, account for just under 70 per cent of the total grocery market during the period.

Figure 4.2 Market share of the four largest grocery companies, 12 weeks to 22 April 2018

Source: www.kantarworldpanel.com

TAXATION

Another consequence of the legal separation of the limited company from its owners is that companies must be accountable to the tax authorities for tax on their profits and gains. This leads to the reporting of tax in the financial statements of limited companies. The charge for tax is shown in the income statement. The tax charge for a particular year is based on that year's profit. For many companies, only 50 per cent of the tax liability is due for payment during the year concerned, so the other 50 per cent will appear on the end-of-year statement of financial position as a current liability. This will be illustrated a little later in the chapter.

Companies are charged **corporation tax** on their profits and gains. It is levied on the company's taxable profit, which may differ from the profit shown on the income statement. This is because tax law does not follow normal accounting rules in every respect. Generally, however, taxable profit and accounting profit are pretty close to one another. The percentage rate of corporation tax tends to vary over time. For the corporation tax year commencing 1 April 2018, the rate is set at 19 per cent and it will remain at this rate for the following tax year. For the tax year commencing 1 April 2020 the rate will be reduced to 18 per cent.

The tax position of companies contrasts with that of sole proprietorships and partnerships, where tax is levied not on the business but on the owner(s). This means that tax will not be reported in the financial statements of unincorporated businesses, as it is a matter between the owner(s) and the tax authorities. There can be tax advantages to trading as a limited company, rather than as a sole proprietor or partner. Although these advantages have been somewhat diminished by recent legislation, they may partly explain the rise in popularity of private limited companies over recent years.

THE ROLE OF THE STOCK EXCHANGE

A **Stock Exchange** typically acts as both an important *primary* and *secondary* capital market for companies. As a primary market, its function is to enable companies to raise new finance. As a secondary market its function is to enable investors to sell their securities (including shares and loan notes) with ease. We have already seen that shares in a company may be transferred from one owner to another. The wish of some investors to sell their shares, coupled with the wish of others to buy those shares, has led to the creation of a formal market in which shares are bought and sold.

As with most stock exchanges, only the shares of certain companies (*listed* companies) may be traded on the **London Stock Exchange**. As at 31 December 2017, just over 1,900 UK companies were listed, either on the 'Main Market' or the Alternative Investment Market (AIM – mainly, newer and smaller businesses). This represents only 1 in about 2,000 of all UK companies (public and private) and roughly 1 in 3.6 public limited companies. However, many of these listed companies are massive. Nearly all of the UK businesses that are 'household names' (for example, Tesco, Next, BT, Vodafone, BP, easyJet (all on Main Market) and Fevertree, Asos, Boohoo (AIM)) are listed companies.

Activity 4.3

As mentioned earlier, the change in ownership of shares does not directly affect a particular company. Why, in that case, do many public companies seek to have their shares traded on a recognised Stock Exchange?

Investors are generally reluctant to pledge their money unless they can see some way of turning their investment back into cash (an 'exit route'). The shares of a particular company may be valuable because it has bright prospects. Unless this value can be turned into cash, however, the benefit to investors is dubious. After all, we cannot spend shares; we normally need cash. Thus, investors are more likely to buy new shares from a company where they can liquidate their investment (turn it into cash) as and when they wish. Stock Exchanges provide the means of liquidation and, by so doing, make it easier for a company to raise new share capital.

Disadvantages of a listing

A Stock Exchange listing can have certain disadvantages for a business. These include the following:

- Strict rules are imposed on listed businesses, including requirements for levels of financial disclosure additional to those already imposed by International Financial Reporting

Standards (for example, the listing rules require that half-yearly financial reports are published).
- Financial analysts, financial journalists and others tend to monitor closely the activities of listed businesses, especially larger ones. Such scrutiny may not be welcome, particularly if the business is dealing with sensitive issues or is experiencing operational problems.
- It is often claimed that listed businesses are under pressure to perform well over the short term. This pressure may detract from undertaking projects that will yield benefits only in the longer term. If the market becomes disenchanted with the business, and the price of its shares falls, this may make it vulnerable to a takeover bid from another business.
- The costs of obtaining and retaining a listing are high and this may be a real deterrent for some businesses.

Going private

Such are the disadvantages of a stock market listing that many businesses have 'delisted'. This has obviously denied them the advantages of a listing, but it has avoided the disadvantages.

CAPITAL MARKET EFFICIENCY

When share prices at all times rationally reflect all available, relevant information, the market in which they are traded is said to be an **efficient capital market**. This implies that any new information relating to a particular company and its share price will be taken into account quickly and rationally, in terms of size and direction of share price movement.

Activity 4.4

Can you suggest why a capital market like the Stock Exchange should be price efficient?

Many analysts study the performance of listed companies. Between them, they should make a valid assessment of the market value of those companies' shares.

Prices are set in capital markets by the forces of supply and demand. If the consensus view of those active in the market is that the shares of a particular business are underpriced, demand will force the price up.

In a secondary capital market such as the London Stock Exchange, share prices are observed by a large number of people, many of them skilled and experienced. Nearly all of them are incentivised by that great motivator – financial gain. They glean information relating to the business from a variety of sources, including the business itself. This information may include published financial statements, press releases and company 'leaks' as well as industry and economy reports.

Where observers spot what they consider to be an irrational price, they try to take advantage of it, or advise others to do so. For example, an investment analyst employed by a financial institution might assess the worth of a share in Tesco plc at £2.50 while the current share price is only £2.10. The analyst may then contact the investment manager to recommend buying Tesco shares because they are underpriced and there are gains to be made. The increase in demand from large-scale buying tends to increase the share price.

> **Activity 4.5**
>
> **If a capital market is price efficient, does this mean that the current market price of a share in a particular business is the correct price?**
>
> No. A share price is based on expectations concerning its future returns. No one can know for certain what those future returns will be.

Price efficiency does not imply perfect powers of prediction on the part of investors. All it means is that the current price of a share is the best estimate of its future returns on the basis of the available evidence.

Evidence on capital market efficiency

An enormous amount of research has been undertaken on the pricing efficiency of most of the world's capital markets. Although there are some minor anomalies, the evidence on most capital markets (including the London Stock Exchange) is that:

1. the price of a share in any particular business fully, rationally and very rapidly takes account of all relevant *publicly* available information that bears on that business and its shares; and
2. any information that is only *privately* available is not necessarily taken into account in the share price.

This means that it is not possible for investors to make systematic gains from trading on the basis of any information that is publicly available. On the other hand, relevant information that is known only, say, to a director of a particular business, but will become publicly known later, may enable that person to gain from trading in the shares. In most jurisdictions, including the UK, such an action by a person in a privileged position would be illegal.

When we say that it is not possible for investors to make systematic gains from trading on the basis of any information that is publicly available, this is because in an efficient market, any relevant new information about the business will immediately be reflected in the price at which the business's shares are trading. For example, an investor notices that a particular business has just announced unexpectedly winning a contract that will significantly improve its profitability and value. However quickly our investor acts to buy shares in the business, in an attempt to benefit from the expected share price rise, it will be too late; the price will already have risen.

The fact that the market is efficient certainly does not mean that people who invest in shares do not make profits. Through a combination of capital appreciation (rises in share prices) and dividends received from the businesses, investors in UK businesses have earned, on average over the past 120 years, an annual return of the rate of inflation plus a little over 5 per cent. This is significantly higher than returns on lending, say to a building society or holding government bonds, or investing in property (real estate). During some periods, investing in shares would have yielded much higher returns. In other periods, very low (including negative) returns have been incurred.

> **Activity 4.6**
>
> If we look at a graph of the price of a share in a particular business plotted against time, we tend to find that it jumps up and down. This is similar to the effect that we get if we plot a graph of a series of random numbers.
> Does this mean that share price movements are arbitrary?

No, it does not mean this. The share price movements mentioned above occur because new information does not arise in a gradual or systematic way but in a random, unexpected way. The share price movements will, however, be a rational and timely response to the new information coming to light.

MANAGING A COMPANY

A limited company may have a legal personality, but it is not a human being capable of making decisions and plans about the business and exercising control over it. People must undertake these management tasks. The most senior level of management of a company is the board of directors.

Directors are elected by shareholders to manage the company on a day-to-day basis on their behalf. By law there must be at least one director for a private limited company and two for a public limited company. In a small company, the board may be the only level of management and consist of all of the shareholders. In larger companies, the board may consist of ten or so directors out of many thousands of shareholders. (The directors are normally shareholders although they do not have to be.) Below the board of directors of the typical large company could be several layers of management comprising many thousands of people.

In recent years, the issue of **corporate governance** has generated much debate. The term is used to describe the ways in which companies are directed and controlled. The issue of corporate governance is important because, with larger companies, those who own the company (that is, the shareholders) are usually divorced from the day-to-day control of the business. The shareholders employ the directors to manage the company for them. Given this position, it may seem reasonable to assume that the best interests of shareholders will guide the directors' decisions. However, in practice this does not always seem to be the case. The directors may be more concerned with pursuing their own interests, such as increasing their pay and 'perks' (such as expensive motor cars, overseas visits and so on) and improving their job security and status. As a result, a conflict can occur between the interests of shareholders and the interests of directors.

The problems and issues associated with corporate governance will be explored in detail in Chapter 7.

FINANCING LIMITED COMPANIES

Equity (the owners' claim)

The equity of a sole proprietorship is normally encompassed in one figure on the statement of financial position. In the case of companies, things are a little more complicated, although the same broad principles apply. With companies, equity is divided between shares (for example, the original investment), on the one hand, and **reserves** (that is, profits and gains subsequently made), on the other. There is also the possibility that there will be more than one type of shares and of reserves. Thus, within the basic divisions of share capital and reserves, there will usually be further subdivisions. This might seem quite complicated, but we shall shortly consider the reasons for these subdivisions and all should become clearer.

The basic division

When a company is first formed, those who take steps to form it (the promoters) will decide how much needs to be raised from potential shareholders to set the company up with the necessary assets to operate. Example 4.1 illustrates this.

Example 4.1

Some friends decide to form a company to operate an office cleaning business. They estimate that the company will need £50,000 to obtain the necessary assets. Between them, they raise the cash, which they use to buy shares in the company, on 31 March 2017, with a **nominal value** (or **par value**) of £1 each.

At this point the statement of financial position of the company would be:

Statement of financial position as at 31 March 2017

	£
Net assets (all in cash)	50,000
Equity	
Share capital	
50,000 shares of £1 each	50,000

The company now buys the necessary non-current assets (vacuum cleaners and so on) and inventories (cleaning materials) and starts to trade. During the first year, the company makes a profit of £10,000 This, by definition, means that the equity expands by £10,000. During the year, the shareholders (owners) make no drawings of their equity, so at the end of the year the summarised statement of financial position looks like this:

Statement of financial position as at 31 March 2018

	£
Net assets (various assets less liabilities*)	60,000
Equity	
Share capital	
50,000 shares of £1 each	50,000
Reserves (revenue reserve)	10,000
Total equity	60,000

* We saw in Chapter 2 that Assets = Equity + Liabilities. We also saw that this can be rearranged to Assets − Liabilities = Equity.

The profit is shown as a reserve, known as a **revenue reserve**, because it arises from generating revenue (making sales). Note that we do not simply merge the profit with the share capital: we must keep the two amounts separate in order to satisfy company law. There is a legal restriction on the maximum drawings of the shareholders equity (for example, as a **dividend**) that can be made. This maximum is defined by the amount of revenue reserves and so it is helpful to show these separately. We shall look at why there is this restriction, and how it works, a little later in the chapter.

SHARE CAPITAL

Ordinary shares

Ordinary shares represent the basic units of ownership of a business. They are issued by all companies and are often known as *equities*. Ordinary shareholders are the primary risk takers as they share in the profits of the company only after other claims have been satisfied. There are no upper limits on the amount by which they may benefit. The potential rewards available to ordinary shareholders reflect the risks that they are prepared to take. Since ordinary shareholders take most of the risks, power normally rests in their hands. Usually, only the ordinary shareholders are able to vote on issues that affect the company, such as the appointment of directors.

The nominal value of such shares is at the discretion of those who start up the company. For example, if the initial share capital is to be £50,000 this could be two shares of £25,000 each, 5 million shares of one penny each or any other combination that gives a total of £50,000. All shares must have equal value.

Activity 4.7

The initial financial requirement for a new company is £50,000. There are to be two equal shareholders. Would you advise them to issue two shares of £25,000 each? Why?

Such large-denomination shares tend to be unwieldy and difficult to sell. If one of the shareholders wished to liquidate her shareholding, she would have to find a single buyer. Where, however, the shareholding consisted of shares of smaller denomination, the price per share would be lower and the whole shareholding could probably be sold more easily to various potential buyers. It would also be possible for the original shareholder to sell just part of the shareholding and retain a part.

In practice, £1 is the normal maximum nominal value for shares. Shares of 25 pence each and 50 pence each are among the more common. BT plc, the telecommunications business, has ordinary shares with a nominal value of 5 pence each (although their market value at 19 January 2018 was £2.67 per share).

Preference shares

In addition to ordinary shares, some companies issue **preference shares**. These shares guarantee that *if a dividend is paid*, the preference shareholders will be entitled to the first part of it up to a maximum value. This maximum is normally defined as a fixed percentage of the nominal value of the preference shares. If, for example, a company issues one million preference shares of £1 each with a dividend rate of 6 per cent, this means that the preference shareholders are entitled to receive the first £60,000 (that is, 6 per cent of £1 million) of any dividend that is paid by the company for a particular year. Any dividend payment in excess of £60,000 goes to the ordinary shareholders.

Real World 4.5 below describes the types of preference shares issued by one large company.

Real World 4.5

Having a preference

BP plc, the energy company, has two types of £1 preference share in issue, one with a dividend rate of 8 per cent and another with a dividend rate of 9 per cent. Both types of preference share are cumulative, which means that any unpaid dividends are carried forward for payment when a dividend is next declared. The unpaid dividends will be paid before ordinary shareholders receive a dividend. Not all preference shares are cumulative. Where non-cumulative preference shares are issued, any dividends not paid for a particular period are foregone.

Source: BP plc, Share information, www.bp.com [accessed 19 January 2018].

It is open to the company to issue shares of various classes – perhaps with some having unusual conditions – but in practice it is rare to find other than straightforward ordinary and preference shares. Even preference shares are not very common. Although a company may have different classes of shares with each class giving holders different rights, within each class all shares must have equal rights. The rights of the various classes of shareholders, as well as other matters relating to a particular company, are contained in that company's set of rules, known as the *memorandum and articles of association*. A copy of these rules must be lodged with the Registrar of Companies, who makes it available for inspection by the general public.

Altering the nominal value of shares

As we have already seen, the promoters of a new company may make their own choice of the nominal (par) value of the shares. This value need not be permanent. At a later date the shareholders can decide to change it.

Suppose that a company has 1 million ordinary shares of £1 each and a decision is made to change the nominal value of the shares from £1 to £0.50 - in other words to halve the value. To maintain the total nominal value of the share capital intact, the company would then issue each shareholder exactly twice as many shares, each with half the original nominal value. Thus, each shareholder would retain a holding of the same total nominal value as before. This process is known, not surprisingly, as **splitting** the shares. The opposite, reducing the number of shares and increasing their nominal value per share to compensate, is known as **consolidating**. Since each shareholder would be left, after a split or consolidation, with exactly the same proportion of ownership of the company's assets as before, the process should have no effect on the total value of the shares held.

Both splitting and consolidating may be used to help make the shares more marketable. Splitting may help avoid share prices becoming too high and consolidating may help avoid share prices becoming too low. It seems that investors do not like either extreme. In addition, some Stock Exchanges do not allow shares to be traded at too low a price.

Real World 4.6 provides an example of a share split by one business.

Real World 4.6

Doing the splits

Air Partner plc, the UK based international private charter flight provider, announced a share split where in place of each five pence share, shareholders will receive five one penny shares. The business explained the reason for this as follows:

> The Board of directors believes that the Company's share price has risen to a point where it is appropriate to recommend that each existing ordinary share of five pence be split into five new ordinary shares of one penny each. The Board believes that this split will improve the liquidity of the market in the Company's shares, reduce the percentage spread between the bid and offer prices and increase the attractiveness of the Company's shares to potential investors. A long term aim of the Board is to attract and retain a diverse shareholder base with an appropriate balance between retail and institutional investors for a public company listed on the premium segment of the London Stock Exchange.

Source: Air Partner plc (2017) Statement from the business, 6 January.

RESERVES

The shareholders' equity consists of share capital and reserves. As mentioned earlier, reserves are profits and gains that a company has made and which still form part of the shareholders' equity. One reason that past profits and gains may no longer continue to be part of equity is that they have been paid out to shareholders (as dividends and so on). Another reason is that reserves will be reduced by the amount of any losses that the company might suffer. In the same way that profits increase equity, losses reduce it.

Activity 4.8

Are reserves amounts of cash? Can you think of a reason why this is an odd question?

To deal with the second point first, it is an odd question because reserves are a claim, or part of one, on the assets of the company, whereas cash is an asset. So reserves cannot be cash.

Reserves are classified as either revenue reserves or **capital reserves**. In Example 4.1 we came across a revenue reserve. This reserve represents the company's retained trading profits as well as gains on the disposal of non-current assets. *Retained earnings*, as they are most often called, represent overwhelmingly the largest source of new finance for UK companies. Capital reserves arise for two main reasons:

- issuing shares at above their nominal value (for example, issuing £1 shares at £1.50);
- revaluing (upwards) non-current assets.

Where a company issues shares at above their nominal value, UK law requires that the excess of the issue price over the nominal value be shown separately.

Activity 4.9

Can you think why shares might be issued at above their nominal value? (*Hint*: This would not usually happen when a company is first formed and the initial shares are being issued.)

Once a company has traded and has been successful, the shares would normally be worth more than the nominal value at which they were issued. If additional shares are to be issued to new shareholders to raise finance for further expansion, unless they are issued at a value higher than the nominal value, the new shareholders will be gaining at the expense of the original ones.

Example 4.2 shows how this works.

Example 4.2

Based on future prospects, the net assets of a company are worth £1.5 million. There are currently 1 million ordinary shares in the company, each with a nominal value of £1. The company wishes to raise an additional £0.6 million of cash for expansion and has decided to raise it by issuing new shares. If the shares are issued for £1 each (that is 600,000 shares), the total number of shares will be:

$$1.0m + 0.6m = 1.6m$$

and their total value will be the value of the existing net assets plus the new injection of cash:

$$£1.5m + £0.6m = £2.1m$$

This means that the value of each share after the new issue will be:

$$£2.1m/1.6m = £1.3125$$

The current value of each share is:

$$£1.5m/1.0m = £1.50$$

so the original shareholders will lose:

$$£1.50 - £1.3125 = £0.1875 \text{ a share}$$

and the new shareholders will gain:

$$£1.3125 - £1.0 = £0.3125 \text{ a share}$$

The new shareholders will, no doubt, be delighted with this outcome; the original ones will not.

Things could be made fair between the two sets of shareholders described in Example 4.2 by issuing the new shares at £1.50 each. In this case, it would be necessary to issue 400,000 shares to raise the necessary £0.6 million. £1 a share of the £1.50 is the nominal value and will be included with share capital in the statement of financial position (£400,000 in total).

The remaining £0.50 is a share premium, which will be shown as a capital reserve known as the **share premium account** (£200,000 in total).

It is not clear why UK company law insists on the distinction between nominal share values and the premium. In some other countries (for example, the United States) with similar laws governing the corporate sector, there is not this distinction. Instead, the total value at which shares are issued is shown as one comprehensive figure on the company's statement of financial position.

Real World 4.7 shows the equity of one very well-known business.

Real World 4.7

Flying funds

Ryanair Holdings plc, the no-frills airline, had the following share capital and reserves as at 31 March 2017:

	€ million
Share capital (Ordinary shares)	7.3
Share premium	719.4
Retained earnings	3,456.8
Other reserves and capital	239.5
Total equity	**4,423.0**

Note how the nominal share capital figure is only a small fraction of the share premium account figure. This implies that Ryanair has issued shares at much higher prices than their nominal value. This reflects its trading success since the company was first formed. As at 31 March 2017, retained earnings (profits) made up nearly four fifths of the total for share capital and reserves.

Source: Information taken from Ryanair Holdings plc, Annual Report 2017, p. 137.

BONUS SHARES

It is always open to a company to take reserves of any kind (irrespective of whether they are capital or revenue) and turn them into share capital. This will involve transferring the desired amount from the reserve concerned to share capital and then distributing the appropriate number of new shares to the existing shareholders. New shares arising from such a conversion are known as **bonus shares**. Example 4.3 illustrates how bonus issues work.

A bonus issue simply takes one part of the equity (a reserve) and puts it into another part (share capital). The transaction has no effect on the company's assets or liabilities, so there is no effect on shareholders' wealth. Issues of bonus shares have become less common in recent years, perhaps because of the lack of business profitability during the recent past.

Note that a bonus issue is not the same as a share split. A split does not affect the reserves.

Example 4.3

The summary statement of financial position of a company at a particular point in time is as follows:

Statement of financial position

	£
Net assets (various assets less liabilities)	128,000
Equity	
Share capital	
50,000 shares of £1 each	50,000
Reserves	78,000
Total equity	128,000

The directors decide that the company will issue existing shareholders with one new share for every share currently owned by each shareholder. The statement of financial position immediately following this will appear as follows:

Statement of financial position

	£
Net assets (various assets less liabilities)	128,000
Equity	
Share capital	
100,000 shares of £1 each	100,000
Reserves	28,000
Total equity	128,000

We can see that the reserves have decreased by £50,000 and share capital has increased by the same amount. To complete the transaction, 50,000 new ordinary shares of £1 each, which have been created from reserves, will be issued to the existing shareholders.

Activity 4.10

A shareholder of the company in Example 4.3 owned 100 shares before the bonus issue. How will things change for this shareholder as regards the number of shares owned and the value of the shareholding?

The answer should be that the number of shares would double, from 100 to 200. Now the shareholder owns one five-hundredth of the company (that is, 200/100,000). Before the bonus issue, the shareholder also owned one five-hundredth of the company (that is, 100/50,000). The company's assets and liabilities have not changed as a result of the bonus issue and so, logically, one five-hundredth of the value of the company should be identical to what it was before. Thus, each share is worth half as much as it used to be.

Activity 4.11

Can you think of any reasons why a company might want to make a bonus issue if it has no economic consequence? Try to think of at least one reason.

We think that there are three possible reasons:

- *Share price.* To lower the value of each share in order to make the shares more marketable. This has a similar effect to share splitting.
- *Shareholder confidence.* To provide the shareholders with a 'feel-good factor'. It is believed that shareholders like bonus issues because they seem to make them better off, although in practice they should not affect their wealth.
- *Lender confidence.* Where reserves arising from operating profits and/or realised gains on the sale of non-current assets (revenue reserves) are used to make the bonus issue, it has the effect of taking part of the shareholders' equity that could be withdrawn and locking it up. The amount transferred becomes part of the permanent equity base of the company. (We shall see a little later in this chapter that there are severe restrictions on the extent to which shareholders may make drawings from their equity.) An individual or business contemplating lending money to the company may insist that the extent to which shareholders can withdraw their funds is restricted as a condition of making the loan. This point will be explained shortly.

Real World 4.8 provides an example of a bonus share issue, where it seemed that the main motive was to make the share price more manageable. The 'feel-good' factor, however, also seems to play a part.

Real World 4.8

Is it really a bonus?

Medusa Mining is a gold producer that is listed on various international stock markets. In 2010, it announced a one-for-ten bonus issue of shares to all shareholders of the company.

In a statement, the company said that it had achieved several significant milestones in the last calendar year and that the bonus issue was in recognition of the invaluable support the company had received from its shareholders. The bonus issue was also designed to encourage greater liquidity in Medusa shares.

Geoff Davis, managing director of Medusa, said: 'The board is extremely pleased to be in a position to reward shareholders as a result of the company having rapidly expanded its production over the last 12 months and having met all targets on time.'

Source: Adapted from 'Medusa Mining', www.proactiveinvestors.co.uk, 8 March 2010.

SHARE CAPITAL JARGON

Before leaving our detailed discussion of share capital, it might be helpful to clarify some of the jargon relating to shares that is used in company financial statements.

Share capital that has been issued to shareholders is known as the **issued share capital** (or **allotted share capital**). Sometimes, but not very often, a company may not require shareholders to pay the whole amount that is due to be paid for the shares at the time of issue. This may happen where the company does not need the money all at once. Some money would normally be paid at the time of issue and the company would 'call' for further instalments until the shares were **fully paid shares**. That part of the total issue price that has been called is known as the **called-up share capital**. That part that has been called and paid is known as the **paid-up share capital**.

BORROWINGS

Most larger companies borrow money to supplement that raised from share issues and ploughed-back profits. Company borrowing is often on a long-term basis, perhaps on a ten-year contract. The contract, which is legally binding, will specify the rate of interest, the interest payments date and the repayment date for the amount borrowed. Lenders may be banks and other professional providers of loan finance, such as pension funds and insurance companies.

Many companies borrow in such a way that individual investors are able to lend only part of the total amount required. This is particularly the case with the larger, Stock Exchange listed, companies and involves them making an issue of **loan notes**. Although such an issue may be large, investors, whether individuals or institutions, can each take up a small slice of the issue. In some cases, these slices of loans can be bought and sold through the Stock Exchange. This means that investors do not have to wait the full term of their loan to obtain repayment. They can sell their slice of the loan to another would-be lender at some point during the loan term. This flexibility can make loan notes an attractive investment to certain investors. Loan notes are often known as **loan stock**, **bonds** or **debentures**.

Some of the features of financing by loan notes, particularly the possibility that the loan notes may be traded on the Stock Exchange, can lead to confusing loan notes with shares. We should be clear, however, that shares and loan notes are not the same thing.

Activity 4.12

What is the essential difference in status within a company between ordinary shareholders and a loan notes holders?

Ordinary shareholders are the owners of the company who share in the profits and losses of the company. We saw earlier that they are the main risk takers and are given voting rights. Holders of loan notes are simply lenders that receive interest on their investment. They have no ownership stake in the company.

Long-term loans are usually secured on assets of the company. This would give the lender the right, if the company fails to make the contractual payments, to seize the assets concerned, sell them and use the cash to rectify this failure. A mortgage granted to a private individual buying a house or an apartment is a very common example of a secured loan.

Long-term financing of companies can be depicted as in Figure 4.3.

It is important to the prosperity and stability of a company that it strikes a suitable balance between finance provided by the shareholders (equity) and from borrowing.

Companies derive their long-term finance from three sources: new share issues, retained earnings and long-term borrowings. For a typical company, the sum of the first two (jointly known as 'equity finance') exceeds the third. Retained earnings usually exceed either of the other two in terms of the amount of finance raised in most years.

Figure 4.3 Sources of long-term finance for a typical limited company

Real World 4.9 shows the long-term borrowings of Rolls-Royce Holdings plc, the engine-building business, at 31 December 2017.

Real World 4.9

Borrowing at Rolls-Royce

The following extract from the annual financial statements of Rolls-Royce plc sets out the sources of the company's long-term borrowings (non-current liabilities) as at 31 December 2017:

	£m
Unsecured	
Bank loans	572
6.75% notes 2019	519
2.375% notes 2020	362
2.125% notes 2021	701
3.625% notes 2025	726
3.375% notes 2026	412
Secured	
Obligations under finance leases	114
	3,406

Source: Rolls-Royce Holdings plc Annual Report and Accounts 2017 p. 148, note 15.

Note the large number of sources of the company's borrowings. This is typical of most large companies and probably reflects a desire to exploit all available means of raising finance, each of which may have advantages and disadvantages. Normally, a lender would accept a lower rate of interest where the loan is secured as there is less risk involved. It should be said that whether a loan to a company like Rolls-Royce is secured or unsecured is usually pretty academic. It is unlikely that such a large and profitable company would fail to meet its obligations.

RAISING SHARE CAPITAL

After an initial share issue, a company may decide to make further issues of new shares in order to finance its operations. These new share issues may be undertaken in various ways. They may involve direct appeals to investors or may employ the services of financial intermediaries. The most common methods of share issues are set out in Figure 4.4.

There are five main methods of issuing shares. Bonus issues differ from the other methods in that they do not lead to an injection of cash for the business. During the lifetime of a particular company, it may use all five of these approaches to issue new shares, though only public limited companies are allowed to make appeals to the general public.

Figure 4.4 Common methods of share issue

Let us now examine, in turn, each of the four methods of raising funds through a share issue that have been identified.

Rights issues

Rights issues are made by established companies wishing to raise additional funds by the issue of new shares to their existing shareholders. The new shares are offered to shareholders in proportion to their existing holding. Company law gives existing shareholders the first right of refusal to buy any new shares issued for cash by a company. Only where shareholders agree to waive this right can the shares be offered to outside investors.

The company (in effect, the existing shareholders) normally prefers existing shareholders to buy the shares through a rights issue, irrespective of the legal position. This is for two reasons:

1 Ownership (and, therefore, control) of the business remains in the same hands; there is no 'dilution' of control.
2 The costs of making the issue (advertising, complying with various company law requirements) tend to be lower if the shares are offered to existing shareholders. Fees incurred for rights issue are broadly 2 to 3 per cent of the total funds raised, depending on the size of the issue (see Reference 1 at the end of the chapter). Since much of the cost is fixed, the percentage tends to be higher for smaller rights issues.

To encourage existing shareholders to exercise their 'rights' to buy, the new shares are offered at a discount to the current market price of the existing shares.

Activity 4.13

Earlier in the chapter, the point was made that issuing new shares at below their current worth was to the advantage of the new shareholders at the expense of the old ones. In view of this, does it matter that rights issues are always made at below the current value of the shares?

The answer is that it does not matter *in these particular circumstances*, because, in a rights issue, the existing shareholders and the new shareholders are the same people. Moreover, the shareholders will hold the new shares in the same proportion as they currently hold the existing shares. Thus, shareholders will gain on the new shares exactly as much as they lose on the existing ones. In the end, no one is better or worse off as a result of the rights issue being made at a discount.

Calculating the value of the rights offer received by shareholders is quite straightforward, as shown in Example 4.4.

Example 4.4

Shaw Holdings plc has 20 million ordinary shares of 50p in issue. These shares are currently valued on the Stock Exchange at £1.60 per share. The directors have decided to make a one-for-four issue (that is, one new share for every four shares held) at £1.30 per share.

The first step in the valuation process is to calculate the price of a share following the rights issue. This is known as the *ex-rights price* and is simply a weighted average of the price of shares before the issue of rights and the price of the rights shares. In this example, we have a one-for-four rights issue. The theoretical ex-rights price is therefore calculated as follows:

	£
Price of four shares before the rights issue (4 × £1.60)	6.40
Price of taking up one rights share	1.30
	7.70
Theoretical ex-rights price = £7.70/5	= £1.54

As the price of each share, in theory, should be £1.54 following the rights issue and the price of a rights share is £1.30, the value per share of the rights offer will be the difference between the two:

$$£1.54 - £1.30 = £0.24 \text{ per share}$$

Market forces will usually ensure that the actual and theoretical price of rights shares will be fairly close.

The level of discount applied to rights shares will vary. In recent years, it has often been 30 to 40 per cent to the theoretical ex rights price (see Reference 2 at the end of the chapter). By offering a significant discount, the risk that the market price will fall below the rights price is reduced. This should increase the prospects of a successful issue. A significant discount may, however, convey the impression that the business is in distress and desperate for funds.

Activity 4.14

An investor with 2,000 shares in Shaw Holdings plc (see Example 4.4) has contacted you for investment advice. She is undecided whether to take up the rights issue, sell the rights or allow the rights offer to lapse.

Calculate the effect on the net wealth of the investor of each of the options being considered.

Before the rights issue the position of the investor was:

	£
Current value of shares (2,000 × £1.60)	3,200

If she takes up the rights issue, she will be in the following position:

	£
Value of holding after the rights issue ((2,000 + 500) × £1.54)	3,850
Cost of buying the rights shares (500 × £1.30)	(650)
	3,200

If the investor sells the rights, she will be in the following position:

	£
Value of holding after the rights issue (2,000 × £1.54)	3,080
Sale of the rights (500 × £0.24)	120
	3,200

If the investor lets the rights offer lapse, she will be in the following position:

	£
Value of holding after rights issue (2,000 × £1.54)	3,080

As we can see, the first two options should leave her in the same position concerning net wealth as before the rights issue. Before the rights issue she had 2,000 shares worth £1.60 each, or £3,200 in total. However, she will be worse off if she allows the rights offer to lapse than under the other two options.

In practice, businesses will typically sell the rights on behalf of those investors who allow them to lapse. The businesses will then pass on the proceeds to ensure that they are not worse off as a result of the issue.

When considering a rights issue, the directors must first think about the amount of funds to be raised. This will depend on the future plans and commitments of the business. The directors must then decide on the issue price of the rights shares. This decision is not normally of critical importance. In Example 4.4, the business made a one-for-four issue with the price of the rights shares set at £1.30. The same amount could have been raised, however, by making a one-for-two issue and setting the rights price at £0.65, a one-for-one issue and setting the price at £0.325, and so on. The issue price that is finally decided upon will not affect the value of the underlying assets of the business or the proportion of the underlying assets and earnings to which each shareholder is entitled. However, the directors must ensure that the issue price is not above the current market price of the shares.

Activity 4.15

Why must the directors ensure that the issue price is not above the current market price of the shares?

If the issue price were above the current market value, it would be cheaper for existing shareholders to buy new shares in the market. They would not, therefore, be prepared to subscribe to the rights issue.

Real World 4.10 describes how one large UK business, Cobham plc, made a rights issue to strengthen its financial position by reducing its level of borrowing. Cobham specialises in electronics, particularly relating to defence applications.

Real World 4.10

Wrongs and rights

Cobham is offering a steep 41 per cent discount on shares issued in a £512 million rescue fundraising as it attempts to woo investors who have been buffeted by five profit warnings in less than two years. The defence equipment company's announcement of a two for five rights issue at 75p a share comes the day after Cobham revealed that it is under investigation by the UK's Financial Conduct Authority for the manner in which it handled sensitive information ahead of a previous £500 million rights issue in 2016. The company's shares held steady in midday trading at 127p. David Lockwood, the chief executive appointed in December to turn around the struggling group, said the funds would help to bring its debt down to sustainable levels, after having come close to breaching bank covenants. 'It is the first step in . . . both reassuring our customers and giving us the flexibility to drive operational improvements.'

Cobham needs to bolster its balance sheet (statement of financial position) to fulfil promises on some big, but troublesome defence contracts. In February the group revealed it was taking a £150 million charge for delays to certification of its wing aerial refuelling technology to be used on the KC-46 tanker being developed by Boeing for the US Air Force. It also booked a further £574 million in impairment charges against many of the businesses acquired in an ill-judged acquisition spree under previous management. Investors will have stumped up £1 billion in just under a year when the rights issue closes on April 12. Once the cash is in, the company could become vulnerable to a takeover, rumours of which have dogged Cobham for some time. However, analysts suggested that investors who have seen the shares tumble from 290p in 2015 might be prepared to give the new management team installed at the turn of the year the benefit of the doubt.

At 75p, the new shares will be issued at a 41 per cent discount to the close on Monday, and a 33 per cent reduction on the theoretical price of the shares after accounting for the enlarged equity base.

Source: Extracts from Hollinger, P. (2017) Cobham offers investors steep discount on rights issue, ft.com, 28 March. © The Financial Times Limited 2017. All rights reserved.

Offers for sale and public issues

When a business wishes to sell new shares to the general investing public, it may make an **offer for sale** or a **public issue**. In the former case, the shares are sold to an *issuing house* (in effect, a wholesaler of new shares), which then sells them on to potential investors. In the latter case, the shares are sold by the business making the share issue direct to potential investors. The advantage of an offer for sale, from the business's viewpoint, is that the sale proceeds of the shares are certain.

In practical terms, the net effect on the business is much the same whether there is an offer for sale or a public issue. As we have seen, the administrative costs of a public issue can be very large. Some share issues by Stock Exchange listed businesses arise from the initial listing of the business, often known as an *initial public offering (IPO)*. Other share issues are undertaken by businesses that are already listed and that are seeking additional finance from investors; usually such an issue is known as a *seasoned equity offering (SEO)*.

Private placings

A **private placing** does not involve an invitation to the public to subscribe for shares. Instead the shares are 'placed' with selected investors, such as large financial institutions. This can be a quick and relatively cheap form of raising funds, because savings can be made in advertising and legal costs. It can, however, result in the ownership of the business being concentrated in a few hands. Shares placed with investors may be offered at a discount to the current market price. This will normally be much lower than the discounts offered when a rights issue is made. For Stock Exchange listed businesses, a maximum discount of 10 per cent to the current market price is permitted.

Real World 4.11 describes how a placing was used by a well-known business to fund its activities.

Real World 4.11

Fashionably placed

Boohoo.com plc, the online fashion retailer raised around £50 million in June 2017, through a share placing. About £20 million of this was used to expand its warehousing capacity. The new warehousing was completed in January 2018.

Source: Boohoo.com plc (2017) Interim results for the six months ended 31 August 2017, 27 September.

Placings may be carried out in conjunction with a public offer or a rights issue. Where, for example, a public offer, or rights issue, is expected to raise less than is needed, a placing may be used to bridge the funding gap.

Placings are an extremely popular way of issuing shares among listed businesses. During 2017, they accounted for around 80 per cent of the total amount raised from shares issued by newly listed businesses (see Reference 1 at the end of the chapter). **Real World 4.12** indicates that they also account for a significant proportion of the total amount raised from shares issued by already-listed businesses.

Real World 4.12

Raising the issue

Table 4.1 reveals the percentage of the total amount raised from issuing shares, according to issuing method, by businesses already listed on the Main Market of the London Stock Exchange.

Table 4.1 Percentage of total funds raised through different issuing methods by already-listed businesses 2013–17

	2017	2016	2015	2014	2013
	%	%	%	%	%
Public offer	6.7	3.3	3.7	2.1	1.0
Placing	51.1	39.9	46.5	46.7	31.5
Public offer and placing	22.2	20.2	9.5	13.6	10.3
Rights issue	20.0	36.6	40.3	37.6	57.2
	100.0	100.0	100.0	100.0	100.0

We can see that, together, placings and rights issues account for a huge percentage of the total amount raised each year.

Source: Based on figures in: London Stock Exchange, Main Market Factsheet, Table 3, covering the five-year period ending 31 December 2017, www.londonstockexchange.com.

WITHDRAWING EQUITY

As we have seen, companies are legally obliged to distinguish, in the statement of financial position, between that part of the shareholders' equity that may be withdrawn and that part which may not. The withdrawable part consists of profits arising from trading and from the disposal of non-current assets. It is represented in the statement of financial position by *revenue reserves*.

Paying dividends is the most usual way of enabling shareholders to withdraw part of their equity. An alternative is for the company to buy its own shares from those shareholders wishing to sell them. This is usually known as a 'share repurchase'. The company would then normally cancel the shares concerned. Share repurchases usually involve only a small proportion of the shareholders, unlike a dividend which involves them all.

The total of revenue reserves appearing in the statement of financial position is rarely the total of all trading profits and profits on disposals of non-current assets generated since the company was first formed. This total will normally have been reduced by at least one of the following:

- corporation tax paid on those profits;
- any dividends paid or amounts paid to purchase the company's own shares; and
- any losses from trading and the disposal of non-current assets.

The non-withdrawable part consists of share capital plus profits arising from shareholders buying shares in the company and from upward revaluations of assets still held. It is represented in the statement of financial position by *share capital* and *capital reserves*.

Figure 4.5 shows the important division between the part of the shareholders' equity that can be withdrawn and the part that cannot.

The law does not specify the size of the non-withdrawable part of shareholders' equity. However, for a company to gain the confidence of prospective lenders and suppliers, the bigger the non-withdrawable part, the better.

> Total equity finance of limited companies consists of share capital, capital reserves and revenue reserves. Only the revenue reserves (which arise from realised profits and gains) can be used to fund a dividend or a share repurchase. In other words, the maximum legal withdrawal is the amount of the revenue reserves.

Figure 4.5 Availability for withdrawal of various parts of the shareholders' equity

Real World 4.13 describes how one company contravened the rules concerning the withdrawal of equity.

Real World 4.13

What's the odds of that happening?

Betfair returned £80 million to investors in violation of accounting rules, the gambling company has admitted. The embarrassing breach – which occurred in 2011, 2012 and 2013 before being noticed – consisted of Betfair paying out more in dividends and share buy-backs than it was legally permitted to.

Betfair announced its first dividend as a public company in June 2011, partly to reassure investors who had seen the company's shares halve since its flotation six months earlier. It paid out £30 million in relation to the 2011, 2012 and 2013 financial years, and also bought back £50 million in shares. However, the payments did not comply with a rule change on how a company's realised profits and distributable reserves are defined.

Betfair said in its latest annual report that, 'as a result of certain changes to the technical guidance issued by the Institute of Chartered Accountants in England and Wales in October 2010, the Company did not have sufficient distributable reserves to make those distributions and so they should not have been paid by the Company to its shareholders.'

Deed polls have now been used to ensure that investors do not have to repay the dividends, and the company's annual general meeting in September will be asked to approve the cancellation of ordinary shares affected by the buyback.

Source: Mance, H. (2014) Betfair admits to £80m payouts mistake, ft.com, 3 August. © The Financial Times Limited 2014. All rights reserved.

Activity 4.16

Why are limited companies required to distinguish different parts of their shareholders' equity, whereas sole-proprietorship and partnership businesses are not?

The reason stems from the limited liability that company shareholders enjoy but which owners of unincorporated businesses do not. If a sole proprietor or partner withdraws all of the equity, the position of the lenders and credit suppliers of the business is not weakened since they can legally enforce their claims against the sole proprietor or partner as an individual. With a limited company, however, the right to enforce claims against individual owners does not exist. To protect the company's lenders and credit suppliers, therefore, the law insists that the non-withdrawable part of shareholders' equity is clearly distinguished.

Let us now look at an example that illustrates how this protection of lenders and suppliers works.

Example 4.5

The summary statement of financial position of a company at a particular date is as follows:

Statement of financial position

	£
Total assets	43,000
Equity	
Share capital	
10,000 shares of £1 each	10,000
Reserves (revenue)	33,000
Total equity	43,000

A bank has been asked to make a £25,000 long-term loan to the company. If the loan is granted, the statement of financial position immediately following would appear as follows:

Statement of financial position (after the loan)

	£
Total assets	68,000
Equity	
Share capital	
10,000 shares of £1 each	10,000
Reserves (revenue)	33,000
	43,000
Non-current liability	
Borrowings – loan	25,000
Total equity and liabilities	68,000

As things stand, there are assets with a total carrying amount of £68,000 to meet the bank's claim of £25,000. It would be possible and perfectly legal, however, for the company to withdraw part of the shareholders' equity (through a dividend or share repurchase) equal to the total revenue reserves (£33,000). The statement of financial position would then appear as follows:

Statement of financial position (after withdrawal)

	£
Total assets (£68,000 − £33,000)	35,000
Equity	
Share capital	
10,000 shares of £1 each	10,000
Reserves [revenue (£33,000 − £33,000)]	–
	10,000
Non-current liabilities	
Borrowings – bank loan	25,000
Total equity and liabilities	35,000

This leaves the bank in a very much weaker position, in that there are now total assets with a carrying amount of £35,000 to meet a claim of £25,000 – bear in mind that the potential disposal proceeds of the assets may well fall far short of the carrying amount. Note that the difference between the amount of the borrowings (bank loan) and the total assets equals the equity (share capital and reserves) total. Thus, the equity represents a margin of safety for lenders and suppliers. The larger the amount of the equity that can be withdrawn by shareholders, the smaller the potential margin of safety for lenders and suppliers.

Activity 4.17

Can you recall the circumstances in which the non-withdrawable part of a company's capital could be reduced, without contravening the law? This was mentioned earlier in the chapter.

It can be reduced as a result of the company sustaining trading losses, or losses on disposal of non-current assets, which exceed the withdrawable amount of shareholders' equity.

THE MAIN FINANCIAL STATEMENTS

The financial statements of a limited company are, in essence, the same as those of a sole proprietor or partnership. There are, however, some differences of detail. We shall now consider these. Example 4.6 sets out the income statement and statement of financial position of a limited company.

Example 4.6

Da Silva plc
Income statement for the year ended 31 December 2018

	£m
Revenue	840
Cost of sales	(520)
Gross profit	320
Wages and salaries	(98)
Heat and light	(18)
Rent and rates	(24)
Motor vehicle expenses	(20)
Insurance	(4)
Printing and stationery	(12)
Depreciation	(45)
Audit fee	(4)
Operating profit	95
Interest payable	(10)
Profit before taxation	85
Taxation	(24)
Profit for the year	61

Statement of financial position as at 31 December 2018

	£m
ASSETS	
Non-current assets	
Property, plant and equipment	203
Intangible assets	100
	303
Current assets	
Inventories	65
Trade receivables	112
Cash	36
	213
Total assets	516
EQUITY AND LIABILITIES	
Equity	
Ordinary shares of £0.50 each	200
Share premium account	30
Other reserves	50
Retained earnings	25
	305
Non-current liabilities	
Borrowings	100
Current liabilities	
Trade payables	99
Taxation	12
	111
Total equity and liabilities	516

Let us now go through these statements and pick out those aspects that are unique to limited companies.

The income statement

The main points for consideration in the income statement are as follows:

Profit

We can see that, following the calculation of operating profit, two further measures of profit are shown:

- The first of these is the **profit before taxation**. Interest charges are deducted from the operating profit to derive this figure. In the case of a sole proprietor or partnership business, the income statement would end here.
- The second measure of profit is the profit for the reporting period (usually a year). As the company is a separate legal entity, it is liable to pay tax (known as corporation tax) on the profits generated. This measure of profit represents the amount that is available for the shareholders.

Audit fee

Companies beyond a certain size are required to have their financial statements audited by an independent firm of accountants, for which a fee is charged. As we shall see in Chapter 5, the purpose of the audit is to lend credibility to the financial statements. Although it is also open to sole proprietorships and partnerships to have their financial statements audited, relatively few do so. Audit fee is, therefore, an expense that is most often seen in the income statement of a company.

Figure 4.6 shows an outline of the income statement for a limited company.

The statement of financial position

The main points for consideration in the statement of financial position are as follows:

Taxation

For many companies, the amount that appears as part of the current liabilities represents 50 per cent of the tax on the profit for the year 2017. It is, therefore, 50 per cent (£12 million) of the charge that appears in the income statement (£24 million) the other 50 per cent will already have been paid. The unpaid 50 per cent will be paid shortly after the statement of financial position date. These payment dates are set down by law.

Other reserves

This will include any reserves that are not separately identified on the face of the statement of financial position. It may include a *general reserve*, which normally consists of trading profits that have been transferred to this separate reserve for reinvestment ('ploughing back') into the operations of the company. It is not necessary to set up a separate reserve for this purpose. The trading profits could remain unallocated and still swell the retained earnings of the company. It is not entirely clear why directors decide to make transfers to general reserves, since the profits concerned remain part of the revenue reserves, and as such they still remain available for dividend.

```
Sales revenue
    ↓ less
Cost of sales
    ↓ equals
Gross profit
    ↓ less
Operating expenses
    ↓ equals
Operating profit
    ↓ less
Non-operating expenses
(for example, interest payable)
    ↓ plus
Non-operating income
(for example, interest receivable)
    ↓ equals
Profit before taxation
    ↓ less
Taxation
    ↓ equals
Profit for the period
```

Figure 4.6 The layout of the income statement for a limited company

Activity 4.18

Can you think of a reason why the directors may wish to make a transfer to general reserves from retained earnings?

The most plausible explanation seems to be that directors feel that placing profits in a separate reserve indicates an intention to invest the funds, represented by the reserve, in the company. Therefore, they should not be used to pay a dividend or to fund a share repurchase.

Retained earnings appearing on the statement of financial position are, of course, also a reserve, but that fact is not indicated in its title.

DIVIDENDS

Although most companies pay dividends to shareholders, they are under no legal obligation to do so. The decision whether to pay dividends will be influenced by commercial factors such as the financial resources of the company, future commitments and shareholder expectations. It must also take account of the legal restraints on the withdrawal of equity, as discussed earlier.

Dividends are paid out of the revenue reserves and should be deducted from these reserves (usually retained earnings) when preparing the statement of financial position. Shareholders are often paid an annual dividend, perhaps in two parts. An 'interim' dividend may be paid part way through the year and a 'final' dividend shortly after the year end.

Dividends declared by the directors during the year but still unpaid at the year end *may* appear as a liability in the statement of financial position. To be recognised as a liability, however, they must be properly authorised before the year-end date. This normally means that the shareholders must approve the dividend by that date.

Large businesses tend to have a clear and consistent policy towards the payment of dividends. Any change in the policy provokes considerable interest and is usually interpreted by shareholders as a signal of the directors' views concerning the future. For example, an increase in dividends may be taken as a signal from the directors that future prospects are bright: a higher dividend is seen as tangible evidence of their confidence.

Real World 4.14 provides an example of one well-known business that restored its dividend after a difficult period.

Real World 4.14

Sending a signal

Tesco chief Dave Lewis will this week attempt to confirm the supermarket giant's comeback by restoring its dividend, even as the alleged 'colossal fraud' that blew a hole in its finances is laid bare in court.

Mr Lewis, who was drafted in to lead a salvage operation at Tesco three years ago after investigators uncovered hundreds of millions of pounds of missing profits, scrapped the dividend months into his reign to help repair the balance sheet.

Its expected return as part of Tesco's half-year results on Wednesday comes as investor nerves are tested by the high-profile trial of three former senior executives accused of masterminding a scheme to 'cook the books'. The trial of Christopher Bush, Tesco UK's former managing director, Carl Rogberg, the company's former UK finance director, and John Scouler, former food commercial director, began on Friday.

Bruno Monteyne, an analyst at Bernstein, has said that, while the size of any dividend may be small, it will be 'important symbolically, signalling the next stage of the Tesco recovery to the market'.

Source: Extract from Armstrong, A. (2017) "Tesco to signal comeback with return to dividend", *Daily Telegraph*, 30 September.

Dividend policy

The fact that directors of profitable businesses can decide the amount of dividends to be paid to shareholders raises the question of how large each year's dividend should be. The traditional view is that dividend payments should be maximised. The belief is that the higher the dividend payments, the more attractive the ordinary shares will become. This, in turn, will lead to higher share prices and more wealthy shareholders. Since the 1950s, however, this traditional view has been subject to increasing challenge.

The main thrust of the critics' argument is that, since the shareholders own the business, why should transferring some of the business's assets to shareholders through a cash dividend make them better off? What shareholders are gaining, through the dividend, they are losing through their business being less well off. Funds handed to shareholders as dividends means less being retained within the business for investment in wealth-generating projects.

An alternative, more modern, view is that the interests of shareholders are best served by the directors retaining, and investing, the funds that the shareholders might otherwise receive as dividends, provided that those funds would generate higher returns than the shareholders could individually achieve by reinvesting them. Where the directors cannot generate higher returns, however, the shareholders would be worse off. This means that the directors should only retain earnings where they can be invested at a rate at least as high as the shareholders' opportunity cost of funds. The residue should be paid as a dividend.

Not all businesses follow the modern view on dividend policy. One that does is Asos plc (the online fashion and beauty retailer). Asos was formed in 2004, but has yet to pay a dividend, despite being profitable for every year up to the time of writing. This is because it needed the funds to expand. **Real World 4.15**, an extract from the business's 2017 annual report, explains the situation.

Real World 4.15

Dividends out of fashion

The Board has again decided not to declare a dividend. We generate a significant return on invested capital, and we firmly believe the right thing for the business and our shareholders is to invest in the opportunities that lie ahead.

Source: Asos plc, 2017 Annual report, p. 19.

Self-assessment question 4.1

The summarised statement of financial position of Dev Ltd at a particular point in time is as follows:

Statement of financial position

	£
Net assets (various assets less liabilities)	235,000
Equity	
Share capital: 100,000 shares of £1 each	100,000
Share premium account	30,000
Revaluation reserve	37,000
Retained earnings	68,000
Total equity	235,000

Required:

(a) Without any other transactions occurring at the same time, the company made a one-for-five rights share issue at £2 per share payable in cash. This means that each shareholder was offered one share for every five already held. All shareholders took up their rights. Immediately afterwards, the company made a one-for-two bonus issue. Show the statement of financial position immediately following the bonus issue, assuming that the directors wanted to retain the maximum dividend payment potential for the future.

(b) Explain what external influence might cause the directors to choose not to retain the maximum dividend payment possibilities.

(c) Show the statement of financial position immediately following the bonus issue, assuming that the directors wanted to retain the *minimum* dividend payment potential for the future.
(d) What is the maximum dividend that could be paid before and after the events described in (a) if the minimum dividend payment potential is achieved?
(e) Lee owns 100 shares in Dev Ltd before the events described in (a). Assuming that the net assets of the company have a value equal to their carrying amount on the statement of financial position, show how these events will affect Lee's wealth.
(f) Looking at the original statement of financial position of Dev Ltd, shown above, what four things do we know about the company's status and history that are not specifically stated on the statement of financial position?

The solution to this question can be found at the back of the book, starting on page 305.

SUMMARY

The main points of this chapter may be summarised as follows:

Main features of a limited company

- It is an artificial person that has been created by law.
- It has a separate life to its owners and is granted a perpetual existence.
- It must take responsibility for its own debts and losses but its owners are granted limited liability.
- To safeguard those dealing with a limited company, limited liability status is included as part of the business name, restrictions are placed on the ability of owners to withdraw equity and annual financial statements are made publicly available.
- A public company can offer its shares for sale to the public; a private company cannot.
- A limited company is governed by a board of directors elected by the shareholders.

The Stock Exchange

- The Stock Exchange is an important primary and secondary market in capital for large businesses. However, a Stock Exchange listing can have certain drawbacks for a business.
- The Stock Exchange is broadly seen as an *efficient capital market*. New information that becomes publicly available is quickly and rationally reflected in share prices. This leads to share prices representing the best estimate of the 'true' value of shares, on the basis of publicly known information.

Financing a limited company

- The share capital of a company can be of two main types: ordinary shares and preference shares.
- Holders of ordinary shares (equities) are the main risk-takers and are given voting rights; they form the backbone of the company.
- Holders of preference shares are given a right to a fixed dividend before ordinary shareholders receive a dividend.

- Reserves are profits and gains made by the company and form part of the ordinary shareholders' claim.
- Borrowings provide another major source of finance.

Share issues
- Share issues that involve the payment of cash by investors can take the form of a rights issue, public issue, offer for sale or a private placing.
- A rights issue is made to existing shareholders. Most share issues are of this type as the law requires that shares that are to be issued for cash must first be offered to existing shareholders. Rights issue costs are relatively low.
- A public issue involves a direct issue to the public and an offer for sale involves an indirect issue to the public.
- A private placing is an issue of shares to selected investors.
- A bonus issue does not involve the receipt of cash in exchange for shares issued.

Withdrawing equity
- Reserves are of two types: revenue reserves and capital reserves.
- Revenue reserves arise from trading profits and from realised profits on the sale of non-current assets.
- Capital reserves arise from the issue of shares above their nominal value or from the upward revaluation of non-current assets.
- Revenue reserves can be withdrawn as dividends by the shareholders whereas capital reserves normally cannot.

Financial statements of limited companies
- The financial statements of limited companies are based on the same principles as those of sole-proprietorship and partnership businesses. However, there are some differences in detail.
- The income statement has two measures of profit displayed after the operating profit figure: profit before taxation and profit for the year.
- The income statement also shows audit fees and tax on profits for the year.
- The statement of financial position will show any unpaid tax and any unpaid, but authorised, dividends as current liabilities.
- The share capital plus the reserves make up 'equity'.

KEY TERMS

limited liability	directors
public limited company	corporate governance
private limited company	reserves
corporation tax	nominal value
Stock Exchange	par value
London Stock Exchange	revenue reserve
efficient capital market	dividend

ordinary shares	paid-up share capital
preference shares	loan notes
splitting	loan stock
consolidating	bonds
capital reserves	debentures
share premium account	rights issues
bonus shares	offer for sale
issued share capital	public issue
allotted share capital	private placing
fully paid shares	profit before taxation
called-up share capital	

REFERENCES

1 London Stock Exchange (2017) *Main Market Factsheet*, December, Table 3.
2 Association of British Insurers (2013) *Encouraging Equity Investment*, July, p. 32.

FURTHER READING

If you would like to explore the topics covered in this chapter in more depth, we recommend the following:

Alexander D., Britton A., Jorissen, A., Hoogendorn M. and Van Mourik C. (2017) *International Financial Reporting and Analysis*, Cengage Learning EMEA, 7th edn, Chapter 10.

Elliott, B. and Elliott, J. (2017) *Financial Accounting and Reporting*, 18th edn, Pearson, Chapters 3, 12 and 22.

Melville, A. (2017) *International Financial Reporting: A Practical Guide*, 6th edn, Pearson, Chapter 1.

Thomas, A. and Ward, A.M. (2015) *Introduction to Financial Accounting*, 8th edn, McGraw-Hill Education, Chapters 28 and 29.

CRITICAL REVIEW QUESTIONS

Solutions to these questions can be found at the back of the book, starting on page 312.

4.1 You and a friend have decided to set up in business offering a bicycle delivery service in your local area. You feel that you can raise enough funds from your own resources to get the business going. You have calculated that you can finance your planned future expansion from profits. You intend to create a limited company to own the business. Would a public limited company or a private one be more appropriate? Explain your reasons.

4.2 The London Stock Exchange has the power to suspend dealing in shares of businesses that have failed to comply with particular regulations. Why is this seen as a punishment for the business concerned?

4.3 'For a capital market to be efficient requires that there are certain individuals that have superior powers of prediction.' Is this statement true?

4.4 Issues of new preference shares are extremely rare these days. Suggest reasons why this is the case.

EXERCISES

Solutions to exercises with coloured numbers can be found at the back of the book, starting on page 319.

Basic-level exercises

4.1 Comment on the following quote:

'Limited companies can set a limit on the amount of debts that they will meet. They tend to have reserves of cash as well as share capital, and they can use these reserves to pay dividends to the shareholders. Many companies have preference shares as well as ordinary shares. The preference shares give a guaranteed dividend. The shares of many companies can be bought and sold on the Stock Exchange. Shareholders selling their shares can represent a useful source of new finance to the company.'

4.2 Comment on the following quotes:

(a) 'Bonus shares increase the shareholders' wealth because, after the issue, they have more shares, but each one of the same nominal value as they had before.'
(b) 'By law, once shares have been issued at a particular nominal value, they must always be issued at that value in any future share issues.'
(c) 'By law, companies can pay as much as they like by way of dividends on their shares, provided that they have sufficient cash to do so.'
(d) 'Companies do not have to pay tax on their profits because the shareholders have to pay tax on their dividends.'

4.3 Briefly explain each of the following expressions that you have seen in the financial statements of a limited company:

(a) dividend
(b) audit fee
(c) share premium account.

Intermediate-level exercises

4.4 Iqbal Ltd started trading on 1 July 2013. During the first five years of trading, the following occurred:

Year ended 30 June	Trading profit/(loss) £	Profit/(loss) on sale of non-current assets £	Upward revaluation of non-current assets £
2014	(15,000)	–	–
2015	8,000	–	10,000
2016	15,000	5,000	–
2017	20,000	(6,000)	–
2018	22,000	–	–

Required:
Assume that the company paid the maximum legal dividend each year. Under normal circumstances, how much would each year's dividend be?

4.5 Hudson plc's outline statement of financial position as at a particular date was as follows:

	£m
Net assets (assets less liabilities)	72
Equity	
£1 Ordinary shares	40
General reserve	32
Total equity	72

The directors made a one-for-four bonus issue, immediately followed by a one-for-four rights issue at a price of £1.80 per share.

Required:
Show the statement of financial position of Hudson plc immediately following the two share issues.

Advanced-level exercises

4.6 The following is a draft set of simplified financial statements for Pear Limited for the year ended 30 September 2018:

Income statement for the year ended 30 September 2018

	£000
Revenue	1,456
Cost of sales	(768)
Gross profit	688
Salaries	(220)
Depreciation	(249)
Other operating costs	(131)
Operating profit	88
Interest payable	(15)
Profit before taxation	73
Taxation at 30%	(22)
Profit for the year	51

Statement of financial position as at 30 September 2018

	£000
ASSETS	
Non-current assets	
Property, plant and equipment	
Cost	1,570
Depreciation	(690)
	880
Current assets	
Inventories	207
Trade receivables	182
Cash at bank	21
	410
Total assets	1,290

	£000
EQUITY AND LIABILITIES	
Equity	
Share capital	300
Share premium account	300
Retained earnings at beginning of year	104
Profit for year	51
	755
Non-current liabilities	
Borrowings (10% loan notes repayable 2020)	300
Current liabilities	
Trade payables	88
Other payables	20
Taxation	22
Borrowings (bank overdraft)	105
	235
Total equity and liabilities	1,290

The following information is available:

1. Depreciation has not been charged on office equipment with a carrying amount of £100,000. This class of assets is depreciated at 12 per cent a year using the reducing-balance method.
2. A new machine was purchased, on credit, for £30,000 and delivered on 29 September 2018 but has not been included in the financial statements. (Ignore depreciation.)
3. A sales invoice to the value of £18,000 for September 2018 has been omitted from the financial statements. (The cost of sales figure is stated correctly.)
4. A dividend of £25,000 had been approved by the shareholders before 30 September 2018, but was unpaid at that date. This is not reflected in the financial statements.
5. The interest payable on the loan notes for the second half-year was not paid until 1 October 2018 and has not been included in the financial statements.
6. An allowance for trade receivables is to be made at the level of 2 per cent of trade receivables.
7. An invoice for electricity to the value of £2,000 for the quarter ended 30 September 2018 arrived on 4 October 2018 and has not been included in the financial statements.
8. The charge for taxation will have to be revised to take account of any amendments to the taxable profit arising from items 1 to 7. Make the simplifying assumption that tax is payable shortly after the end of the year, at the rate of 30 per cent of the profit before tax.

Required:
Prepare a revised set of financial statements for the year ended 30 September 2018 incorporating the additional information in 1 to 8 above. (Work to the nearest £1,000.)

4.7 Presented below is a draft set of financial statements for Chips Limited.

Income statement for the year ended 30 June 2018

	£000
Revenue	1,850
Cost of sales	(1,040)
Gross profit	810
Depreciation	(220)
Other operating costs	(375)
Operating profit	215
Interest payable	(35)
Profit before taxation	180
Taxation	(60)
Profit for the year	120

Statement of financial position as at 30 June 2018

	Cost £000	Depreciation £000	£000
ASSETS			
Non-current assets			
Property, plant and equipment			
Buildings	800	(112)	688
Plant and equipment	650	(367)	283
Motor vehicles	102	(53)	49
	1,552	(532)	1,020
Current assets			
Inventories			950
Trade receivables			420
Cash at bank			16
			1,386
Total assets			2,406
EQUITY AND LIABILITIES			
Equity			
Ordinary shares of £1, fully paid			800
Reserves at beginning of the year			248
Profit for the year			120
			1,168
Non-current liabilities			
Borrowings (secured 10% loan notes)			700
Current liabilities			
Trade payables			361
Other payables			117
Taxation			60
			538
Total equity and liabilities			2,406

The following additional information is available:

1. Purchase invoices for goods received on 29 June 2018 amounting to £23,000 have not been included. This means that the cost of sales figure in the income statement has been understated.
2. A motor vehicle costing £8,000 with depreciation amounting to £5,000 was sold on 30 June 2018 for £2,000, paid by cheque. This transaction has not been included in the company's records.
3. No depreciation on motor vehicles has been charged. The annual rate is 20 per cent of cost at the year end.
4. A sale on credit for £16,000 made on 1 July 2018 has been included in the financial statements in error. The cost of sales figure is not affected.
5. A half-yearly payment of interest on the secured loan due on 30 June 2018 has not been paid.
6. The tax charge should be 30 per cent of the reported profit before taxation. Assume that it is payable, in full, shortly after the year end.

Required:
Prepare a revised set of financial statements incorporating the additional information in 1 to 6 above. (Work to the nearest £1,000.)

4.8 Rose Limited is a wholesaler and retailer of high-quality teas and coffees. Approximately half of sales are on credit. Abbreviated and unaudited financial statements are as follows:

Rose Limited
Income statement for the year ended 31 March 2018

	£000
Revenue	12,080
Cost of sales	(6,282)
Gross profit	5,798
Labour costs	(2,658)
Depreciation	(625)
Other operating costs	(1,003)
Operating profit	1,512
Interest payable	(66)
Profit before taxation	1,446
Taxation	(434)
Profit for the year	1,012

Statement of financial position as at 31 March 2018

	£000
ASSETS	
Non-current assets	2,728
Current assets	
Inventories	1,583
Trade receivables	996
Cash	26
	2,605
Total assets	5,333
EQUITY AND LIABILITIES	
Equity	
Share capital (50p shares, fully paid)	750
Share premium	250
Retained earnings	1,468
	2,468
Non-current liabilities	
Borrowings – secured loan notes	300
Current liabilities	
Trade payables	1,118
Other payables	417
Tax	434
Borrowings – overdraft	596
	2,565
Total equity and liabilities	5,333

Since the unaudited financial statements for Rose Limited were prepared, the following information has become available:

1. An additional £74,000 of depreciation should have been charged on fixtures and fittings.
2. Invoices for credit sales on 31 March 2018 amounting to £34,000 have not been included; cost of sales is not affected.
3. Trade receivables totalling £21,000 are recognised as having gone bad, but they have not yet been written off.
4. Inventories which had been purchased for £2,000 have been damaged and are unsaleable. This is not reflected in the financial statements.
5. Fixtures and fittings to the value of £16,000 were delivered just before 31 March 2018, but these assets were not included in the financial statements and the purchase invoice had not been processed.
6. Wages for Saturday-only staff, amounting to £1,000 have not been paid for the final Saturday of the year. This is not reflected in the financial statements.
7. Tax is payable at 30 per cent of profit before taxation. Assume that it is payable shortly after the year end.

Required:
Prepare revised financial statements for Rose Limited for the year ended 31 March 2018, incorporating the information in 1 to 7 above. (Work to the nearest £1,000.)

Chapter 5

ACCOUNTING FOR LIMITED COMPANIES (2)

INTRODUCTION

This chapter continues our examination of the financial statements of limited companies. We begin by considering the importance of accounting rules in preparing financial statements and the main sources of these rules. The accounting rules in place enjoy widespread support and are generally considered to have had a beneficial effect on the quality of financial information provided to users. There are, however, potential problems with imposing accounting rules. In this chapter, we shall consider these problems and how they might affect the financial statements. We shall also consider the efforts made to ensure that a coherent conceptual framework underpins the accounting rules.

Over the years, the published annual financial reports of larger companies have greatly increased in scope. They now include a comprehensive set of financial statements for users. A detailed consideration of the various rules relating to these statements is beyond the scope of this book; however, we shall take a look at the key rules that shape their form and content. To accompany the financial statements, the directors must provide comments, and supplementary information, concerning the performance and position of the company. In this chapter, we outline the key topics that the directors must address.

Despite the proliferation of accounting rules and the increasing supply of financial information to users, concerns have been expressed over the quality of some published financial reports. We end the chapter by looking at some well-publicised accounting scandals and the problem of creative accounting.

Learning outcomes

When you have completed this chapter, you should be able to:

- discuss the case for and against a rule-based approach to the preparation of financial statements;
- prepare a statement of financial position, statement of comprehensive income and statement of changes in equity in accordance with International Financial Reporting Standards;
- describe the role and content of the directors' report and the strategic report; and
- discuss the threat posed by creative accounting and describe the main methods used to distort the fair presentation of position and performance.

THE DIRECTORS' DUTY TO ACCOUNT

For all companies, except the very small ones, it is not practical for all shareholders to be involved in the management of the company. Instead, they appoint directors to act on their behalf. This separation of ownership from day-to-day control creates a need for directors to be accountable for their stewardship (management) of the company's assets. To fulfil this need, the directors must prepare financial statements that fairly represent the financial position and performance of the business. Fair representation involves selecting appropriate accounting policies, making reasonable accounting estimates and keeping to the relevant accounting rules when preparing the statements. To avoid mistaken, or deliberately misleading, statements appearing in the financial statements appropriate internal control systems must be maintained.

Activity 5.1

Do you think that, in practice, the directors will undertake the task of preparing the financial statements themselves?

Probably not – they will normally delegate this task to the accounting staff. Nevertheless, they will retain responsibility for the financial statements and must monitor the work done.

Each of the company's shareholders has the right to be sent a copy of the financial statements produced by the directors. A copy must also be sent to the Registrar of Companies, which is then made available for public inspection. A Stock Exchange listed company has the additional obligation to publish its financial statements on its website.

Activity 5.2

It can be argued that the publication of financial statements is vital to a well-functioning private sector. Why might this be the case? Try to think of at least one reason.

There are at least two reasons:

- Unless shareholders receive regular information about the performance and position of a business they will encounter problems in evaluating their investment. As a result, they would probably be reluctant to invest.
- Suppliers of labour, goods, services and loans need information about the financial health of a business. They would probably be reluctant to engage in commercial relationships where a company does not provide this information. The fact that a company has limited liability increases the risks involved in dealing with it.

In both cases, the functioning of the private sector of the economy will be adversely affected by the absence of financial statements.

THE NEED FOR ACCOUNTING RULES

The obligation on directors to prepare and publish financial statements has led to the creation of a framework of rules concerning their form and content. Without rules, there is a much greater risk that unscrupulous directors will employ accounting policies and practices that portray an unrealistic view of financial health. There is also a much greater risk that the financial statements will not be comparable over time, or with those of other businesses. Accounting rules can narrow areas of differences and reduce the variety of accounting methods. This should help ensure that businesses treat similar transactions in a similar way.

Example 5.1 illustrates the problems that may arise where businesses can exercise choice over the accounting policies used.

Example 5.1

Rila plc and Pirin plc are both wholesalers of electrical goods. Both commenced trading on 1 March 2018 with an identical share capital. Both acquired identical property, plant and equipment on 1 March and both achieved identical trading results during the first year of trading. The following financial information relating to both businesses is available:

	£m
Ordinary £1 shares fully paid on 1 March 2018	60
Non-current assets (at cost) acquired on 1 March 2018	40
Revenue for the year to 28 February 2019	100
Purchases of inventories during the year to 28 February 2019	70
Expenses for the year to 28 February 2019 (excluding depreciation)	20
Trade receivables as at 28 February 2019	37
Trade payables as at 28 February 2019	12
Cash as at 28 February 2019	5

The non-current assets held by both businesses are leasehold buildings that have five years left to run on the lease. Inventories for both businesses have been valued at the year end at £16 million on a FIFO basis and £12 million on a LIFO basis.

When preparing their financial statements for the first year of trading,

- Rila plc decided to write off the cost of the leasehold buildings at the end of the lease period. Pirin plc adopted the straight-line basis of depreciation for the leasehold buildings.
- Rila plc adopted the FIFO method of inventories valuation and Pirin plc adopted the LIFO method.

The income statements and the statements of financial position for the two businesses, ignoring taxation, will be as follows:

Income statements for the year to 28 February 2019

	Rila plc £m	Pirin plc £m
Revenue	100	100
Cost of sales		
Rila plc (£70m − £16m)	(54)	
Pirin plc (£70m − £12m)		(58)
Gross profit	46	42
Expenses (excluding depreciation)	(20)	(20)
Depreciation		
Rila plc	(−)	
Pirin plc (£40m/5)		(8)
Profit for the year	26	14

Statements of financial position as at 28 February 2019

	Rila plc £m	Pirin plc £m
ASSETS		
Non-current assets		
Property, plant and equipment at cost	40	40
Accumulated depreciation	(−)	(8)
	40	32
Current assets		
Inventories	16	12
Trade receivables	37	37
Cash	5	5
	58	54
Total assets	98	86
EQUITY AND LIABILITIES		
Equity		
Share capital	60	60
Retained earnings	26	14
	86	74
Current liabilities		
Trade payables	12	12
Total equity and liabilities	98	86

Although the two businesses are identical in terms of funding and underlying trading performance, the financial statements create an impression that the financial health of each business is quite different. The accounting policies selected by Rila plc help to portray a much rosier picture. We can see that Rila plc reports a significantly higher profit for the year and higher assets at the year end.

Depreciation and inventories valuation are not the only areas where choices might be exercised. Nevertheless, they illustrate the potential impact of different accounting choices over the short term.

Accounting rules should help to create greater confidence in the integrity of financial statements. This should make it easier to raise funds from investors and to build stronger relationships with customers and suppliers. We must be realistic, however, about what can be achieved through regulation. Problems of manipulation and of concealment can still occur even within a highly regulated environment (and examples of both will be considered later in the chapter). Nevertheless, the scale of these problems should be reduced where accounting rules are in place.

Problems of comparability between businesses can also still occur. Accounting is not a precise science. Even within a regulated environment, estimates and judgements must be made and these may vary according to who makes them. Furthermore, no two businesses are identical (unlike those in Example 5.1). Different accounting policies may therefore be applied to fit different circumstances.

SOURCES OF ACCOUNTING RULES

In recent years, there has been an increasing trend towards both the internationalisation of business and the integration of financial markets. This has helped to strengthen the case for the international harmonisation of accounting rules. By adopting a common set of rules, users of financial statements are better placed to compare the financial health of companies based in different countries. It can also relieve international companies of some of the burden of preparing financial statements. Different financial statements are no longer needed to comply with the rules of the particular countries in which these companies operate.

The International Accounting Standards Board (IASB) is an independent body that is at the forefront of the move towards harmonisation. The Board, which is based in the UK, is dedicated to developing a single set of high-quality, globally accepted, accounting rules. These aim to provide transparent and comparable information in financial statements. The rules, which are known as **International Accounting Standards** (IASs) or **International Financial Reporting Standards** (IFRSs), deal with key issues such as:

- what information should be disclosed;
- how information should be presented;
- how assets should be valued; and
- how profit should be measured.

Activity 5.3

We have already come across some IASs and IFRSs in earlier chapters. Try to recall at least two topics where financial reporting standards were mentioned.

We came across financial reporting standards when considering:

1. the valuation and impairment of assets (Chapter 2);
2. depreciation and impairment of non-current assets (Chapter 3); and
3. the valuation of inventories (Chapter 3).

The growing authority of the IASB

Over recent years the authority of the IASB has gone from strength to strength. The first major boost came when the European Commission required nearly all companies listed on the stock exchanges of European Union member states to adopt IFRSs for reporting periods commencing on or after 1 January 2005. As a result, nearly 7,000 companies in 25 different countries switched to IFRSs. Since this landmark development, the authority of the IASB has continued to grow. Of the 166 countries that the IASB profiles, 144 (87 per cent) require the use of IFRS Standards for all, or most, public companies and financial institutions listed in their capital markets (such as stock exchanges). (See Reference 1 at the end of the chapter.)

Non-listed UK companies are not required to adopt IFRSs but have the option to do so. It is possible, however, that IFRSs will eventually become a requirement for all UK companies.

Adopting IFRSs

The EU requirement to adopt IFRSs, mentioned earlier, overrides any laws in force in member states that could either hinder or restrict compliance with them. The ultimate aim is to achieve a single framework of accounting rules for companies from all member states. The EU recognises that this will be achieved only if individual governments do not add to the requirements imposed by the various IFRSs. Thus, it seems that accounting rules developed within individual EU member countries will eventually disappear. For the time being, however, the EU accepts that the governments of member states may need to impose additional disclosures for some corporate governance matters and regulatory requirements.

In the UK, company law requires disclosure relating to various corporate governance issues. There is, for example, a requirement to disclose details of directors' remuneration in the published financial statements, which goes beyond anything required by IFRSs. Furthermore, the Financial Conduct Authority (FCA), in its role as the UK listing authority, imposes rules on Stock Exchange listed companies. These include the requirement to publish a condensed set of interim (half-yearly) financial statements in addition to the annual financial statements. (Interim statements are not required by the IASB although, if prepared, there is an appropriate standard.)

Figure 5.1 sets out the main sources of accounting rules for Stock Exchange listed companies.

International Financial Reporting Standards provide the basic framework of accounting rules for nearly all Stock Exchange listed companies. These rules are augmented by company law and by the Financial Conduct Authority (FCA) in its role as the UK listing authority.

Figure 5.1 Sources of external accounting rules for a UK public limited company listed on the London Stock Exchange

Real World 5.1 provides a list of IASB standards that were in force as at 5 February 2018. It gives some idea of the range of topics that are covered. The IASB continues its work and so changes to this list will occur over time.

Real World 5.1

International standards

The following is a list of the International Accounting Standards (IASs) and International Financial Reporting Standards (IFRSs) in force as at 5 February 2018. (The latter term is used for standards issued from 2003 onwards.) Several standards have been issued and subsequently withdrawn, which explains the gaps in the numerical sequence. In addition, several have been revised and reissued.

IAS 1	*Presentation of Financial Statements*
IAS 2	*Inventories*
IAS 7	*Statement of Cash Flows*
IAS 8	*Accounting Policies, Changes in Accounting Estimates and Errors*
IAS 10	*Events after the Reporting Period*
IAS 11	*Construction Contracts*
IAS 12	*Income Taxes*
IAS 16	*Property, Plant and Equipment*
IAS 17	*Leases*[1]
IAS 18	*Revenue*[2]
IAS 19	*Employee Benefits*
IAS 20	*Accounting for Government Grants and Disclosure of Government Assistance*
IAS 21	*The Effects of Changes in Foreign Exchange Rates*
IAS 23	*Borrowing Costs*
IAS 24	*Related Party Disclosures*
IAS 26	*Accounting and Reporting by Retirement Benefit Plans*
IAS 27	*Separate Financial Statements*
IAS 28	*Investments in Associates*
IAS 29	*Financial Reporting in Hyperinflationary Economies*
IAS 32	*Financial Instruments: Presentation*
IAS 33	*Earnings per Share*
IAS 34	*Interim Financial Reporting*
IAS 36	*Impairment of Assets*
IAS 37	*Provisions, Contingent Liabilities and Contingent Assets*
IAS 38	*Intangible Assets*
IAS 39	*Financial Instruments: Recognition and Measurement*
IAS 40	*Investment Property*
IAS 41	*Agriculture*
IFRS 1	*First-time Adoption of International Financial Reporting Standards*
IFRS 2	*Share-based Payment*
IFRS 3	*Business Combinations*
IFRS 4	*Insurance Contracts*

IFRS 5	Non-current Assets Held for Sale and Discontinued Operations
IFRS 6	Exploration for and Evaluation of Mineral Resources
IFRS 7	Financial Instruments: Disclosures
IFRS 8	Operating Segments
IFRS 9	Financial Instruments[1]
IFRS 10	Consolidated Financial Statements
IFRS 11	Joint Arrangements
IFRS 12	Disclosure of Interests in Other Entities
IFRS 13	Fair Value Measurement
IFRS 14	Regulatory Deferral Accounts
IFRS 15	Revenue from Contracts with Customers
IFRS 16	Leases
IFRS 17	Insurance Contracts

1 Will be superseded by IFRS 16
2 Will be superseded by IFRS 15

Source: Adapted from list on International Accounting Standards Board website, www.ifrs.org [accessed 5 February 2018]. © Copyright IFRS Foundation. Copyright © International Financial Reporting Standards Foundation All rights reserved. Reproduced by Pearson Education with the permission of the International Financial Reporting Standards Foundation®. Reproduction and use rights are strictly limited. No permission granted to third parties to reproduce or distribute. The International Accounting Standards Board, the International Financial Reporting Standards Foundation, the authors and the publishers do not accept responsibility for any loss caused by acting or refraining from acting in reliance on the material in this publication, whether such loss is caused by negligence or otherwise.

PROBLEMS WITH STANDARDS

There is broad agreement that financial reporting standards have improved the quality of financial statements. Nevertheless, we should be alert to the potential problems associated with their use. These include the following:

Standards may inhibit change

By setting out rigid procedures to be followed, the development of new and better procedures may be stifled. Progress in financial reporting may, therefore, depend on businesses having the freedom to experiment and innovate. Unless this happens, accounting practice may become ossified.

Although this argument has some appeal, history has shown that financial reporting standards are changed when they prove to be ineffective or inadequate. Over the years, numerous standards have been either modified or withdrawn. Furthermore, developing a new standard involves wide consultation with interested parties and much debate about what constitutes best practice. Thus, financial reporting standards can provide the stimulus for new thinking.

Standards may impose false conformity

No two businesses are identical: each will have its own characteristics and operating methods. When common standards are imposed, there is a risk that the unique aspects of each business will be obscured.

Again, this argument has some appeal, but it can be taken too far. Differences between businesses can be overstated while their common features are understated. Furthermore, there is nothing to prevent standards from offering a limited choice between accounting methods. This may help in reflecting individual characteristics.

> ### Activity 5.4
>
> Can you think of a financial reporting standard that allows some choice of accounting method? (*Hint*: Think back to Chapter 3).
>
> The inventories standard permits some choice over inventories costing methods and the depreciation standard permits some choice over depreciation methods.

Finally, a business can, in exceptional circumstances, depart from a financial reporting standard where it conflicts with the overriding requirement to provide a fair presentation of financial health. Businesses do not, therefore, have to comply with unreasonable rules.

Standards involve consensus seeking

Financial reporting standards affect particular interest groups who must be prepared to accept them. Unless this occurs, standards cannot be implemented effectively. The development of standards may, therefore, be influenced more by the need to achieve consensus than by technical considerations of what is the best approach to adopt. Where this occurs, the quality of financial statements will suffer.

To date, there is no evidence to suggest that this has been a major problem. In order to command authority, standard setters must be responsive to the groups affected. In a democracy, this is how authority is legitimised. The goal that they must seek to achieve, however, is to make rules that are both technically sound and broadly acceptable.

Standards can be costly

There is now an intricate web of financial reporting standards surrounding large businesses. The costs of complying with these rules are high and are borne by shareholders. Each additional standard that incurs costs for businesses means that less is available for distribution to shareholders. There is an assumption that the benefits of standards outweigh their costs, but what if this is not the case? Before adding to the burden of rules, the likely costs and benefits should be assessed.

Standards can be complex

There is a concern that international financial reporting standards have made financial statements far too complex. They have lost sight of their original purpose and have made financial statements less, rather than more, useful to users. This has led to calls for better regulation. To avoid excessive complexity, international financial reporting standards are meant to be based on principles, rather than on legalistic rules. The concern raised suggests that a principles-based approach has not been implemented properly.

Real World 5.2 gives an indication of the type of criticism levelled at the annual financial reports of financial institutions.

> ### Real World 5.2
>
> **Complexity is standard practice**
>
> Banks and other financial companies are publishing annual reports that are overly complicated and indigestible, prompted in part by regulatory requirements that have swelled the numbers of disclosures, analysts have complained. Nearly two-thirds of analysts questioned by accountancy firm EY said they found annual reports and accounts to be 'too complex', while a similar proportion indicated the tomes being published by firms are hard to digest.
>
> Reports from big lenders for 2013 confirmed the scale of the paper mountain, with HSBC publishing an annual report weighing in at nearly 600 pages while Barclays produced a document that was 444 pages. A decade ago HSBC's annual report was half the current length.
>
> The gripes about the tsunami of paperwork come as the UK's Financial Reporting Council attempts to foster more clarity and concision in corporate reporting.
>
> A fifth of the analysts went so far as saying the reports are not 'fit for purpose'. The companies' governance report was ranked as the least useful section, closely followed by the chairman's statement to shareholders.
>
> Isabelle Santenac, EY's head of financial services audit for Europe, the Middle East, India and Africa, said: 'The IFRS accounting standards both made the accounts more complex and significantly increased the disclosures. Regulators regularly ask for more information with an objective of greater transparency. But there is a need to find the right balance between giving very detailed information and being as clear and concise as possible.'
>
> Source: Extracts from Fleming, H. and Agnew, H. (2014) Bank annual reports too long or complex, ft.com, 8 June. © The Financial Times Limited 2014. All rights reserved.

ACCOUNTING RULES OR ACCOUNTING CHOICE?

The alternative to a rule-based approach is to give businesses the freedom to choose their accounting methods. Rather than creating standards for all to follow, the shareholders of each business should decide how much and what kind of information they need. Competitive forces, so it is argued, should ensure that managers are responsive to shareholders' needs.

> ### Activity 5.5
>
> What sort of competitive forces should ensure that managers are responsive as suggested?
>
> These include competition for investors' funds and competition for managers' jobs.

It would be nice to think that the supply of financial information could be left to competitive forces. There are times, however, when these forces are weak. There are also times when managers have an incentive to conceal relevant information from shareholders.

> ### Activity 5.6
>
> **What sort of information might managers have an incentive to conceal?**
>
> Managers may wish to conceal information that would cast doubt on their ability or integrity or might prevent the business from obtaining funds. This may include information relating to excessive management rewards, poor business performance or weak financial health.
>
> Managers also have an incentive to select accounting methods and policies that enhance profits, particularly if they are linked to managerial rewards. This point will be considered further when we discuss creative accounting later in the chapter.

Given the management incentives described, there is a risk that shareholders will not receive the information they need. Financial reporting standards combat this risk by imposing discipline on managers when preparing financial statements. This disciplinary role was an important impetus to the creation of standards.

With freedom of choice comes the problem of comparability. Differences in shareholder needs and the strength of competitive forces between businesses can lead to differences in both the quantity and quality of information disclosed. This, of course, leads us back to the central purpose of financial reporting standards.

THE NEED FOR A CONCEPTUAL FRAMEWORK

In Chapters 2 and 3 we came across various accounting conventions such as the prudence, historic cost and going concern conventions. These were developed as a practical response to particular problems that were confronted when preparing financial statements. They have stood the test of time and are still of value to preparers today. However, they do not provide, and were never designed to provide, a **conceptual framework**, or framework of principles, to guide the development of financial statements. As we grapple with increasingly complex financial reporting problems, the need to have a sound understanding of *why* we account for things in a particular way becomes more pressing. Knowing *why* we account, rather than simply *how* we account, is vital if we are to improve the quality of financial statements.

In recent years, much effort has been expended in trying to develop a clear conceptual framework to guide us in the future development of accounting. This framework should provide clear answers to such fundamental questions as:

- Who are the main users of financial statements?
- What is the purpose of financial statements?
- What qualities should financial information possess?
- What are the main elements of financial statements?
- How should these elements be defined, recognised and measured?

If these questions can be answered, accounting rule makers, such as the IASB, will be in a stronger position to identify best practice and to develop more coherent and consistent rules. This should, in turn, increase the credibility of financial reports in the eyes of users. It may even help reduce the possible number of rules.

Accounting for Limited Companies (2) 171

> **Activity 5.7**
>
> Can you think how it may help reduce the number of rules required?
>
> Some issues may be resolved by reference to the application of general principles rather than by the generation of further rules.

THE IASB FRAMEWORK

The quest for a conceptual framework began in earnest in the 1970s when the Financial Accounting Standards Board (FASB) in the US devoted a large amount of time and resources to this task. This resulted in a broad framework, which other rule-making bodies, including the IASB, then drew upon to develop their own frameworks. The main aim of the IASB conceptual framework is to provide a firm foundation for the development of International Financial Reporting Standards (IFRSs). It seeks to ensure that IFRSs are underpinned by a clear set of principles. These principles, however, should also provide guidance to preparers when reporting events not covered by a particular IFRS and should help both users and preparers in the interpretation of current IFRSs.

History shows that the IASB conceptual framework is not set in stone. It is revised over time to take account of developments in accounting and the changing business environment. In 2018, the IASB produced its latest version of the *Conceptual Framework for Financial Reporting*. This states that the objective of general purpose financial reporting is '*to provide financial information about the reporting entity that is useful to existing and potential investors, lenders and other creditors in making decisions relating to providing resources to the entity*'. Note that it is the providers of finance that are seen as the primary users of general-purpose financial reports. This is because investors, lenders and other creditors largely rely on these reports to make their investment decisions. Although other users may find general-purpose financial reports useful, the reports are not particularly aimed at them.

The IASB framework sets out the qualitative characteristics that make financial statements useful. These are the same as those discussed in Chapter 1.

> **Activity 5.8**
>
> Can you recall what they are?
>
> The fundamental characteristics identified are relevance and faithful representation: it is these characteristics that make information useful. Characteristics that enhance the quality of financial reports are comparability, timeliness, verifiability and understandability. These enhancing characteristics are of secondary importance. In the absence of relevance and faithful representation, they cannot make information useful.

The IASB conceptual framework also recognises that producing financial information incurs costs, which should be justified by the benefits provided.

The framework discusses three important accounting conventions that were covered in earlier chapters: going concern, prudence and accruals. It states that financial statements should normally be prepared on the assumption that a business is a going concern. Where, however, this assumption cannot be applied, a different basis for preparation must be used. This basis should then be described in the financial statements. The framework defines prudence as the exercise of caution when making judgements under conditions of uncertainty. More controversially, prudence is viewed, as supporting the concept of neutrality, a component of faithful representation. This is a point to which we shall return later. The IASB framework supports the accruals convention as a better means of assessing past and future performance than a system based on cash inflows and outflows. Nevertheless, information regarding cash flows is seen as useful when assessing financing and investing activities, liquidity and solvency.

The IASB conceptual framework goes on to identify the main elements of financial statements. Those relating to the measurement of financial position are assets, liabilities and equity. Those relating to the measurement of performance are income and expense. Each of these elements is defined and corresponds to those discussed in Chapters 2 and 3. The procedure for recognising each of the main elements, as well as the way in which they should be presented and disclosed in the financial statements, is also discussed.

Finally, the IASB conceptual framework discusses different measurement bases for assets and liabilities. These include historic cost and current value measures, such as current cost and fair value. No attempt is made to support a particular measurement basis. Instead, the framework states that, when selecting a particular measurement basis, the nature of the information produced must be considered. This information must be useful to users, which means that it must possess the qualitative characteristics of relevance, faithful representation and so on. Furthermore, the cost constraint should be applied when selecting an appropriate measurement basis. (See Reference 2 at the end of the chapter.)

Activity 5.9

Which do you think is likely to be the less costly measurement basis to employ: one based on historic cost or one based on current values?

A measurement basis that employs historic cost will normally prove to be far less costly. Establishing the cost of acquisition is usually fairly straightforward, assuming proper records are kept. Establishing current value, on the other hand, can be time consuming and can involve out-of-pocket search costs. (Similar search costs, however, can be incurred under historic cost when calculating impairment and depreciation charges for an asset.)

The general approach to developing a conceptual framework has attracted some criticism. It has been suggested, for example, that the IASB framework is too broad in nature to provide useful guidance for the development of financial reporting standards, or to help deal with emerging accounting issues. It has also been suggested that the framework is merely descriptive and fails to provide theoretical underpinning to the financial statements.

There has also been criticism of specific issues covered. The recent version of the conceptual framework, for example, has sparked controversy for asserting that prudence supports the concept of neutrality. This runs counter to traditional practice, where prudence and neutrality are not seen as comfortable bedfellows. Rather, prudence is taken to mean that more convincing evidence is required for recognising assets and income than for liabilities and expenses. Despite such criticism, however, IASB's efforts in developing a principles-led approach to standard setting are widely supported.

THE AUDITORS' ROLE

Shareholders are required to elect a qualified and independent person or, more usually, a firm to act as **auditors**. The auditors' main duty is to report whether, in their opinion, the financial statements do what they are supposed to do, namely to show a true and fair view of the financial performance, position and cash flows of the company. To form an opinion, auditors must carefully scrutinise the financial statements and the underlying evidence upon which those statements are based. This will involve an examination of the accounting principles followed, the accounting estimates made and the robustness of the company's internal control systems. Following this examination, the auditors should be able to assess the risks of misstatements arising from either fraud or error. Their opinion must accompany the financial statements provided for shareholders and the Registrar of Companies.

The relationship between the shareholders, the directors and the auditors is illustrated in Figure 5.2. This shows that the shareholders elect the directors to act on their behalf, in the day-to-day running of the company. The directors are then required to 'account' to the shareholders on the performance, position and cash flows of the company, on an annual basis. The shareholders also elect the auditors, who then report back to the shareholders.

The directors are appointed by the shareholders to manage the company on the shareholders' behalf. The directors are required to report each year to the shareholders, principally by means of financial statements, on the company's performance, position and cash flows. To give greater confidence in the statements, the shareholders also appoint auditors to investigate the reports and to express an opinion on their reliability.

Figure 5.2 The relationship between the shareholders, the directors and the auditors

The audit and its relationship to the management of the company will be discussed in more detail in Chapter 7.

THE FRAMEWORK OF ANNUAL FINANCIAL REPORTS

Over the years, there has been a trend towards greater disclosure in the published annual financial reports of limited companies. Various reasons have been put forward to explain this trend. They include the increasing complexity of business, the increasing sophistication of users and a growing recognition that other groups with a stake in the business, apart from shareholders, require information.

The content of annual financial reports now ventures way beyond the main financial statements. A wide range of information is provided and the reporting boundaries are ill defined. As well as financial information, annual reports often contain information concerning social matters (such as community involvement) and environmental matters (such as carbon emissions). This has led to a growing debate as to whether this kind of information should be included. Questions raised include: 'Does this information fit with the objectives of financial reporting? Should more appropriate forms of reporting be devised to convey this information?'

Whatever the outcome of this debate, it has exposed the need for a more coherent reporting framework. A useful starting point in developing this framework is to identify the core components of annual financial reports. It has been argued that three core components have evolved over time (see Reference 3 at the end of the chapter). These are set out in Figure 5.3.

Financial statements	Corporate governance	Management commentary
The main financial statements, prepared in accordance with generally agreed accounting rules, along with explanatory notes.	Reports to shareholders on the way in which the directors have managed and controlled the business.	Contextual information to help understand the financial statements. This information both supplements and complements the financial statements.

Three core components have evolved over time.

Figure 5.3 The core components of financial reports

In the sections that follow, we turn our attention to two of these three components: the main financial statements and management commentary. The third component, corporate governance, will be considered in detail in Chapter 7.

PRESENTING THE FINANCIAL STATEMENTS

Let us begin by examining the main financial statements and the rules that surround them. In doing so, our main focus will be on the IASB rules and, in particular, those contained in IAS 1 *Presentation of Financial Statements*. This standard is very important as it sets out the structure and content of the main financial statements and the principles to be followed in their preparation.

It might be helpful to have a set of the most recent financial statements of a Stock Exchange listed company available as you work through this section. They should all be available on the Internet. Select a listed company that interests you and go to its website.

The financial statements identified in IAS 1 are as set out in Figure 5.4.

Accounting for Limited Companies (2)

IAS 1 *Presentation of Financial Statements* requires the preparation of the five statements shown.

Figure 5.4 Financial statements required under IAS 1

Each of the financial statements identified in Figure 5.4 should be presented with equal prominence.

According to the standard, these financial statements should normally cover a one-year period and should be accompanied by comparative information for the previous year. Thus, at the end of each reporting period companies should normally produce two of each of the statements, plus the related notes. In practice, virtually all companies satisfy this requirement by showing the equivalent figures for the previous year in a separate column in the current year's statements.

Comparative narrative information should also be provided if needed for a better grasp of current period results – for example, as background to an ongoing legal dispute.

Fair representation

Before considering the various financial statements, it is important to note that IAS 1 contains an overriding requirement that these statements provide a *fair representation* of a company's financial position, financial performance and cash flows. There is a presumption that this will occur as long as they are drawn up in accordance with current IASB standards. Only in very rare circumstances would this not be the case. Where the financial statements have applied all relevant IASB standards, this fact should be clearly stated in the notes.

Activity 5.10

IAS 1 says that the financial statements are required to show a 'fair representation' of financial health. It does not say that the statements should show a 'correct' or an 'accurate' representation of financial health. Why, in your opinion, does it not use those words? (*Hint*: Think of depreciation of non-current assets.)

Accounting can never really be said to be 'correct' or 'accurate' as these words imply that there is a precise value that an asset, claim, revenue or expense could have. This is simply not true in many, if not most, cases.

Depreciation provides a good example of where 'correct' or 'accurate' would not be appropriate. The annual depreciation expense is based on judgements about the future

> concerning the expected useful life and residual value of an asset. If all relevant factors are taken into account and reasonable judgements are applied, it may be possible to achieve a fair representation of the amount of the cost or fair value of the asset that is consumed for a particular period. However, a uniquely correct figure for depreciation for a period cannot be achieved.

Let us now consider each of the financial statements in turn.

Statement of financial position

IAS 1 does not prescribe the layout for this financial statement but does set out the *minimum* information that should be presented on the face of the statement of financial position. This includes the following:

- property, plant and equipment;
- investment property;
- intangible assets;
- financial assets (such as shares and loan notes of other companies held as assets);
- inventories;
- trade and other receivables;
- cash and cash equivalents;
- trade and other payables;
- provisions (a provision is a liability that is of uncertain timing or amount – such as a possible obligation arising from a legal case against the company that has yet to be determined);
- financial liabilities (other than payables and provisions shown above);
- tax liabilities; and
- issued share capital and reserves (equity).

Additional information should also be shown where it is relevant to an understanding of the financial position of the business.

The standard requires that, on the statement of financial position, a distinction is normally made between current assets and non-current assets and between current liabilities and non-current liabilities. However, for certain types of business, such as financial institutions (such as banks), the standard accepts that it may be more appropriate to order items according to their liquidity (that is, their nearness to cash).

Some of the assets and claims listed above may have to be sub-classified to comply with particular standards or because of their size or nature. This means that, sub-classifications are required for assets such as property, plant and equipment, trade receivables and inventories as well as for claims such as provisions and reserves. Certain details relating to share capital, such as the number of issued shares and their nominal value, must also be shown. To avoid cluttering up the statement of financial position, however, this additional information can be shown in the notes. In practice, most companies use notes for this purpose.

Statement of comprehensive income

This statement extends the conventional income statement to include certain other gains and losses that affect shareholders' equity. It may be presented either in the form of a single statement or as two separate statements, comprising an income statement (such as we have considered so far) and a **statement of comprehensive income**. This choice of presentation, however, may be a transitional arrangement as the IASB's preference is for a single statement.

Again, the layout of the statement of comprehensive income is not prescribed, but IAS 1 sets out the *minimum* information to be presented on the face of the statement. This includes:

- revenue;
- finance costs;
- impairment losses;
- profits or losses arising from discontinued operations;
- share of the profits or losses of associates or joint ventures;
- tax expense;
- profit or loss;
- total other comprehensive income (as well as certain items such as the share of other comprehensive income from associate and joint ventures); and
- total comprehensive income (profit or loss plus other comprehensive income).

As a further aid to understanding, all material expenses should be separately disclosed. However, they need not be shown on the face of the income statement, they can appear in the notes to the financial statements. The kind of material items that may require separate disclosure include:

- write-down of inventories to net realisable value;
- write-down of property, plant and equipment;
- disposals of investments;
- restructuring costs;
- discontinued operations; and
- litigation settlements.

This is not an exhaustive list and, in practice, other material expenses may require separate disclosure.

The standard suggests two possible ways in which expenses can be presented on the face of the income statement. Expenses can be presented either:

- according to their nature, for example as depreciation, employee expenses and so on; or
- according to business functions, such as administrative activities and distribution (where, for example, depreciation of delivery lorries will be included in distribution expenses).

The choice between the two possible ways of presenting expenses will depend on which one the directors believe will provide the more relevant and reliable information.

To understand what additional information must be presented, apart from that already in a conventional income statement, we should remember that, broadly, the conventional income statement shows all *realised* gains and losses for the period. It also includes some unrealised losses (that is, losses relating to assets still held).

Activity 5.11

Identify two types of unrealised loss that may appear in the conventional income statement. (*Hint*: Think back to Chapter 3.)

Unrealised losses may include:

- impairment losses following the revaluation of non-current assets; and
- inventories written down to net realisable value.

Unrealised gains and some unrealised losses, however, do not pass through the conventional income statement, but, instead, go directly to equity. In the case of limited companies, a separate revaluation reserve (forming part of total equity) is created for each type of revaluation. In an earlier chapter, we came across an example of an unrealised gain that did not pass through the conventional income statement.

Activity 5.12

Can you think of this example? (*Hint*: Think back to Chapter 2.)

The example that we met earlier is where a business revalues its land and buildings. The gain arising is not shown in the conventional income statement, but is transferred directly to the equity of the owners. (See Activity 2.18 on page 61.) For a limited company, this gain is transferred to a separate revaluation reserve.

Land and buildings are not the only assets to which this rule relates, but these types of asset, in practice, provide the most common example of unrealised gains.

An example of unrealised gains, or losses, that has not been mentioned so far, arises from those arising from holding marketable equity shares. Any such gains, or losses, will bypass the income statement and be taken directly to a reserve.

A weakness of conventional accounting is that no robust principle can be applied in order to determine precisely what should, and what should not, be included in the income statement. Losses arising from the impairment of property, plant and equipment, as we have seen, appear in the income statement. However, losses arising from holding marketable equity shares that are available for sale do not. In principle, there is no significant difference between these two types of loss, but the difference in treatment is ingrained in conventional accounting practice.

The statement of comprehensive income attempts to overcome the deficiencies mentioned by taking into account unrealised gains as well as any unrealised losses not reported in the conventional income statement. It extends the conventional income statement by including these items immediately beneath the profit for the year figure. An illustration of this statement is shown in Example 5.2. Here, expenses are presented according to business function and comparative figures for the previous year are shown alongside the figures for the current year.

Example 5.2

Malik plc
Statement of comprehensive income for the year ended 30 June

	2018 £m	2017 £m
Revenue	100.6	97.2
Cost of sales	(60.4)	(59.1)
Gross profit	40.2	38.1
Other income	4.0	3.5
Distribution expenses	(18.2)	(16.5)

	2018	2017
	£m	£m
Administration expenses	(10.3)	(11.2)
Other expenses	(2.1)	(2.4)
Operating profit	13.6	11.5
Finance charges	(2.0)	(1.8)
Profit before tax	11.6	9.7
Tax	(2.9)	(2.4)
Profit for the year	8.7	7.3
Other comprehensive income		
Revaluation of property, plant and equipment	20.3	6.6
Gains on holding equity investments available for sale	12.5	4.0
Tax related to other comprehensive income	(6.0)	(2.0)
Other comprehensive income net of tax	26.8	8.6
Total comprehensive income for the year	35.5	15.9

This example adopts a single-statement approach to presenting comprehensive income. The alternative two-statement approach simply divides the information shown into two separate parts. The income statement, which is the first statement, begins with the revenue and ends with the profit for the reporting period. The statement of comprehensive income, which is the second statement, begins with the profit for the reporting period and ends with the total comprehensive income.

Statement of changes in equity

The **statement of changes in equity** reveals the changes in share capital and reserves that took place during the reporting period. It reconciles the figures for these items at the beginning of the period with those at the end. This is achieved by showing the effect of the total comprehensive income for the reporting period on the share capital and reserves as well as share issues and redemptions during the period. The effect of dividends during the period may also be shown in this statement, although dividends can be shown in the notes instead.

To see how a statement of changes in equity may be prepared, let us consider Example 5.3.

Example 5.3

At 1 January 2018 Miro plc had the following equity:

Miro plc

	£m
Share capital (£1 ordinary shares)	100
Revaluation reserve	20
Translation reserve	40
Retained earnings	150
Total equity	310

During 2018, the company made a profit for the year from normal business operations of £42 million and reported an upward revaluation of property, plant and equipment of £120 million (net of any tax payable if the unrealised gains were realised). A loss on exchange differences on translating the results of foreign operations of £10 million was also reported under 'Other comprehensive income'. To strengthen its financial position, the company issued 50 million ordinary shares during the year at a premium of £0.40. Dividends for the year were £27 million.

This information for 2018 can be set out in a statement of changes in equity as follows:

Statement of changes in equity for the year ended 31 December 2018

	Share capital £m	Share premium £m	Revaluation reserve £m	Translation reserve £m	Retained earnings £m	Total £m
Balance as at 1 January 2018	100	–	20	40	150	310
Changes in equity for 2018						
Profit for the period[1]					42	42
Other comprehensive income for the year[2]			120	(10)		110
Issue of ordinary shares[3]	50	20	–	–	–	70
Dividends[4]	–	–	–	–	(27)	(27)
Balance at 31 December 2018	150	20	140	30	165	505

Notes:
1 The profit for the year is added to retained earnings.
2 The effect of each component of comprehensive income on the various elements of shareholders' equity must be separately disclosed. The revaluation gain and the loss on translating foreign operations are each allocated to a specific reserve.
3 The premium on the share price is transferred to a specific reserve.
4 We have chosen to show dividends in the statement of changes in equity rather than in the notes. They represent an appropriation of equity and are deducted from retained earnings.

Statement of cash flows

The statement of cash flows should help users to assess the ability of a company to generate cash and to assess the company's need for cash. The presentation requirements for this statement are set out in IAS 7 *Statement of Cash Flows*.

Notes

The notes play an important role in helping users to understand the financial statements. They will normally contain the following:

- a declaration that the financial statements comply with relevant financial reporting standards;
- a summary of the measurement bases used and other significant accounting policies applied (for example, the basis of inventories valuation);
- any dividends proposed;
- information concerning the objectives and policies for managing capital;

- information relevant to an understanding of the financial statements but not presented elsewhere;
- information required by accounting standards but not presented elsewhere; and
- key assumptions made concerning the future and major sources of estimation uncertainty.

These notes to accompany the financial statements must be presented in a systematic manner.

General points

The standard provides support for three key accounting conventions when preparing the financial statements. These are:

- the going concern convention;
- the accruals convention (except for the statement of cash flows); and
- the consistency convention.

These conventions were discussed in Chapters 2 and 3.

Finally, to improve the transparency of financial statements, the standard states that:

- offsetting liabilities against assets, or expenses against income, is not allowed unless specifically permitted by a particular accounting standard. It is not acceptable, for example, to offset a bank overdraft against a positive bank balance (where a company has both); and
- material items must be shown separately.

MANAGEMENT COMMENTARY

Many businesses create complex organisational structures, operating systems and financing methods. These features must be accommodated within the financial statements if those statements are to faithfully portray financial position and performance. The statements, as a consequence, can become lengthy, detailed and difficult to understand. To provide a clearer picture, a management commentary can be very helpful. It involves a review of the results and the disclosure of any further information relevant to an understanding of financial health.

Activity 5.13

What do you think are the main qualitative characteristics that information contained in a management commentary should possess? (*Hint*: Think back to Chapter 1.)

To be useful, the information should exhibit the characteristics for accounting information in general, which we identified in Chapter 1. Thus, the information should be relevant and faithfully represented. It should also be comparable, verifiable, timely and understandable. The fact that we may be dealing with narrative information does not alter the need for these characteristics to be present.

In the UK, a management commentary has become part of the financial reporting landscape. We shall now consider two narrative reports, the directors' report and the strategic report, which both supplement and complement the main financial statements. Each of these forms part of the management commentary.

DIRECTORS' REPORT

For many years, the directors have been required to prepare a report to shareholders relating to each reporting period. The content of the **directors' report** is prescribed by law and includes assorted topics such as financing decisions, business activities, future prospects and broader social aspects. For larger companies the report must cover, among other things, the following matters:

- the names of those who were directors during the reporting period;
- any recommended dividend;
- the acquisition by a public listed company of its own shares;
- the involvement of employees in the affairs of the company;
- the employment and training of disabled persons;
- important events affecting the company since the year end;
- financial risk management objectives and policies;
- greenhouse gas emissions by a public listed company;
- likely future developments in the business; and
- research and development activities.

In addition to disclosing the information mentioned above, the directors' report must contain a declaration that the directors are not aware of any other information that the auditors might need in preparing their audit report. There must also be a declaration that the directors have taken steps to ensure that the auditors are aware of all relevant information. The auditors do not carry out an audit of the directors' report. However, they do check to see that the information in the report is consistent with that contained in the audited financial statements.

While this report provides useful information, there is a strong case for revising its role, form and content. It contains a disjointed collection of items that lacks an underlying theme. It seems little more than a repository for miscellaneous items. The structure and presentation of the report is not tightly prescribed and so, in practice, comparisons between companies can be difficult. Furthermore, its relationship with the strategic report, which also provides additional information about the business and which is discussed below, is not clear.

STRATEGIC REPORT

The overall aim of the **strategic report** is to provide context for the financial statements and so help shareholders assess how well the directors have performed in promoting the success of the company. The content of the report has five main themes, which are summarised in Figure 5.5.

Directors of all but the smallest companies are legally obliged to produce a strategic report. The report produced should be fair, balanced and understandable. This means that both positive and negative aspects of performance, position and future prospects should be covered. The report must not be biased and there should be no omissions of important information. Although the report should be concise, it should also be comprehensive. This means that it must convey all information relevant to an understanding of business performance and position.

Accounting for Limited Companies (2)

Figure 5.5 Strategic report: content themes

The strategic reports prepared by Stock Exchange listed companies must disclose more than those of other companies, including disclosures concerning its strategy and business model. Figure 5.6 summarises their main features.

Strategic management	Business environment	Business performance
How the entity intends to generate and preserve value	The internal and external environment in which the entity operates	How the entity has developed and performed and its position at the year end
Strategy	Principal risks and uncertainties	Analysis of performance and position
Business model	Environmental, employee, social, community, human rights, anti-corruption and anti-bribery matters	Key performance indicators (KPIs)
		Employee gender diversity

We can see that the strategic report covers three broad areas. These are interrelated and should not be treated in isolation.

Figure 5.6 The main features of the strategic report

Source: Guidance on the Strategic Report, Financial Reporting Council, July 2018, p. 40.

Activity 5.14

Stock Exchange listed companies are required to disclose more information about their business than other companies? Try to think of at least one reason for this requirement.

Various arguments can be made in favour of greater accountability from such companies. They include:

- Greater transparency concerning the companies' business operations should help investors make more informed decisions. This is particularly important with Stock Exchange listed companies since their shares are frequently traded. Share prices may, therefore,

- be set in a more efficient manner, which can contribute towards the smooth functioning of capital markets.
- Stock Exchange listed companies tend to be larger, have more economic power and have more stakeholders than other companies. Their impact on the economy and society as a whole, therefore, tends to be greater. This, in turn, creates an obligation for them to account more fully for their operations and actions.

We saw earlier that Stock Exchange listed companies must, along with other matters, report on their strategy and business model. **Real World 5.3** illustrates how one listed company reports these elements.

Real World 5.3

Equipped for the future

VP plc is a specialist equipment rental group operating in the UK, Ireland and mainland Europe. It offers products and services to a diverse range of markets including rail, transmission, water, civil engineering, construction, house building, oil and gas. The business has summed up its strategy and business model as follows:

> Our aim is to generate sustainable value creation for shareholders and other stakeholders through our expertise in asset management, by exceeding customer expectations, maintaining and utilising our financial strength and retaining and attracting the best people.

Resilient & proven model
- specialist equipment rental
- market leading positions in niche sectors
- diverse markets in UK and Overseas

First class asset management
- buy quality products at competitive prices
- maintain assets through rental life cycles
- use strong balance sheet and cash generation for fleet growth and acquisitions

Enhancing our offer
- embrace change and innovate
- take long term view
- continue to exceed customer expectations
- provide value added services

Building on core attributes
- retain and attract the best people
- safe and sustainable business
- product service reliability and operational excellence

Figure 5.7 VP plc business model

Source: Business Model and Strategy © Vp plc 2018 www.vpplc.com/investors/business-model-and-strategy [accessed 2 January 2019].

The auditors have the same duty towards the strategic report as that of the directors' report. They must give an opinion as to whether the information it contains is consistent with the financial statements and complies with legal requirements. Where there are any material misstatements they must be disclosed. Both narrative reports are, therefore, subject to independent scrutiny.

ACCOUNTING STANDARDS AND ACCOUNTING POLICIES

In earlier chapters, we have considered a number of financial reporting standards, for example those relating to depreciation and to the valuation of inventories. We shall now discuss two other important standards. Both of these have a broad application and relate to general accounting policies that should be followed.

IAS 8 *Accounting Policies, Changes in Accounting Estimates and Errors*

IAS 8 sets out the criteria for selecting and changing accounting policies and the appropriate treatment for disclosing these policies. It also sets out the treatment for disclosing changes in accounting estimates and for the correction of errors. A key aim of the standard is to improve the comparability of financial statements both over time and between different businesses.

Accounting policies

Accounting policies are the principles, rules and conventions used to prepare the financial statements. Wherever possible, they should be determined by reference to appropriate financial reporting standards. (The standard on inventories, for example, will provide policies to be followed in this area.) In the absence of an appropriate standard, managers must make suitable judgements to ensure that users receive relevant and reliable information.

The general rule is that, once a particular policy has been selected and applied, it should not be changed. This is designed to ensure consistency in approach. However, an accounting policy may be changed where:

1 it is required by a new financial reporting standard; or
2 it will result in more relevant and reliable information being provided to users.

If a new financial reporting standard requires changes to be made, the name of the standard, and any transitional arrangements, should be disclosed. If it is a voluntary change, the reasons why it will result in more relevant and reliable information should be disclosed. In both cases, the nature of the change in policy and the amount of the adjustment on relevant items and on earnings per share for both the current and the prior period should be disclosed.

Changes in accounting estimates

Managers are normally required to make various estimates when preparing financial statements.

Activity 5.15

What estimates will normally be required? Try to think of at least three. (*Hint*: Think back to Chapter 3.)

They will normally include estimates of:

- the amount of bad debts incurred;
- the net realisable value of inventories;
- the useful life of non-current assets;
- the fair value of non-current assets;
- the residual value of non-current assets; and
- the amount of accrued expenses (such as electricity) incurred.

These estimates may need revision in the light of new information. If a revised estimate affects assets, liabilities or equity, it should be adjusted in the period of the change. If it affects profit, it should be revised in the period affected. This may be in the period of change and/or in future periods.

Activity 5.16

Try to think of an example of an estimate that will normally affect only the period of change and an example of one that will normally affect the period of change and future periods.

Normally, estimates of bad debts will only affect the period of change whereas a change in the estimated useful life of a non-current asset will affect the period of change and future periods.

Both the nature and amount of a change in estimate affecting the current period or future periods should be disclosed. If it is impracticable to estimate the amount, this fact must be disclosed.

Errors

Errors are omissions or misstatements in the financial statements. They may arise for a variety of reasons, which include arithmetical mistakes, oversights, misinterpretation of facts and fraud. Sometimes these errors are significant in nature and/or size and are not discovered until a later period. In such a situation, the general rule is that the relevant figures for the earlier period(s) in which the errors occurred should be restated for comparison purposes. If the errors occurred before the prior periods presented for comparison, then the opening balances of assets, liabilities and equity for the earliest prior period presented should be restated. The nature of the errors and their effect on relevant items and on earnings per share for the current and the prior period(s) should also be disclosed.

IAS 10 *Events After the Reporting Period*

The main aim of IAS 10 is to clarify the circumstances in which financial statements should be adjusted for events that took place after the reporting period (or accounting period). The standard deals with events that occur between the end of the reporting period and the date when the financial statements are authorised to be issued both to the shareholders and to the general public. Two types of events are identified:

1. those providing evidence of conditions that existed before the end of the reporting period (adjusting events); and
2. those indicating conditions arising after the end of the reporting period (non-adjusting events).

The standard requires that financial statements should incorporate only the adjusting events.

Activity 5.17

Vorta plc received the following information between the end of the reporting period and the date at which the financial statements were authorised for issue:

1. Inventories which were reported in the statement of financial position at an estimated net realisable value of £250,000 were sold immediately after the year end for £200,000.
2. There was a decline of £150,000 in the market value of investments after the end of the reporting period.
3. An error was discovered which indicated that the trade receivables figure on the statement of financial position was understated by £220,000.

Which of the above are adjusting events?

Items 1 and 3 meet the definition of an adjusting event whereas item 2 meets the definition of a non-adjusting event. This is because, with items 1 and 3, we have received additional information on the position at the year end. With item 2, a change has occurred *after the year end*.

The standard clarifies two important points concerning events after the reporting period. First, if a dividend is declared for equity shareholders after the reporting period, it should not be treated as a liability in the financial statements. In other words, it is a non-adjusting event. In the past, it had been normal practice to treat such dividends as liabilities. Secondly, if it becomes clear after the reporting period that the business will cease trading, the going concern assumption will not apply. As a result, the financial statements must be prepared using a different basis for valuation. Assets, for example, would normally have to be shown at their estimated realisable values.

The date at which the financial statements were authorised for issue to shareholders and to others must be disclosed. This is important to understanding what events should and should not be included. There should also be disclosure of who authorised the issue.

Activity 5.18

Who do you think will normally authorise the issue of the financial statements?

It is normally the board of directors.

Where non-adjusting events are significant, they are capable of influencing users' decisions. The standard therefore requires significant non-adjusting events to be disclosed by way of a note. A major restructuring, a plan to discontinue an operation and the proposed purchase of a major asset are examples of non-adjusting events that might be disclosed. The standard requires the nature of the event and its likely financial effect be disclosed. If the financial effect cannot be reliably estimated, this fact should be disclosed.

Real World 5.4 sets out two transactions described in the notes to the financial statements of A G Barr plc, makers of the well-known drink IRN-BRU. They deal with non-adjusting events occurring between the statement of financial position date and the date of issue of the financial statements.

Real World 5.4

Non-adjusting events

In February 2017, the Group entered into three revolving credit facilities over periods of 3 to 5 years with Royal Bank of Scotland plc, Bank of Scotland plc and HSBC Bank plc. These facilities provide £60m of Sterling debt facilities to 2019/20, reducing to £20m for the period to 2021/22.

On 1 February 2017, the Group completed on the sale of the Walthamstow distribution site. The asset was held for sale at 28 January 2017. Total proceeds of £3.8m were received against a net book value of £1.3m, giving rise to a gain on sale of £2.5m, which will be recognised in the year to 27 January 2018. The Group has entered into a 3-year operating lease to continue to operate from the site for the short term.

Source: A G Barr plc, Annual Report and Accounts 2017 p.128.

Figure 5.8 summarises the main points to be considered when applying IAS 10.

There are key questions that need to be asked and answered when applying IAS 10.

Figure 5.8 Applying IAS 10

CREATIVE ACCOUNTING

Despite the proliferation of accounting rules and the independent checks that are imposed, concerns over the quality of published financial statements surface from time to time. There are occasions when directors apply particular accounting policies, or structure particular transactions, in such a way as to portray a picture of financial health that is in line with what they want users to see, rather than what is a true and fair view of financial position and performance. Misrepresenting the performance and position of a business in this way is often called **creative accounting** and it poses a major problem for accounting rule makers and for society generally.

Activity 5.19

Why might the directors of a company engage in creative accounting? Try to think of at least two reasons.

There are many reasons, including:

- to get around restrictions (for example, to report sufficient profit to pay a dividend);
- to avoid government action (for example, the taxation of profits);
- to hide poor management decisions;
- to achieve sales revenue or profit targets, thereby ensuring that performance bonuses are paid to the directors;
- to attract new share capital or long-term borrowing by showing an apparently healthy financial position; and
- to satisfy the demands of major investors concerning levels of return.

Creative accounting methods

There are many ways in which unscrupulous directors can manipulate the financial statements. They usually involve adopting novel or unorthodox practices for reporting key elements of the financial statements, such as revenue, expenses, assets and liabilities. They may also involve the use of complicated or obscure transactions in an attempt to hide the underlying economic reality. The manipulation carried out may be designed either to bend the rules or to break them.

We shall now consider some of the more important ways in which rules may be bent or broken.

Misstating revenue

Some creative accounting methods are designed to overstate the revenue for a period. These methods often involve the early recognition of sales revenue or the reporting of sales transactions that have no real substance. **Real World 5.5** provides examples of both types of revenue manipulation.

Real World 5.5

Overstating revenue

Types of revenue manipulation include:

- *Early recognition of revenue.* A business may report the sale of goods as soon as an order has been placed, rather than when the goods are delivered to, and accepted by, the customer. This will boost current revenues and profits and is known as 'pre-dispatching'.
- *Passing goods to distributors.* A business may force its distributors to accept more goods than they can sell. This will again boost current revenues and profits and is known as 'channel stuffing' or 'trade loading'.
- *Artificial trading.* This involves businesses in the same industry selling the same items between themselves to boost sales revenue. One example is where telecoms businesses sell unused fibre optic capacity to each other. This is known as 'hollow swaps'. Another example is where energy businesses sell energy between themselves for the same price and at the same time. This is known as 'round tripping' or 'in and out trading'.

Note that artificial trading between similar businesses will inflate the sales revenue for a period but will not inflate reported profits. Nevertheless, this may still benefit the business. Sales revenue growth has become an important yardstick of performance for some investors and can affect the value they place on the business.

Source: Based on information in: Dirty laundry: how companies fudge the numbers, *The Times*, Business Section, 22 September 2002, News Syndication.

The manipulation of revenue has been at the heart of many of the accounting scandals recently exposed. Given its critical role in the measurement of performance, this is, perhaps, not surprising. **Real World 5.6** discusses how the reported revenues of one UK software business have been hotly disputed. It was acquired by a US computer giant, which concluded that, as a result of this and other alleged irregularities, the price paid was far too much. It, therefore, reported a huge impairment charge soon after the acquisition.

Real World 5.6

Recomputing the numbers

Autonomy, the UK software company at the centre of massive fraud allegations, booked revenues from uncompleted transactions at the end of a number of quarters to meet sales targets, according to claims levelled in a document from the US Air Force.

The accusations, made against Autonomy founder Mike Lynch and five other former executives, contain the first details of the alleged accounting irregularities that US computer group Hewlett-Packard has said forced it to take an $8.8 billion write-off in 2012, a year after buying the UK company. Also named in the letter are two US government contractors, MicroTech and Capax Global, that acted as resellers of Autonomy's software and played a role in the disputed transactions. A representative for Mr Lynch responded that Autonomy's accounting had been in compliance with international accounting standards.

The allegations, which were first reported by the Washington Post, detail three transactions that had not been completed when Autonomy recorded revenues on them. One of the deals later fell through, while another was completed for less than the amount Autonomy recorded.

Under one of the contracts, Autonomy was said to have booked $11 million in revenue at the end of March 2010 on a transaction involving MicroTech and an unnamed end customer. The final sale failed to materialise, with Autonomy only receiving $500,000 on the contract. After an auditor queried the large uncollected debt from MicroTech at the end of the year, according to the claims, Autonomy made a payment of $9.6 million to the contractor under the heading 'Advanced technology innovation centre' and MicroTech wired back the same amount to cover some of the money it owed Autonomy.

Autonomy booked a further $15.7 million of revenue in two instalments on the final days of March and June the following year on a separate deal involving Capax, even though the ultimate sales transactions had not been completed, according to the Air Force document. The deal was later completed for $14.1 million.

In the third case, a $1.95 million sale was booked in December 2010, six months before it was finalised.

Source: Waters, R. (2014) Autonomy beset by revenues allegation, ft.com, 5 January.
© The Financial Times Limited 2014. All rights reserved.

In November 2018, Mike Lynch was charged with fraud by a federal court in Los Angeles.

Massaging expenses

Some creative accounting methods focus on the manipulation of expenses. Those expenses that rely on directors' estimates of the future or their choice of accounting policy are particularly vulnerable to manipulation.

Activity 5.20

Can you identify the kind of expenses where the directors make estimates or choices in the ways described? Think back to Chapter 3 and try to identify at least two.

These include certain expenses that we discussed in Chapter 3, such as:

- depreciation of property, plant and equipment;
- amortisation of intangible assets, such as goodwill;
- inventories (cost of sales); and
- allowances for trade receivables.

By changing estimates about the future (for example, the useful life or residual value of an asset), or by changing accounting policies (for example, switching from FIFO to AVCO), it may be possible to derive an expense figure and, consequently, a profit figure, that suits the directors.

The incorrect 'capitalisation' of expenses may also be used as a means of manipulation. This involves treating expenses as if they were amounts incurred to acquire or develop non-current assets, rather than amounts consumed during the period. Businesses that build their own assets are often best placed to undertake this form of malpractice.

Activity 5.21

What would be the effect on the profits and total assets of a business of incorrectly capitalising expenses?

Both would be artificially inflated. Reported profits would increase because expenses would be reduced. Total assets would be increased because the expenses would be incorrectly treated as non-current assets.

Real World 5.7 provides an example of one business that capitalised expenses on a huge scale.

Real World 5.7

Sorry – wrong numbers

One particularly notorious case of capitalising expenses is alleged to have occurred in the financial statements of WorldCom (now renamed MCI). This company, which is a large US telecommunications business, is alleged to have overstated profits by treating certain operating expenses, such as basic network maintenance, as capital expenditure. This happened over a fifteen-month period during 2001 and 2002. To correct for this overstatement, profits had to be reduced by a massive $3.8 billion.

Source: Based on two personal views on WorldCom posted on the ft.com site, 27 June 2002.
© The Financial Times Limited 2002. All rights reserved.

Concealing 'bad news'

Some creative accounting methods focus on the concealment of losses or liabilities. The financial statements can look much healthier if these can somehow be eliminated. One way of doing this is to create a 'separate' entity that will take over the losses or liabilities.

Real World 5.8 describes how one large business concealed losses and liabilities.

Real World 5.8

For a very special purpose

Perhaps the most well-known case of concealment of losses and liabilities concerned the Enron Corporation. This was a large US energy business that used 'special purpose entities' (SPEs) as a means of concealment. SPEs were used by Enron to rid itself of problem assets that were falling in value, such as its broadband operations. In addition, liabilities were transferred to these entities to help Enron's statement of financial position look healthier. The company had to keep its gearing ratios (the relationship between borrowing and equity) within particular limits to satisfy credit-rating agencies and SPEs were used to achieve this. The SPEs used for concealment purposes were not independent of the company and should have been consolidated in the statement of financial position of Enron, along with their losses and liabilities.

> When these, and other accounting irregularities, were discovered in 2001, there was a restatement of Enron's financial performance and position to reflect the consolidation of the SPEs, which had previously been omitted. As a result of this restatement, the company recognised $591 million in losses over the preceding four years and an additional $628 million worth of liabilities at the end of 2000.
>
> The company collapsed at the end of 2001.
>
> *Source*: William Thomas, C. (2002) The rise and fall of Enron, *Journal of Accountancy*, vol. 194, no. 3. This article represents the opinions of the author, which are not necessarily those of the Texas Society of Certified Public Accountants.

Misstating assets

There are various ways in which assets may be misstated. These include:

- using asset values that are higher than the assets' fair market values;
- capitalising costs that should have been written off as expenses, as described earlier; and
- recording assets that are not owned, or which do not exist.

Real World 5.9 describes how one large business is alleged to have overstated some of its assets.

Real World 5.9

It's worth . . . less

Anglo-Australian mining giant Rio Tinto has been charged with fraud in the US and fined £27.4 million in the UK after being accused of overstating the value of African coal assets. The FTSE 100 company and two of its top former executives were charged in the US of hiding losses by inflating the value of assets in Mozambique, which Rio bought in 2011 for $3.7 billion and sold a few years later for $50 million.

America's financial regulator, the Securities and Exchange Commission, filed a complaint in federal court in Manhattan. It alleges that Rio Tinto, its former chief executive, Tom Albanese, and its former chief financial officer, Guy Elliott, failed to follow accounting standards and company policies to accurately value and record its assets.

As the project began to suffer setbacks, resulting in the rapid decline of the value of the coal assets, Albanese and Elliott sought to hide or delay disclosure of the nature and extent of the adverse developments from Rio Tinto's board of directors, auditors, and investors, the SEC alleges.

'Rio Tinto and its top executives allegedly failed to come clean about an unsuccessful deal that was made under their watch. They tried to save their own careers at the expense of investors by hiding the truth,' said Steven Peikin, co-director of the SEC's enforcement division.

The miner said it intends to 'vigorously defend itself' against the allegations.

Source: Extract from: Rio Tinto charged with fraud in US and fined £27.4m in UK, www.theguardian.com, 18 October 2017.

Inadequate disclosure

Directors may misrepresent or try to conceal certain information. This may relate to commitments made, illegal behaviour, key changes in accounting policies or estimates, significant events and so on. **Real World 5.10** reveals how one large bank allegedly tried to conceal its actions in order to avoid the legal consequences.

> **Real World 5.10**
>
> ## Standard practice?
>
> New York State's financial watchdog has accused Standard Chartered of hiding $250 billion of transactions with the Iranian government, leaving 'the US financial system vulnerable to terrorists, weapons dealers, drug kingpins and corrupt regimes'. The UK-based bank's shares fell more than 6 per cent after the New York state Department of Financial Services (DFS) issued an order just before the London market closed on Monday, which included a threat to revoke the bank's licence to operate in the state, and called it a 'rogue institution'.
>
> The order said that between 2001 and 2010 Standard Chartered concealed from US authorities roughly 60,000 transactions for Iranian clients, amounting to about $250 billion and generating 'hundreds of millions of dollars' in fees for the bank. Among the Iranian clients were the Central Bank of Iran and two state-owned institutions, Bank Saderat and Bank Melli. The US has had economic sanctions in place against Iran since 1979. They were toughened in 1995 to place strict limits on dealing with Iranian customers by US banks, including foreign banks with operations in the US. The New York regulator, led by Benjamin Lawsky, superintendent of financial services, alleged that StanChart had falsified records and evaded US sanctions.
>
> **FT** *Source*: Braithewaite, T. and Goff, S. (2012) StanChart accused of hiding Iran dealings, ft.com, 7 August. © The Financial Times Limited 2012. All rights reserved.

Figure 5.9 summarises the main methods of creative accounting.

There are five main methods of creative accounting.

Figure 5.9 The main methods of creative accounting

Checking for creative accounting

When the financial statements of a business are being examined, a number of checks may be carried out to help gain a feel for their reliability. These can include checks to see whether:

- the reported profits are significantly higher than the operating cash flows for the period (as shown in the business's statement of cash flows), which may suggest that profits have been overstated;

- the tax charge is low in relation to reported profits, which may suggest, again, that profits are overstated, although there may be other, more innocent, explanations;
- the valuation methods used for assets held are based on historic cost or fair values, and, if the latter approach has been used, why and how the fair values were determined;
- there have been changes in accounting policies over the period, particularly in key areas such as revenue recognition, inventories valuation and depreciation;
- the accounting policies adopted are in line with those adopted by the rest of the industry;
- the auditors' report gives a 'clean bill of health' to the financial statements; and
- the 'small print' (that is the notes to the financial statements) is being used to hide significant events or changes.

Real World 5.11 describes the emphasis that one analyst places on this last check.

Real World 5.11

Taking note

Alistair Hodgson, investment manager at private client stockbroker Pilling and Co, says 'I almost look at the notes more than I look at the main figures at first. The notes tend to hold the key to anything that looks strange. I look to pick out things that the auditor has told the company to declare – the kind of thing they might not want to declare, but they have got to do so in order to make the accounts honest.'

Source: Smith, S. (2005) It pays to read between the lines, *Financial Times,* 17 September.
© The Financial Times Limited 2005. All rights reserved.

Checks may also be carried out to provide confirmation of positive financial health. These may include checks to see whether:

- the business is paying increased dividends; and/or
- the directors are buying shares in the business.

Although the various checks described are useful, they cannot be used to guarantee the reliability of the financial statements. Some creative accounting practices may be very deeply seated and may go undetected for years.

Creative accounting and economic growth

Some years ago, there was a wave of creative accounting scandals, particularly in the US but also in Europe. It seems, however, that this wave has now subsided. As a result of action taken by various regulatory bodies, the behaviour of companies is now subject to stricter controls. Corporate governance procedures have been strengthened and tighter financial reporting rules have been imposed. Creative accounting has now become a more risky and difficult process for those who attempt it. However, it will never disappear completely and a further wave of creative accounting scandals may occur in the future.

The wave of creative accounting scandals coincided with a period of strong economic growth. During good economic times, investors and auditors become less vigilant, making it easier to manipulate the figures. We must not, therefore, become too complacent. Things may change again when we next experience a period of strong growth.

Real World 5.12 concludes this chapter by identifying some key features of businesses that engage in creative accounting.

Real World 5.12

Spotting a wrong 'un

We all know why companies manipulate their earnings. They do it because they can. Accounting principles necessarily allow some discretion beyond the direct moves that show up in cash terms each quarter. And there are rewards for manipulation – stronger earnings will be greeted by higher share prices. That means cheaper equity finance for the company, and more pay for any executives whose remuneration is linked to share performance. The tricky part is to work out who is manipulating. That requires a good grasp of forensic accounting. And the really useful knowledge for investors would be to spot companies before they start cooking their books. New research from a group of academics at the University of Southern California, the University of Houston, the University of Hong Kong and Cambridge University's Judge Business School appears to do just that. After studying all the companies that fell foul of US regulators for manipulation between 1985 and 2010, they boiled down the search for future manipulators into internal and external factors.

Internally the key driver, and this should surprise nobody, is the power of the chief executive officer. CEOs with power concentrated in themselves – measured by standard corporate governance measures such as whether they also have the role of chairman, and how many independent directors sit on the board – tend to get their own way. Manipulation is much more likely.

Externally, the key factor is earnings expectations themselves. Once companies see that brokers' analysts have higher forecasts for them, they feel pressure from the market to try harder (through manipulation) to beat those forecasts. Also, as big institutions raise their stakes, they feel greater pressure to meet expectations.

Perhaps the most surprising finding is that legitimately consistent and rising earnings are a first warning flag. There is what Jennifer Chu of the Judge Business School describes as a 'slippery slope'. Companies with a regular record of growth and of outperforming expectations become accustomed to the rich equity valuation that comes with it. They do not want to suffer the sharp sell-off that would accompany an admission of reality.

Source: Extract from Authers, J. (2017) How to spot companies at risk of earnings manipulation: academic research underlines the dangers of chief executives with too much power, ft.com, 7 September. © The Financial Times Limited 2017. All rights reserved.

Self-assessment question 5.1

You have overheard the following statements:

(a) 'Dividends announced between the end of the reporting period and the date at which the financial reports are authorised for publication, which relate to the reporting period just ended, should be treated as a liability in the statement of financial position at the end of that period.'
(b) 'IAS 1 provides support for three key accounting conventions – accruals, historic cost and consistency.'
(c) 'IAS 1 permits bank overdrafts to be offset against positive bank balances when preparing the statement of financial position.'

(d) 'Accounting policies can only be changed if it is required by a new financial reporting standard.'
(e) 'All non-adjusting events occurring between the end of the reporting period and the date at which the financial statements are authorised for issue should be ignored.'
(f) 'The strategic report should be prepared by the company's auditors rather than by the directors of the company.'

Required:
Critically comment on each of the statements.

The solution to this question can be found at the back of the book, starting on page 305.

SUMMARY

The main points of this chapter may be summarised as follows:

Directors' duty
- Separation of ownership from day-to-day control creates a need for directors to be accountable.
- To fulfil this need, the directors have a duty to prepare and publish financial statements.
- Shareholders have a right to receive a copy of the published financial statements.

The need for accounting rules
- Accounting rules are necessary in order to avoid unacceptable accounting practices and to improve the comparability of financial statements.
- This should give greater confidence in the integrity of financial statements.

Source of accounting rules
- The International Accounting Standards Board (IASB) has become an important source of rules.
- Company law and the London Stock Exchange are also sources of rules for UK companies.

Problems with standards
- Various problems may arise from using financial reporting standards:
  - they may inhibit change
  - they may impose false conformity
  - they involve consensus seeking
  - they can be costly
  - they can introduce complexity.
- The alternative is to allow accounting choice. This, however, leads to the risk of manipulation, inadequate disclosure and lack of comparability.

Conceptual framework
- This helps to underpin financial reporting standards.
- The IASB framework sets out the objective of general purpose financial reports, the primary user groups, the qualitative characteristics, the elements of financial statements and the different measurement bases that may be used.

The role of auditors

- Auditors are required to report to shareholders whether, in their opinion, the financial statements provide a true and fair view of the financial health of a business.
- They are elected by the shareholders.

Financial reporting framework

- Company reports consist of three core components: the main financial statements, corporate governance disclosure and a management commentary.

Presenting financial statements

- IAS 1 sets out the structure and content of financial statements.
- It requires preparation of a statement of financial position, a statement of comprehensive income, a statement of changes in equity and a statement of cash flows. In addition, explanatory notes are required.
- The financial statements must provide a fair representation of the financial health of a company, which will only normally be achieved by sticking to relevant IASB standards.
- IAS 1 sets out information to be shown in the various financial statements and some of the accounting conventions and principles to be followed in preparing the statements.

Management commentary

- A management commentary reviews the financial results. It aims to complement and supplement the financial statements.
- The directors' report contains information of a financial and non-financial nature. It includes such diverse matters as any recommended dividend, the involvement of employees in company affairs and important events since the year end. It lacks any underlying theme.
- The strategic report aims to provide context for the financial statements and so help shareholders assess how well the directors have performed in promoting the success of the company. It should be fair, balanced and understandable.
- The strategic report of Stock Exchange listed companies must provide additional information, including the strategy and business model adopted.

Accounting standards and accounting policies

- IAS 8 sets out the criteria for selecting and changing accounting policies.
- It also sets out the treatment for disclosing changes in accounting estimates and for the correction of errors.
- IAS 10 aims to clarify when financial statements should be adjusted for events that took place after the reporting period.
- Only events that provide evidence of conditions before the end of the reporting period lead to adjustments to the financial statements.

Creative accounting

- This involves using accounting practices to show what the directors would like users to see rather than what is a fair representation of reality.
- The main forms of creative accounting involve misstating revenues, massaging expenses, concealing bad news, misstating assets and inadequate disclosure.

KEY TERMS

International Accounting Standards
International Financial Reporting Standards
conceptual framework
auditors
statement of comprehensive income
statement of changes in equity
directors' report
strategic report
creative accounting

REFERENCES

1 *Analysis of the IFRS jurisdiction profiles,* www.ifrs.org [accessed 2 January 2019].
2 International Accounting Standards Board (2018) *Conceptual Framework for Financial Reporting,* pp. 28–31.
3 FRC (2012). *Thinking about disclosures in a broader context: A roadmap for a disclosure framework,* Discussion paper, Financial Reporting Council, www.frc.org.uk, October.

FURTHER READING

If you would like to explore the topics covered in this chapter in more depth, we recommend the following:

Alexander, D., Britton, A., Jorissen, A. Hoogendoorn and Van Mourik C. (2017) *International Financial Reporting and Analysis,* 7th edn, Cengage Learning EMEA, Chapters 2, 3, and 8.

Elliott, B. and Elliott, J. (2017) *Financial Accounting and Reporting,* 18th edn, Pearson, Chapters 3, 6 and 7.

International Accounting Standards Board, *The Conceptual Framework for Financial Reporting,* March 2018.

International Accounting Standards Board, *2017 A Guide through IFRS (Green Book),* IAS 1 *Presentation of Financial Statements.*

CRITICAL REVIEW QUESTIONS

Solutions to these questions can be found at the back of the book, starting on page 312.

5.1 There is a risk that managers will be inhibited from providing meaningful management commentaries. Instead, their commentaries may be uninformative and written in a bland form. Can you think why managers may feel inhibited? What might be done to overcome any concerns they may have?

5.2 'Searching for an agreed conceptual framework for accounting rules is likely to be a journey without an ending.' Discuss.

5.3 Why are accounting rules needed when preparing financial statements? Can you see any difficulties arising from harmonising accounting rules between different countries?

5.4 What are the main methods of creative accounting? How might the problem of creative accounting in developing countries be mitigated by harmonising accounting rules across national boundaries?

EXERCISES

Solutions to exercises with coloured numbers can be found at the back of the book, starting on page 319.

Basic-level exercises

5.1 'Financial reporting standards eliminate the need for accountants to make judgements and so lower their professional status.' Do you agree?

5.2 The size of annual financial reports published by limited companies has increased steadily over the years. Can you think of any reasons, apart from the increasing volume of accounting regulation, why this has occurred?

Intermediate-level exercises

5.3 Thor plc has the following events occurring between the end of the reporting period and the date the financial statements were authorised for issue:

1. The discovery that, during the reporting period, an employee had defrauded the business of £120,000.
2. The bankruptcy of a customer who owes the business £280,000. This sum was outstanding at the end of the reporting period.
3. A fire occurring after the reporting period that destroyed a large factory owned by Thor plc.
4. An increase in the value of land held by Thor plc by £10 million that occurred as a result of a change in the planning laws, which occurred after the end of the reporting period.

According to IAS 10 *Events After the Reporting Period,* how should each of these events be treated?

5.4 What are the potential benefits arising from developing a conceptual framework for accounting? What are the possible drawbacks?

Advanced-level exercises

5.5 The following information was extracted from the financial statements of I. Ching (Booksellers) plc for the year to 31 May 2018:

	£000
Finance charges	40
Cost of sales	460
Distribution expenses	110
Revenue	943
Administrative expenses	212
Other expenses	25
Gain on revaluation of property, plant and equipment	20
Loss on foreign currency translations on foreign operations	15
Tax on profit for the year	24
Tax on other components of comprehensive income	1

Required:
Prepare a statement of comprehensive income for the year ended 31 May 2018 that is set out in accordance with the requirements of IAS 1 *Presentation of Financial Statements*.

5.6 Manet plc had the following share capital and reserves as at 1 June 2017:

	£m
Share capital (£0.25 ordinary shares)	250
Share premium account	50
Revaluation reserve	120
Currency translation reserve	15
Retained earnings	380
Total equity	**815**

During the year to 31 May 2018, the company revalued property, plant and equipment upwards by £30 million and made a loss on foreign exchange translation of foreign operations of £5 million (and which is treated as other comprehensive income.). The company made a profit for the year from normal operations of £160 million and the dividend for the year to 31 May 2018 was £80 million.

Required:
Prepare a statement of changes in equity for the year ended 31 May 2018 in accordance with the requirements of IAS 1 *Presentation of Financial Statements*.

5.7 Professor Myddleton argues that financial reporting standards should be limited to disclosure requirements and should not impose rules on companies as to how to measure particular items in the financial statements. He states:

> The volume of accounting instructions is already high. If things go on like this, where will we be in 20 or 30 years' time? On balance I conclude we would be better off without any standards on accounting measurement. There could still be some disclosure requirements for listed companies, though probably less than now.

Do you agree with this idea? Discuss.

5.8 You have overheard the following statements:

(a) 'The role of independent auditors is to prepare the financial statements of the company.'
(b) 'International Accounting Standards (IASs) apply to all UK companies, but London Stock Exchange listed companies must also adhere to International Financial Reporting Standards (IFRSs).'
(c) 'All listed companies in the European Union states must follow IASs and IFRS Standards.'
(d) 'According to IAS 1, companies' financial statements must show an "accurate representation" of what they purport to show.'
(e) 'IAS 1 leaves it to individual companies to decide the format that they use in the statement of financial position.'
(f) 'The statement of changes in equity deals with unrealised profits and gains, for example an upward revaluation of a non-current asset.'

Critically comment on each of these statements.

Chapter 6

ANALYSING AND INTERPRETING FINANCIAL STATEMENTS

INTRODUCTION

In this chapter, we consider the analysis and interpretation of the financial statements. We shall see how the use of financial (or accounting) ratios can help to assess the financial performance and position of a business. We shall also take a look at the problems encountered when applying financial ratios.

Financial ratios can be used to examine various aspects of financial health and are widely used by external users, such as shareholders and lenders, and by managers. They can be very helpful to managers in a wide variety of decision areas, such as profit planning, working capital management and financial structure.

Learning outcomes

When you have completed this chapter, you should be able to:

- identify the major categories of ratios that can be used for analysing financial statements;
- calculate key ratios for assessing the financial performance and position of a business;
- explain the significance of the ratios calculated; and
- discuss the limitations of ratios as a tool of financial analysis.

FINANCIAL RATIOS

Financial ratios provide a quick and relatively simple means of assessing the financial health of a business. A ratio simply relates one figure appearing in the financial statements to another figure appearing there (for example, operating profit in relation to sales revenue) or, perhaps, to some resource of the business (for example, operating profit per employee).

Ratios can be very helpful when comparing the financial health of different businesses. Differences may exist between businesses in the scale of operations. As a result, a direct comparison of, say, the operating profit generated by each business, may be misleading. By expressing operating profit in relation to some other measure (for example, capital employed), the problem of scale is eliminated. This means that a business with an operating profit of £10,000 and capital employed of £100,000 can be compared with a much larger business with an operating profit of £80,000 and capital employed of £1,000,000 by the use of a simple ratio. The operating profit to capital employed ratio for the smaller business is 10 per cent (that is, $(10,000/100,000) \times 100\%$) and the same ratio for the larger business is 8 per cent (that is, $(80,000/1,000,000) \times 100\%$). These ratios can be directly compared, whereas a comparison of the absolute operating profit figures might be much less meaningful. The need to eliminate differences in scale through the use of ratios can also apply when comparing the performance of the same business from one time period to another.

By calculating a small number of ratios, it is often possible to build up a revealing picture of the position and performance of a business. It is not surprising, therefore, that ratios are widely used by those who have an interest in businesses and business performance. Ratios are not difficult to calculate but they can be difficult to interpret.

Ratios help us to identify which questions to ask, rather than provide the answers. They can help to highlight the financial strengths and weaknesses of a business, but cannot explain why those strengths or weaknesses exist or why certain changes have occurred. They provide a starting point for further analysis. Only a detailed investigation will reveal the underlying reasons.

Ratios can be expressed in various forms, for example as a percentage or as a proportion. The way that a particular ratio is presented will depend on the needs of those who will use the information. Although it is possible to calculate a large number of ratios, only a few, based on key relationships, tend to be helpful to a particular user. Many of the ratios that could be calculated from the financial statements (for example, rent payable in relation to current assets) may not be considered because there is not usually any clear or meaningful relationship between the two items.

There is no generally accepted list of ratios that can be applied to the financial statements, nor is there a standard method of calculating many ratios. Variations in both the choice of ratios and their calculation will be found in practice. It is important, therefore, to be consistent in the way in which ratios are calculated for comparison purposes. The ratios that we shall discuss are very popular – presumably because they are seen as useful for decision-making purposes.

FINANCIAL RATIO CLASSIFICATIONS

Ratios can be grouped into categories, with each category relating to a particular aspect of financial performance or position. The following broad categories provide a useful basis for explaining the nature of the financial ratios to be dealt with. There are five of them:

- *Profitability.* Businesses generally exist with the primary purpose of creating wealth for their owners. Profitability ratios provide an indication of the degree of success in achieving this purpose. They normally express the profit made in relation to other key figures in the financial statements, or to some business resource.
- *Efficiency.* Ratios may be used to measure the efficiency with which particular business resources, such as inventories or employees, have been used. These ratios are also referred to as *activity* ratios.
- *Liquidity.* It is vital to the survival of a business that there are sufficient liquid resources available to meet maturing obligations (that is, amounts owing that must be paid in the near future). Liquidity ratios examine the relationship between liquid resources and amounts due for payment in the near future.
- *Financial gearing.* This category of ratios is concerned with the relationship between the contribution to financing a business made by the owners and the contribution made by lenders. The relationship is important because it has an important effect on the level of risk associated with a business. Gearing ratios help to reveal the extent to which loan finance is employed and the consequent effect on the level of risk borne by a business.
- *Investment.* Ratios may be used by shareholders, who are not involved with managing the business, to assess the returns (such as profits and dividends) from their shares.

These five key aspects of financial health that ratios seek to examine are summarised in Figure 6.1.

Ratios can be used to examine each of the areas that we have discussed.

Figure 6.1 The key aspects of financial health

The analyst must be clear *who* the target users are and *why* they need the information. Different users of financial information are likely to have different information needs. This will, in turn, determine the ratios that they find useful. Shareholders, for example, are likely to be interested in their returns in relation to the level of risk associated with their investment. Profitability, investment and gearing ratios should, therefore, be of particular interest. Long-term lenders are likely to be concerned with the long-term viability of the business and, to assess this, profitability and gearing ratios should be of interest. Short-term lenders, such as suppliers of goods and services on credit, are likely to be interested in the ability of the business to repay the amounts owing in the short term.

Activity 6.1

Which of one the above category of ratios should be of most value for short-term lenders?

Liquidity ratios, which focus on the ability to meet maturing obligations, are likely to be of most value.

THE NEED FOR COMPARISON

Merely calculating a ratio will not tell us very much about the position or performance of a business. If, for example, a ratio revealed that a retail business was generating £100 in sales revenue per square metre of floor space, it would not be possible to deduce from this information alone whether this particular level of performance was good, bad or indifferent. It is only when we compare this ratio with some 'benchmark' that the information can be interpreted and evaluated.

Activity 6.2

Can you think of any benchmarks or bases that could be used to compare a ratio that you have calculated from the financial statements of your business for a particular period? (*Hint*: There are three main possibilities.)

You may have thought of the following bases:

- past periods for the same business;
- similar businesses for the same or past periods; and/or
- planned performance for the business.

We shall now take a closer look at these three in turn.

Past periods

By comparing the ratio that we have calculated with the same ratio, but for a previous period, it is possible to detect whether there has been an improvement or deterioration in performance. Indeed, as we shall see later in the chapter, it is often useful to track particular ratios over time (say, five or ten years) to see whether it is possible to detect trends. The comparison of ratios from different periods can create problems, however. In particular, there is always the possibility that trading conditions were quite different in the periods being compared. There is the further problem that, when comparing the performance of a single business over time, operating inefficiencies may not be clearly exposed. For example, the fact that sales revenue per employee has risen by 10 per cent over the previous period may at first sight appear to be satisfactory. This may not be the case, however, if similar businesses have shown an improvement of 50 per cent for the same period or had much better sales revenue per employee to start with. Finally, there is the problem that inflation may have distorted the figures on which the ratios are based. Inflation can lead to an overstatement of profit and an understatement of asset values, as will be discussed later in the chapter.

Similar businesses

In a competitive environment, a business must consider its performance in relation to that of other businesses operating in the same industry. Survival may well depend on its ability to achieve comparable levels of performance. A useful basis for comparing a particular ratio, therefore, is the ratio achieved by similar businesses during the same period. This basis is not, however, without its problems. Competitors may have different year ends and so trading conditions may not be identical. They may also have different accounting policies, which can have a significant effect on reported profits and asset values (for example, different methods of calculating depreciation or valuing inventories). Finally, it may be difficult to obtain the financial statements of competitor businesses. Sole proprietorships and partnerships, for example, are not obliged to make their financial statements available to the public. In the case of limited companies, there is a legal obligation to do so. However, a diversified business may not provide a breakdown of activities that is sufficiently detailed to enable comparisons to be made.

Planned performance

Ratios may be compared with targets that management developed before the start of the period under review. The comparison of actual performance with planned performance can be a useful way of assessing the level of achievement attained. Indeed, planned performance often provides the most valuable benchmark against which managers may assess their own business. However, planned performance must be based on realistic assumptions if it is to be worthwhile for comparison purposes.

Planned, or target, ratios may be prepared for each aspect of the business's activities. When developing these ratios, account will normally be taken of past performance and the performance of other businesses. This does not mean, however, that the business should seek to achieve either of these levels of performance. Neither of them may provide an appropriate target.

We should bear in mind that those outside the business do not normally have access to the business's plans. For such people, past performance and the performances of other, similar, businesses may provide the only practical benchmarks.

CALCULATING THE RATIOS

Probably the best way to explain financial ratios is through an example. Example 6.1 provides a set of financial statements from which we can calculate important ratios.

Example 6.1

The following financial statements relate to Alexis plc, which operates a wholesale carpet business:

Statements of financial position (balance sheets) as at 31 March

	2017 £m	2018 £m
ASSETS		
Non-current assets		
Property, plant and equipment (at cost less depreciation)		
Land and buildings	381	427
Fixtures and fittings	129	160
	510	587
Current assets		
Inventories	300	406
Trade receivables	240	273
Cash at bank	4	–
	544	679
Total assets	1,054	1,266
EQUITY AND LIABILITIES		
Equity		
£0.50 ordinary shares (Note 1)	300	300
Retained earnings	263	234
	563	534
Non-current liabilities		
Borrowings – 9% loan notes (secured)	200	300
Current liabilities		
Trade payables	261	354
Taxation	30	2
Short-term borrowings (all bank overdraft)	–	76
	291	432
Total equity and liabilities	1,054	1,266

Income statements for the year ended 31 March

	2017 £m	2018 £m
Revenue (Note 2)	2,240	2,681
Cost of sales (Note 3)	(1,745)	(2,272)
Gross profit	495	409
Operating expenses	(252)	(362)
Operating profit	243	47
Interest payable	(18)	(32)
Profit before taxation	225	15
Taxation	(60)	(4)
Profit for the year	165	11

Notes:

1. The market value of the shares of the business at the end of the reporting period was £2.50 for 2017 and £1.50 for 2018.
2. All sales and purchases are made on credit.
3. The cost of sales figure can be analysed as follows:

	2017 £m	2018 £m
Opening inventories	241	300
Purchases (Note 2)	1,804	2,378
	2,045	2,678
Closing inventories	(300)	(406)
Cost of sales	1,745	2,272

4. At 1 April 2016, the trade receivables stood at £223 million and the trade payables at £183 million.
5. A dividend of £40 million had been paid to the shareholders in respect of each of the years.
6. The business employed 13,995 staff at 31 March 2017 and 18,623 at 31 March 2018.
7. The business expanded its capacity during 2018 by setting up a new warehouse and distribution centre.
8. At 1 April 2016, the total of equity stood at £438 million and the total of equity and non-current liabilities stood at £638 million.

A BRIEF OVERVIEW

Before we start our detailed examination of the ratios for Alexis plc (in Example 6.1), it is helpful to take a quick look at what information is obvious from the financial statements. This will usually pick up some issues that ratios may not be able to identify. It may also highlight some points that could help us in our interpretation of the ratios. Starting at the top of the statement of financial position, the following points can be noted:

- *Expansion of non-current assets.* These have increased by about 15 per cent (from £510 million to £587 million). Note 7 mentions a new warehouse and distribution centre, which may account for much of the additional investment in non-current assets. We are not told when this new facility was established, but it could have been well into the year. If so, not much benefit would arise in terms of additional sales revenue or cost saving during 2018. Sales revenue, in fact, expanded by about 20 per cent (from £2,240 million to £2,681 million) – greater than the expansion in non-current assets.

- *Major expansion in the elements of working capital.* Inventories increased by about 35 per cent, trade receivables by about 14 per cent and trade payables by about 36 per cent between 2017 and 2018. These are major increases, particularly in inventories and payables (which are linked because the inventories are all bought on credit – see Note 2).
- *Reduction in the cash balance.* The cash balance fell from £4 million (in funds) to a £76 million overdraft, between 2017 and 2018. The bank may be putting the business under pressure to reverse this, which could create difficulties.
- *Apparent debt capacity.* Comparing the non-current assets with the long-term borrowings implies that the business may well be able to offer security on further borrowing. This is because potential lenders usually look at the value of assets that can be offered as security when assessing loan requests. Understandably, lenders seem particularly attracted to land and buildings as security. For example, at 31 March 2018, non-current assets had a carrying amount (the value at which they appeared in the statement of financial position) of £587 million, but long-term borrowing was only £300 million (though there was also an overdraft of £76 million). Carrying amounts are not often a reliable guide to current market values. Thus, land and buildings, which tend to increase in value during periods of inflation, may have market values that exceed their carrying amount.
- *Lower operating profit.* Though sales revenue expanded by 20 per cent between 2017 and 2018, both cost of sales and operating expenses rose by a greater percentage, leaving both gross profit and, particularly, operating profit massively reduced. The level of staffing, which increased by about 33 per cent (from 13,995 to 18,623 employees – see Note 6), may have greatly affected the operating expenses. (Without knowing when the additional employees were recruited during 2018, we cannot be sure of the effect on operating expenses.) Increasing staffing by 33 per cent must put an enormous strain on management, at least in the short term. It is not surprising, therefore, that 2018 was not successful for the business – not, at least, in profit terms.

Having had a quick look at what is fairly obvious, without calculating any financial ratios, we shall now go on to calculate and interpret those relating to profitability, efficiency, liquidity, gearing and investment.

PROFITABILITY

The following ratios may be used to evaluate the profitability of the business:

- return on ordinary shareholders' funds ratio;
- return on capital employed ratio;
- operating profit margin ratio; and
- gross profit margin ratio.

We shall now look at each of these in turn.

Return on ordinary shareholders' funds (ROSF)

The **return on ordinary shareholders' funds ratio** compares the amount of profit for the period available to owners, with their average investment in the business during that same period. The ratio (which is normally expressed in percentage terms) is as follows:

$$\text{ROSF} = \frac{\text{Profit for the year (less any preference dividend)}}{\text{Ordinary share capital + Reserves}} \times 100$$

The profit for the year (less any preference dividend) is used in calculating the ratio, because this figure represents the amount of profit that is attributable to the owners.

In the case of Alexis plc, the ratio for the year ended 31 March 2017 is:

$$\text{ROSF} = \frac{165}{(438 + 563)/2} \times 100 = 33.0\%$$

Note that, when calculating the ROSF, the average of the figures for ordinary shareholders' funds as at the beginning and at the end of the year has been used. This is because an average figure is normally more representative. The amount of shareholders' funds was not constant throughout the year, yet we want to compare it with the profit earned during the whole period. We know, from Note 8, that the amount of shareholders' funds at 1 April 2016 was £438 million. By a year later, however, it had risen to £563 million, according to the statement of financial position as at 31 March 2017.

The easiest approach to calculating the average amount of shareholders' funds is to take a simple average based on the opening and closing figures for the year. This is often the only information available, as is the case for us with Alexis plc. Averaging is normally appropriate for all ratios that use figures taken at a single point in time (such as shareholders' funds) where they are related to a figure covering a period (such as profit for the year).

Where the beginning-of-year figure is unavailable, it will be necessary to rely on just the year-end figure. This is not ideal but, when this approach is consistently applied, it can still produce useful ratios.

Activity 6.3

Calculate the ROSF for Alexis plc for the year to 31 March 2018.

The ratio for 2018 is:

$$\text{ROSF} = \frac{11}{(563 + 534)/2} \times 100 = 2.0\%$$

Broadly, businesses seek to generate as high a value as possible for this ratio. However, a high value should not be achieved by jeopardising future returns through, for example, taking on more risky activities. We can see that the 2018 ratio is poor by any standards;

a bank deposit account will normally yield a better return. Why did things go so badly wrong in 2018? As we look at other ratios, we should find some clues.

Return on capital employed (ROCE)

The **return on capital employed ratio** is a fundamental measure of business performance. This ratio expresses the relationship between the operating profit generated during a period and the average long-term capital invested in the business.

The ratio is expressed in percentage terms and is as follows:

$$\text{ROCE} = \frac{\text{Operating profit}}{\text{Share capital + Reserves + Non-current liabilities}} \times 100$$

Note, in this case, that the profit figure used is the operating profit (that is, the profit *before* interest and taxation), because the ratio attempts to measure the returns to all suppliers of long-term finance before any deductions for interest payable on borrowings, or payments of dividends to shareholders, are made.

For the year to 31 March 2017, the ratio for Alexis plc is:

$$\text{ROCE} = \frac{243}{(638 + 763)/2} \times 100 = 34.7\%$$

(The capital employed figure, which is the total equity plus non-current liabilities, at 1 April 2016 is given in Note 8.)

ROCE is considered by many to be a primary measure of profitability. It compares inputs (capital invested) with outputs (operating profit) so as to reveal the effectiveness with which funds have been deployed. Once again, an average figure for capital employed should be used where the information is available.

Activity 6.4

Calculate the ROCE for Alexis plc for the year to 31 March 2018.

The ratio for 2018 is:

$$\text{ROCE} = \frac{47}{(763 + 834)/2} \times 100 = 5.9\%$$

This ratio tells much the same story as ROSF; namely a poor performance, with the return on the assets being less than the rate that the business pays for most of its borrowed funds (that is, 9 per cent for the loan notes).

Real World 6.1 provides some indication of the levels of ROCE achieved by businesses in different European countries.

REAL WORLD 6.1

Comparing profitability

Average ROCE ratios for non-financial businesses in different European countries for the five-year period ending in 2016 are shown in Figure 6.2.

The chart reveals a steady improvement in average ROCE for businesses in three of the five different countries over the period. For Italy and France, there has also been an improvement but it has been less steady over time.

Figure 6.2 The average ROCE of companies in different European countries

Source: Eurostat database (2017) 'Gross return on capital employed, before taxes, of non-financial corporations', October, http://ec.europa.eu/eurostat/tgm/.

Operating profit margin

The **operating profit margin ratio** relates the operating profit for the period to the sales revenue. The ratio is expressed as follows:

$$\text{Operating profit margin} = \frac{\text{operating profit}}{\text{sales revenue}} \times 100$$

Operating profit (that is, profit before interest and taxation) is used in this ratio as it represents the profit from trading operations before interest payable is taken into account. It is normally the most appropriate measure of operational performance, when making comparisons. This is because differences arising from the way in which the business is financed will not influence the measure.

For the year ended 31 March 2017, Alexis plc's operating profit margin ratio is:

$$\text{Operating profit margin} = \frac{243}{2{,}240} \times 100 = 10.8\%$$

This ratio compares one output of the business (operating profit) with another output (sales revenue). It can vary considerably between types of business. Supermarkets, for example, tend to operate on low prices and, therefore, low operating profit margins. This is done in an attempt to stimulate sales and thereby increase the total amount of operating profit generated. Jewellers, on the other hand, tend to have high operating profit margins but have much lower levels of sales volume. Factors such as the degree of competition, the type of customer, the economic climate and industry characteristics (such as the level of risk) will influence the operating profit margin of a business. This point is picked up again later in the chapter.

Activity 6.5

Calculate the operating profit margin for Alexis plc for the year to 31 March 2018.

The ratio for 2018 is:

$$\text{Operating profit margin} = \frac{47}{2{,}681} \times 100 = 1.8\%$$

Once again, this indicates a very weak performance compared with that of 2017. In 2017 for every £1 of sales revenue an average of 10.8p (that is, 10.8 per cent) was left as operating profit, after paying the cost of the carpets sold and other expenses of operating the business. By 2018, however, this had fallen to only 1.8p for every £1. The reason for the poor ROSF and ROCE ratios seems partly, if not wholly, due to a high level of other expenses relative to sales revenue. The next ratio should provide us with a clue as to how the sharp decline in this ratio occurred.

Real World 6.2 sets out the target operating profit margins for some well-known car manufacturers.

REAL WORLD 6.2

Profit driven

- BMW has a target operating profit margin of between 8 and 10 per cent.
- Volvo has a target operating profit margin of 10 per cent over the business cycle.
- Nissan has a target operating profit margin of 8 per cent.
- Volkswagen has a target operating profit margin of 6 per cent.
- Daimler has a target profit margin of 9 per cent.
- Renault has set a target operating profit margin of 7 per cent by 2022.
- Ford has a long-term target of achieving an operating profit margin target in excess of 8 per cent.

> We can see that, with the exception of Volkswagen and Renault, target operating profit margins fall within the 8 to 10 per cent range.
>
> Sources: *Fortune* (2016) 'Here's why BMW's profit margins are falling', 4 November; BNN (2017) 'Volvo shares jump over new margin target', www.bnn.ca, 1 September; Greimel, H. (2016) 'Nissan backs off profit targets', *Autonews*, 31 July; McGee, P. (2016) 'VW margin target out of reach for now, admits finance chief', ft.com, 31 May; Daimler Annual report 2016, www.Daimler.com/investors, p. 84; Frost, L. and Guillaume, G. (2017) 'Renault pricing weakness overshadows record first half', europe.autonews.com, 28 July; and Stoll, J. (2017) 'Ford CEO says company could exceed 8 per cent profit margin', *Wall Street Journal*, www.wsj.com.

Gross profit margin

The **gross profit margin ratio** relates the gross profit of the business to the sales revenue generated for the same period. Gross profit represents the difference between sales revenue and the cost of sales. The ratio is therefore a measure of profitability in buying (or producing) and selling goods or services before any other expenses are taken into account. As cost of sales represents a major expense for many businesses, a change in this ratio can have a significant effect on the 'bottom line' (that is, the profit for the period). The gross profit margin ratio is calculated as follows:

$$\text{Gross profit margin} = \frac{\text{Gross profit}}{\text{Sales revenue}} \times 100$$

For the year to 31 March 2017, the ratio for Alexis plc is:

$$\text{Gross profit margin} = \frac{495}{2{,}240} \times 100 = 22.1\%$$

Activity 6.6

Calculate the gross profit margin for Alexis plc for the year to 31 March 2018.

The ratio for 2018 is:

$$\text{Gross profit margin} = \frac{409}{2{,}681} \times 100 = 15.3\%$$

The decline in this ratio means that gross profit was lower *relative* to sales revenue in 2018 than it had been in 2017. Bear in mind that:

Gross profit = Sales revenue − Cost of sales (or cost of goods sold)

This means that cost of sales was higher *relative* to sales revenue in 2018, than in 2017. This could mean that sales prices were lower and/or that the purchase price of carpets had increased. It is possible that both sales prices and purchase prices had reduced, but the former at a greater rate than the latter. Similarly, they may both have increased, but with sales prices having increased at a lesser rate than purchase prices.

Clearly, part of the decline in the operating profit margin ratio is linked to the dramatic decline in the gross profit margin ratio. Whereas, after paying for the carpets sold, for each

£1 of sales revenue, 22.1p was left to cover other operating expenses in 2017, this was only 15.3p in 2018.

Real World 6.3 sets out the gross profit margin and operating profit margin of four large UK food producers.

REAL WORLD 6.3

Food for thought

The gross profit margin and operating profit margin for four large food producers for 2017 are set out in Figure 6.3.

Profitability ratios (per cent) for 2017:

Company	Gross profit margin	Operating profit margin
Finsbury Food Group plc	31.12	4.32
Premier Foods plc	35.03	7.78
The Real Good Food Company plc	24.35	−5.38
Cranswick plc	12.76	6.27

The chart reveals significant variations in both the gross profit margin and operating profit margin between the four businesses.

Figure 6.3 Profitability ratios for 2017 for four food producers

Source: Chart constructed from information in https://markets.ft.com/data/equities/tearsheet/financials, *Financial Times* [accessed 4 November 2017].
© The Financial Times Limited 2017. All Rights Reserved.

The profitability ratios for Alexis plc over the two years can be set out as follows:

	2017 %	2018 %
ROSF	33.0	2.0
ROCE	34.7	5.9
Operating profit margin	10.8	1.8
Gross profit margin	22.1	15.3

Activity 6.7

What do you deduce from a comparison of the declines in the operating profit and gross profit margin ratios?

We can see that the difference in the operating profit margin was 9 per cent (that is, 10.8 per cent to 1.8 per cent), whereas that of the gross profit margin was only 6.8 per cent (that is, from 22.1 per cent to 15.3 per cent). This can only mean that operating expenses were greater, compared with sales revenue in 2018, than they had been in 2017. The decline in both ROSF and ROCE was caused partly, therefore, by the business incurring higher inventories' purchasing costs relative to sales revenue and partly through higher operating expenses compared with sales revenue. We need to compare each of these ratios with their planned levels, however, before we can usefully assess the business's success.

An investigation is needed to discover what caused the increases in both cost of sales and operating expenses, relative to sales revenue, from 2017 to 2018. This will involve checking on what has happened with sales and inventories prices over the period. It will also involve 'drilling down' on operating expenses by examining each of the individual areas of expense. To isolate the reason for the change, further ratios may be calculated such as staff expenses (wages and salaries) to sales revenue. As mentioned earlier, the increase in staffing may well have caused much of the increase in operating expenses.

Real World 6.4 discusses how some operating expenses are controlled by unusual means.

REAL WORLD 6.4

Having a fly in

McKinsey and Company, the international management consultancy, reports that one of its clients, an airline, saves on operating expenses in an unusual way. Some of the planes operated by the airline have seats that could go flat to make it easier for passengers to sleep on overnight flights. It was the policy of the airline to leave the cabin lights off as late in the morning as possible to avoid passengers demand for – and cost of – breakfast.

Source: Information contained in Dichter, A., Sorensen, A. and Saxon, S. (2017) 'Buying and flying: next generation airline procurement', McKinsey and Company, www.mckinsey.com, April.

EFFICIENCY

Efficiency ratios are used to try to assess how successfully the various resources of the business are managed. The following ratios consider some of the more important aspects of resource management:

- average inventories' turnover period ratio;
- average settlement period for trade receivables ratio;
- average settlement period for trade payables ratio;

- sales revenue to capital employed ratio; and
- sales revenue per employee ratio.

We shall now look at each of these in turn.

Average inventories' turnover period

Inventories often represent a significant investment for a business. For some types of business (for example, manufacturers and certain retailers), inventories may account for a substantial proportion of the total assets held. The **average inventories' turnover period ratio** measures the average period for which inventories are being held. The ratio is calculated as follows:

$$\text{Average inventories' turnover period} = \frac{\text{Average inventories held}}{\text{Cost of sales}} \times 365$$

The average inventories for the period can be calculated as a simple average of the opening and closing inventories levels for the year. In the case of a highly seasonal business, however, where inventories levels vary greatly over the year, a monthly average would be more appropriate. For external users, this information is not usually available however. This point about monthly averaging is equally relevant to any asset or claim that varies over the reporting period, including trade receivables and trade payables.

In the case of Alexis plc, the inventories' turnover period for the year ended 31 March 2017 is:

$$\text{Average inventories' turnover period} = \frac{(241 + 300)/2}{1{,}745} \times 365 = 56.6 \text{ days}$$

(The opening inventories figure was taken from Note 3 to the financial statements.)

This means that, on average, the inventories held are being 'turned over' every 56.6 days. So, a carpet bought by the business on a particular day would, on average, have been sold about eight weeks later. A business will normally prefer a short inventories' turnover period to a long one, because holding inventories has costs, such as the opportunity cost of the funds tied up. When judging the amount of inventories to carry, the business must consider such things as the likely demand, the possibility of supply shortages, the likelihood of price rises, the amount of storage space available and their perishability or susceptibility to obsolescence.

This ratio is sometimes expressed in terms of weeks or months rather than days: multiplying by 52 or 12, rather than 365, will achieve this.

Activity 6.8

Calculate the average inventories turnover period for Alexis plc for the year ended 31 March 2018.

The ratio for 2018 is:

$$\text{Average inventories turnover period} = \frac{(300 + 406)/2}{2{,}272} \times 365 = 56.7 \text{ days}$$

The inventories turnover period is virtually the same in both years.

Average settlement period for trade receivables

Selling on credit is the norm for most businesses, except for retailers. Trade receivables are a necessary evil. A business will naturally be concerned with the amount of funds tied up in trade receivables and try to keep this to a minimum. The speed of payment can have a significant effect on the business's cash flow. The **average settlement period for trade receivables ratio** calculates how long, on average, credit customers take to pay the amounts that they owe to the business. The ratio is as follows:

$$\text{Average settlement period for trade receivables} = \frac{\text{Average trade receivables}}{\text{Credit sales revenue}} \times 365$$

A business will normally prefer a shorter average settlement period to a longer one. Once again, funds are being tied up that may otherwise be used for more profitable purposes. While this ratio can be useful, we should bear in mind that it produces an *average* figure for the number of days for which debts are outstanding. This average may be badly distorted by, for example, a few large customers who are very slow or very fast payers.

Since all sales made by Alexis plc are on credit, the average settlement period for trade receivables for the year ended 31 March 2017 is:

$$\text{Average settlement period for trade receivables} = \frac{(223 + 240)/2}{2{,}240} \times 365 = 37.7 \text{ days}$$

(The opening trade receivables figure was taken from Note 4 to the financial statements.)

Activity 6.9

Calculate the average settlement period for Alexis plc's trade receivables for the year ended 31 March 2018.

The ratio for 2018 is:

$$\text{Average settlement period for trade receivables} = \frac{(240 + 273)/2}{2{,}681} \times 365 = 34.9 \text{ days}$$

On the face of it, this reduction in the settlement period is welcome. It means that less cash was tied up in trade receivables for each £1 of sales revenue in 2018 than in 2017. Only if the reduction were achieved at the expense of customer goodwill, or through high out-of-pocket cost, might it be unwelcome. It may have been accomplished, for example, by chasing customers too vigorously or by giving large discounts to customers for prompt payment.

Average settlement period for trade payables

The **average settlement period for trade payables ratio** measures how long, on average, the business takes to pay those who have supplied goods and services to it on credit. The ratio is calculated as follows:

$$\text{Average settlement period for trade payables} = \frac{\text{Average trade payables}}{\text{Credit purchases}} \times 365$$

This ratio provides an average figure, which, like the average settlement period for trade receivables ratio, can be distorted by the payment period for one or two large suppliers.

As trade payables provide a free source of finance for the business, it is not surprising that some businesses attempt to increase their average settlement period for trade payables. This can be taken too far, however, and can result in a loss of goodwill of suppliers.

For the year ended 31 March 2017, Alexis plc's average settlement period for trade payables is:

$$\text{Average settlement period for trade payables} = \frac{(183 + 261)/2}{1{,}804} \times 365 = 44.9 \text{ days}$$

(The opening trade payables figure was taken from Note 4 to the financial statements and the purchases figure from Note 3.)

Activity 6.10

Calculate the average settlement period for trade payables for Alexis plc for the year ended 31 March 2018.

The ratio for 2018 is:

$$\text{Average settlement period for trade payables} = \frac{(261 + 354)/2}{2{,}378} \times 365 = 47.2 \text{ days}$$

There was an increase, between 2017 and 2018, in the average length of time that elapsed between buying goods and services and paying for them. On the face of it, this is beneficial because the business is using free finance provided by suppliers. This may not be so, however, if it results in a loss of supplier goodwill and Alexis plc suffers adverse consequences.

Small businesses often suffer acute cash flow problems because large business customers refuse to pay within a reasonable period. This has led the UK government to introduce a Prompt Payment Code, which sets standards for the payment practices of large businesses. **Real World 6.5** describes how the Code is aimed at improving matters.

REAL WORLD 6.5

Better late than never – new rules for late payers

The Prompt Payment Code, which came into effect in April 2017, is the government's attempt to combat the problem of late payments from buyers to suppliers, a problem which forces 50,000 UK businesses a year to close, according to the Federation of Small Business. The new law aims to increase transparency and focus on a tough new reporting requirement on large British companies. They will be required to publish information about their payment practices and performance on a government approved web service twice per financial year. This means reporting detailed statistics around the time it takes the business to pay invoices, within the six-month reporting period, as well as the proportion of invoices which were paid late and the average time to pay any given invoice. In addition, the business must describe its payment terms, dispute mechanism and any supporting services it offers, such as e-invoicing or supply chain finance.

The government is hopeful that public pressure through the open nature of the report and pressure from companies, suppliers and other third parties comparing reports will push companies to reform their payment practices and reduce the number of invoices paid late. Once the data is public, companies which are shown to be poor payers risk quite a significant public and media backlash. In addition, suppliers will surely take this data into account when it comes to deciding which companies to work for and when negotiating contracts.

Source: Adapted extracts from GT News (2017) 'Are you ready for the Prompt Payment Code?', www.gtnews.com, 11 September.

Sales revenue to capital employed

The **sales revenue to capital employed ratio** (or net asset turnover ratio) examines how effectively the assets of the business are being used to generate sales revenue. It is calculated as follows:

$$\text{Sales revenue to capital employed ratio} = \frac{\text{Sales revenue}}{\text{Share capital + Reserves + Non-current liabilities}}$$

Generally speaking, a higher sales revenue to capital employed ratio is preferred to a lower one. A higher ratio normally suggests that assets are being used more productively in generating revenue. However, a very high ratio may indicate that the business is **overtrading** on its assets. In other words, it has insufficient assets to sustain the level of sales revenue achieved.

When comparing the sales revenue to capital employed ratio for different businesses, factors such as the age and condition of assets held, the valuation bases for assets and whether assets are leased or owned outright can complicate interpretation.

A variation of this formula is to use the total assets less current liabilities (which is equal to long-term capital employed) in the denominator (lower part of the fraction). The same result is obtained.

For the year ended 31 March 2017, this ratio for Alexis plc is:

$$\text{Sales revenue to capital employed} = \frac{2{,}240}{(638 + 763)/2} = 3.20 \text{ times}$$

Activity 6.11

Calculate the sales revenue to capital employed ratio for Alexis plc for the year ended 31 March 2018.

The ratio for 2018 is:

$$\text{Sales revenue to capital employed} = \frac{2{,}681}{(763 + 834)/2} = 3.36 \text{ times}$$

This seems to be an improvement, since, in 2018, more sales revenue was being generated for each £1 of capital employed (£3.36) than was the case in 2017 (£3.20). Provided that overtrading is not an issue, and that the additional sales are generating an acceptable profit, this is to be welcomed.

Sales revenue per employee

The **sales revenue per employee ratio** relates sales revenue generated during a reporting period to a particular business resource – labour. It provides a measure of the productivity of the workforce. The ratio is:

$$\text{Sales revenue per employee} = \frac{\text{Sales revenue}}{\text{Number of employees}}$$

Generally, businesses would prefer a high value for this ratio, implying that they are deploying their staff efficiently.

For the year ended 31 March 2017, the ratio for Alexis plc is:

$$\text{Sales revenue per employee} = \frac{£2{,}240m}{13{,}995} = £160{,}057$$

Activity 6.12

Calculate the sales revenue per employee for Alexis plc for the year ended 31 March 2018.

The ratio for 2018 is:

$$\text{Sales revenue per employee} = \frac{£2{,}681m}{18{,}623} = £143{,}962$$

This represents a fairly significant decline, which merits further investigation. As already mentioned, the number of employees increased quite notably (by about 33 per cent) during 2018. We need to know why this had not generated the additional sales revenue required to maintain the ratio at its 2017 level. It may be because the extra employees were not appointed until late in the year ended 31 March 2018.

The efficiency, or activity, ratios may be summarised as follows:

	2017	2018
Average inventories turnover period	56.6 days	56.7 days
Average settlement period for trade receivables	37.7 days	34.9 days
Average settlement period for trade payables	44.9 days	47.2 days
Sales revenue to capital employed (net asset turnover)	3.20 times	3.36 times
Sales revenue per employee	£160,057	£143,962

Activity 6.13

What do you deduce from a comparison of the efficiency ratios over the two years?

Maintaining the inventories turnover period at the 2017 level may be reasonable, although this will depend on the planned inventories turnover period. In formulating the planned level, the inventories turnover period for other carpet retailers, particularly the market leaders, may have been used. On the face of things, a shorter trade receivables settlement period and a longer trade payables settlement period are both desirable. These changes may, however, have been achieved at the cost of a loss of goodwill among both customers and suppliers.

The increased sales revenue to capital employed ratio seems beneficial, provided the business can manage this increase. The decline in the sales revenue per employee ratio is unwelcome but is probably related to the dramatic increase in the number of employees. As with the inventories turnover period, these other ratios need to be compared with planned, or target, ratios.

RELATIONSHIP BETWEEN PROFITABILITY AND EFFICIENCY

In our earlier discussions concerning profitability ratios, we saw that return on capital employed (ROCE) is regarded as a key ratio by many businesses. The ratio is:

$$\text{ROCE} = \frac{\text{Operating profit}}{\text{Long-term capital employed}} \times 100$$

where long-term capital comprises share capital plus reserves plus long-term borrowings. This ratio can be broken down into two elements, as shown in Figure 6.4. The first ratio is the operating profit margin ratio and the second is the sales revenue to capital employed (net asset turnover) ratio, both of which we discussed earlier.

```
Operating profit
─────────────
Sales revenue
```
multiplied by

```
Sales revenue
────────────────────────
Long-term capital employed
```
equals

Return on capital employed

The ROCE ratio can be divided into two elements: operating profit to sales revenue and sales revenue to capital employed. By analysing ROCE in this way, we can see the influence of both profitability and efficiency on this important ratio.

Figure 6.4 The main elements of the ROCE ratio

By breaking down the ROCE ratio in this manner, we highlight the fact that the overall return on funds employed within the business will be determined both by the profitability of sales and by efficiency in the use of capital.

Example 6.2

Consider the following information, for last year, concerning two different businesses operating in the same industry:

	Antler plc £m	Baker plc £m
Operating profit	20	15
Average long-term capital employed	100	75
Sales revenue	200	300

The ROCE for each business is identical (20%). However, the manner in which that return was achieved by each business is quite different. In the case of Antler plc, the operating profit margin is 10 per cent and the sales revenue to capital employed ratio is 2 times (so, ROCE = 10% × 2 = 20%). In the case of Baker plc, the operating profit margin is 5 per cent and the sales revenue to capital employed ratio is 4 times (and so, ROCE = 5% × 4 = 20%).

Example 6.2 demonstrates that a relatively high sales revenue to capital employed ratio can compensate for a relatively low operating profit margin. Similarly, a relatively low sales revenue to capital employed ratio can be overcome by a relatively high operating profit margin. In many areas of retail and distribution (for example, supermarkets and delivery services), operating profit margins are quite low, but the ROCE can be high, provided assets are used productively (that is, low margin, high sales revenue to capital employed).

> **Activity 6.14**
>
> Show how the ROCE ratio for Alexis plc can be analysed into the two elements for each of the years 2017 and 2018. What conclusions can you draw from your figures?
>
> | | ROCE | = | Operating profit margin | × | Sales revenue to capital employed |
> |---|---|---|---|---|---|
> | 2017 | 34.7% | | 10.8% | | 3.20 |
> | 2018 | 5.9% | | 1.8% | | 3.36 |
>
> As we can see, the relationship between the three ratios holds for Alexis plc for both years. The small apparent differences arise because the three ratios are stated here only to one or two decimal places which led to minor rounding errors.
>
> In 2018, the business was more effective at generating sales revenue (sales revenue to capital employed ratio increased). However, it fell well below the level needed to compensate for the sharp decline in the profitability of sales (operating profit margin). As a result, the 2018 ROCE was well below the 2017 value.

LIQUIDITY

Liquidity ratios are concerned with the ability of the business to meet its short-term financial obligations. The following ratios are widely used:

- current ratio; and
- acid test ratio.

These ratios will now be considered.

Current ratio

The **current ratio** compares the 'liquid' assets (that is, cash and those assets soon to be turned into cash) of the business with the current liabilities. The ratio is calculated as follows:

$$\text{Current ratio} = \frac{\text{Current assets}}{\text{Current liabilities}}$$

Some appear to believe that there is an 'ideal' current ratio (usually 2 times or 2:1) for all businesses. However, this is not the case. Different types of business require different current ratios. A manufacturing business, for example, will normally have a relatively high current ratio because it will hold inventories of finished goods, raw materials and work-in-progress. It will also sell goods on credit, thereby giving rise to trade receivables.

A supermarket chain, on the other hand, will have a relatively low ratio, as it will hold only fast-moving inventories of finished goods and its sales will be for cash rather than on credit.

The higher the current ratio, the more liquid the business is considered to be. As liquidity is vital to the survival of a business, a higher current ratio is often preferable to a lower one. A very high ratio, however, may indicate that excessive amounts are tied up in cash or other liquid assets that are not being used productively.

As at 31 March 2017, the current ratio of Alexis plc is:

$$\text{Current ratio} = \frac{544}{291} = 1.9 \text{ times (or 1.9:1)}$$

Activity 6.15

Calculate the current ratio for Alexis plc as at 31 March 2018.

The ratio as at 31 March 2018 is:

$$\text{Current ratio} = \frac{679}{432} = 1.6 \text{ times (or 1.6:1)}$$

Although this is a decline from 2017 to 2018, it may not be a matter for concern. The next ratio may provide a clue as to whether there seems to be a problem.

Acid test ratio

The **acid test ratio** is very similar to the current ratio, but it represents a more stringent test of liquidity. For many businesses, inventories cannot be converted into cash quickly. (Note that, in the case of Alexis plc, the inventories turnover period was about 57 days in both years (see page 217)). With a business like Alex plc, it is usually better to exclude this particular asset from this measure of liquidity. For a business that turns its inventories over very quickly, such as a supermarket, it will probably be reasonable to include inventories in the calculation.

The acid test ratio is calculated as follows:

$$\text{Acid test ratio} = \frac{\text{Current assets (excluding inventories)}}{\text{Current liabilities}}$$

The acid test ratio for Alexis plc as at 31 March 2017 is:

$$\text{Current ratio} = \frac{679}{432} = 1.6 \text{ times (or 1.6:1)}$$

We can see that the 'liquid' current assets do not quite cover the current liabilities, so the business may be experiencing some liquidity problems.

The minimum level for this ratio is often stated as 1.0 times (or 1:1; that is, current assets (excluding inventories) equal to current liabilities). However, many highly successful businesses, have an acid test ratio below 1.0 times without suffering liquidity problems.

Activity 6.16

Calculate the acid test ratio for Alexis plc as at 31 March 2018.

The ratio as at 31 March 2018 is:

$$\text{Acid test ratio} = \frac{679 - 406}{432} = 0.6 \text{ times}$$

The 2018 ratio is significantly below that for 2017. The 2018 level may well be a cause for concern. The rapid decline in this ratio should lead to steps being taken to understand why this has occurred and, perhaps, action to stop it falling further.

The liquidity ratios for the two-year period may be summarised as follows:

	2017	2018
Current ratio	1.9	1.6
Acid test ratio	0.8	0.6

Activity 6.17

What do you deduce from these liquidity ratios?

There has clearly been a decline in liquidity from 2017 to 2018. This is indicated by both ratios. The decline in the acid-test ratio is particularly worrying as it suggests that the business may struggle to meet its short-term obligations. The apparent liquidity problem may, however, be planned, short term and linked to the increase in non-current assets and the number of employees. When the benefits of the expansion come on stream, liquidity may improve. On the other hand, short-term lenders and suppliers may become anxious by the decline in liquidity. This could lead them to press for payment, which is likely to cause further problems.

Real World 6.6 reveals the liquidity ratios for four leading UK supermarkets.

REAL WORLD 6.6

Checking out liquidity

Figure 6.5 shows the current ratio and acid-test ratio for the financial year ending in 2017 for four leading supermarkets.

> [Chart: Bar chart showing liquidity ratios for four supermarkets]
>
> Liquidity ratios:
> - Tesco: Current ratio 0.79, Acid-test ratio 0.67
> - J Sainsbury: Current ratio 0.74, Acid-test ratio 0.53
> - W Morrison: Current ratio 0.48, Acid-test ratio 0.28
> - Ocado: Current ratio 0.46, Acid-test ratio 0.36
>
> We can see that the liquidity ratios are low for all of the four businesses. However, there is a clear difference between the liquidity ratios of Tesco plc and J. Sainsbury plc, on the one hand, and those of W. Morrison plc and Ocado Group plc, on the other. Ocado Group plc differs from the other three supermarkets insofar that it operates exclusively online.

Figure 6.5 Liquidity ratios for four supermarkets

Source: Chart constructed from information in https://markets.ft.com/data/equities/tearsheet/financials, *Financial Times* [accessed 3 November 2017].
© The Financial Times Limited 2017. All Rights Reserved.

FINANCIAL GEARING

Financial gearing occurs when a business is financed, at least in part, by borrowing rather than by owners' equity. The extent to which a business is geared (that is, financed from borrowing) is an important factor in assessing risk. Borrowing involves taking on a commitment to pay interest charges and to make capital repayments. Where the borrowing is heavy, this can be a significant financial burden; it can increase the risk of the business becoming insolvent. Nevertheless, most businesses are geared to some extent. (Costain Group plc, the builders and construction business, is a rare example of a UK business with little or no borrowings.)

Given the risks involved, we may wonder why a business would want to take on gearing. One reason is that the owners have insufficient funds, so the only way to finance the business adequately is to borrow. Another reason is that gearing can be used to increase the returns to owners. This is possible provided the returns generated from borrowed funds exceed the cost of paying interest. Example 6.3 illustrates this point.

Example 6.3

The long-term capital structures of two new businesses, Lee Ltd and Nova Ltd, are as follows:

	Lee Ltd £	Nova Ltd £
£1 ordinary shares	100,000	200,000
10% loan notes	200,000	100,000
	300,000	300,000

In their first year of operations, each make an operating profit (that is, profit before interest and taxation) of £50,000. The tax rate is 20 per cent of the profit before taxation (but after interest).

Lee Ltd would probably be considered relatively highly geared, as it has a high proportion of borrowed funds in its long-term capital structure. Nova Ltd is much lower geared. The profit available to the shareholders of each business in the first year of operations will be:

	Lee Ltd £	Nova Ltd £
Operating profit	50,000	50,000
Interest payable	(20,000)	(10,000)
Profit before taxation	30,000	40,000
Taxation (20%)	(6,000)	(8,000)
Profit for the year (available to ordinary shareholders)	24,000	32,000

The return on ordinary shareholders' funds (ROSF) for each business will be:

Lee Ltd
$$\frac{24,000}{100,000} \times 100 = 24\%$$

Nova Ltd
$$\frac{32,000}{200,000} \times 100 = 16\%$$

We can see that Lee Ltd, the more highly geared business, has generated a better ROSF than Nova Ltd. This is despite the fact that the ROCE (return on capital employed) is identical for both businesses (that is, (£50,000/£300,000) × 100 = 16.7%).

Note that at the £50,000 level of operating profit, the shareholders of both businesses have generated higher returns as a result of gearing. If both businesses were totally financed by equity, the profit for the year (that is, after taxation) would be £40,000 (that is, £50,000 less 20 per cent taxation), giving an ROSF of 13.3 per cent (that is, £40,000/£300,000).

An effect of gearing is that returns to shareholders become more sensitive to changes in operating profits. For a highly geared business, a change in operating profits will lead to a proportionately greater change in the ROSF ratio.

> **Activity 6.18**
>
> Assume that the operating profit is £70,000 rather than £50,000. What would be the effect of this on ROSF?
>
> The revised profit available to the shareholders of each business in the first year of operations will be:
>
> | | Lee Ltd £ | Nova Ltd £ |
> |---|---|---|
> | Operating profit | 70,000 | 70,000 |
> | Interest payable | (20,000) | (10,000) |
> | Profit before taxation | 50,000 | 60,000 |
> | Taxation (20%) | (10,000) | (12,000) |
> | Profit for the year (available to ordinary shareholders) | 40,000 | 48,000 |
>
> The ROSF for each business will now be:
>
> Lee Ltd
> $$\frac{40,000}{100,000} \times 100 = 40\%$$
>
> Nova Ltd
> $$\frac{48,000}{200,000} \times 100 = 24\%$$

We can see that for Lee Ltd, the higher-geared business, the returns to shareholders have increased by two thirds (from 24 per cent to 40 per cent), whereas for the lower-geared business, Nova Ltd, the benefits of gearing are less pronounced, increasing by only half (from 16 per cent to 24 per cent). The effect of gearing can, of course, work in both directions. So, for a highly geared business, a small decline in operating profit will bring about a much greater decline in the returns to shareholders.

The reason that gearing seems to be beneficial to shareholders is that interest rates for borrowings are low by comparison with the returns that the typical business can earn. On top of this, interest expenses are tax deductible, in the way shown in Example 6.3 and Activity 6.18. This makes the effective cost of borrowing quite cheap. It is debatable, however, whether low interest rates really are beneficial to shareholders. Since borrowing increases the risk to shareholders, there is a hidden cost involved. Many argue that this cost is precisely compensated by the higher returns, giving no net benefit to shareholders. In other words, the apparent benefits of higher returns from gearing are illusory. What are not illusory, however, are the benefits to shareholders from the tax deductibility of interest payments.

> **Activity 6.19**
>
> **If shareholders gain from the tax-deductibility of interest on borrowings, who loses?**
>
> The losers are the tax authority (ultimately the government) and, therefore, other taxpayers.

The effect of gearing is like that of two intermeshing cogwheels of unequal size (see Figure 6.6). The movement in the larger cog (operating profit) causes a more than proportionate movement in the smaller cog (returns to ordinary shareholders).

The two wheels are linked by the cogs, so that a small circular movement in the large wheel (operating profit) leads to a relatively large circular movement in the small wheel (returns to ordinary shareholders).

Figure 6.6 The effect of financial gearing

Two ratios are widely used to assess gearing:

- gearing ratio; and
- interest cover ratio.

We shall now consider each of these in turn.

Gearing ratio

The **gearing ratio** measures the contribution of long-term lenders to the long-term capital structure of a business:

$$\text{Gearing ratio} = \frac{\text{Long-term (non-current) liabilities}}{\text{Share capital + Reserves + Long-term (non-current) liabilities}} \times 100$$

The gearing ratio for Alexis plc, as at 31 March 2017, is:

$$\text{Gearing ratio} = \frac{200}{(563 + 200)} \times 100 = 26.2\%$$

This is a level of gearing that would not normally be considered to be very high.

Activity 6.20

Calculate the gearing ratio of Alexis plc as at 31 March 2018.

The ratio as at 31 March 2018 is:

$$\text{Gearing ratio} = \frac{300}{(534 + 300)} \times 100 = 36.0\%$$

This is a substantial increase in the level of gearing over the year.

Interest cover ratio

The **interest cover ratio** measures the amount of operating profit available to cover interest payable. The ratio may be calculated as follows:

$$\text{Interest cover ratio} = \frac{\text{Operating profit}}{\text{Interest payable}}$$

The ratio for Alexis plc for the year ended 31 March 2017 is:

$$\text{Interest cover ratio} = \frac{243}{18} = 13.5 \text{ times}$$

This ratio shows that the level of operating profit is much higher than the level of interest payable. This means that a large fall in operating profit could occur before operating profit levels failed to cover interest payable. The lower the level of operating profit coverage, the greater the risk to lenders that interest payments will not be met. There will also be a greater risk to the shareholders that the lenders will take action against the business to recover the interest due.

Activity 6.21

Calculate the interest cover ratio of Alexis plc for the year ended 31 March 2018.

The ratio for the year ended 31 March 2018 is:

$$\text{Interest cover ratio} = \frac{47}{32} = 1.5 \text{ times}$$

Alexis plc's gearing ratios are:

	2017	2018
Gearing ratio	26.2%	36.0%
Interest cover ratio	13.5 times	1.5 times

Activity 6.22

What do you deduce from a comparison of Alexis plc's gearing ratios over the two years?

The gearing ratio has changed significantly. This is mainly due to the substantial increase in the contribution of long-term lenders to financing the business. The gearing ratio at 31 March 2018 would not be considered very high for a business that is trading successfully. It is the low profitability that is the problem. The interest cover ratio has fallen dramatically from 13.5 times in 2017 to 1.5 times in 2018. This was partly caused by the increase in borrowings in 2018, but mainly caused by the dramatic fall in profitability in that year. The situation in 2018 looks hazardous. Only a small decline in future operating profits would result in an inability to cover interest payments.

Without knowledge of the planned ratios, it is not possible to reach a valid conclusion on Alexis plc's gearing.

INVESTMENT RATIOS

There are various ratios available that are designed to help shareholders assess the returns on their investment. The following are widely used:

- dividend payout ratio;
- dividend yield ratio;
- earnings per share; and
- price/earnings ratio.

Dividend payout ratio

The **dividend payout ratio** measures the proportion of earnings that is paid out to shareholders in the form of dividends. The ratio is calculated as follows:

$$\text{Dividend payout ratio} = \frac{\text{Dividends announced for the year}}{\text{Earnings for the year available for dividends}} \times 100$$

In the case of ordinary shares, the earnings available for dividend will normally be the profit for the year (that is, the profit after taxation) less any preference dividends relating to the year. This ratio is normally expressed as a percentage.

The dividend payout ratio for Alexis plc for the year ended 31 March 2017 is:

$$\text{Dividend payout ratio} = \frac{40}{165} \times 100 = 24.2\%$$

Activity 6.23

Calculate the dividend payout ratio of Alexis plc for the year ended 31 March 2018.

The ratio for 2018 is:

$$\text{Dividend payout ratio} = \frac{40}{11} \times 100 = 363.6\%$$

This would normally be considered to be a very alarming increase in the ratio over the two years. Paying a dividend of £40 million in 2018 seems very imprudent.

The information provided by this ratio is often expressed slightly differently as the **dividend cover ratio**. Here the calculation is:

$$\text{Dividend cover ratio} = \frac{\text{Earnings for the year available for dividend}}{\text{Dividends announced for the year}}$$

For 2017, the ratio for Alexis plc would be 165/40 = 4.1 times. That is to say, the earnings available for dividend cover the actual dividend paid by just over four times. For 2018, the ratio is 11/40 = 0.3 times.

Dividend yield ratio

The **dividend yield ratio** relates the cash return from a share to its current market value. This can help investors to assess the cash return on their investment in the business. The ratio, expressed as a percentage, is:

$$\text{Dividend yield} = \frac{\text{Dividend per share}}{\text{Market value per share}} \times 100$$

The dividend yield for Alexis plc for the year ended 31 March 2017, therefore, is:

$$\text{Dividend yield} = \frac{0.067^*}{2.50} \times 100 = 2.7\%$$

The shares' market value is given in Note 1 to Example 6.1 (pages 207–208).

* Dividend proposed/number of shares = 40/(300 × 2) = £0.067 dividend per share (the 300 is multiplied by 2 because they are £0.50 shares).

Activity 6.24

Calculate the dividend yield for Alexis plc for the year ended 31 March 2018.

The ratio for 2018 is:

$$\text{Dividend yield} = \frac{0.067^*}{1.5} = 100 = 4.5\%$$

*40/(300 × 2) = £0.067.

Earnings per share

The **earnings per share (EPS)** ratio relates the earnings generated by the business, and available to shareholders, during a period, to the number of shares in issue. For equity (ordinary) shareholders, the amount available will be represented by the profit for the year (profit after taxation) less any preference dividend, where applicable. The ratio for equity shareholders is calculated as follows:

$$\text{Earnings per share} = \frac{\text{Earnings available to ordinary shareholders}}{\text{Number of ordinary shares in issue}}$$

In the case of Alexis plc, the earnings per share for the year ended 31 March 2017 is:

$$\text{EPS} = \frac{£165}{600m} = 27.5p$$

Many investment analysts regard the EPS ratio as a fundamental measure of share performance. The trend in earnings per share over time is used to help assess the investment potential of a business's shares. Although it is possible to make total profit increase through ordinary shareholders investing more in the business, by the business issuing more shares for cash, this will not necessarily lead to an increase in the profitability *per share*.

Real World 6.7 points out the danger of placing too much emphasis on this ratio. The equity fund manager Terry Smith argues that, had more attention been paid to ROCE rather than EPS, investors would have spotted that all was not well with Tesco plc, the supermarket giant. He also takes to task Warren Buffett, the legendary investor, for ignoring his own advice and investing heavily in the business.

REAL WORLD 6.7

A trolley load of problems

In his 1979 letter to shareholders, Mr Buffett stated: 'The primary test of managerial economic performance is the achievement of a high earnings rate on equity capital employed (without undue gearing, accounting gimmickry, etc.) and not the achievement of consistent gains in earnings per share.'

This makes it all the more surprising to me that both Mr Buffett and the many acolytes who have seemingly followed him to the gates of hell in Tesco, ignored this chart:

Figure 6.7 Tesco: the Leahy years

This is not the first such chart that I have come across in which a company reports steadily rising earnings per share (EPS), on which most analysts and 'investors' focus. For them, the rise in EPS seems to have a mesmeric effect like Kaa the snake in *The Jungle Book*. But they ignore the point that more capital is being employed to generate those earnings at ever lower returns. Add in the fact that Tesco has changed its definition of return on capital employed (ROCE) eight times during those years, and there's more than enough material to send investors running for cover – even those who have less aversion than I do to retailers.

Yet much of the commentary about what has gone wrong at Tesco focuses on Philip Clarke, who took over as chief executive from Sir Terry Leahy in 2011, as if everything was going swimmingly until then. Looking at the ROCE line in the chart it is clear that this was not the case.

Moreover, one thing to bear in mind is that if Tesco's ROCE during the Leahy years fell from a very good 19 per cent to a less than adequate 10 per cent, this is an average of returns on capital employed, which includes both capital invested years ago and more recent commitments. To drag the average ROCE down so dramatically it is likely that returns on new investments in those years were not just inadequate, but in some cases negative – as the ill-starred US expansion proved to be.

Even if return on capital employed does not have the same importance for you as it does for me, or Mr Buffett (at least in 1979), consider this: in 14 of the past 18 years (taking us back to 1997 when Sir Terry became chief executive) Tesco's free cash flow less its dividend (with free cash defined as operating cash flow less gross capital expenditure) was a negative number. In plain English, Tesco was not generating enough cash both to invest and to pay its dividend. In half of those 14 years, the proceeds of fixed asset disposals took the numbers back into the black, but that is not exactly a sustainable source of financing.

So guess what they did instead? Yes, they borrowed it. Tesco's gross debt, which was £894 million when Sir Terry took over, peaked at nearly £15.9 billion in 2009.

The company spent much of its free cash on fixed-asset investment and raised debt to help pay the dividend. This is neither healthy nor sustainable, as investors in Tesco have now come to realise.

The concept that this might not be sustainable hardly requires much thought. Neither does charting the ROCE versus the growth in EPS. Yet it is evident that many investors, including it seems Mr Buffett (who has been trimming his Tesco stake in recent years) either didn't do this or ignored the results if they did. It makes me wonder what else they are ignoring.

Source: Smith, T. (2014) 'How investors ignored the warning signs at Tesco', *Financial Times,* 5 September.
© The Financial Times Limited 2014. All Rights Reserved.

It is not usually very helpful to compare the EPS of one business with that of another. Differences in financing arrangements (for example, in the nominal value of shares issued) can make any such comparison meaningless. However, it can be helpful to monitor the changes that occur in this ratio for a particular business over time. As we saw with Tesco's EPS history, the ratio can be misleading, however.

Activity 6.25

Calculate the earnings per share of Alexis plc for the year ended 31 March 2018.

The ratio for 2018 is:

$$\text{EPS} = \frac{£11m}{600m} = 1.8p$$

Price/earnings (P/E) ratio

The **price/earnings ratio** relates the market value of a share to the earnings per share. This ratio can be calculated as follows:

$$\text{P/E ratio} = \frac{\text{Market value per share}}{\text{Earnings per share}}$$

The P/E ratio for Alexis plc as at 31 March 2017 is:

$$\text{P/E ratio} = \frac{£2.50}{27.5p^*} = 9.1 \text{ times}$$

* The EPS figure (27.5p) was calculated on page 234.

This ratio indicates that the market value of the share is 9.1 times higher than its current level of earnings. It is a measure of market confidence in the future of a business. The higher the P/E ratio, the greater the confidence in the future earning power of the business and, consequently, the more investors are prepared to pay in relation to that current earning power.

Activity 6.26

Calculate the P/E ratio of Alexis plc as at 31 March 2018.

The ratio for 2018 is:

$$\text{P/E ratio} = \frac{£1.50}{1.8p} = 83.3 \text{ times}$$

As P/E ratios provide a useful guide to market confidence about the future, they can be helpful when comparing different businesses. However, differences in accounting policies between businesses can lead to different profit and earnings per share figures. This can distort comparisons.

The investment ratios for Alexis plc over the two-year period are as follows:

	2017	2018
Dividend payout ratio	24.2%	363.6%
Dividend yield ratio	2.7%	4.5%
Earnings per share	27.5p	1.8p
P/E ratio	9.1 times	83.3 times

Activity 6.27

What do you deduce from the investment ratios set out above? Can you offer an explanation why the share price has not fallen as much as it might have done, bearing in mind the much poorer trading performance in 2018?

Although the EPS has fallen dramatically, and the dividend payment for 2018 seems very imprudent, the share price has held up reasonably well (fallen from £2.50 to £1.50). Moreover, the dividend yield and P/E ratios have improved in 2018. This is an anomaly of these two ratios, which stems from using a forward-looking value (the share price) in conjunction with historic data (dividends and earnings). Share prices are based on investors' assessments of the business's future. It seems that the 'market' was less happy with Alexis plc at the end of 2018 than at the end of 2017. This is evidenced by the fact that the share price had fallen by £1 a share. The decline in share price, however, was less dramatic than the decline in profit for the year. This suggests that investors believe the business will perform better in the future. Perhaps they feel confident that the large increase in assets and employee numbers occurring in 2018 will yield future benefits; benefits that the business was not able to generate in 2018.

Real World 6.8 provides information about the share performance of a selection of large, well-known UK businesses. This type of information is provided on a daily basis by several newspapers, notably the *Financial Times*.

REAL WORLD 6.8

Market statistics for some well-known businesses

The following data were extracted from the *Financial Times* of 23 November 2017, relating to the previous day's trading of the shares of some well-known businesses on the London Stock Exchange:

Share	Price (pence)	Change (pence)	52-week high	52-week low	Yield %	P/E	Volume (000s)
Marks and Spencer	298.30	−1.60	397.80	296.70	6.27	26.17	8,518.3
HSBC	738.80	+9.20	772.00	518.17	5.12	35.40	31,179.5
National Express	361.2	+6.20	382.67	332.40	3.40	15.70	646.3
Tate and Lyle	692.00	+8.00	796.50	622.00	4.05	12.98	2,943.1
Unilever	4,188.50	−39.00	4,557.50	3,050.50	2.78	23.50	2,163.1
TUI Travel	1,329.00	−6.00	1,374.00	913.76	4.23	16.51	2,058.1

Price	Mid-market price in pence (that is, the price midway between buying and selling price) of the shares at the end of trading on 22 November 2017.
Change	Gain or loss in the mid-market price during 22 November 2017.
High/low	Highest and lowest prices reached by the share during the 52 weeks ended on 22 November 2017.
Yield	Dividend yield, based on the most recent year's dividend and the share price at the end of 22 November 2017.
P/E	Price/earnings ratio, based on the most recent year's (after-tax) profit for the year and the share price at the end of 22 November 2017.
Volume	The number of shares (in thousands) that were bought/sold on 22 November 2017.

So, for example, for the retail business Marks and Spencer plc:

- the shares had a mid-market price of 298.30 pence each at the close of Stock Exchange trading on 22 November 2017;
- the shares had fallen in price by 1.60 pence during trading on 22 November 2017;
- the shares had highest and lowest prices during the previous 52 weeks of 397.80 pence and 296.70 pence, respectively;
- the shares had a dividend yield, based on the 22 November 2017 closing price (and the dividend for the most recent year) of 6.27 per cent;
- the shares had a P/E ratio, based on the 22 November 2017 closing price (and the after-taxation earnings per share for the most recent year) of 26.17;
- during trading on 22 November 2017, 8,518,300 of the business's shares changed hands between buyers and sellers.

FT Source: *Financial Times*, 23 November 2017, p. 35.
© The Financial Times Limited 2017. All Rights Reserved.

Real World 6.9 shows how investment ratios can vary between different industry sectors.

REAL WORLD 6.9

Yielding dividends

Investment ratios can vary significantly between businesses and between industries. To give some indication of the range of variations that occur, the average dividend yield ratios and average P/E ratios for listed businesses in 12 different industries are shown in Figures 6.8 and 6.9, respectively.

These dividend yield ratios are calculated from the current market value of the shares and the most recent year's dividend paid.

Figure 6.8 Average dividend yield ratios for businesses in a range of industries

Some industries pay out lower dividends than others, leading to lower dividend yield ratios. The average for all Stock Exchange listed businesses was 3.60 per cent (as is shown in Figure 6.8), but there is a wide variation with Food Producers at 1.70 per cent and Electricity at 6.30 per cent.

Some types of businesses invest heavily in developing new products, hence their tendency to pay low dividends compared with their share prices. Some of the inter-industry differences in the dividend yield ratio can be explained by the way the ratio is calculated. Share prices at any given moment reflect investors' expectations of future economic prospects; dividends are actual past events. A business may have recently paid a dividend that, based on the investors' assessment of its future economic prospects, is considered high (a high dividend yield).

The P/E ratios are calculated from the current market value of the shares and the most recent year's earnings per share (EPS).

Industry	P/E Ratio
Oil and gas producers	23.65
Construction and materials	86.15
Chemicals	28.90
Industrial engineering	30.96
Pharmaceuticals and biotechnology	29.31
Tobacco	23.36
Travel and leisure	19.78
Media	16.45
Food and drug retailers	22.60
Electricity	8.77
Life assurance	16.61
Beverages	25.56
Average for all SE listed businesses	22.25

Figure 6.9 Average price/earnings ratios for businesses in a range of industries

Businesses that have a high share price relative to their recent historic earnings have high P/E ratios. This may be because their economic prospects are considered bright, which may result from investing heavily in the future at the expense of recent profits (earnings). On the other hand, high P/Es also arise where businesses have recently generated low profits, yet investors believe that their economic prospects are brighter. As is shown in Figure 6.9, the average P/E for all Stock Exchange listed businesses was 22.25 times, but Electricity was as low as 8.77 times and Construction and Materials as high as 86.15 times.

Source: Figures compiled from information in 'Companies and markets', *Financial Times,* 3 November 2017.
© The Financial Times Limited 2017. All Rights Reserved.

TREND ANALYSIS

It is often helpful to see whether ratios are indicating trends. Key ratios can be plotted on a graph to provide a simple visual display of changes occurring over time. The trends occurring within a business may, for example, be plotted against trends for rival businesses or for the industry as a whole for comparison purposes. An example of trend analysis is shown in **Real World 6.10**.

REAL WORLD 6.10

Trend setting

In Figure 6.10, the current ratio of three of the UK's leading supermarkets is plotted over time. Tesco plc was lower than that of its two main rivals, until 2005, when it overtook Morrison and 2009, when it overtook Sainsbury. Since then, however, the ratios of Tesco and Sainsbury have been fairly close and, for the most current year, are almost identical. Morrison has maintained the lowest current ratio over time.

With well-managed businesses like these, it is highly likely that any changes are the result of deliberate policy.

The current ratio for three leading UK supermarket businesses is plotted for the financial years ended during 2007 to 2017. This enables comparison to be made regarding the ratio, both for each of the three businesses over time and between the businesses.

Source: Ratios calculated from information in the annual reports of the three businesses for each of the years 2007 to 2017.

Figure 6.10 Graph plotting current ratio against time

USING RATIOS TO PREDICT FINANCIAL FAILURE

Financial ratios, based on current or past performance, are often used to help predict the future. Normally, both the choice of ratios and the interpretation of results are dependent on the judgement and opinion of the analyst. In recent years, however, attempts have been made to develop a more rigorous and systematic approach to the use of ratios for prediction purposes. In particular, researchers have shown an interest in the ability of ratios to predict the financial failure of a business.

By financial failure, we mean a business either being forced out of business, or being severely adversely affected, by its inability to meet its financial obligations. It is often referred to as 'going bust' or 'going bankrupt'. This is, of course, a likely area of concern for all those connected with the business. It is probably fair to say that attempts to predict financial failure using financial ratios have broadly been successful.

LIMITATIONS OF RATIO ANALYSIS

Although ratios offer a quick and useful method of analysing the position and performance of a business, they suffer from problems and limitations. We will now review some of their shortcomings.

Quality of financial statements

It must always be remembered that ratios are based on financial statements. The quality of ratio analysis will, therefore, depend on the quality of these underlying statements. An important limitation of financial statements is their failure to include all resources controlled by the business. Internally generated goodwill and brands, for example, are excluded from the statement of financial position for failing to meet the strict definition of an asset. Ratios will inherit this limitation. Thus, even though unreported resources may be of great value to the business, key ratios such as ROSF, will not acknowledge their existence.

Activity 6.28

Assume that a business has internally generated goodwill that had been created in earlier years. If this resource were introduced as a non-current asset with an indefinite life in the current statement of financial position, what would be the effect on ROSF, ROCE and the gearing ratio?

The effect of introducing internally generated goodwill will be similar to that of an asset revaluation. Total assets will increase and equity will also increase. An increase in equity will increase the denominator (lower part of the fraction) for all three ratios. This will, in turn, lead to lower ratios than would be the case if the goodwill were not introduced.

When considering the quality of financial statements, there is also the problem of 'creative accounting'.

Inflation

A persistent problem, in most countries, is that the financial results of businesses can be distorted as a result of inflation. One effect of inflation is that the reported value of assets held for any length of time may bear little relation to current values. Generally speaking, the reported value of assets will be understated relative to current prices during a period of inflation. This occurs because they are often reported at their original cost (less any amounts written off for depreciation). This means that comparisons, either between businesses or between periods, will be hindered. A difference in, say, ROCE may simply be due to assets, shown in one of the statements of financial position being compared, having been acquired more recently.

Another effect of inflation is to distort the measurement of profit. In calculating profit, sales revenue is often matched with costs incurred at an earlier time. There is often a time lag between acquiring a particular resource and then using it to help generate sales revenue. Inventories, for example, may be acquired several months before they are sold. The cost of sales figure is usually based on the historic cost of the inventories concerned. This means that, during a period of inflation, this expense will not reflect prices that are current at the time of the sale.

Activity 6.29

How will this affect the profitability ratios mentioned in the chapter?

Expenses will tend to be understated as a result of inflation. This will, in turn, lead to an overstatement of profit. Hence, profitability ratios such as the gross profit margin, operating margin, ROCE and ROSF will also be overstated.

The restricted view given by ratios

It is important not to rely exclusively on ratios, thereby losing sight of information contained in the underlying financial statements. As we saw earlier in this chapter, some items reported in these statements can be vital in assessing position and performance. For example, the total sales revenue, capital employed and profit figures may be useful in assessing changes in absolute size that occur over time, or in assessing differences in scale between businesses. Ratios do not provide such information. When comparing one figure with another, ratios measure *relative* performance and position and, therefore, provide only part of the picture. When comparing two businesses, therefore, it will often be useful to assess the absolute size of profits, as well as the relative profitability of each business. For example, Business A may generate £1 million operating profit and have a ROCE of 15 per cent and Business B may generate £100,000 operating profit and have a ROCE of 20 per cent. Although Business B has a higher level of *profitability,* as measured by ROCE, it generates lower total operating profits and that fact should not be overlooked.

The basis for comparison

We saw earlier that if ratios are to be useful they require a basis for comparison. Moreover, it is important that we compare like with like. Where the comparison is with another business, there can be difficulties. No two businesses are identical: the greater the differences between the businesses being compared, the greater are the limitations of ratio analysis. Furthermore, any differences in accounting policies, financing methods (gearing levels) and financial year ends will add to the problems of making comparisons between businesses.

Statement of financial position ratios

Because the statement of financial position is only a 'snapshot' of the business at a particular moment in time, any ratios based on statement of financial position figures, such as the liquidity ratios, may not be representative of the financial position of the business for the year as a whole. It is common, for example, for a seasonal business to have a financial year end that coincides with a low point in business activity. Inventories and trade receivables may therefore be low at the year end. As a result, the liquidity ratios may also be low. A more representative picture of liquidity can only really be gained by taking additional measurements at other points in the year.

? SELF-ASSESSMENT QUESTION 6.1

Both Ali plc and Bhaskar plc operate wholesale electrical stores throughout the UK. The financial statements of each business for the year ended 31 December last year are as follows:

Statements of financial position as at 31 December last year

	Ali plc £m	Bhaskar plc £m
ASSETS		
Non-current assets		
Property, plant and equipment (cost less depreciation)		
Land and buildings	360.0	510.0
Fixtures and fittings	87.0	91.2
	447.0	601.2
Current assets		
Inventories	592.0	403.0
Trade receivables	176.4	321.9
Cash at bank	84.6	91.6
	853.0	816.5
Total assets	1,300.0	1,417.7
EQUITY AND LIABILITIES		
Equity		
£1 ordinary shares	320.0	250.0
Retained earnings	367.6	624.6
	687.6	874.6
Non-current liabilities		
Borrowings – Loan notes	190.0	250.0
Current liabilities		
Trade payables	406.4	275.7
Taxation	16.0	17.4
	422.4	293.1
Total equity and liabilities	1,300.0	1,417.7

Income statements for the year ended 31 December last year

	Ali plc £m	Bhaskar plc £m
Revenue	1,478.1	1,790.4
Cost of sales	(1,018.3)	(1,214.9)
Gross profit	459.8	575.5
Operating expenses	(308.5)	(408.6)
Operating profit	151.3	166.9
Interest payable	(19.4)	(27.5)
Profit before taxation	131.9	139.4
Taxation	(32.0)	(34.8)
Profit for the year	99.9	104.6

All purchases and sales were on credit. The market values of a share in Ali plc and Bhaskar plc at the end of the year were £6.50 and £8.20 respectively.

Required:
For each business, calculate two ratios that are concerned with each of the following aspects:

- profitability;
- efficiency;
- liquidity;
- gearing; and
- investment (ten ratios in total).

What can you conclude from the ratios that you have calculated?

The solution to this question can be found at the back of the book on pages 305.

SUMMARY

The main points of this chapter may be summarised as follows.

Ratio analysis

- Compares two related figures, usually both from the same set of financial statements.
- Is an aid to understanding what the financial statements really mean.
- Is an inexact science so results must be interpreted with caution.
- Usually requires the business's performance for past periods, the performance of similar businesses and/or planned performance as benchmark ratios.
- Can often benefit from a brief overview of the financial statements to provide insights that may not be revealed by ratios and/or may help in the interpretation of them.

Profitability ratios

- Are concerned with assessing the effectiveness of the business in generating profit.

- Most commonly found in practice are the return on ordinary shareholders' funds (ROSF), return on capital employed (ROCE), operating profit margin and gross profit margin.

Efficiency ratios

- Are concerned with assessing the efficiency of using assets/resources.
- Most commonly found in practice are the average inventories turnover period, average settlement period for trade receivables, average settlement period for trade payables, sales revenue to capital employed and sales revenue per employee.

Liquidity ratios

- Are concerned with assessing the ability to meet short-term obligations.
- Most commonly found in practice are the current ratio and the acid test ratio.

Gearing ratios

- Are concerned with assessing the relationship between equity and debt financing.
- Most commonly found in practice are the gearing ratio and interest cover ratio.

Investment ratios

- Are concerned with assessing returns to shareholders.
- Most commonly found in practice are the dividend payout ratio, the dividend yield ratio, earnings per share (EPS) and the price/earnings ratio.

Uses of ratios

- Individual ratios can be tracked to detect trends, for example by plotting them on a graph.
- Ratios can be used to predict financial failure.

Limitations of ratio analysis

- Ratios are only as reliable as the financial statements from which they derive.
- Inflation can distort the information.
- Ratios give a restricted view.
- It can be difficult to find a suitable benchmark (for example, another business) to compare with.
- Some ratios could mislead due to the 'snapshot' nature of the statement of financial position.

KEY TERMS

return on ordinary shareholders' funds ratio (ROSF)
return on capital employed ratio (ROCE)
operating profit margin ratio
gross profit margin ratio
average inventories' turnover period ratio
average settlement period for trade receivables ratio
average settlement period for trade payables ratio
sales revenue to capital employed ratio
overtrading
sales revenue per employee ratio
current ratio
acid test ratio
financial gearing
gearing ratio
interest cover ratio
dividend payout ratio
dividend cover ratio
dividend yield ratio
dividend per share
earnings per share (EPS)
price/earnings ratio

FURTHER READING

If you would like to explore the topics covered in this chapter in more depth, we recommend the following:

Alexander D., Britton, A., Jorissen, A., Hoogendoorn, M., and van Mourik, C. (2017) *International Financial Reporting and Analysis*, Cengage Learning, 7th edn, Chapters 29–31.

Cope A., Robinson T., Henry E., Pirie W. and Broihahn M. (2015) *International Financial Statement Analysis*, 3rd edn, CFA Institute, Chapter 7.

Elliott, B. and Elliott, J. (2017) *Financial Accounting and Reporting*, 18th edn, Pearson, Chapters 28 and 29.

Subramanyam, K and Wild, J. (2015) *Financial Statement Analysis*, 11th edn, McGraw-Hill Higher Education, Chapters 6 and 8.

CRITICAL REVIEW QUESTIONS

Solutions to these questions can be found at the back of the book on page 312.

6.1 Some businesses operate on a low operating profit margin (for example, a supermarket chain). Does this mean that the return on capital employed from the business will also be low?

6.2 What potential problems arise particularly for the external analyst from the use of statement of financial position figures in the calculation of financial ratios?

6.3 Two businesses operate in the same industry. One has an inventories turnover period that is longer than the industry average. The other has an inventories turnover period that is shorter than the industry average. Give three possible explanations for each business's inventories turnover period ratio.

6.4 In the chapter it was mentioned that ratios help to eliminate some of the problems of comparing businesses of different sizes. Does this mean that size is irrelevant when interpreting and analysing the position and performance of different businesses?

EXERCISES

Solutions to exercises with coloured numbers can be found at the back of the book on pages 319.

Basic-level exercises

6.1 Set out below are ratios relating to three different businesses. Each business operates within a different industrial sector.

Ratio	A plc	B plc	C plc
Operating profit margin	3.6%	9.7%	6.8%
Sales to capital employed	2.4 times	3.1 times	1.7 times
Average inventories turnover period	18 days	N/A	44 days
Average settlement period for trade receivables	2 days	12 days	26 days
Current ratio	0.8 times	0.6 times	1.5 times

Required:
State, with reasons, which one of the three businesses is:
(a) a holiday tour operator;
(b) a supermarket chain;
(c) a food manufacturer.

6.2 Amsterdam Ltd and Berlin Ltd are both wholesalers serving broadly the same market, but they seem to take a different approach to it according to the following information:

Ratio	Amsterdam Ltd	Berlin Ltd
Return on capital employed (ROCE)	20%	17%
Return on ordinary shareholders' funds (ROSF)	30%	18%
Average settlement period for trade receivables	63 days	21 days
Average settlement period for trade payables	50 days	45 days
Gross profit margin	40%	15%
Operating profit margin	10%	10%
Average inventories turnover period	52 days	25 days

Required:
Describe what this information indicates about the differences in approach between the two businesses. If one of them prides itself on customer service and one of them on competitive prices, which do you think is which and why?

Intermediate-level exercises

6.3 The directors of Helena Beauty Products Ltd have been presented with the following abridged financial statements:

Helena Beauty Products Ltd
Income statement for the year ended 31 December

	Year before last		Last year	
	£000	£000	£000	£000
Sales revenue		3,600		3,840
Cost of sales				
Opening inventories	320		400	
Purchases	2,240		2,350	
	2,560		2,750	
Closing inventories	(400)	(2,160)	(500)	(2,250)
Gross profit		1,440		1,590
Expenses		(1,360)		(1,500)
Operating profit		80		90
Corporation tax		(15)		(20)
Profit before taxation		65		70
Interest payable		–		–
Profit for the year		65		70

Statement of financial position as at 31 December

	Year before last	Last year
	£000	£000
ASSETS		
Non-current assets		
Property, plant and equipment	1,900	1,860
Current assets		
Inventories	400	500
Trade receivables	750	960
Cash at bank	8	4
	1,158	1,464
Total assets	3,058	3,324
EQUITY AND LIABILITIES		
Equity		
£1 ordinary shares	1,650	1,700
Share premium account	–	116
Retained earnings	1,018	1,058
	2,668	2,874
Current liabilities	390	450
Total equity and liabilities	3,058	3,324

Required:

Using six ratios, comment on the profitability (three ratios) and efficiency (three ratios) of the business.

6.4 Threads Limited manufactures nuts and bolts, which are sold to industrial users. The abbreviated financial statements for each of the last two years are as follows:

Income statements for the year ended 31 December

	Year before last £000	Last year £000
Revenue	1,180	1,200
Cost of sales	(680)	(750)
Gross profit	500	450
Operating expenses	(200)	(208)
Depreciation	(66)	(75)
Operating profit	234	167
Interest	(–)	(8)
Profit before taxation	234	159
Taxation	(80)	(48)
Profit for the year	154	111

Statements of financial position as at 31 December

	Year before last £000	Last year £000
ASSETS		
Non-current assets		
Property, plant and equipment	702	687
Current assets		
Inventories	148	236
Trade receivables	102	156
Cash	3	4
	253	396
Total assets	955	1,083
EQUITY AND LIABILITIES		
Equity		
Ordinary share capital (£1 shares, fully paid)	500	500
Retained earnings	256	295
	756	795
Non-current liabilities		
Borrowings – Bank loan	–	50
Current liabilities		
Trade payables	60	76
Other payables and accruals	18	16
Taxation	40	24
Short-term borrowings (all bank overdraft)	81	122
	199	238
Total equity and liabilities	955	1,083

Dividends were paid on ordinary shares of £70,000 and £72,000 in respect of the year before last and last year, respectively.

Required:

(a) Calculate the following financial ratios for *both* years (using year-end figures for statement of financial position items):
- return on capital employed
- operating profit margin
- gross profit margin
- current ratio
- acid test ratio
- settlement period for trade receivables
- settlement period for trade payables
- inventories turnover period.

(b) Comment on the performance of Threads Limited from the viewpoint of a business considering supplying a substantial amount of goods to Threads Limited on usual trade credit terms.

Advanced-level exercises

6.5 The financial statements for Harridges plc are given below for the two years ended 31 December for each of the last two years. Harridges plc operates a large chain of retail stores.

Harridges Ltd
Income statement for the years ended 31 December

	Year before last £m	Last year £m
Sales revenue	2,600	3,500
Cost of sales	(1,560)	(2,350)
Gross profit	1,040	1,150
Wages and salaries	(320)	(350)
Overheads	(260)	(200)
Depreciation	(150)	(250)
Operating profit	310	350
Interest payable	(50)	(50)
Profit before taxation	260	300
Taxation	(105)	(125)
Profit for the year	155	175

Statement of financial position as at 31 December

	Year before last £m	Last year £m
ASSETS		
Non-current assets		
Property, plant and equipment	1,265	1,525
Current assets		
Inventories	250	400
Trade receivables	105	145
Cash at bank	380	115
	735	660
Total assets	2,000	2,185
EQUITY AND LIABILITIES		
Equity		
Share capital: £1 shares fully paid	490	490
Share premium	260	260
Retained earnings	350	450
	1,100	1,200
Non-current liabilities		
Borrowings – 10% loan notes	500	500
Current liabilities		
Trade payables	300	375
Other payables	100	110
	400	485
Total equity and liabilities	2,000	2,185

Dividends were paid on ordinary shares of £65 million and £75 million in respect of the year before last and last year, respectively.

Required:
(a) Choose and calculate eight ratios that would be helpful in assessing the performance of Harridges plc. Use end-of-year values and calculate ratios for both years.
(b) Using the ratios calculated in (a) and any others you consider helpful, comment on the business's performance from the viewpoint of a prospective purchaser of a majority of shares.

Chapter 7

GOVERNING A COMPANY

INTRODUCTION

In Chapter 4, we saw that corporate governance, which concerns the way in which companies are directed and controlled, has become an important issue. Strenuous efforts have been made to improve standards of corporate governance, particularly for large listed companies. In this chapter, we consider the framework of rules that has been created to ensure that appropriate checks and balances are in place and that key governance issues are addressed.

We continue our examination of corporate governance matters by considering the role and composition of the board of directors. As part of this examination, we shall explore the roles of chair and non-executive director and the contribution of each role towards good governance. We shall see that each role raises issues which must be resolved if the board is to operate in a smooth and effective manner.

An important aspect of corporate governance is the annual audit. We discussed the audit process briefly in Chapter 5 and saw how it seeks to lend credibility to the financial statements. In this chapter, we take a look at what the audit process involves and the contribution made by each of the key players. We also identify problems that may arise when carrying out, and when reviewing, the audit of a company's financial statements.

For a number of years, the remuneration of directors has been a thorny issue in corporate governance. In this chapter, we discuss the remuneration policies adopted by companies and the performance measures used as a basis for incentivising directors. We also discuss the extent to which the measures identified help align the interests of directors with those of shareholders.

A framework of rules plays an important role in monitoring and controlling the behaviour of directors. However, shareholders also have responsibilities. In the final part of this chapter, we shall consider how shareholders may act to improve accountability and to restrain the excesses of directors.

Learning outcomes

When you have completed this chapter, you should be able to:

- discuss the need for corporate governance rules and the principles upon which these rules are based;
- explain the role and composition of the board of directors and discuss the main issues surrounding the roles of chair and non-executive director;
- describe the audit process and the contribution of the key players to this process;
- explain the main issues and problems associated with the remuneration of directors;
- discuss the importance of shareholder involvement in the corporate governance process and outline the different forms of shareholder involvement that may be found.

CORPORATE GOVERNANCE

With larger companies, ownership is usually separated from day-to-day control of operations. As a result, a conflict of interest may arise between the directors and the shareholders. There is a risk that the directors will pursue their own interests rather than those of the shareholders. If this occurs, it is clearly a problem for the shareholders; however, it may also be a problem for society as a whole.

Activity 7.1

Can you think why directors pursuing their own interests, rather than those of shareholders, may be a problem for society as a whole?

If shareholders believe that their funds will be mismanaged, they will be reluctant to invest. A shortage of funds will lead to companies making fewer investments. Furthermore, the costs of finance will increase as companies compete for what limited funds are available. A lack of concern for shareholders can therefore have a profound effect on the performance of individual companies and, with this, the health of the economy.

To avoid these problems, most competitive market economies have a framework of rules to help monitor and control the behaviour of directors. These rules are usually based around three guiding principles:

- *Disclosure.* This lies at the heart of good corporate governance. Adequate and timely disclosure can help shareholders to judge the performance of the directors. Where performance is considered unsatisfactory this will be reflected in the price of shares. Changes should then be made to ensure the directors regain the confidence of shareholders.
- *Accountability.* This involves setting out the duties of the directors and establishing an adequate monitoring process. In the UK, company law requires that the directors act in the best interests of the shareholders. This means, among other things, that they must not try to use their position and knowledge to make gains at the expense of the shareholders. The law also requires larger companies to have their annual financial statements independently audited. The purpose of an independent audit is to lend credibility to the financial statements prepared by the directors. We shall consider this point in more detail later in the chapter.

- *Fairness.* Directors should not be able to benefit from access to 'inside' information that is not available to shareholders. As a result in the UK, both the law and the Stock Exchange place restrictions on the ability of directors to buy and sell the shares of the company. This means, for example, that the directors cannot buy or sell shares immediately before the announcement of the annual profits or before the announcement of a significant event such as a planned merger.

These principles are set out in Figure 7.1.

The three principles should guide rule makers in their work.

Figure 7.1 Principles underpinning a framework of rules

Strengthening the framework of rules

The number of rules designed to safeguard shareholders has increased considerably over the years. This has been in response to weaknesses in corporate governance procedures, which have been exposed through well-publicised company failures and frauds, excessive pay increases to directors and evidence that some financial reports were being 'massaged' so as to mislead shareholders.

Many believe, however, that shareholders must shoulder some of the blame for any weaknesses. Ownership, by market value, of the shares listed on the London Stock Exchange is dominated by institutional investors such as insurance businesses, banks and pension funds and so on (see Real World 7.12). They are often massive operations, owning large quantities of the shares of the companies in which they invest. These institutional investors employ specialist staff to manage their share portfolios. Yet, despite their size and expertise, they have often demonstrated little concern with corporate governance matters. As a consequence, directors' behaviour has not been closely monitored. In recent times, however, there has been a significant change. Institutional investors are now engaging much more with the companies in which they invest. We shall return to this point towards the end of the chapter.

THE BOARD OF DIRECTORS

Before we consider corporate governance issues in more detail, it might be helpful to clarify the role and composition of the board of directors. The board governs the company on behalf of the shareholders and is responsible for promoting their interests. It is led by a chair and, for a listed public company, the board will normally include both executive and non-executive directors.

The chair

The **chair** is the senior director. This individual is elected by the other directors and chairs board meetings. We shall discuss the chair's role in more detail a little later in the chapter.

Executive directors

Executive directors are salaried employees with senior management responsibilities. The finance directors of most large companies, for example, are full-time employees. In addition to being a board member and taking part in board decisions, the finance director is responsible for managing the finance function within the company.

Non-executive directors

Non-executive directors act purely as directors; they are not full-time employees of the company. They have often gained experience through their association with other companies or organisations. It is common, for example, for non-executive directors to be executive directors of other companies. In recent years, the role of non-executive director has taken on increasing importance, which, in turn, reflects the increasing attention paid to corporate governance matters.

The **UK Corporate Governance Code**, which we shall discuss shortly, draws a distinction between non-executive directors and *independent* non-executive directors. The term 'independent' in this context implies freedom from other significant links to the company, to its directors or to major shareholders. According to the UK Code, independence may be impaired for a variety of reasons such as where a person had been an employee of the company within the previous five years, or had a significant business relationship with the company within the past three years, or receives remuneration from the company apart from a director's fee.

To try to ensure an effective presence of independent, non-executive directors, the UK Code states that at least half the board, excluding the chair, should consist of independent, non-executive directors. A senior independent non-executive director should be appointed from among the independent non-executive directors to act as a sounding board for the board chair. The chair should also be an independent non-executive director, at the time of being appointed.

Although executive directors are much more deeply involved in running the company than non-executive directors, both have the same legal obligations towards the shareholders of the company. We shall discuss the role of non-executive directors in some detail a little later.

THE UK CORPORATE GOVERNANCE CODE

In recent years, there has been a real effort to address the problems of poor corporate governance. This has led to the creation of a code of best practice, known as the UK Corporate Governance Code. The UK Code is produced by the Financial Reporting Council, an independent regulator that seeks to promote high quality corporate governance and accountability. The first version of the UK Code was published in 1992 and revised versions have been published every few years since then. The 2018 version is divided into five sections and sets out a number of key principles. **Real World 7.1** below describes these principles.

Real World 7.1

The UK Corporate Governance Code

The UK Code is based on the following key principles:

Board leadership and company purpose

- A successful company is led by an effective and entrepreneurial board, whose role is to promote the long-term sustainable success of the company, generating value for shareholders and contributing to wider society.
- The board should establish the company's purpose, values and strategy, and satisfy itself that these and its culture are aligned. All directors must act with integrity, lead by example and promote the desired culture.
- The board should ensure that the necessary resources are in place for the company to meet its objectives and measure performance against them. The board should also establish a framework of prudent and effective controls, which enable risk to be assessed and managed.
- In order for the company to meet its responsibilities to shareholders and stakeholders, the board should ensure effective engagement with, and encourage participation from, these parties.
- The board should ensure that workforce policies and practices are consistent with the company's values and support its long-term sustainable success. The workforce should be able to raise any matters of concern.

Division of responsibilities

- The chair leads the board and is responsible for its overall effectiveness in directing the company. They should demonstrate objective judgement throughout their tenure and promote a culture of openness and debate. In addition, the chair facilitates constructive board relations and the effective contribution of all non-executive directors, and ensures that directors receive accurate, timely and clear information.
- The board should include an appropriate combination of executive and non-executive (and, in particular, independent non-executive) directors, such that no one individual or small group of individuals dominates the board's decision-making. There should be a clear division of responsibilities between the leadership of the board and the executive leadership of the company's business.
- Non-executive directors should have sufficient time to meet their board responsibilities. They should provide constructive challenge, strategic guidance, offer specialist advice and hold management to account.
- The board, supported by the company secretary, should ensure that it has the policies, processes, information, time and resources it needs in order to function effectively and efficiently.

Company success and evaluation

- Appointments to the board should be subject to a formal, rigorous and transparent procedure, and an effective succession plan should be maintained for board and senior management. Both appointments and succession plans should be based on merit and objective criteria and, within this context, should promote diversity of gender, social and ethnic backgrounds, cognitive and personal strengths.

- The board and its committees should have a combination of skills, experience and knowledge. Consideration should be given to the length of service of the board as a whole and membership regularly refreshed.
- Annual evaluation of the board should consider its composition, diversity and how effectively members work together to achieve objectives. Individual evaluation should demonstrate whether each director continues to contribute effectively.

Audit, risk and internal control

- The board should establish formal and transparent policies and procedures to ensure the independence and effectiveness of internal and external audit functions and satisfy itself on the integrity of financial and narrative statements.
- The board should present a fair, balanced and understandable assessment of the company's position and prospects.
- The board should establish procedures to manage risk, oversee the internal control framework, and determine the nature and extent of the principal risks the company is willing to take in order to achieve its long-term strategic objectives.

Remuneration

- Remuneration policies and practices should be designed to support strategy and promote long-term sustainable success. Executive remuneration should be aligned to company purpose and values, and be clearly linked to the successful delivery of the company's long-term strategy.
- A formal and transparent procedure for developing policy on executive remuneration and determining director and senior management remuneration should be established. No director should be involved in deciding their own remuneration outcome.
- Directors should exercise independent judgement and discretion when authorising remuneration outcomes, taking account of company and individual performance, and wider circumstances.

Source: Extracts from The UK Corporate Governance Code, Financial Reporting Council, July 2018, pp. 4–13, www.frc.org.uk. © Financial Reporting Council (FRC). All rights reserved. For further information, please visit www.frc.org.uk or call +44 (0)20 7492 2300.

The 2018 UK Code places great emphasis on how the principles described above have been applied in practice. Listed companies are required to provide a statement to shareholders on the approach taken. Because of its importance, this statement should not be produced in a formulaic way. The UK Code states that a 'tick box' approach, which has been a growing trend in corporate governance reporting, is unacceptable.

The UK Code acknowledges there may be circumstances where non-compliance with a particular provision is justified. Nevertheless, a recent survey found that 66 per cent of the largest 350 listed companies declare full compliance with the UK Code provisions. A common reason for non-compliance centres around the independence of the chair and non-executive directors (see Reference 1 at the end of the chapter).

The UK Code has the backing of the London Stock Exchange. This means that companies listed on the London Stock Exchange are expected to comply with the requirements of the UK Code or must give shareholders good reason why they do not. Failure to do one of these can lead to the company's shares being suspended from listing.

Activity 7.2

Why might this be an important sanction against a non-compliant company?

A major advantage of a Stock Exchange listing is that it enables investors to sell their shares whenever they wish. A company that is suspended from listing would find it hard and, therefore, expensive to raise funds from investors because there would be no ready market for the shares.

It is generally believed that the Code has improved the quality of information available to shareholders. It has also resulted in better checks on the powers of directors, and provided greater transparency in corporate affairs. However, rules can only be a partial answer. Ultimately, good corporate governance behaviour depends on a healthy **corporate culture**. This term refers to the values, attitudes and behaviour displayed towards the company's various stakeholders and to the wider community. To be effective, governance rules rely on corporate decision making that reflect high standards of integrity, openness and accountability.

Rulemaking is a tricky business. Where corporate governance rules are too tightly drawn, entrepreneurial spirit may be stifled and risk taking may be discouraged. However, problems can also arise where rules are too loosely drawn.

Activity 7.3

Can you think of a possible problem with corporate governance rules that are too loosely drawn?

In this case, it would be easier for unscrupulous directors to find ways around them.

Thus, when creating corporate governance rules, a balance must somehow be struck between the need to protect shareholders and other stakeholders and the need to encourage entrepreneurial behaviour.

TASKS OF THE BOARD

To help ensure that the company succeeds in its purpose, the board is charged with various tasks. The main tasks are to:

1 *Decide on the strategic direction of the company.* The degree of involvement in strategy setting tends to vary between boards. In some cases, the full board will establish the strategic aims but will delegate responsibility for developing a strategic plan to an **executive committee**. This is a committee made up of some of the board members, which usually includes the **chief executive officer (CEO)**, who leads the management team, and the

other executive directors. Once the committee has developed a plan, it will be put before the full board for approval.

2 *Exercise control.* To try to ensure that things go according to plan and resources are properly allocated, the board must exercise control. This is often done through board committees. Each committee is made up of some board members who report to the full board on their progress and findings. The key committees are mentioned below.

The main areas over which the board must exercise control include:

- *Carrying out the strategic plan.* Having developed a strategic plan, the executive committee will usually be charged with its successful implementation.
- *Checking the integrity of the financial statements.* The UK Corporate Governance Code states that a separate board committee, known as the audit committee, should be set up to promote the reliability of the financial reporting systems.
- *Evaluating and managing risk.* Although a separate risk management committee may be formed, the audit committee may take on this responsibility.
- *Nominating and remunerating directors.* The UK Corporate Governance Code states that a nomination committee and a remuneration committee should each be established to help provide formal and transparent procedures in these areas.
- *Assessing board performance.* Appraisals based on contributions made, or outcomes achieved, should be carried out on individual directors and on the board as a whole.

The control function of the board will be discussed in more detail in later sections.

3 *Maintain external relations.* The board is responsible for promoting the interests of the company and establishing good relationships with shareholders. Relationships with major shareholders are often helped through informal meetings involving key board members. These meetings, which usually involve a free exchange of views between board members and shareholders, may help the shareholders to adopt a long-term perspective on company performance. They may also help in securing support when the board has to make difficult decisions.

The main tasks discussed are summarised in Figure 7.2.

These three main tasks have been discussed in the text.

Figure 7.2 The main tasks of the board of directors

CHAIRING THE BOARD

We have seen that the role of chair is to lead and manage the board of directors. The chair should try to ensure that the board operates as an effective decision-making body and that board meetings are conducted in a business-like manner. To fulfil the role, the chair will normally be expected to:

- hold frequent board meetings so that key issues and problems can be dealt with at the appropriate time;
- try to ensure that the board agenda properly reflects the key issues and problems confronting the company;
- provide board members with relevant, reliable and timely information to help in their deliberations;
- provide enough time at board meetings for key issues and problems to be discussed thoroughly;
- allow all directors the opportunity to voice their opinions at board meetings; and
- guide discussions so that the focus does not deviate from key strategic issues and problems.

The chair should play a crucial role in defining the culture of the board and, through this, the company as a whole. It is important, therefore, that the chair tries to foster a good working relationship between board members by providing a supportive environment where directors feel valued and where a climate of trust prevails.

> **Activity 7.4**
>
> In trying to establish a supportive environment, should the chair try to ensure that boardroom conflict is avoided?
>
> No. There are occasions when conflict between board members is beneficial. It can help ensure that issues are thoroughly aired and that important proposals are given proper scrutiny.

The chair will act as an important link between the board and the shareholders. When the board wishes to inform shareholders of its proposals and decisions, the chair will normally take a lead role. Similarly, when shareholders wish to respond to board proposals and decisions, or to raise concerns, they will often relay their views to the board through the chair. Good communication skills are, therefore, a vital ingredient of a successful chair.

Finally, the chair should ensure that board performance is subject to proper scrutiny. The UK Code states that performance of individual directors, board committees and the board, as a whole, should be evaluated on an annual basis. Furthermore, the chair should act on the results. The criteria for assessing board performance will be considered later in the chapter.

Separating the roles of chair and CEO

We have seen that the role of the chair is to lead the board of directors and the role of the chief executive officer is to lead the management team. The UK Corporate Governance Code states that the same individual should not occupy both roles.

> **Activity 7.5**
>
> **What risks are associated with a single individual occupying both roles?**
>
> Where the two roles are combined, too much power may be concentrated in the hands of a single individual. This power may be used to dominate the board and to marginalise the contribution of others. It may also be used to plunder the company's resources through excessive pay, bonuses and 'perks'. When the company is performing well, these abuses of power may be overlooked but, when things turn sour, the issue of accountability will inevitably surface.

Having a separate chair may provide a number of benefits. The chair may be a useful source of support for the chief executive when the occasion demands. Where, for example, problems that create controversy among board members arise, they are more likely to be resolved when the chair and chief executive adopt the same stance. A chair can also act as a sounding board for new ideas and provide advice for the chief executive. In many cases, chairs have occupied the position of chief executive at an earlier point in their careers and are older, and more widely experienced, than the chief executive. They are often, therefore, well placed to undertake these supportive roles.

Having a separate chair may also help in smoothing the path of succession. Where a chief executive leaves the company, the continued presence of the chair can help to 'steady the ship' and provide a sense of continuity during the period of transition (see Reference 2 at the end of the chapter). The chair can also help a newly appointed chief executive to settle in and to become familiar with the issues and challenges to be faced.

Finally, a separate chair may help the company to cope more effectively with the demands of modern business. The skills and time required to fulfil both roles are likely to be beyond the capacity of a single individual. It is argued that only by separating the roles can proper attention be given both to corporate governance matters and to managing the company.

Is separation always the best solution?

There is little doubt that a powerful, combined chair and chief executive can create problems for a company. What is less certain, however, is whether a 'one size fits all' approach is the best solution for dealing with this issue. There may be circumstances where combining the roles may be appropriate. A company in difficulties, for example, may benefit from a single, strong leader who has a clear vision and who can act in a decisive and fairly unconstrained manner.

Where a board of directors intends to combine the roles of chair and chief executive, the UK Code requires major shareholders to be consulted prior to any appointment. In addition, the reasons for the decision should be communicated to all shareholders.

Problems in separating the roles

There are potential problems in separating the roles of chair and chief executive, which can be overlooked.

Activity 7.6

Can you think of potential problems that may arise from separating the two roles?

Responsibilities may become hazy and this, in turn, may result in a lack of clear direction. There is also a risk that the two individuals occupying the roles simply do not get on. They may have conflicting personalities. They may also have conflicting views over the way in which each role should be carried out and the general direction in which the company should be heading. A breakdown in relationships can lead to endless power struggles, which may badly affect the performance of the company.

Perhaps a clinching argument in favour of separating the two roles would be that it leads to a more effective business performance, perhaps evidenced by superior shareholder returns. There is, however, no clear evidence to suggest that this is the case.

Making separation work

Separating the two roles will only be successful if the two individuals concerned strike up a good working relationship. Thus, the board should appoint individuals whose personalities appear to mesh. The board should ideally also appoint two individuals with complementary skills and knowledge (see Reference 3 at the end of the chapter). This will help to fill any gaps and should help to build mutual respect between the chair and the chief executive.

The two roles should be clearly defined and everyone should be made aware of the responsibilities and duties associated with each role. Defining the roles, however, may be difficult. In a fast-changing environment, new issues arise that can result in boundary disputes. Resolving these disputes will depend a great deal on the mutual trust and respect the two individuals have for each other.

The chair, who is often a former chief executive, must resist any temptation to intervene in the management of the company. The role of the chair demands that a different approach be taken. It requires a willingness to operate in the background and to keep ego and ambition firmly in check.

Should the chief executive go on to become chair?

The UK Corporate Governance Code recommends that the chief executive should not go on to become chair of the same company.

Activity 7.7

Can you think of a potential problem that may arise from allowing the chief executive to relinquish this post and then become the chair?

The main risk here is that the individual will be unable to give up the reins of management easily and will still become involved in operating decisions.

The chair's involvement in day-to-day management issues can create disharmony and can have a detrimental effect on company performance. It can generate confusion and can undermine the decisions of the current chief executive. The chair must not, however, become too detached from management issues. This would allow the chief executive too much freedom in running the company (see Reference 4 at the end of the chapter).

Allowing the chief executive to become chair can also increase the risk of defensive behaviour. The new chief executive may try to score points by criticising the decisions made, and results achieved, when the former chief executive (and now the chair) managed the company. The chair, on the other hand, may try to justify past decisions and actions. This may lead to criticism of the new chief executive and attempts to undermine any proposals for change.

Despite these points, there are possible disadvantages in preventing the chief executive from becoming chair.

Activity 7.8

Can you think what these disadvantages might be?

The most important is the loss to the company of the chief executive's expertise and experience. This loss can be particularly severe where the company's operations are unique or highly complex. In these circumstances, recruiting a suitable outside chair may be extremely difficult. A further disadvantage of not allowing the chief executive to become chair is that a sense of continuity may be lost.

THE ROLE OF NON-EXECUTIVE DIRECTORS

In the past, the image of the non-executive director was that of an avuncular figure offering kindly guidance and advice to the board concerning the direction of the company. This was not seen as an unduly onerous role and any time spent on the company's affairs could be confined to board meetings and in perusing background documents for the various agenda items. Whatever truth such an image may have contained, it is not a faithful portrayal of the current role of the non-executive director of a UK listed public company. An important consequence of strengthening corporate governance standards, which was discussed earlier, has been to increase the demands placed on the non-executive directors.

Non-executive directors are expected to contribute towards each of the functions of the board mentioned above and the contribution they make will largely depend on their background, experience and personal qualities. As we have seen, often non-executive directors of a listed public company are, or have been, executive directors of another listed public company and so will usually have experience of the commercial world as well as expertise in a particular field, such as finance or marketing. As a result, non-executive directors can often play a valuable role in discussions on strategy. They may make useful suggestions and may constructively challenge the assumptions and decisions of the executive directors.

> **Activity 7.9**
>
> How might the fact that non-executive directors are not engaged in the day-to-day running of the company be of help in board discussions?
>
> They are more detached from company problems and this allows them to provide a more objective view. This may be of particular value during periods of change or crisis, when an objective view can help executive directors to maintain perspective.

Non-executive directors can also play an important role in monitoring and controlling the activities of the company. In working towards the strategic plan, control mechanisms involving plans, budgets, quality indicators and benchmarking may be used. The experience and skills of non-executive directors may enable them to identify weaknesses in the current control systems and to suggest ways of improving them. They may also be able to highlight areas of poor performance.

Non-executives have an important role in the various board committees that are set up to control the activities of the company. It was mentioned earlier that, to promote the integrity of financial information, an audit committee is usually set up. The UK Corporate Governance Code states that this committee should consist entirely of independent non-executive directors. It was also mentioned that listed companies normally have a remuneration committee that is charged with recommending to the board the remuneration of the executive directors and the chair. The UK Code states that this committee should also consist of independent non-executive directors. This means that non-executives have enormous influence over the remuneration of executive directors and, where there are performance-related elements, will be involved in setting targets and in monitoring the performance of the executive directors. The roles of both the audit committee and the remuneration committee will be considered in more detail later in the chapter.

Finally, the UK Code states that the nomination committee should have a majority of independent non-executive directors as members. We have seen that listed companies normally have such a committee. Its role is to lead the nomination process for new directors. This involves identifying the skills, knowledge and experience required for the board and preparing appropriate job specifications.

The board and large shareholders often maintain a dialogue through informal meetings, which non-executives may attend. This can help them to understand the concerns of shareholders. At times, non-executives may become the shareholders' communications channel to the board of directors. Shareholders may be particularly reliant on this channel if they have already voiced concerns to the chair, or to the executive directors, and have not received satisfactory replies.

Non-executive directors may help to raise the profile of the company. They often enjoy a good reputation within their particular field and may have strong links with a wide range of bodies, including government agencies and foreign companies. These links may be extremely valuable in developing new contacts and in promoting the company's interests.

Role conflict

The different roles that non-executives are expected to play provide potential for conflict. In developing strategy, co-operation between the executive and non-executive directors is essential. All directors are expected to work together as part of a team in pursuit of a common purpose. However, the monitoring role that non-executive directors have means that they must assess the performance of executive directors. Disputes between executive and non-executive directors can easily arise over the company's financial systems, control systems and remuneration systems. Given this potential conflict, non-executive directors must tread carefully and must retain a certain distance from the executive directors to maintain their independence.

Relations with the executive directors

The potential for disputes may make the non-executive and executive directors wary of each other. Executive directors may resent the presence of non-executives on the board because they believe that the non-executives:

- are monitoring their behaviour and, effectively, acting as 'corporate police officers';
- do not fully understand the nature of the company's business; and
- do not devote enough time and effort in carrying out their duties.

Non-executives, on the other hand, may sense that executives are acting in an unhelpful or guarded manner towards them. They may feel that executive directors are seeking to undermine their position by:

- withholding key information or reports;
- failing to provide important information at the required time; and
- holding informal meetings on important matters to which the non-executives are not invited.

The chair of the board can play an important part in overcoming these suspicions and problems.

Activity 7.10

What do you think the chair could do? (Try to think of at least two possible initiatives the chair could take.)

The chair can take various initiatives, such as trying to ensure that the board's procedures are transparent and that informal meetings of cliques are discouraged. Where doubts exist over the competence of particular directors, the chair should see that appropriate training and development opportunities are made available. To allow any suspicions and problems to be aired, the chair should arrange meetings between executive and non-executive directors. Finally, the chair should try to ensure that all directors receive timely and relevant information.

Maintaining independence

There is a danger that non-executive directors will not provide an independent voice. They may come under the influence of the executive directors and fail to challenge decisions and so ensure proper accountability. The fact that non-executives are often executive directors of other companies can result in feelings of empathy with the executive directors on the board.

Activity 7.11

How might shareholders intervene to ensure that the risk of non-executive directors not being sufficiently independent is avoided, or at least reduced?

Shareholders can become involved in the appointment of the non-executive directors, perhaps by identifying and proposing suitable candidates. Once appointed, regular meetings with shareholders may help to strengthen their independence from the executive directors, as well as their commitment to the shareholders' interests.

The role of non-executive directors can be very time-consuming. Despite this, some individuals hold multiple non-executive directorships. This may prevent them from devoting sufficient time to the affairs of each company. The UK Code does not specify a minimum time commitment for non-executive directors, but does state that they should have sufficient time to be able to carry out their duties effectively.

To encourage a diligent attitude, non-executives should be properly rewarded for the time spent on company business and for the responsibilities that they take on. There is a risk, however, of paying non-executives too handsomely for their efforts.

Activity 7.12

What problem may arise from paying non-executive directors large salaries?

It may compromise their independence. Where non-executives are paid fairly modest salaries, based on the time spent carrying out their duties, the amounts will usually form only a small proportion of their total income. This may help them retain a greater degree of independence when making decisions.

Real World 7.2 gives an impression of the remuneration awarded to non-executive directors in the UK's largest listed businesses.

Real World 7.2

Time to get on board

A survey by KPMG, the accountants and management consultants, provides the following average (median) figures for the remuneration of non-executive directors in the UK's 100 listed businesses.

	£000
Basic fees	
Chair	400
Non-executive director	69
Additional fees	
Audit committee chair	23
Remuneration committee chair	20
Nomination committee chair	17
Audit committee member	14
Remuneration committee member	12
Nomination committee member	10

Half of the largest 100 listed businesses pay additional fees for membership of board committees.

Source: Extracts from Guide to Directors' Remuneration 2017, KPMG, pp. 68, 71 and 72.

THE AUDIT PROCESS

External audit

As we saw in Chapter 5, **external audit** forms an important element of corporate governance. To understand what it entails, we must first be clear about the roles and responsibilities of directors and auditors concerning the published financial statements.

Company law requires the directors to prepare annual financial statements that provide a true and fair view of the state of affairs of the company. This will involve:

- selecting suitable accounting policies and applying them consistently;
- making estimates and judgements that are reasonable and prudent;
- stating whether appropriate accounting standards have been adopted;
- presenting information in a way that is relevant, reliable comparable and understandable; and
- applying the going concern convention where it is appropriate to do so.

In addition to preparing the annual financial statements, the law also obliges the directors to keep proper accounting records and to safeguard the assets of the company.

External auditors are appointed by, and report to, the shareholders. They are normally an independent firm of accountants and their role is to form an opinion concerning the integrity of the annual financial statements prepared by the directors. In forming their opinion, the auditors must bring to bear their professional scepticism and judgement. The audit process will involve examining the available accounting records, reviewing the key assumptions and estimates employed and evaluating the internal controls in operation. It will also involve checking to see whether the accounting policies adopted are appropriate, whether key information is adequately disclosed and whether the financial statements are properly presented and structured.

External auditors must inform shareholders of any significant problems that have been unearthed during the audit process. By law, the audit report must include any instances where:

- adequate accounting records have not been kept;
- information and explanations needed to undertake the audit have not been received;
- the financial statements are not in agreement with the underlying accounting records; and
- certain disclosures concerning directors' remuneration are not made.

In addition, there are auditing rules that require auditors to report where other information within the annual report is inconsistent with the financial statements, or is otherwise misleading.

External auditors take on additional responsibilities for Stock Exchange listed companies. These include checking the directors' required statement on the long-term viability of the business and, where the going concern basis for preparing the financial statements is used, that it is appropriate to do so.

Following an examination of all the relevant information, the auditors provide shareholders with an independent opinion as to whether:

- the financial statements provide a true and fair view of the state of affairs of the company and comply with legal and other regulatory requirements;
- information contained within the directors' report and strategic report is consistent with the financial statements and comply with legal requirements; and
- the reporting of certain details concerning directors' remuneration complies with the law.

These opinions are contained within an audit report, which forms part of the published annual report. Where the auditors have no concerns to raise, an 'unmodified opinion' is provided. This should provide reasonable assurance to shareholders that the financial statements are free from any serious misstatements arising from either fraud or error. There is, however, no guarantee that this is the case.

In practice, the audit process does not always operate smoothly. There are times when auditors fail to spot errors and fraud. **Real World 7.3** below reveals one such time.

Real World 7.3

Ringing the changes

BT has appointed KPMG as its new auditor following a review of its accounting practices prompted by a scandal in its Italian division, ending a relationship with rival PwC that lasted more than three decades. The move comes after a whistleblower exposed fraud at BT Italia, triggering a £530 million write-off and wiping a fifth off the telecoms group's market value in January.

The telecoms company was due to carry out a review of its auditors in 2019 but brought the process forward after it became aware of issues at its Italian unit, part of its Global Services division. There was unease from some at the company that PwC had failed to spot the scale of the problems in Italy, which were only brought to the company's attention by a whistleblower and through a subsequent investigation by KPMG.

It was the second time in a decade that auditing problems were uncovered in BT's Global Services division. In 2008–9, the company took a £1.6 billion writedown after optimistic profitability estimates went unchallenged.

Source: Extracts from Bond, D. and Khan, M. (2017) BT appoints KPMG as auditor after Italian scandal, ft.com, 8 June. © The Financial Times Limited 2017. All rights reserved.

Two key issues have emerged from past audit failures – the gap in expectations between auditors and shareholders and auditor independence. It is to these issues that we now turn.

The expectations gap

Over the years, there has been much discussion of the **expectations gap** in auditing. This refers to the difference between what external auditors believe their responsibilities and duties to be and what shareholders believe them to be. As seen earlier, external auditors are broadly concerned with checking the integrity of the accounting system and seeing whether the financial statements are properly presented. They are not primarily concerned with the detection of errors and fraud. However, when auditors fail in this respect, the reaction of shareholders suggests that they have a different view of the auditors' role.

From time to time, auditors complain that shareholders do not fully understand the nature and limitations of the audit process. When checking the integrity of accounting systems, for example, auditors often rely on sampling techniques. They do not normally examine every accounting transaction for the period.

Activity 7.13

Why do you think auditors rely on sampling techniques?

For a company of any size, the huge number of transactions undertaken during a financial period would make an examination of each transaction impossible.

While sampling techniques can help to assess the overall reliability of the accounting system, they cannot guarantee the absence of errors and fraud. Shareholders must, therefore, be realistic about what is achievable from an audit. Narrowing the expectations gap is not, however, simply about educating shareholders. Auditors must understand that shareholders need relevant feedback for their investment decisions.

In recent years, the auditors' report for listed businesses has become much more informative in response to the problems mentioned. It now includes an overview of the scope of the audit. It also describes key audit matters, such as the most significant risks of misstatements that have been identified, including those having the greatest effect on the audit strategy and on how audit resources were allocated. The auditors' report also includes the auditors' response to risks of misstatement and any observations relating to them. Finally, the report includes an explanation as to what the auditors regard as a material amount when performing the audit.

Real World 7.4 explains the view taken by the external auditors of Ocado Group plc, the online grocer, as to the appropriate threshold for what should be considered a material amount for the financial statements as whole.

Real World 7.4

Auditing in the material world

We define materiality as the magnitude of misstatement in the financial statements that makes it probable that the economic decisions of a reasonably knowledgeable person would be changed or influenced. We use materiality both in planning the scope of our audit work and in evaluating the results of our work. Based on our professional judgement, we determined materiality for the financial statements as a whole as follows:

Group materiality	We determined materiality for the group to be £6 million (2016: £5 million).
Basis for determining materiality	We determined materiality to be £6 million based on revenue. As a percentage materiality is 0.4% of revenue (2016: 0.4% of revenue).
	Parent company materiality was determined as less than 0.5% of total assets.
Rationale for the benchmark applied	This has been based on professional judgement and the requirement of auditing standards. We believe revenue to be the financial measure most relevant to users of the financial statements given Ocado's performance, in particular its levels of profitability and the significant investment in technology.
	It also provides a consistent basis to the approach taken by the previous auditor.

Source: Independent Auditors Report, Annual report and Accounts 53 weeks ended 3 December 2017, Ocado plc.

Auditor independence and audit quality

In the past, the external auditors of large UK listed companies were rarely replaced. Instead they tended to enjoy long tenures.

> ### Activity 7.14
>
> Can you think of an argument in favour of long tenures for auditors?
>
> More effective audits may be undertaken if the audit firm has a detailed knowledge of the strengths and weaknesses of the company's policies and processes. This knowledge may only be gained through a long-term relationship with the company.
>
> A further argument in favour of long tenures is that 'switching costs' have to be incurred whenever there is a change of auditor. A new auditor must be initiated in the policies and processes that the business operates, which can be very time consuming.

Long tenures, however, run the risk of a cosy relationship developing between the auditors and directors, thereby undermining auditor independence. The external auditors may, for example, be reluctant to revisit earlier decisions relating to accounting policies and processes. In order to maintain good relations, they may feel inhibited from challenging directors on matters about which they have previously agreed. Replacing the auditors avoids this kind of problem. A new chapter begins and earlier decisions can be viewed through fresh eyes. Rather than following a well-trodden path based on previous audit work, a more critical and rigorous approach may be introduced.

To strengthen the independence of auditors, new rules require UK listed companies to change external auditors after a maximum period of 20 years. The audit must, however, be put out to tender at the mid-point of 10 years. A key question is whether strengthening auditor independence in this way will, in turn, lead to an improvement in audit quality. Research carried out to date has usually examined situations where auditor rotations have been carried out on a voluntary basis. The results of this research are mixed. (See Reference 5 at the end of the chapter.) Furthermore, it is already established practice for the partner in the firm of auditors who is responsible for conducting the audit of a large listed business to be rotated every five years. This may pre-empt some of the problems of long audit tenures.

A further issue relating to auditor independence concerns the provision of non-audit services. In the past, auditors have often provided significant non-audit services to client companies. These services, which can take various forms such as tax advice, financial advice and bookkeeping, are often well paid. Whereas it is the shareholders that appoint the auditors in respect of their statutory audit work, the directors have responsibility for making the appointment for the non-audit services.

> ### Activity 7.15
>
> How might the provision of non-audit services undermine auditor independence?
>
> By undertaking non-audit services, the auditors will, in effect, have two clients within the same company – the directors and the shareholders. When performing an audit on behalf of the shareholders, there is a risk that the auditors will try to avoid upsetting the directors for fear of losing non-audit revenue.

Providing non-audit services may also involve the auditors carrying out a 'self-review'. This occurs where the auditors make recommendations as part of their non-audit services and then, as part of the audit process, evaluate the validity of these recommendations when implemented.

New rules now prohibit audit firms from providing a wide range of non-audit services to their client-listed businesses. The prohibited services include those relating to bookkeeping, employee payrolls, various human resource, legal and tax services, the design of internal controls and risk management procedures, management decision making and financing matters. Furthermore, the law imposes a cap on fees generated from non-audit services that have not been prohibited.

For some years, concerns have been expressed about the lack of competition within the audit market. The audit of large companies is carried out by only a handful of audit firms and there are doubts that the recent changes to the rules described above will change matters. **Real World 7.5** describes the problems confronted by regulators.

Real World 7.5

Four play

Britain's audit market is overwhelmingly dominated by four firms – EY, Deloitte, KPMG and PwC. Despite new regulation designed to increase choice and competition, the so-called big four audit 98 per cent of FTSE 350 companies. Recent high-profile accounting scandals at UK companies including Rolls-Royce and Tesco – which have involved KPMG and PwC respectively – have meant the continuing concentration is worrying some investors.

Latest market share figures, compiled by PwC, show that 99 of Britain's 100 biggest listed companies are audited by the big four. That is the same as in 2011, before rules were changed to make companies tender their audit every decade, and change auditors every 20. 'It's very clear that tendering has done nothing to improve choice,' says Prof Guy Jubb of Edinburgh Business School's Centre for Accounting and Society and former head of governance at Standard Life.

Audit reform, which sprung from the global financial crisis and took effect in 2014, was supposed to introduce choice and competition in an environment of decades-long, cosy relationships between companies and auditors. Before it appointed a new auditor in 2015, Barclays had been with PwC for 120 years, for example. Last year 68 companies tendered their audit, the highest yearly total since the rule change. But hopes of drawing in new competitors have not materialised and people in the industry say firms outside the big four are increasingly reticent to participate in resource-draining audit tenders for large listed UK companies.

Annual audits for FTSE 100 companies are big catches. PwC, for example, received fees of $111.1 million from HSBC last year, of which $71.3 million were for auditing. But firms argue that switching clients means investing time and money getting to know new businesses, which can hit audit profitability. Mr Persico adds that 'beyond the big four, I don't think there is competition'. He says 'willingness to merge' is the only way smaller players would get to the major leagues. However, Sue Almond, head of audit and assurance at Grant Thornton, says audit tendering processes have helped to increase the group's non-audit work for FTSE 100 companies, which is up by a third since 2013. With scrutiny of Britain's financial accounts in so few hands, there is also a recurring fear one firm will fail. Should one of the big four have 'a crisis of confidence and go into meltdown, because of serious audit quality or reputational issues, you (could) find yourself going rapidly from the big four to the big three,' says Mr Jubb.

Source: Extracts from Cornish, C. (2017) Auditor merry-go-round fails to shake-up cosy market, ft.com, 29 May. © The Financial Times Limited 2017. All rights reserved.

Concerns have also been raised over the quality of audits undertaken by the big four audit firms. Recently, four out of ten audits inspected by the International Forum of Independent Audit Regulators found serious deficiencies in the audits that the big four carried out. (See Reference 6 at the end of the chapter.) Nevertheless, company shareholders rarely show any enthusiasm to change auditors. **Real World 7.6** below provides one example, however, of shareholders sacking one of the big four auditors over the quality of its work.

Real World 7.6

You're fired!

SIG, the building materials group, suffered a large shareholder revolt on Thursday after investors rejected the reappointment of Deloitte as auditor just months after the company admitted repeatedly overstating its profits in previous years.

More than 78 per cent of investors voted against Deloitte's reappointment, in a rare move against an auditor by shareholders. Auditor re-election is usually one of the least controversial aspects of an annual meeting, with the majority of these resolutions gaining support of at least 95 per cent from shareholders.

"The board takes the views of shareholders extremely seriously, and takes this opportunity to inform shareholders that it is committed to carrying out an EU audit regulation compliant audit tender for the role of external auditor, as soon as practicable," a statement from the company said.

"The board intends to consult with shareholders over coming weeks on the timing of that audit tender process and the resulting appointment of a new auditor."

In February, the company said it had discovered misstatements after a whistleblowing allegation about irregularities at its core UK insulation and exteriors business.

It added that a review with auditors at Deloitte and KPMG had found a number of balances related to rebates and other "potential recoveries" from suppliers had been overstated, "in some cases intentionally".

Earlier in the year, the company also said it had overstated its cash balances by around £20m at the end of 2016 and £27m in its 2017 half-year results.

One governance expert described the vote against Deloitte as "unprecedented".

Source: Mooney, A. (2018) *SIG shareholders reject reappointment of Deloitte as auditors*, ft.com 10 May. © The Financial Times Limited 2018. All rights reserved.

It seems that regulators are losing patience with the big four firms and with the quality of audits being carried out. A thorough review of the audit market, along with the role and responsibilities of auditors, seems imminent. Various changes have been suggested, including:

- setting a limit to the number of large listed companies the big four firms can audit;
- requiring larger audit firms to share audits of large listed companies with smaller audit firms;
- passing responsibility for the appointment of auditors of large listed companies to a regulatory authority, such as the Stock Exchange;
- encouraging smaller audit firms to merge to enable them to challenge the big four firms;
- separating audit firms completely from their consulting activities in order to avoid conflicts of interest;
- ensuring that auditors have a clearer duty to exercise judgement rather than to simply 'tick boxes';
- imposing larger penalties on auditors that fail to identify significant problems; and
- expanding the role of auditors to include a responsibility for detecting fraud.

Two points are worth making concerning any further regulatory changes. Firstly, improving the quality of audits will come at a cost. Auditors will have to devote more time and invest in new technology, to further check the accuracy and completeness of financial reports. The additional cost this incurs must be borne by the shareholders. Secondly, some regulation could be avoided if shareholders became more proactive in monitoring the activities of auditors. On the whole, they tend to be passive, even in the face of egregious failures by auditors. There are cases where, following the failure to detect significant fraud or errors, shareholders have overwhelmingly voted to re-appoint the auditors.

Internal audit

Many large companies have an **internal audit** function – although there is no legal requirement to have one. The purpose of an internal audit is to reassure directors about the company's control, risk management and governance procedures. In particular, reassurance is needed about the integrity and reliability of the financial control and accounting systems. An important task of internal audit is, therefore, to review:

- the financial control systems to see whether they are effective in safeguarding the company's assets and in preventing errors and fraud; and
- the accounting systems to see whether they provide reliable information that meets the needs of management and complies with relevant regulations.

The review process will normally highlight areas of weakness and make recommendations based on best practice. It can, therefore, be an important catalyst for improvement.

As internal auditors regularly review the company's accounting and financial control systems, the external auditors may take this into account when planning the scope and nature of the external audit work. External auditors must retain full responsibility for the external audit but may place confidence in the work carried out by competent and experienced internal auditors.

In addition to the risks associated with its accounting systems, a company has to manage many other kinds of risk. How these other risks are managed is vital to good corporate governance.

Activity 7.16

What other kinds of risks may a company face? Try to think of at least three.

They can include:

- risks to its reputation for quality products or fair dealing;
- risks to IT systems from malfunction or security breaches;
- risks of suppliers failing to deliver what is needed on time;
- risks to the health and safety of employees and customers; and
- risks of changes in market demand.

You may have thought of others.

The internal audit function is often charged with reviewing the procedures for managing these other risks. When doing so, a proactive approach may be taken. This means assessing not only how well the procedures cope with managing current risks but also how well they would cope with managing future risks.

Real World 7.7 explains how serious failures in the internal control systems of a well-known car rental business contributed towards investors actively seeking change.

> **Real World 7.7**
>
> ## Losing control at Hertz
>
> Carl Icahn, the activist investor, has made a move on Hertz, the US car rental group, revealing an 8.48 per cent stake and saying he could seek seats on the board, a day after the company said it expected this year's earnings to be 'well below' its previous guidance.
>
> Mr Icahn said in a filing to the Securities and Exchange Commission, the US regulator, that his group of companies had a 'lack of confidence in management' at Hertz, but had taken the stake in the belief that the shares were undervalued. He added that his representatives planned to meet Hertz's management and directors to discuss 'shareholder value, accounting issues, operational failures, [and] underperformance relative to its peers'.
>
> The company said it was facing additional costs for the accounting review it has launched to fix the errors in its reporting. Hertz said that these extra costs, and the potential revisions resulting from the accounting review, meant that it was withdrawing its previous guidance that underlying earnings per share this year would be in the range $1.70 to $2.00, which would have been an increase of about 13.5 per cent on the $1.63 reported for 2013.
>
> The company said in June that it would have to restate its 2011 accounts, while the 2012 and 2013 statements would need to be revised to correct errors, and might also need to be withdrawn and formally restated if the accounting review determined that the errors were material. The problems identified included the treatment of depreciation for some assets, and allowances for 'doubtful accounts' in Brazil.
>
> The company said it had uncovered 'at least one material weakness' in its internal control over financial reporting, and that 'disclosure controls and procedures were ineffective at December 31, 2013'.
>
> Source: Extracts from Crooks, E. (2014) Icahn signals a move on Hertz, ft.com, 20 August.
> © The Financial Times Limited 2014. All rights reserved.

In carrying out their duties, internal auditors try to be both independent and objective. As employees of the company, however, they cannot enjoy the same degree of independence as external auditors. Nevertheless, their independence can be strengthened where the audit committee, rather than executive directors, determines the nature and scope of their duties. Their independence can be further strengthened where the audit committee takes responsibility for appointing and, where necessary, removing, the head of internal audit.

A little earlier, we mentioned the extent that external auditors may be inclined to rely on the work of internal auditors. Naturally, the external auditors will tend to place more confidence in the work of internal auditors, where the internal auditors have a measure of independence, in the way discussed in the previous paragraph.

We shall now go on to consider the role of audit committees in some detail.

Audit committees

The UK Corporate Governance Code places audit committees at the heart of the financial reporting and control process. The responsibilities of the audit committee have increased in recent years following the introduction of international financial reporting standards and tougher overseas corporate governance rules, such as the Sarbanes–Oxley Act in the US. This Act was introduced in the wake of accounting scandals and applies to a number of large UK listed companies that also list their shares in the US.

The role of the audit committee

The UK Corporate Governance Code recommends that an audit committee should have delegated authority for trying to ensure that financial reporting and internal control principles are properly applied. In essence, the role concerns the oversight and assessment of work carried out by others. Although the committee receives its terms of reference from the board of directors, these tend to be in line with the guidelines set out in **Real World 7.8**.

> **Real World 7.8**
>
> **That's the way to do it**
>
> The Financial Reporting Council, which is responsible for setting the UK Corporate Governance Code, has set out the following guidelines for the role and responsibilities of audit committees:
>
> - to monitor the integrity of the financial statements and related information such as the strategic report;
> - to review the company's internal controls and risk management systems (unless this task has been delegated to other committees);
> - to review the need for an internal audit function and, where one exists, to assess its role, resourcing and effectiveness;
> - to make formal recommendation to the board of directors for the appointment and removal of the external auditors and to approve their terms of engagement and remuneration;
> - to review and monitor the independence, expertise and effectiveness of the external auditors;
> - to review the annual work plan of the external auditors;
> - to establish and implement policies concerning non-audit services carried out by the external auditors;
> - to report to the board of directors on how the committee discharged its responsibilities; and
> - to communicate with shareholders its role, the work carried out and any significant issues considered.
>
> Source: Summarised from Guidance on Audit Committees, Financial Reporting Council, April 2016, pp. 6–15.
> © Financial Reporting Council (FRC). All rights reserved. For further information, please visit www.frc.org.uk or call +44 (0)20 7492 2300.

The audit committee will also review the risk management systems of the company where the board, or a separate risk committee, does not take on this task.

Members of the audit committee do not have to be qualified accountants. The UK Corporate Governance Code imposes only a modest requirement that at least one committee member should have 'recent and relevant financial experience'. To be effective, members must, however, possess integrity, judgement and character. They may need to pursue enquiries when faced with determined opposition from senior managers or directors.

> **Activity 7.17**
>
> Do you think that *all* members of the committee should be qualified accountants? Try to think of the case for and against this idea.

There is an argument for having at least some qualified accountants on the committee. An important part of the committee's role can involve carrying out a detailed examination of complex accounting issues. To deal effectively with these issues, a high level of technical expertise will usually be needed.

> The committee must, however, fulfil other roles that do not demand a high level of accounting expertise. These roles may well require other skills, such as those relating to IT, law, risk management and so on. Furthermore, committee members may be put under enormous pressure to agree to controversial accounting policies. When faced with such pressure, the personal qualities mentioned earlier can be more important than formal accounting qualifications.

The UK Code states that the audit committee should consist of at least three or, in the case of smaller companies, two independent non-executive directors. Furthermore, the chair of the board should not be a committee member. To be effective, it should have direct access to key individuals such as the chief executive, the finance director and the heads of the internal and external audit teams. It must also have the authority and resources to carry out its responsibilities.

The audit committee should meet at least three times each year (see Reference 7 at the end of the chapter) and sufficient time should be devoted to each meeting. Only members of the committee are normally entitled to attend these meetings, although others may be invited to attend if needed. Some meetings should be timed to coincide with important events such as the start of the annual audit and the announcement of the annual results. In practice, it seems that audit committees meet at least four times a year, excluding teleconference calls (see Reference 8 at the end of the chapter).

The review process

When reviewing the company's internal controls, the committee should examine the effectiveness of the processes put in place by the internal and external audit teams. The committee must be satisfied that the internal controls are operating smoothly and that recommendations for improvement have been implemented. When reviewing the company's risk management systems, the committee should check that key risk areas are being monitored and that any control failures, or emerging risks, are quickly identified and dealt with. The committee must also be satisfied that risk management is not simply a 'box-ticking' exercise and that everyone appreciates its importance.

When reviewing the internal audit function, the committee should agree the remit that the internal auditors have been given by the board and the resources that they have been allocated. The committee should look at the internal audit work plan and receive regular updates on the work carried out. It should also receive feedback on the responses by management to recommendations provided by the internal auditors. To boost their independence and status, internal auditors are often given direct access to the audit committee and to the chair.

When reviewing the external audit process, the audit committee should consider the experience, expertise and resources of the audit team. It should also review the effectiveness of the audit process. This will usually involve scrutinising audit plans and procedures and seeing how they fit with the work carried out by the internal auditors. It will also involve checking that sufficient time is spent on the audit and that key risk areas are receiving attention. To monitor progress, there should be meetings with the external auditor. Topics for discussion may include any major issues that have been identified and whether they have been resolved. They may also include a review of key audit decisions and any errors that have been unearthed.

To ensure the independence of the auditors is not threatened, the committee should monitor any non-audit services undertaken by the external auditors.

> **Activity 7.18**
>
> **What do you think the audit committee should consider when reviewing the non-audit services provided?**
>
> It should consider:
>
> - the type of non-audit work carried out;
> - the fees provided for the work carried out;
> - whether the external auditors are the most suitable candidates for the work carried out; and
> - the regulations concerning the provision of non-audit work.

Each year, the audit committee should recommend to shareholders whether the external auditors should be reappointed. (See Reference 9 at the end of the chapter.)

When reviewing the financial statements, the audit committee should pay particular attention to:

- the accounting policies adopted and whether they conform to the industry norm;
- any changes to accounting policies;
- the estimates and judgements made in key areas such as bad debts, provisions, depreciation and so on;
- any unusual items, such as large write-offs, or unusual relationships, such as very high bad debts to sales revenue figure; and
- any unusual trends in financial performance or position.

This should help to identify irregular accounting practices or fraudulent behaviour.

The committee should also review other information presented in the annual reports that relate to the financial statements, such as the strategic report. It can then advise the board whether the annual reports, as a whole, are fair, balanced and understandable.

The audit committee will produce a report for shareholders to be included within the annual report. The report sets out the main features of the committee including its role, membership and frequency of meetings. It also sets out how the committee has gone about its work. This should include a description of significant issues examined by the committee and how they were addressed. It should also explain how the effectiveness of the external auditors was assessed and how their independence was protected. In practice, the quality of audit committee reports can vary considerably. Not all contain useful information. Some would benefit from a more focused approach that provides more detail concerning key issues and decisions.

Audit committee reports are presented to the annual general meeting of shareholders, which the chair of the audit committee should attend. This allows shareholders the opportunity to question the chair on any matters for which the committee has responsibility.

Problems with audit committees

Over time, the audit committee has had to take on increased responsibilities and its work has been subject to much greater scrutiny. This places committee members under considerable pressure, which may, in turn, promote a cautious approach. A 'compliance' mentality may develop that inhibits creativity and risk taking, which are essential to long-term prosperity (see Reference 10 at the end of the chapter). The pressures mentioned may also discourage individuals from chairing the audit committee, or even becoming a member of it. A great deal of time and effort is normally required to undertake the work involved and an individual's reputation may suffer irreparable damage if things go wrong.

The composition of the audit committee is a contentious issue. We saw earlier that only one committee member is required to have recent and relevant financial experience. Furthermore, no member is required to possess a professional accountancy qualification. This raises the risk that the audit committee will lack the depth and breadth of expertise to handle highly technical accounting issues. Where only one committee member has relevant financial experience, there is also the risk that the burden of dealing with these issues will not be evenly spread. These problems may be mitigated by the committee seeking outside, independent advice; nevertheless, there remains a strong case for requiring a higher minimum level of financial literacy for audit committee members.

Finally, the costs involved in carrying out the tasks of an audit committee are very high. It is not always clear whether the benefits gained outweigh these costs. This is an important issue that has probably not received sufficient attention by researchers.

REMUNERATING DIRECTORS

Setting an appropriate level of remuneration for directors is not an easy task. It can, however, be vitally important to the success of the company. In this section, we consider some key issues that surround this area.

Remuneration policy

The remuneration package of an executive director of a large listed company is usually made up of two elements:

- a fixed element, which is largely in the form of a base salary but will also include benefits such as pension contributions, medical insurance, company car and so on; and
- a variable element, which rewards directors on the basis of both short-term and long-term results.

This latter element is designed to motivate directors to improve performance.

The short-term, variable element usually takes the form of an annual bonus, typically expressed as a multiple of base salary. Not all of the bonus may be paid at the year end; some may be deferred. Deferral may be undertaken on a voluntary or compulsory basis.

Activity 7.19

Why might part of the annual bonus be deferred on a compulsory basis?

One reason is to reduce the risk of paying directors a large sum on the basis of only one year's performance. Instead, a part of the bonus is paid at a later date, subject to satisfactory performance during the deferral period. A further reason for deferral is that it can provide a financial incentive for directors to stay with the company. Directors may become ineligible for the deferred part of a bonus if they leave before the end of the deferral period.

The deferred part of the bonus will normally be invested in company shares during the deferral period, which is often three years. Where part of the bonus is deferred, the directors may receive matching shares to compensate for the deferred amount.

Annual bonuses are paid to directors for achieving prescribed levels of performance. This often relies on the use of profit-based measures (such as operating profit and earnings per share) in conjunction with non-financial measures (such as those relating to personal performance).

The long-term performance reward normally takes the form of a **performance share plan (PSP)**. Under this type of plan, the directors are awarded a specified number of shares in the company. These shares are again awarded for achieving predefined levels of performance. The shares may be awarded on an 'all or nothing basis', that is, all of the shares will be awarded if the performance level is reached and none will be awarded if it is not. Alternatively, shares may be awarded on a sliding scale according to the actual level of performance achieved. Awarding shares, in addition to the number specified, may be used to reward exceptional performance. The shares will be awarded to directors at the end of the performance period, which is typically three to five years.

Under a performance share plan, directors may be awarded **restricted shares**. This type of share is issued to the directors immediately, but the shares are not owned outright. They may be forfeited under certain circumstances, such as where the directors fail to reach the prescribed level of performance, or where they leave the company before the end of the performance period. Restricted shares are rarely issued in the UK.

Share awards will transfer to directors some of the risks and rewards of being a shareholder. This may help directors to think more like shareholders and to strive to enhance shareholder wealth. The process for awarding shares, however, can provoke much head scratching. Finding an appropriate performance measure, setting the appropriate performance level for triggering a bonus award and determining the number of shares to be awarded to directors are all areas fraught with difficulties.

The main elements of the remuneration package for an executive director of a listed public company are summarised in Figure 7.3.

An executive director will normally receive a fixed element and a variable element, with the latter being performance-related.

Figure 7.3 The main elements of remuneration for an executive director of a listed public company

In large listed companies, the variable (performance-related) element typically accounts for a large proportion of the total remuneration for executive directors. In practice, however, the variable element may contain a hidden fixed element. Few directors of large companies receive no annual bonus at all (see Reference 11 at the end of the chapter). The methods used to calculate the variable element of directors' remuneration can be very complicated. This can make it difficult to discover the link between the amounts awarded to directors and the company's financial results.

Real World 7.9 provides an impression of how the total remuneration for executive directors of the UK's largest companies is made up.

Real World 7.9

Just rewards?

KPMG, the accounting and consulting firm, revealed in its 2017 Guide to Directors' Remuneration the following median figures and other details relating to annual basic salaries, annual bonuses and performance share payments for executive directors in the 100 largest listed UK companies.

	Chief Executive	Finance Director	Other executive directors
Basic salary	£871,000	£552,000	£546,000
Total annual bonus received (as percentage of salary)	130%	124%	138%
Maximum permitted bonus deferral (as percentage of salary)	50%	50%	50%
Deferral period	3 years	3 years	3 years
PSP maximum award (as a percentage of salary)	250%	205%	200%
PSP actual award (as percentage of salary)	245%	201%	196%
Total earnings	£3,478,000	£2,128,000	£1,951,000

Source: Guide to Directors' Remuneration 2017, KPMG, Extracts from Summary, p. 2.

A comparison of the data in Real Worlds 7.2 and 7.9 reveals a huge gulf between the remuneration received by part-time, non-executive directors and that received by full-time, executive directors.

The UK Code regards a performance-related element for the remuneration of non-executive directors as inappropriate. It takes the view that non-executive directors should be rewarded on the basis of the time spent and responsibilities undertaken on behalf of the company.

Activity 7.20

Do you agree with this position? Should non-executive directors, as well as executive directors, have a performance-related element to their remuneration?

The view taken is that offering performance-related remuneration may undermine their independence. Not all countries, however, adopt this view.

Tenure and service contracts

The UK Code requires that all directors submit themselves for annual re-election by shareholders. This is designed to encourage greater accountability. There are, however, concerns that it can be disruptive and can encourage short-term thinking among board members. The chair should not remain in position for more than nine years, according to the Code.

Directors are normally given service contracts, but these should not provide immunity against poor performance. Where directors have underperformed, the board must be prepared to terminate their contracts. To prevent the risk of overcompensation when contracts are terminated, the UK Code states that notice periods should be no longer than one year and any compensation awarded should exclude rewards for poor performance. In practice, however, poor performance may prove no obstacle to receiving a handsome payout. **Real World 7.10** provides a recent example of where directors were accused of being rewarded for failure.

Real World 7.10

Rewarding failure?

The main lobby group representing UK bosses has savaged the 'highly inappropriate' pay packets awarded to directors running the now-collapsed construction giant Carillion. Roger Barker, head of corporate governance at the Institute of Directors, said the collapse of the company 'suggests that effective governance was lacking at Carillion'. He added: 'There are some worrying signs. The relaxation of clawback conditions for executive bonuses in 2016 appears in retrospect to be highly inappropriate. It does no good to the reputation of UK business when top managers appear to benefit in spite of the collapse of the organisations that they are responsible for.'

His comments on clawback refer to a change in the company's pay policy made in 2016 that limited the criteria under which the company could demand the repayment of executive bonuses. Previously the firm could ask for cash back if the business went bust but the revised policy said it could only do so in the event of gross misconduct or if the financial results had been misstated.

Much of the criticism has centred on Richard Howson, Carillion's former chief executive from 2012 until a shock profit warning last July resulted in his stepping down. Howson earned £1.5 million in 2016, including £591,000 in bonuses. He continued to work for the firm until last autumn after stepping down as chief executive and is due to stay on the payroll, receiving his £660,000 salary and £28,000 benefits for another year, until October 2018.

Vince Cable, the Liberal Democrat leader and former business secretary, said he hoped that bonuses paid to Carillion's chief executive would be clawed back. In an interview with the BBC's Daily Politics he said it was 'an absolute outrage' that senior executives should receive 'rewards for failure in this way'.

Source: Extracts from Goodley, S. (2018) Carillion's 'highly inappropriate' pay packets criticised, *Guardian*, 15 January.

Remuneration committee

The remuneration committee is the cornerstone of the UK Code's attempt to ensure that directors' rewards are appropriate. The UK Code states that this committee should be responsible for setting remuneration for the chair, executive directors and for senior management. For larger companies, the committee should consist of at least three (and for smaller companies at least two) independent non-executive directors.

Although this committee is meant to prevent executive directors from being over-rewarded, critics point out that, in recent years, directors' pay and benefits have increased at a much faster rate than have corporate profits and sales (or the pay and benefits in other occupations). Furthermore, studies have shown that the relationship between directors' pay and performance is not a very clear one (see Reference 12 at the end of the chapter).

The composition of the remuneration committee means that non-executive directors are responsible for determining the awards of executive directors. We have seen, however, that non-executive directors are often executive directors of other companies, which creates the risk that they will be sympathetic to a high-reward culture. To act as a counterweight, there have been calls for a representative of the workforce to be a member of the remuneration committee.

Activity 7.21

What objections may be raised to having a workforce representative on this committee? Try to think of at least one.

A number of objections have been raised. They include:

- the risk that the representative will not understand the company's strategy and the broader business context with which remuneration decisions are made;
- the difficulty of finding workforce representative that would truly reflect the views of the whole workforce, particularly for large international companies;
- the difficulty of finding a representative willing to challenge the directors and, perhaps, put at risk future career prospects; and
- the risk that the authority of the board will be weakened by having a workforce representative on a board committee.

The revised UK Code does not support the idea of a workers' representative but is sympathetic towards the workforce exerting a greater influence on board decisions generally. It requires the board of directors to engage with the workforce in order to understand its views and states that this should normally be done through one, or more, of the following mechanisms:

- a director appointed from the workforce;
- a workforce advisory panel; and/or
- a designated non-executive director.

Whether this greater engagement provides a moderating influence on directors' remuneration remains to be seen.

In addition to problems of committee membership, there are problems with the way in which the committee operates. It is to these problems that we now turn.

Problems with the process

Various studies have pointed to problems with the way in which remuneration committees operate. One study by Main and others (see Reference 13 at the end of the chapter) interviewed 22 independent non-executive directors with experience of remuneration committees and found that the companies for which they served held, on average, 4.8 committee meetings per year. These meetings were tightly scheduled and often fairly brief (on average 1.5 hours). Despite the importance of their role, it seems that these committees do not devote much time to carrying it out. The study also found that it was quite common for the chief executive officer and chair to be present at remuneration committee meetings.

> **Activity 7.22**
>
> **Why might the presence of the CEO and chair be a problem?**
>
> While it may be useful for the committee to receive their input at times, there is a danger that the independence of the committee will be compromised by their presence.

There is some evidence that committee members lack the experience and training to carry out their tasks effectively (see Reference 14 at the end of the chapter). This can be a particular problem when hiring a new chief executive officer. The pool of talent for chief executives is small and it is a 'seller's market'. As a result, to recruit a suitable candidate, the committee may be tempted to offer more than is necessary. Incumbent chief executive officers may also be over-rewarded. They are often powerful personalities with considerable influence over other board members. There is a risk that committee members will be too deferential and will err on the side of generosity in contract negotiations.

There is some concern as to how market data is used by remuneration committees in formulating appropriate reward packages. Too great a focus on market trends and statistics can lead to a 'ratcheting effect' on executive directors' rewards. This occurs when the data is used to justify increases in rewards because companies do not want to be seen paying below-average rewards to directors. The upward pressure on the average level of rewards occurs without a corresponding increase in performance.

Non-executive directors

Setting up a remuneration committee does not deal with the problem of who decides the pay of the non-executive directors.

> **Activity 7.23**
>
> **Who do you think should decide the pay of the non-executive directors?**
>
> The UK Corporate Governance Code states that this should be done in accordance with the company's documents of incorporation, or by the board of directors. In the latter case, the executive directors largely decide the pay of the non-executive directors (a point which may not be lost on those non-executive directors serving on the remuneration committee!).

Reporting directors' remuneration

Listed companies are required by law to prepare an annual directors' remuneration report that consists of two parts. The first part is concerned with remuneration policy. It must set out each element of remuneration to which each director is entitled and how it supports the company's strategy and performance. Shareholders are given a binding vote, at least every three years, whether to approve this part of the report. The second part must set out how the remuneration policy was implemented during the financial year. It will contain a figure for the total pay each director receives, which includes all benefits received such as salaries, pension benefits, benefits in kind and share awards. Reporting this single figure should help comparisons to be made over time and between companies. Shareholders are given an advisory vote each year as to whether to approve this part of the report.

The chair of the remuneration committee will normally attend the shareholders' meeting to deal with any issues that may arise.

> **Activity 7.24**
>
> How might these requirements to publish influence the level of directors' remuneration?
>
> Publishing a remuneration report, as well as seeking shareholder approval for remuneration policy and remuneration payments, may help to moderate the level of directors' remuneration.

There is some concern, however, that the reporting requirements could have unintended consequences. It has been suggested, for example, that the disclosure of sensitive, pay-related, information could increase the ratcheting effect on directors' pay.

PERFORMANCE MEASURES

We saw earlier that much of the remuneration received by executive directors is performance-related. Various performance measures can be used as a basis for rewarding directors and we shall go on to consider some of the more popular of these. Before doing so, however, it is useful to identify the characteristics that a good performance measure should possess. Perhaps the key characteristics are that it should:

- be in line with the objectives and strategy of the company;
- lead to a convergence of directors' and shareholders' interests;
- reflect the achievement of the directors; and
- be robust and not easily distorted by particular policies, financing arrangements or manipulative practices.

No single performance measure perfectly encapsulates all of these characteristics. In practice, therefore, companies often employ a combination of measures. When calculating an annual bonus for executive directors, for example, the majority of large UK companies use three or more measures (see Reference 11 at the end of the chapter).

Let us now turn our attention to three of the more popular performance measures found in practice.

Total shareholder return

Total shareholder return (TSR) is a measure that investors employ to assess value created. It is also used as a basis for rewarding directors. The total return from a share is made up as follows:

1. the increase (or decrease) in share value over a period plus (minus); and
2. any dividends paid during the period.

This total return is usually expressed as a percentage of the start-of-period share price.
To illustrate how total shareholder return is calculated, let us assume that a company started trading after issuing shares of £0.50 each at their nominal value (P_0) and by the end of the first

year of trading the shares had increased in value to £0.55 (P_1). Furthermore, the company paid a dividend of £0.06 (D_1) per share during the period. We can calculate the total shareholder return as follows:

$$\text{Total shareholder return} = \frac{D_1 + (P_1 - P_0)}{P_0} \times 100\%$$

$$= \frac{0.06 + (0.55 - 0.50)}{0.50} \times 100\% = 22\%$$

The figure calculated has little information value when taken alone. It can only really be used to assess performance when compared with some benchmark.

Activity 7.25

What benchmark would be most suitable?

Perhaps the best benchmark to use would be the returns made by similar companies operating in the same industry over the same period of time.

Where this benchmark is used, returns generated will be compared with those generated from other investment opportunities with the same level of risk.

TSR and directors' rewards

Using TSR as a basis for rewarding directors has been subject to much criticism. This measure has a number of serious flaws, which include the following:

- Share prices reflect investors' views concerning future returns. This means that directors receive rewards based on expected future performance rather than on actual performance, though it can be argued that the dividend plus the increase in the share price has actually occurred.
- Prices quoted for the shares of a listed company may not provide a reliable guide to their 'true' value. There may be times when investors' perceptions about the value of shares become detached from underlying reality.
- Share price movements may be beyond the control of directors. (For this reason, TSR-based incentives have been described as a lottery for directors.)
- Directors may achieve higher share returns by simply taking on higher-risk projects. This policy shift may not, however, align with the risk appetite of investors.
- The contribution of individual directors to changes in TSR cannot normally be determined.
- Finding similar companies against which to assess relative performance may be difficult. There is also the risk that unsuitable companies will be deliberately selected by directors to make their performance appear better than it is.
- TSR can be manipulated over the short term (by, for example, the timing of important announcements).

Economic value added (EVA®)

Performance targets based on **economic value added (EVA®)** offer another approach. This measure has been developed and trademarked by a US management consultancy firm, Stern Stewart. EVA®, however, is based on the idea of economic profit, which has been around for many years. The measure reflects the point made earlier that for a company to be profitable in an economic sense, it must generate returns that exceed the returns required by investors. It is not enough simply to make an accounting profit, because this measure does not take full account of the returns required by investors.

EVA® indicates whether the returns generated exceed the returns required by investors. The formula is:

$$EVA® = NOPAT - (R \times C)$$

where:

NOPAT = Net operating profit after tax
R = Returns required by investors (that is, the cost of capital)
C = Capital invested (that is, the net assets of the company).

Activity 7.26

Dena plc has net assets of £250 million and the required return from investors is 10 per cent. The company made a net operating profit of £50 million for the year and the appropriate tax rate is 20 per cent. What is the EVA® for the year?

EVA® will be:

$$(£50 - (20\% \times £50m)) - (10\% \times £250m) = £15m$$

Only when EVA® is positive can we say that the company is increasing shareholder wealth. To maximise shareholder wealth, managers must increase EVA® by as much as possible.

Activity 7.27

What can managers do in order to increase EVA®? (*Hint*: use the formula shown above as your starting point.)

The formula suggests that in order to increase EVA®, managers may try to:

- Increase NOPAT. This may be done either by reducing expenses or by increasing sales revenue.
- Use capital invested more efficiently. This means selling off assets that are not generating returns that exceed their cost and investing in assets that do; and/or
- reduce the required rates of return for investors. This may be achieved by changing the capital structure in favour of long-term borrowing (which tends to be cheaper to service than share capital).

EVA® relies on conventional financial statements to measure the wealth created for shareholders. However, the NOPAT and capital figures shown on these statements are used only as a starting point. They have to be adjusted because of the problems and limitations of conventional measures. According to Stern Stewart, the major problem is that profit and capital are understated because of the conservative bias in accounting measurement. Profit may be understated as a result of arbitrary write-offs such as research and development expenditure written off and as a result of excessive provisions being created (such as allowances for trade receivables). Capital may also be understated because assets are reported at their original cost (less amounts written off), which can produce figures considerably below current market values. In addition, certain assets such as internally generated goodwill and brand names are normally omitted from the financial statements because no external transactions have occurred.

Stern Stewart has identified more than a hundred adjustments that could be made to the conventional financial statements to eliminate the conservative bias. However, it believes that, in practice, only a handful of adjustments to the accounting figures of any particular company tend to be needed. Unless an adjustment is going to have a significant effect on the calculation of EVA®, it is really not worth making.

EVA and directors' rewards

Under EVA®, directors can receive rewards based on achievement over a particular period. Where that period is only one year, directors are given an incentive to increase EVA® over the short term. This may be achieved, however, by cutting back on investment. To encourage a longer-term perspective, rewards should be based on the ability of directors to improve EVA® over a number of years.

The amount of EVA® generated during a period is rarely reported to shareholders. This means that shareholders will be unable to check whether rewards given to directors are appropriate.

Earnings per share

We may recall that the earnings per share (EPS) ratio is calculated as follows:

$$\text{Earnings per share} = \frac{\text{Earnings available to ordinary shareholders}}{\text{Number of ordinary shares in issue}}$$

When used as a basis for directors' incentive plans, a particular level of growth in EPS is usually required in order to trigger rewards.

A major difficulty with using this measure for rewarding directors is that an increase in EPS does not necessarily lead to an increase in shareholder wealth. EPS may be increased by embarking on higher risk ventures with higher prospective returns. This higher risk will, however, be reflected in a lower share price. A further difficulty is that EPS can be increased in the short term by changing certain management decisions and accounting policies.

Activity 7.28

Can you think how EPS could be increased in the short term by changes in management decisions and accounting policies?

Management can decide to restrict expenditure on discretionary items such as training, research and nurturing brands. Changes in accounting policies, such as changing the point at which revenue is recognised, and changes in depreciation methods can also increase EPS in the short term.

Other measures of performance, such as return on capital employed, profit before interest and tax or some measure of cash flow generated, are used in practice to reward executive directors. They often suffer, however, from the same sort of problems that afflict EPS.

Real World 7.11 provides some insight to the popularity of the measures discussed among larger UK listed businesses.

Real World 7.11

Measure for measure

The KPMG survey mentioned earlier found that PSPs continue to be the most common form of LTIP for the largest 100 listed companies. Furthermore, TSR and EPS are the most popular measures for inclusion in PSPs. The findings of the survey are set out in Figure 7.4.

Figure 7.4 Target measures for inclusion in PSPs

- Pure TSR: 6%
- TSR and other: 35%
- Pure EPS: 3%
- EPS and other: 16%
- TSR and EPS: 10%
- TSR, EPS and other: 21%
- Other: 9%

The measures falling under the category 'Other' include measures such as profits, cash flow, share price targets and return on capital.

Source: Guide to Directors' Remuneration 2017, KPMG, p. 59.

ASSESSING BOARD PERFORMANCE

It was mentioned earlier that the performance of the board should be subject to regular evaluation. This raises the question as to who should carry out the evaluation. The choice is effectively between the board members themselves or an external party, such as a firm of management consultants. In practice, it seems that boards prefer self-evaluation. The UK Code, however, states that, for larger companies, an external evaluation should be undertaken at least every three years.

Activity 7.29

What are the advantages and disadvantages of board members, rather than an external party, evaluating board performance?

The main advantage is that the board members have an intimate knowledge of the company's business and of board operations. They should therefore be in a position to ask more searching questions. A further advantage is that there is a low risk that confidentiality will be breached.

> A disadvantage is that shareholders might view this as being rather too cosy an arrangement. They may feel that an external party would provide a more objective and a more rigorous assessment of board performance. This may give more credibility to the process (although the cost is likely to be much higher).

A second question raised concerns the areas of performance that should be evaluated. Some possible areas, based on the UK Corporate Governance Code and other sources of good practice, are set out in Table 7.1.

Table 7.1 Evaluating board performance

Company objectives	■ Are the objectives of the company clearly set out? ■ Is the board fully committed to these objectives? ■ Are the objectives used as a framework for board decisions? ■ Is there a regular board review of progress towards the achievement of the objectives?
Controlling the company	■ Is the system of internal control and reporting regularly reviewed by the board? ■ Are the risk management and reporting systems regularly reviewed by the board?
Board structure and roles	■ Are the roles and responsibilities of the board clearly defined? ■ Is the relationship between the board and key board committees appropriate and clear? ■ Are the roles of the chair and non-executive directors appropriate and clear?
Board meetings	■ Are board meetings called with sufficient frequency to permit timely decisions? ■ Is relevant material, including written agendas and minutes of previous meetings, sent to directors prior to a board meeting? ■ Are all directors required to attend board meetings and what is their attendance record? ■ Do the discussions at board meetings focus on strategic rather than operational issues? ■ Are urgent problems arising between board meetings properly managed and reported?
Board composition	■ Is there a separation of the roles of chair and chief executive? ■ Does the board reflect an appropriate balance between executive and non-executive directors? ■ Does the board membership reflect an appropriate mix of age, skills and experience? ■ Is the membership of important board committees, such as remuneration and audit committees, appropriate? ■ Do the tenure agreements of board members provide the opportunity to refresh the board over time?
Board discussions and decisions	■ Does the board work together in an effective manner? ■ Do board discussions result in appropriate decisions being made? ■ Are board decisions implemented and monitored? ■ Are board members given the time and opportunity to express their views on key issues? ■ Is the contribution of all directors at board meetings satisfactory? ■ Are board discussions and decisions dominated by key individuals?
Board relations with shareholders	■ Are there appropriate policies in place for communicating with shareholders? ■ Are the communication channels established between the board and institutional and private shareholders appropriate? ■ Are shareholders satisfied that their views are heard and considered by the board?
Board appointments and development	■ Are rigorous procedures in place for the appointment of new directors? ■ Are there clearly defined and appropriate procedures in place for appraising the performance of individual directors? ■ Are appropriate training and development programmes (including induction programmes) available to board members? ■ Has the board developed clear succession plans?

THE RISE OF SHAREHOLDER ACTIVISM

Improving corporate governance has focused mainly on developing a framework of rules for managing listed companies. Whilst rules are important, it is also important for the shareholders, who own the companies, to play their part by actively monitoring and controlling directors' behaviour. We shall now identify the main shareholders of listed companies and discuss their role in establishing good corporate governance. We also consider why there has been greater shareholder activism in recent years.

Who are the main shareholders?

Real World 7.12 provides an analysis of the ownership of shares in UK listed companies at the end of 2016.

Real World 7.12

Going overseas

The breakdown of ownership of UK listed shares as at 31 December 2016 is shown in Figure 7.5.

Category	%
Rest of the world	53.9
Insurance companies	4.9
Pension funds	3.0
Individuals	12.4
Unit trusts	9.5
Investment trusts	2.1
Other financial institutions	8.1
Charities, church, etc.	1
Private non-financial companies	2.2
Public sector	1.1
Banks	1.8

Figure 7.5 Beneficial ownership of UK shares by UK investors, 31 December 2016

> Looking at the changes in the ownership of listed shares over the years shows two striking features:
>
> 1. the value of listed shares owned by overseas residents has gone up progressively from 30.7 per cent in 1998 to 53.9 per cent in 2016; and
> 2. the value of listed shares held by UK individuals has fallen from 16.7 per cent in 1998 to 12.3 per cent in 2016.
>
> However, the percentage of shares held by each group appears to have stabilised in the past few years.
>
> There is no reason to believe that the 53.9 per cent of shares owned by non-UK shareholders is any more weighted towards individuals than is the case with UK shareholders.
>
> Source: *Ownership of UK Quoted Shares 2016*, Table 4, Office for National Statistics, 29 November 2017. Office for National Statistics licensed under the Open Government Licence v.3.0.

Activity 7.30

The rise of financial institutions means that private individuals have less direct investment in listed shares than in the past. Does that mean they have less financial interest in listed shares?

No. It means that individuals are tending to invest through the institutions, for example by making pension contributions rather than buying shares directly. Ultimately, all of the investment finance must come from individuals.

The concentration of ownership of listed shares means that financial institutions have enormous voting power. As result, there is the potential to exercise significant influence over the way in which Stock Exchange listed companies are directed and controlled. In the past, however, these institutions have been reluctant to exercise this power. They have been criticised for being too passive and for allowing the directors of companies too much independence.

What can shareholders do?

There are two main ways in which shareholders can try to control the behaviour of directors. These are by:

- introducing incentive plans for directors that link their remuneration to the share performance of the company. In this way, the interests of directors and shareholders should become more closely aligned; and
- closely monitoring the actions of the directors and exerting influence over the way in which they use company resources.

The first issue was picked up earlier. It is the second issue to which we now turn.

Getting active

In the past, financial institutions chose to take a non-interventionist approach to the affairs of a company. Instead, they confined their investment activities to deciding whether to buy, hold or sell shares in a particular company. They appear to have taken the view that the costs of actively engaging with directors and trying to influence their decisions are too high in relation to the likely benefits. It is worth pointing out that these costs are borne by the particular financial institution that becomes actively involved, whereas the benefits are spread across all shareholders. (This phenomenon is often referred to as the 'free-rider' problem.)

Waking the sleeping giants

In recent years, financial institutions have begun to play a more active role in corporate governance. More time is being invested in monitoring the actions of directors and in engaging with them over key decisions. This change of heart has occurred for a variety of reasons. One important reason is that the increasing concentration of share ownership has made it more difficult for financial institutions to simply walk away from an investment in a poorly performing company by selling its shares.

Activity 7.31

Why might it be a problem for a financial institution that holds a substantial number of shares in a poorly performing company to simply sell the shares?

Where a substantial number of shares are held, a decision to sell can have a significant impact on the market price, perhaps leading to heavy losses.

A further reason why it may be difficult to disinvest is that a company's shares may be included in a stock market index (such as the FTSE 100 or FTSE 250). Certain types of financial institution, such as investment trusts or unit trusts, may offer investments that are designed to 'track' the particular index and so they become locked into a company's shares in order to reflect the index. In both situations outlined, therefore, a financial institution may have little choice but to stick with the shares held and try to improve performance by seeking to influence the actions and decisions of the directors.

It is also worth mentioning that financial institutions have experienced much greater competitive pressures in recent years. There have been increasing demands from clients for them to demonstrate their investment skills, and so justify their fees, by either outperforming benchmarks or beating the performance of rival financial institutions. This, in turn, has led the institutions to be less tolerant towards underperforming boards of directors.

Finally, the regulatory environment has favoured greater activism on the part of financial institutions. This point will be considered in more detail a little later.

Forms of activism

It is important to clarify the term 'shareholder activism' as it can take various forms. In its simplest form, it involves taking a more active role in voting for or against the resolutions put before the annual general meeting or any extraordinary general meeting of the company. This form of activism is seen by the UK government as being vital to good corporate governance. The government is keen to see much higher levels of participation than currently exist, and expects institutional shareholders to exercise their right to vote. In the past, financial institutions have often indicated their dissent by abstaining from a vote rather than by outright opposition to a resolution. However, they are now more prepared to use their vote to oppose resolutions of the board of directors.

A particularly rich source of contention between shareholders and directors' concerns directors' remuneration. **Real World 7.13** provides an example of a fairly recent falling out.

> **Real World 7.13**
>
> ## Revolting shareholders
>
> Ryanair faces a fresh shareholder revolt at its annual meeting this month after adviser groups called on investors to vote against executive pay. An influential trio of advisers – Institutional Shareholder Services, Glass Lewis and Pirc – have recommended investors vote against the low-cost carrier's advisory pay report, flagging concerns about 'poor disclosure' and bonus payments.
>
> Europe's biggest airline by passenger numbers has frequently clashed with shareholders at its annual meetings. Last year, almost a fifth of investors revolted on pay, marking the third year in a row when the airline faced significant protests over its remuneration policies. ISS, Glass Lewis and Pirc, whose recommendations are widely used by asset managers and pension funds when deciding how to vote, said the total pay of Michael O'Leary, Ryanair's chief executive, was not excessive, but expressed concerns about how his bonus was calculated. Mr O'Leary's total pay last year was €3.26 million, including a bonus.
>
> Glass Lewis said it had 'severe reservations about supporting the remuneration report at this time'. 'We believe shareholders should be concerned by the structure of the company's executive remuneration programme and the inadequacy of disclosure regarding several aspects of executive compensation,' it said. ISS said: 'While there has been some improvement, the overall level of disclosure remains lacking and does not allow for visibility between the vigour of targets set against performance achieved by the company.'
>
> Mr O'Leary has repeatedly dismissed concerns about pay structures at the airline and big bonuses at listed companies. 'My view of shareholders voting against my pay package is: if you don't like it, don't vote against it – sell your shares,' Mr O'Leary said last week.
>
> The calls for a rebellion at Ryanair come as institutional investors increasingly show their teeth at annual meetings. Eighteen out of 20 big investors, including BlackRock, cast fewer votes in favour of management recommendations at AGMs in the year to the end of June, compared with the previous 12 months, according to data from Proxy Insight.
>
> *Source*: Extracts from Mooney, D. (2017) Ryanair faces fresh shareholder rebellion over executive pay ft. com, 7 September. © The Financial Times Limited 2017. All rights reserved.

The latest version of the UK Code has sought to defuse some of the tensions relating to this issue by laying down various principles concerning how directors' remuneration should be managed and calculated. Thus, when setting directors' remuneration, the remuneration committee must try to promote long-term business success and must take account of wider company pay policy. The UK Code also requires that account be taken, among other things, of the need for clarity and simplicity when calculating rewards and the reputational risk arising from granting excessive rewards. To prevent undue reliance on formulaic calculations, the UK Code expects the remuneration committee to exercise discretion and independent judgement. Finally, it requires the committee to explain, in an annual report, the rationale for the remuneration policies adopted and the level of engagement that took place with shareholders and with the wider workforce concerning these policies.

The UK Code requires boards to be sensitive to shareholder dissatisfaction, which includes dissatisfaction over directors' remuneration. Where 20 per cent, or more, of shareholder votes have been cast against a board resolution, the board should seek feedback from shareholders on the contentious issue. It should also explain in the annual report what impact this feedback had on board decisions and what further action is proposed.

Shareholder revolts over directors' remuneration often catch the headlines but are still fairly unusual occurrences. During 2017, there were only two instances among the largest 350 listed businesses where a majority of votes were cast against the directors' remuneration report. (See Reference 15 at the end of the chapter.) Nevertheless, the benefits for shareholders of flexing their muscles and voting against resolutions put forward by the directors may go beyond their immediate, intended objective: other boards of directors may take note of shareholder dissatisfaction and adjust their behaviour in an attempt to avoid a similar fate. The cost of voting need not be high as there are specialist agencies which offer research and advice to financial institutions on how their votes should be cast.

Another form of activism involves meetings and discussions between representatives of a particular financial institution and the board of directors of a company. At such meetings, a wide range of issues affecting the company may be discussed.

Activity 7.32

What might financial institutions wish to discuss with the directors of a company? Try to think of at least two financial and two non-financial aspects of the company.

Some of the more important aspects that are likely to attract their attention include:

- objectives and strategies adopted;
- trading performance;
- internal controls;
- policies regarding mergers and acquisitions;
- major investments and disinvestments;
- adherence to the recommendations of the UK Corporate Governance Code;
- corporate social responsibility; and
- directors' incentive schemes and remuneration.

This is not an exhaustive list. For shareholders, as owners of the company, anything that might have an impact on their wealth should be a matter of concern.

This form of activism requires a fairly high degree of involvement with the company, and some of the larger financial institutions have dedicated teams for this purpose. This can be, therefore, a costly exercise.

Meetings between financial institutions and the managers of the companies, in which they hold shares, can be a useful mechanism for exchanging views and for gaining a greater understanding of the needs and motivations of each party. This may help to pre-empt public arguments between the board of directors and financial institutions, which is rarely the best way to resolve issues.

The final form of activism involves intervention in the affairs of the company. This, however, can be very costly, depending on the nature of the problem. Where strategic and operational issues raise concerns, intervention can be very costly indeed. Identifying the weaknesses and problems relating to these issues requires a detailed understanding of the nature of the business. This implies close monitoring by relevant experts who can analyse the issues and then propose feasible solutions. The costs associated with such an exercise would normally be prohibitive, although the costs may be mitigated through some kind of collective action by financial institutions.

Not all forms of intervention in the affairs of a company, however, need be costly. Where, for example, there are corporate governance issues to be addressed, such as a failure to adhere to the recommendations of the UK Corporate Governance Code, a financial institution may nominate individuals for appointment as non-executive directors who can be relied upon to ensure that necessary changes are made. This should involve relatively little cost for the financial institution.

The main forms of shareholder activism are summarised in Figure 7.6.

There are three main forms of shareholder activism, as explained in the text.

Figure 7.6 The main forms of shareholder activism

UK Stewardship Code

To improve the quality of engagement between financial institutions and investee businesses, the Financial Reporting Council (FRC) has published the **UK Stewardship Code**. This sets out key principles concerning the way in which financial institutions should engage with investee businesses. They relate to financial institutions:

- establishing policies relating to stewardship and voting procedures, along with periodic reporting of how these policies were actioned.
- checking on investee businesses
- establishing the circumstances under which stewardship activities are intensified and accepting the need, at times, to act in concert with other shareholders.
- disclosing conflicts of interest arising from stewardship activities and how they are resolved.

The Code also offers guidance on how these principles should be enacted.

Real World 7.14 describes how Thomas Miller Investment (TMI) will escalate its stewardship activities so as to protect shareholder value. This relates to the fourth requirement of the Code identified above.

The UK Stewardship Code, like the UK Governance Code, operates on a 'comply or explain' basis. It is designed to provide principles and guidance rather than rigid rules. Financial institutions that are signatories to the code are graded, or tiered, by the FRC according to the quality and transparency of the information provided.

Real World 7.14

Getting active

As a general policy we aim to support the management of the companies in which we invest but our dialogue with companies is a robust one and we will form our own views on the strategy and governance of a business. On occasion our views may differ from those of management or the Board and this may give rise to an escalation in our engagement. Factors taken into account prior to an escalation include an assessment of the materiality of the matter in dispute, the size of our shareholding, the timeframe of the investment thesis and the ownership profile of the business in question. Escalation can also occur when we become aware of differences between directors. Our specific response will always be determined on a case by case basis and there will be instances when we choose to sell our shares.

When escalation is deemed appropriate our first step is often to make contact with other significant shareholders to determine whether they share our views or concerns. Following these conversations, we will speak to the company's advisers and/or independent directors for a further exchange of views. Our strong preference is to achieve our objectives in a consensual and confidential manner but when differences with a company remain we may consider joint engagement with other shareholders, escalating concerns if necessary to regulators and more public forms of dissent, although as a general policy we do not favour using the media to help achieve our objectives. If differences with a company remain unresolved we may vote against the Board in a general meeting or even requisition an extraordinary general meeting to enable all investors to vote on the matter in dispute. We would not normally intervene on an operational matter but topics which have given rise to escalation in the past include the need for management and/or Board change, strategy, capital structure, M&A, protection of shareholder rights, remuneration and other ESG-related issues.

Source: (2018) *Responsible Investment Policy* Fidelity International, February, P.4.

Shareholder activism and short-term behaviour

Shareholder activism is generally regarded as a force for good. There are times, however, when this may not be the case. Some shareholders engage with companies simply in order to extract short-term gains. **Real World 7.15** warns of the problems this can create.

The future of shareholder activism

Shareholder activism appears to be taken an increasing hold. In a study of 400 activist campaigns in the US, McKinsey and Co found that shareholder activism is becoming more frequent and target businesses are becoming larger in size. Perhaps unsurprisingly, the study also found that activism is often provoked by the underperformance of a business in relation to industry peers. While three quarters of activist campaigns began by taking a collaborative approach, almost half of these eventually turned hostile (see Reference 16 at the end of the chapter.)

> **Real World 7.15**
>
> ## Ignoring the long term
>
> Terry Smith, a successful fund manager, has warned against activist shareholders who seek only short-term gains. He has argued:
>
> When an activist shareholder becomes involved in a company, the modus operandi is often something like this.
>
> 1. Acquire a stake in the company, usually via on-market purchases;
> 2. Campaign noisily for change, which can entail the company trying to sell itself to an acquirer, splitting itself into a number of listed entities for each of its activities, taking on more debt, buying back its own shares, or some combination of these;
> 3. The share price rises as a result of excitement about this activity, which it is claimed will 'create shareholder value' and benefit all investors;
> 4. Sell the shares at a profit.
>
> Nothing wrong with that, you might think, and certainly not from the point of view of the activist. But there is plenty wrong for those of us who are long-term investors and actually want to own the shares to gain from their ability to compound in value over time. We are often left trying to make sense of fragmented businesses, new management teams, higher gearing, the costs of separation or integration and financial statements which are rendered incomprehensible by many adjustments.
>
> This particular problem of activism comes from confusing creating shareholder value with making the share price go up. One should lead to the other, but when short-term share price movements become the main objective, as they clearly are with many activists, the inevitable by-product is future problems for the business and its long-term shareholders.
>
> *Source:* Smith, T (2015) Shareholder value is an outcome not an objective, ft.com 6 February.
> © The Financial Times Limited 2015. All rights reserved.

A key question to be asked is whether shareholder activism makes any real difference to financial performance. Early research in the US was not encouraging for those who urge large investing institutions to take a more active approach. However, a more recent study of 2,000 active interventions found that the operating performance of US businesses was improved for a five-year period following the interventions (see Reference 17 at the end of the chapter). The McKinsey study mentioned above also found a positive effect from activist interventions. The study states:

> Our analysis of 400 activist campaigns (out of 1,400 launched against US companies over the past decade) finds that, among large companies for which data are available, the median activist campaign reverses a downward trajectory in target-company performance and generates excess shareholder returns that persist for at least 36 months. (p. 1)

The key elements required for good corporate governance, which have just been discussed, are summarised in Figure 7.7.

Figure 7.7 Key elements for ensuring good corporate governance

Self-assessment question 7.1

The board of directors of Hexworthy Publishers plc recently endured a stormy annual general meeting of shareholders. During this meeting, the directors were subjected to intense scrutiny and criticism. Two of the non-executive directors were not re-elected for office by shareholders and all members of the remuneration committee resigned when a proposed new long-term performance share plan for directors was comprehensively rejected.

At the meeting, shareholders expressed grave concerns over the way in which the company was being managed and felt that they were not being properly informed of key decisions. They were also concerned that the share price had fallen significantly over the past three years while directors' remuneration had increased significantly over the same period.

The board of directors met to decide how to respond to the anger of shareholders. At this meeting, it was decided to appoint Parix Consulting to carry out a thorough review of board performance. Parix Consulting would also be charged with advising the directors on the composition of the new remuneration committee and the ways in which communications between shareholders and the board could be improved.

Required:
Assume that you are a partner in Parix Consulting.

(a) Identify the sources of information that may be used to help evaluate the performance of the board of directors. (Use the checklist set out in Table 7.1 on p. 290 as the basis for carrying out this task.)
(b) Suggest a possible composition for the remuneration committee that may help to restrain excessive pay awards to executive directors.
(c) Set out recommended forms of communication with the shareholders, which incorporate corporate governance rules and good practice, for consideration by the board of directors.

The solution to this question can be found at the back of the book, starting on page 305.

SUMMARY

The main points of this chapter may be summarised as follows:

Corporate governance
- Corporate governance issues arise because of the separation of ownership from control of the company.
- Corporate governance rules are based around the principles of disclosure, accountability and fairness.
- The UK Corporate Governance Code, which applies to UK Stock Exchange listed companies, adopts a 'comply-or-explain' approach. It contains principles and guidance on corporate governance matters as well as annual reporting requirements.

The board of directors
- The board governs the company on behalf of the shareholders.
- It is responsible for setting the strategic direction, exercising control and nurturing relations with shareholders and others.
- The chair must lead and manage the board of directors.
- The chair's role involves ensuring that the board operates effectively, providing advice and support to directors, communicating with shareholders and ensuring that the performance of the board and the directors is subject to regular scrutiny.
- The UK Corporate Governance Code states that the roles of chair and chief executive should not be occupied by the same person. Furthermore, the chief executive should not go on to become chair of the same company.
- The board is made up of executive and non-executive directors, all of which have the same legal obligation to the shareholders of the company.

The role of non-executive directors
- Non-executive directors are part-time and do not engage in the day-to-day running of the company.
- This more detached role allows them to take a more objective view of issues confronting the company.

- Non-executive directors contribute to the main tasks of the board and also play a key role in board committees concerned with the nomination of directors, the remuneration of executive directors and the integrity of financial statements.
- The role of non-executive directors contains the potential for conflict between the need to work with executive directors as part of a team and the need to monitor and assess the performance of executive directors on behalf of the shareholders.

The audit process
- An external audit is required by all but the smallest companies.
- External auditors are appointed by, and report to, the shareholders. Their role is to examine the annual financial statements that have been prepared by the directors.
- Differences in perception can arise between external auditors and shareholders concerning the role of auditors.
- Various measures have been put in place to strengthen the independence of external auditors.
- Many large companies have an internal audit function to provide reassurance to directors about the reliability of the company's control and financial reporting systems.
- The UK Corporate Governance Code states that an audit committee should be created to ensure financial reporting and internal control principles are properly applied and for maintaining an appropriate relationship with the external auditors.
- The terms of reference of the committee will be determined by the board of directors.
- An audit committee report will be prepared for shareholders and presented at the AGM.

Remunerating directors
- The UK Corporate Governance Code states that executive directors' remuneration should be designed to promote strategy and long-term sustainable success of the company.
- The remuneration of executive directors will usually include a fixed element and a variable element, with the latter being linked to the achievement of performance targets.
- The variable element normally rewards short-term performance through an annual bonus and long-term performance through share awards.
- The remuneration committee is the cornerstone of the UK Corporate Governance Code's attempt to ensure that directors' rewards are appropriate.
- Various problems in the way in which a remuneration committee functions may have contributed to excessive rewards being paid to directors.

Performance measures
- Performance targets should be consistent with the objectives and strategy of the company, align the interests of directors with those of shareholders, reflect the achievement of the directors and be robust.
- TSR (total shareholder return) measures changes in shareholder wealth. To assess relative performance, similar companies must be used as a benchmark.

- EVA® (economic value added) indicates whether the returns generated exceed the returns required by investors. It relies on conventional financial statements to measure the wealth created but adjusts these to reflect the conservative bias in accounting measurement.
- EPS (earnings per share) can be used as a performance target by setting a particular level of growth required.
- Most listed public companies use a variety of measures and incentives to reward executive directors rather than relying on a single measure.

Assessing board performance
- The board should be subject to regular evaluation, which may be carried out by the board itself or by an external party.
- Areas of performance to be evaluated may include achievement of company objectives, control exercised over the company's activities, board structure and roles, board meetings, board composition, board discussions and decisions, relations with shareholders and board appointments and development.

The rise of shareholder activism
- Institutional shareholders have taken a more active role in the affairs of listed companies in recent years.
- Activism takes the form of using their votes, meetings with directors and intervention in a company's affairs.
- There is some evidence to suggest that activism can improve returns to shareholders.

KEY TERMS

chair	remuneration committee
executive directors	external audit
non-executive directors	expectations gap
UK Corporate Governance Code	internal audit
corporate culture	performance share plan (PSP)
executive committee	restricted shares
chief executive officer (CEO)	total shareholder return (TSR)
audit committee	economic value added (EVA®)
risk management committee	UK Stewardship Code
nomination committee	

REFERENCES

1. Grant Thornton (2017) *Corporate Governance Review 2017*, www.grantthornton.co.uk.
2. Kimbell, D. and Neff, T. (2006) Separating the roles of chairman and chief executive: Looking at both sides of the debate, *Spencer Stuart Research and Insight*, July, p. 2.
3. Stiles, P. and Taylor, B. (2001) *Boards at Work*, Oxford University Press, p. 108.
4. Owen, G. and Kirchmaier, T. (2006) *The Changing Role of the Chairman: Impact of Corporate Governance Reform in the UK 1995–2005 on Role, Board Compensation and Appointment*, March.

5. Cameran M., Negri G. and Pettinicchio A. (2015) The audit mandatory rotation rule: The state of the art, *Journal of Financial Perspectives*, Vol. 3, issue 2.
6. FT View (2018) What the public should expect from auditors, ft.com, 14 March.
7. Financial Reporting Council (2016) *Guidance on Audit Committees*, April, p. 4, frc.org.uk.
8. KPMG's Audit Committee Institute, *2015 Global Audit Committee Survey*, p. 32.
9. Financial Reporting Council (2016) *Guidance on Audit Committees*, April, p. 10, frc.org.uk.
10. Sulkowicz, K. (2003) New organisational and psychological challenges of the audit committee, *Audit Committee Quarterly*, Audit Committee Institute, issue 8.
11. KPMG (2014), *KPMG's Guide to Directors Remuneration 2014*, kpmg.co.uk, p. 50.
12. Girma, S., Thompson, S. and Wright, P. (2007) Corporate governance reforms and executive compensation determination: Evidence from the UK, *The Manchester School*, Vol. 75, pp. 65–81.
13. Main, B., Jackson, C., Pymm, J. and Wright, V. (2007) Questioning the remuneration committee process, Working Paper, 21 February.
14. Lincoln, D., Young, D., Wilson, T. and Whiteley, P. (2006) *The Role of the Board Remuneration Committee*, PARC Research Report, March.
15. KPMG (2017) *Guide to Directors' Remuneration 2017*, kpmg.co.uk, p. 9
16. Criac, J., De Backer R. and Sanders J. (2014) *Preparing for Bigger, Bolder, Shareholder Activists*, www.mckinsey.com, March.
17. Bebchuk, L., Brav, A. and Jiang, W. (2015) *The Long-term Effects of Hedge Fund Activism*, NBER Working Paper Number 21227, June.

FURTHER READING

If you would like to explore the topics covered in this chapter in more depth, we recommend the following:

Mallin, C. (2016) *Corporate Governance*, 5th edn, Oxford University Press, Chapters 3, 6, 8 and 9.

Millichamp A and Taylor J. (2018) *Auditing*, 11th edn, Cengage Learning, Chapters 1, 2, 7 and 9.

Open University (2016) *Influences on Corporate Governance*, Open University.

Tricker, B. (2015) *Corporate Governance Principles, Policies and Practices*, Oxford University Press, Chapters 13, 14 and 16.

CRITICAL REVIEW QUESTIONS

Solutions to these questions can be found at the back of the book, starting on page 312.

7.1 Assume that you have been asked by the chair of a large listed business to prepare a report highlighting the main areas to be used as a basis for evaluating the performance of the chief executive. Identify and briefly discuss five areas that could be included in the report.

7.2 What are the benefits of separating the roles of chair and chief executive? Should such a separation be made compulsory?

7.3 A large listed business wishes to improve its payroll accounting systems and is seeking outside help to do this. The external auditors are a large firm of accountants that has a consultancy arm. What are the advantages and disadvantages of allowing the external auditors to undertake this task?

7.4 A large listed business has become the target of a shareholder activist. What steps should the board of directors take in response to this event?

EXERCISES

Solutions to exercises with **coloured numbers** can be found at the back of the book, starting on page 319.

Basic-level exercise

7.1 Identify five ways in which the independence of an auditor of a large listed company may be strengthened.

Intermediate-level exercises

7.2 Assume that the chair of the board of directors of a large public listed company has asked you to develop a set of criteria against which the performance of a non-executive director could be appraised. Based on the discussion of the non-executive's role found in the chapter, identify at least six criteria that you might select.

7.3 Reviewing the risk management systems within a company goes beyond the traditional role of internal audit. What changes may have to be made to the internal audit function to enable it to carry out this enhanced role?

7.4 The board of directors of a listed company is likely to place considerable emphasis on maintaining good communications and strong relationships with its institutional shareholders. What are the main benefits and problems of doing this?

Advanced-level exercise

7.5 The newly appointed chair of Vorak plc has been told that considerable tension and suspicion exists between the executive and non-executive directors on the board. The executive directors question the competence of the non-executive directors and the non-executive directors believe that important information is being withheld from them. Assuming that the concerns of each group are well founded, what advice would you give to the chair as to how to ease the tension and promote a better working relationship between the two groups?

SOLUTIONS TO SELF-ASSESSMENT QUESTIONS

Chapter 2

2.1 Simonson Engineering

(a) The statement of financial position should be set out as follows:

Simonson Engineering
Statement of financial position as at 30 September 2018

	£
ASSETS	
Non-current assets	
Property, plant and equipment	
Property	72,000
Plant and machinery	25,000
Fixtures and fittings	9,000
Motor vehicles	15,000
	121,000
Current assets	
Inventories	45,000
Trade receivables	48,000
Cash in hand	1,500
	94,500
Total assets	215,500
EQUITY AND LIABILITIES	
Equity	
Closing balance*	120,500
Non-current liabilities	
Long-term borrowings	51,000
Current liabilities	
Trade payables	18,000
Short-term borrowings	26,000
	44,000
Total equity and liabilities	215,500
* The equity is calculated as follows:	
Opening balance	117,500
Profit	18,000
	135,500
Drawings	(15,000)
Closing balance	120,500

(b) The statement of financial position shows:

- The biggest investment in assets is property, followed by trade receivables and inventories. These, combined, account for more than 76% of the value of assets held.
- The investment in current assets accounts for 44% of the total investment in assets.

- The total long-term finance is divided 70% equity and 30% long-term borrowings. There is, therefore, not excessive reliance on long-term borrowings.
- The current assets (which are cash or near cash) cover the current liabilities (which are maturing obligations) by a ratio of more than 2:1.

(c) The revised statement of position will be as follows:

Simonson Engineering
Statement of financial position as at 30 September 2018

	£
ASSETS	
Non-current assets	
Property, plant and equipment	
Property	115,000
Plant and machinery	25,000
Motor vehicles	15,000
Fixtures and fittings	9,000
	164,000
Current assets	
Inventories	38,000
Trade receivables	48,000
Cash in hand	1,500
	87,500
Total assets	251,500
EQUITY AND LIABILITIES	
Equity	
Closing balance (120,500 + 43,000 − 7,000)	156,500
Non-current liabilities	
Long-term borrowings	51,000
Current liabilities	
Trade payables	18,000
Short-term borrowings	26,000
	44,000
Total equity and liabilities	251,500

Chapter 3

3.1 TT and Co.

Statement of financial position as at 31 December 2017

	£
ASSETS	
Delivery van (12,000 − 2,500)	9,500
Inventories (143,000 + 12,000 − 74,000 − 16,000)	65,000
Trade receivables	
(152,000 − 132,000 − 400)	19,600
Cash at bank (50,000 − 25,000 − 500 − 1,200	750
− 12,000 − 33,500 − 1,650 − 12,000 + 35,000	
+ 132,000 − 121,000 − 9,400)	
Prepaid expenses (5,000 + 300)	5,300
Total assets	100,150
EQUITY AND LIABILITIES	
Equity (50,000 + 26,900)	76,900
Trade payables (143,000 − 121,000)	22,000
Accrued expenses (630 + 620)	1,250
Total equity and liabilities	100,150

Income statement for the year ended 31 December 2017

	£
Sales revenue (152,000 + 35,000)	187,000
Cost of goods sold (74,000 + 16,000)	(90,000)
Gross profit	97,000
Rent	(20,000)
Rates (500 + 900)	(1,400)
Wages (33,500 + 630)	(34,130)
Electricity (1,650 + 620)	(2,270)
Bad debts	(400)
Van depreciation ((12,000 − 2,000)/4)	(2,500)
Van expenses	(9,400)
Profit for the year	26,900

The statement of financial position could now be rewritten in a more stylish form as follows:

Statement of financial position as at 31 December 2017

	£
ASSETS	
Non-current assets	
Property, plant and equipment	
Delivery van at cost	12,000
Accumulated depreciation	(2,500)
	9,500
Current assets	
Inventories	65,000
Trade receivables	19,600
Prepaid expenses	5,300
Cash	750
	90,650
Total assets	100,150
EQUITY AND LIABILITIES	
Equity	
Closing balance	76,900
Current liabilities	
Trade payables	22,000
Accrued expenses	1,250
	23,250
Total equity and liabilities	100,150

Chapter 4

4.1 Dev Ltd

(a) The summarised statement of financial position of Dev Ltd, immediately following the rights and bonus issue, is as follows:

Statement of financial position

	£000
Net assets (235 + 40 (cash from the rights issue))	275
Equity	
Share capital: 180,000 shares @ £1 ((100 + 20) + 60)	180
Share premium account (30 + 20 − 50)	–
Revaluation reserve (37 − 10)	27
Retained earnings	68
	275

Note that the bonus issue of £60,000 is taken from capital reserves (reserves unavailable for dividends) as follows:

	£000
Share premium account	50
Revaluation reserve	10
	60

More could have been taken from the revaluation reserve and less from the share premium account without making any difference to dividend payment possibilities.

(b) There may be pressure from a potential lender for the business to limit its ability to pay dividends. This would place lenders in a more secure position because the maximum buffer, or safety margin, between the value of the assets and the amount owed by the business is maintained. It is not unusual for potential lenders to insist on locking in shareholders' funds in this way as a condition of granting the loan.

(c) The summarised statement of financial position of Dev Ltd, immediately following the rights and bonus issue, assuming a minimum dividend potential objective, is as follows:

Statement of financial position

	£000
Net assets (235 + 40 (cash from the rights issue))	275
Equity	
Share capital: 180,000 shares @ £1 ((100 + 20) + 60)	180
Share premium account (30 + 20)	50
Revaluation reserve	37
Retained earnings (68 − 60)	8
	275

(d) Before the bonus issue, the maximum dividend was £68,000. Now it is £8,000. The bonus issue has therefore locked in an additional £60,000 of assets and thereby restricted the business's ability to pay dividends.

(e) Before the issues, Lee had 100 shares worth £2.35 (£235,000/100,000) each or £235 in total. Lee would be offered 20 shares in the rights issue at £2 each or £40 in total. After the rights issue, Lee would have 120 shares worth £2.2917 (£275,000/120,000) each or £275 in total.

The bonus issue would give Lee 60 additional shares. After the bonus issue, Lee would have 180 shares worth £1.5278 (£275,000/180,000) each or £275 in total.

None of this affects Lee's wealth. Before the issues, Lee had £235 worth of shares and £40 more in cash. After the issues, Lee has the same total wealth but all £275 is in the value of the shares.

(f) The things that we know about the company are as follows:
- It is a private (as opposed to a public) limited company, as it has 'Ltd' (limited) as part of its name, rather than plc (public limited company).
- It has made an issue of shares at a premium, almost certainly after it had traded successfully for a period. (There is a share premium account. It would be unlikely that the original shares, issued when the company was first formed, would have been issued at a premium.)
- Some of the assets in the statement of financial position have been upwardly revalued by at least £37,000. (There is a revaluation reserve of £37,000. This may be only what is remaining after an earlier bonus issue used part of this reserve.)
- The company has traded at an aggregate profit (though there could have been losses in some years), net of tax and any dividends paid. (There is a positive balance on retained earnings.)

Chapter 5

5.1 Comments

(a) Dividends announced between the end of the reporting period and the date at which the financial reports are authorised for publication should *not* be treated as a liability in the statement of financial position at the end of that period. IAS 1 specifically precludes the treatment of such dividends as liabilities.

(b) IAS 1 provides support for three key accounting conventions – accruals, going concern and consistency. It does not specifically support the historic cost convention.

(c) IAS 1 does not permit bank overdrafts to be offset against positive bank balances when preparing the statement of financial position. For the sake of relevance they should be shown separately.

(d) IAS 8 states that accounting policies should be changed if it is required by a new financial reporting standard *or* if it leads to more relevant and reliable information being reported.

(e) IAS 10 states that *significant* non-adjusting events occurring between the end of the reporting period and the date at which the financial statements are authorised should be disclosed by way of note. The standard requires the nature of the event and its likely financial effect to be disclosed.

(f) Preparing a strategic report may present a problem for accountants. For information to be credible to all interested parties, accountants should be as neutral as possible in measuring and reporting the financial performance and position of the business. The strategic report requires some interpretation of results and there is always a risk of bias, or at least the perception of bias among some users, in what items are reported and how they reflect on business performance. The board of directors is charged with running the business and it is logical that the directors accept full responsibility for preparing the report. This should be made clear to users.

Chapter 6

6.1 Ali plc and Bhaskar plc

To answer this question, you may have used the following ratios:

	Ali plc	Bhaskar plc
Return on ordinary shareholders' funds ratio	$99.9/687.6 \times 100 = 14.5\%$	$104.6/874.6 \times 100 = 12.0\%$
Operating profit margin ratio	$151.3/1{,}478.1 \times 100 = 10.2\%$	$166.9/1{,}790.4 \times 100 = 9.3\%$
Inventories turnover period ratio	$592.0/1{,}018.3 \times 12 = 7.0$ months	$403.0/1{,}214.9 \times 12 = 4.0$ months
Settlement period for trade receivables ratio	$176.4/1{,}478.1 \times 12 = 1.4$ months	$321.9/1{,}790.4 \times 12 = 2.2$ months
Current ratio	$\dfrac{853.0}{422.4} = 2.0$	$\dfrac{816.5}{291.3} = 2.8$
Acid test ratio	$\dfrac{(853.0 - 592.0)}{422.4} = 0.6$	$\dfrac{(816.5 - 403.0)}{291.3} = 1.4$
Gearing ratio	$\dfrac{190}{(687.6 + 190)} \times 100 = 21.6\%$	$\dfrac{250}{(874.6 + 250)} \times 100 = 22.2\%$
Interest cover ratio	$\dfrac{151.3}{19.4} = 7.8$ times	$\dfrac{166.9}{27.5} = 6.1$ times
Earnings per share	$\dfrac{99.9}{320.0} = £0.31$	$\dfrac{104.6}{250.0} = £0.42$
Price earnings ratio	$\dfrac{£6.50}{£0.31} = 21.0$ times	$\dfrac{£8.20}{£0.42} = 19.5$ times

310 Financial Accounting Reporting and Analysis

(Note: It is not possible to use any average ratios because only the end-of-year figures are provided for each business.)

Ali plc seems more effective than Bhaskar plc at generating returns for shareholders indicated by the higher ROSF ratio. This may be partly caused by Ali plc's higher operating profit margin.

Both businesses seem to have a very high inventories turnover period; this probably needs to be investigated. This ratio is particularly high for Ali plc. Both may suffer from poor inventories management.

Ali plc has a lower settlement period for trade receivables than Bhaskar plc. This may suggest that Bhaskar plc needs to exert greater control over trade receivables.

Ali plc has a much lower current ratio and acid test ratio than Bhaskar plc. The acid test ratio of Ali plc is substantially below 1.0, which may suggest a liquidity problem.

The gearing ratio of each business is quite similar. Neither business seems to have excessive borrowing. The interest cover ratios are also similar: they indicate that both businesses have good profit coverage for their interest charges.

Earnings per share is significantly higher for Ali plc than for Bhaskar plc. However, the P/E ratio for Ali plc is slightly higher. This latter ratio suggests that the market considers Ali plc to have slightly better prospects than Bhaskar plc.

To draw better comparisons between the two businesses, it would be useful to calculate other ratios from the financial statements. It would also be helpful to calculate ratios for both businesses over (say) five years as well as key ratios of other businesses operating in the same industry.

Chapter 7

7.1 Hexworthy and Parix

(a) The sources of information that may be used may include the following:

- documents setting out the:
  - strategic plan of the company;
  - board structure and roles;
  - board appointments procedures;
  - operations of the board;
  - minutes of board meetings;
  - meeting agendas and background information;
  - criteria for directors' appraisal;
- interviews with board members;
- interviews with and/or questionnaires sent to senior management and shareholders;
- attendance and observation at board meetings;
- attendance and observation at meetings with shareholders, including the AGM;
- company website and published material, including the annual reports;
- CVs of board members;
- performance reports (such as monthly budget reports and sales reports) received by the board; and
- information relating to training and development programmes carried out.

This is not an exhaustive list. You may have thought of other sources of information.

(b) The remuneration committee must be sensitive to the needs of shareholders and others with respect to directors' rewards. This has led some to argue that the committee should include an employee representative and, or, a shareholder representative. Perhaps, as a further brake on excessive rewards, the committee should also exclude from membership any non-executive director who is also an executive director of a large listed company. Such suggestions would, however, fly in the face of normal practice and could create various problems. A more conventional suggestion is to ensure that the committee has a chair who has the experience and emotional intelligence required to anticipate problems and to be aware of the risks involved.

(c) Communication with shareholders can take various forms. The following are either required by law or are considered to be good practice:

- distribution of annual reports and interim reports to all shareholders as well as their publication on the company's website;
- timely releases throughout the year concerning major developments;
- a chairman's address at the annual general meeting;
- an address by the chairman of the audit committee and the chairman of the remuneration committee at the annual general meeting;
- an opportunity for shareholders to question the board of directors at the annual general meeting;
- publication of notice of all shareholder meetings on the website;
- dedicated staff to manage the company website and deal with shareholder queries;
- prompt publication of announcements and press releases on the company website;
- briefings for major shareholders and analysts and their publication on the company website;
- regular meetings between major shareholders and the chairman and chief executive;
- regular meetings between non-executive directors and major shareholders; and
- email newsletters setting out new developments, financial results, announcements and so on to major shareholders and analysts.

SOLUTIONS TO CRITICAL REVIEW QUESTIONS

Chapter 1

1.1 Accounting, like a spoken language, is a form of communication. It provides those with an interest in a business with a common means of understanding its financial health and performance. However, while a spoken language is general purpose in nature and can cover a wide range of different issues, the language of accounting is restricted to financial issues. It does not, therefore, have the same breadth of 'vocabulary' as a spoken language.

1.2 The main users of financial information for a university and the purposes for which they need information may be summed up as follows:

Students	Whether to enrol on a course of study. This would probably involve an assessment of the university's ability to continue to operate and to fulfil students' needs.
Other universities and colleges	How best to compete with the university. This might involve using the university's performance in various aspects as a 'benchmark' when evaluating their own performance.
Employees	Whether to take up or to continue in employment with the university. Employees might assess this by considering the ability of the university to continue to provide employment and to reward employees adequately for their labour.
Government/funding authority	How efficient and effective the university is in undertaking its various activities. Possible funding needs that the university may have.
Local community representatives	Whether to allow/encourage the university to expand its premises. To assess this, the university's ability to continue to provide employment for the community, to use community resources and to help fund environmental improvements might be considered.
Suppliers	Whether to supply the university with goods and services on credit. This would involve an assessment of the university's ability to pay for any goods and services supplied.
Lenders	Whether to lend money to the university and/or whether to require repayment of any existing loans. This would involve assessing the university's ability to pay interest and to repay the principal.
Board of governors and managers (faculty deans and so on)	Whether the performance of the university requires improvement. Performance to date would be compared with earlier plans or some other 'benchmark' to decide whether action needs to be taken. Whether there should be a change in the university's future direction. In making such decisions, management will need to look at the university's ability to perform and at the opportunities available to it.

We can see that the users of accounting information and their needs are broadly similar to those of a private sector business.

1.3 Not-for-profit organisations do not pursue profit as their *primary* objective. However, this does not mean that they are indifferent about, or uninterested in, making a profit. By creating wealth (profit), they are usually better placed to pursue their primary objective, such as the relief of suffering or the education of students, more effectively.

A not-for-profit organisation will normally need to account to those with a stake in the organisation how wealth was generated and how it was applied in pursuit of its stated objectives. Hence, it will have a keen interest in monitoring and reporting the inflows and outflows of wealth over time. A good accounting system and sound financial practice can therefore be as vital for this type of organisation as it is for a business.

1.4 We can never be sure what is going to happen in the future, the best we can often do is to make judgements based on past experience. Thus, information concerning past flows of cash and wealth in the recent past may well be useful in helping to form judgements about possible future outcomes.

Chapter 2

2.1 The owner seems unaware of the business entity convention in accounting. This convention requires a separation of the business from the owner(s) of the business for accounting purposes. The business is regarded as a separate entity and the statement of financial position is prepared from the perspective of the business rather than that of the owner. As a result, funds invested in the business by the owner are regarded as a claim that the owner has on the business. In the standard layout of the statement of financial position, this claim will be shown alongside other claims on the business from outsiders.

2.2 A statement of financial position does not show what a business is worth, for two major reasons:

1. Only those items that can be measured reliably in monetary terms are shown on the statement of financial position. Thus, things of value such as the reputation for product quality, skills of employees and so on will not normally appear in the statement of financial position.
2. The historic cost convention results in assets often being recorded at their outlay cost rather than their current value. For certain assets, the difference between historic cost and current value may be significant.

2.3 The statement of financial position is a static financial statement, showing only the situation at a single moment in time, whereas the other two major statements – the income statement and statement of cash flows – are dynamic, showing flows of wealth and cash over time. We saw in Chapter 1 that a business exists in order to generate wealth for its owners. The amount of wealth (profit) generated for a particular period is revealed in the income statements. As a result, this statement tends to be the main focus of attention for many users. The statement of cash flows is also of critical importance. In order to survive over time, a business must have an uninterrupted capacity to pay its debts when they fall due. This means that there must be sufficient cash available when needed.

Apart from its static nature, we saw in the answer to Question 2.2 above, that the statement of financial position provides only a restricted view of financial health. Nevertheless, the statement of financial position still offers important insights and should not be regarded as of secondary importance. To understand the financial health of a business all three major financial statements must be examined.

2.4 Some object to the idea of humans being treated as assets for inclusion on the statement of financial position. It is seen as demeaning for humans to be listed alongside inventories, plant and machinery and other assets. Others argue, however, that humans are often the most valuable resource of a business and that placing a value on this resource will help bring to the attention of managers the importance of nurturing and developing this 'asset'.

Humans are likely to meet the criterion of an asset relating to future potential benefits, otherwise there would be little point in employing them. The criterion relating to exclusive right

Chapter 3

3.1 When preparing the income statement, it is not always possible to determine accurately the expenses that need to be matched to the sales revenue for the period. It is perhaps only at some later point that the true position becomes clear. Nevertheless, we must try to include all relevant expenses and so estimates of the future have to be made. These estimates may include accrued expenses, depreciation charges and bad debts incurred. The income statement would lose much of its usefulness if we were to wait for all uncertainties to become clear.

3.2 Depreciation attempts to allocate the cost or fair value, less any residual value, of an asset over its useful life. Depreciation does not attempt to measure the fall in value of the asset during a particular accounting period. Thus, the carrying amount of the asset appearing on the statement of financial position normally represents the unexpired part of its cost, or fair value, rather than its current market value.

3.3 The convention of consistency aims to provide some uniformity in the application of accounting policies. In certain areas, there may be more than one method of accounting for an item, for example inventories. The convention of consistency states that, having decided on a particular accounting policy, a business should continue to apply the policy in successive periods. While this policy helps to ensure that more valid comparisons can be made of business performance *over time,* it does not ensure that valid comparisons can be made *between businesses.* Different businesses may still consistently apply different accounting policies.

3.4 An expense is that element of the cost incurred that is used up during the reporting period. An asset is that element of cost that is carried forward on the statement of financial position and which will normally be used up in future periods. Thus, both assets and expenses arise from costs being incurred. The major difference between the two is the period over which the benefits (arising from the costs incurred) accrue.

Chapter 4

4.1 A private limited company would seem to be more appropriate. The principal advantage of a public limited company is its ability to offer issues of new shares to the general public. This does not seem not to be a consideration for this particular business, since you and your friend feel that you can finance the start up and planned expansion from your own resources. Being a private company means that neither you nor your friend could sell shares to a third party without you both agreeing to it. This may well be something that you would both prefer, at this stage.

4.2 Some businesses arrange, at significant economic cost, to have their shares listed on the London Stock Exchange (LSE). They do this because they see the need for shareholders to have an easy means of selling their shares whenever they choose to do so. Unless investors have the opportunity to sell their shares through the LSE, they will be reluctant to take up shares issued by a business. This will make it more difficult and, probably, more costly for the business to raise equity finance. This means that the LSE barring the business's shares from being traded will be to the great disadvantage of the business.

4.3 This statement is untrue. All that is required for a market to be efficient is active trading by investors researching the various factors affecting each business's economic fortunes. Between them, these investors will generate, through their buying and selling activities, a share price that represents the best estimate of the share's true value. In effect, a business's current share price represents a consensus view among investors of the share's true worth.

4.4 Companies would generally prefer not to issue preference shares because they impose a moral obligation to pay a dividend. Failure to pay a preference dividend may be embarrassing for the company and show it in a bad light to investors. Preference shareholders do not have a right to receive a dividend. They only have a right to receive the first slice of any dividend declared.

From a potential shareholder's perspective, preference shares would not provide the greater certainty of returns that a loan would give. At the same time, preference shares do not give their holders the level of returns associated with ordinary shares.

Chapter 5

5.1 Managers may shy away from an open and meaningful evaluation of the performance and position of a business because of the risk of litigation. If legal action may result from making statements in good faith or making predictions that prove to be inaccurate, managers will be advised by their lawyers to be very guarded and to stick to making only bland statements. To avoid this risk, managers acting in good faith could be awarded some sort of legal protection (safe harbour). This should help to improve the quality of their commentaries. In the UK, the directors' liability for the strategic report is protected by a 'safe harbour' provision.

5.2 Accounting is an evolving subject. It is not static and the conceptual framework that is laid down at any particular point in time may become obsolete. This may occur as a result of changes in our understanding of the nature of accounting information and its impact on users, or as a result of changes in the economic environment within which accounting is employed. We must accept, therefore, that accounting principles will continue to evolve and those currently employed must be regularly reviewed.

5.3 Accounting rules impose an important discipline on managers. They help to ensure that unscrupulous directors do not exploit their position and portray an unrealistic view of financial health. They are also important for the purpose of comparability, both over time and between businesses.

Harmonisation may lead to sovereignty-related problems. Each country has its own tax laws, banking laws, financial regulations and stock exchange rules. International accounting rules may well conflict with these national rules. Furthermore, international rules may not fit well with the local business culture and the way in which businesses operate.

Harmonisation may also lead to some businesses, which operate solely within the confines of its own country, having to comply with international rules.

5.4 The main methods of creative accounting are misstating revenues, massaging expenses, misstating assets, concealing 'bad news' and inadequate disclosure.

Harmonisation of accounting rules will often draw on best practice occurring in highly developed countries. Other countries may well have weaker rules in place, leading to poor quality financial reporting. By harmonising accounting rules, businesses operating within those countries will need to comply with more demanding rules for financial reporting.

Chapter 6

6.1 The fact that a business operates on a low operating profit margin indicates that only a small operating profit is being produced for each £1 of sales revenue generated. However, this does not necessarily mean that the ROCE will be low. If the business is able to generate sufficient sales revenue, the operating profit may be very high even though the operating profit per £1 of sales revenue is low. If the overall operating profit is high, this can lead, in turn, to a high ROCE, since it is the total operating profit that is used as the numerator (top part of the fraction) in this ratio. Many businesses (including supermarkets) pursue a strategy of 'low margin, high sales revenue'.

6.2 The statement of financial position is drawn up at a single point in time – typically, the end of the reporting period. As a result, the figures shown on the statement represent the position at that single point in time and may not be representative of the position during the period. Wherever possible, average figures (perhaps based on monthly figures) should be used. However, an external user may have access only to the opening and closing statements of financial position for the year and so a simple average based on these figures may be all that it is possible to calculate. Where a business is seasonal in nature or is subject to cyclical changes, this simple averaging may not be sufficient.

6.3 Three possible reasons for a long inventories turnover period are:
- poor inventories controls, leading to excessive investment in inventories;
- inventories hoarding in anticipation of price rises, shortages or increased future sales;
- to be able to offer customers a wide range of products or to be able to supply promptly at all times.

A short inventories turnover period may be due to:
- tight inventories controls, reducing excessive investment in inventories and/or the amount of obsolete and slow-moving inventories;
- an inability to finance the required amount of inventories to meet sales demand;
- a difference in the mix of inventories carried by similar businesses (for example, greater investment in perishable goods which are held for a short period only).

These are not exhaustive lists; you may have thought of other reasons.

6.4 Size may well be an important factor when comparing businesses:
- Larger businesses may be able to generate economies of scale in production and distribution to an extent not available to smaller businesses.
- Larger businesses may be able to raise finance more cheaply, partly through economies of scale (for example, borrowing larger amounts) and partly through being seen as less of a risk to the lender.
- Smaller businesses may be able to be more flexible and 'lighter on their feet' than can the typical larger business.

These and other possible factors may lead to differences in performance and position between larger and smaller businesses.

Chapter 7

7.1 The main areas identified to evaluate a chief executive may include:
- setting a vision for the business and communicating the path towards that vision to employees;
- building an effective team of executive directors to manage the business;
- ensuring the business is properly resourced, in terms of finance, human resources and capacity to fulfil the vision that has been set;
- building a culture across the business that promotes openness, participation and high ethical standards; and
- achieving the financial and other targets set to achieve the stated vision.

You may have thought of others.

7.2 The main benefits of separation are that:
- it ensures that a single individual does not have too much power;
- the chairman can offer support and act as a mentor to the CEO;
- it can smooth the path of succession; and
- it can ensure that the responsibilities of both roles will be carried out more effectively than would be the case if a single individual occupied both roles.

There may be points in the history of a company when it would benefit from a strong leader with the required authority to be decisive and to overcome strong opposition. However, following this path would carry considerable risk.

7.3 The external auditors may have an intimate knowledge of the accounting and payroll systems that are currently in operation and may be well placed to suggest improvements that suit the company's needs. There may, therefore, be a saving of time and cost if they are given the task. However, there is always a risk that the external auditors will receive too high a proportion of the total fees received from the company in the form of consultancy work. This runs the risk of compromising the auditors' independence. New EU legislation now prohibits this kind of work being undertaken by the external auditors.

7.4 When approached by a shareholder activist, the board of directors should first:
- establish the underlying motivation of the activist, the tactics used and the past history of activism;
- evaluate the proposals that the activist wishes to see implemented; and
- ascertain the degree of support among other shareholders to the proposals.

To deal with the proposals, the board should:
- set up a team of senior directors to create a dialogue with the activist and to advise the board on any developments;
- prepare a detailed response to the proposals raised by the activist;
- establish whether there are any areas where collaboration with the activist is possible; and
- create a dialogue with other shareholders to ensure they are fully informed of the position of the board and the actions taken.

SOLUTIONS TO SELECTED EXERCISES

Chapter 2

2.1 Paul

Statement of cash flows for Thursday

	£
Opening balance (from Wednesday)	59
Cash from sale of wrapping paper	47
Cash paid to purchase wrapping paper	(53)
Closing balance	**53**

Income statement for Thursday

	£
Sales revenue	47
Cost of goods sold	(33)
Profit	**14**

Statement of financial position as at Thursday evening

	£
Cash	53
Inventories of goods for resale (23 + 53 − 33)	43
Total assets	**96**
Equity	**96**

2.2 Paul (continued)

Equity

	£
Cash introduced by Paul on Monday	40
Profit for Monday	15
Profit for Tuesday	18
Profit for Wednesday	9
Profit for Thursday	14
Total business wealth (total assets)	**96**

Thus the equity, all of which belongs to Paul as sole owner, consists of the cash he put in to start the business plus the profit earned each day.

2.3 Helen

Income statement for day 1

	£
Sales revenue (70 × £0.80)	56
Cost of sales (70 × £0.50)	(35)
Profit	**21**

Statement of cash flows for day 1

	£
Cash introduced by Helen	40
Cash from sales	56
Cash for purchases (80 × £0.50)	(40)
Closing balance	56

Statement of financial position as at end of day 1

	£
Cash balance	56
Inventories of unsold goods (10 × £0.50)	5
Total assets	61
Equity	61

Income statement for day 2

	£
Sales revenue (65 × £0.80)	52.0
Cost of sales (65 × £0.50)	(32.5)
Profit	19.5

Statement of cash flows for day 2

	£
Opening balance	56.0
Cash from sales	52.0
Cash for purchases (60 × £0.50)	(30.0)
Closing balance	78.0

Statement of financial position as at end of day 2

	£
Cash balance	78.0
Inventories of unsold goods (5 × £0.50)	2.5
Total assets	80.5
Equity	80.5

Income statement for day 3

	£
Sales revenue ((20 × £0.80) + (45 × £0.40))	34.0
Cost of sales (65 × £0.50)	(32.5)
Profit	1.5

Statement of cash flows for day 3

	£
Opening balance	78.0
Cash from sales	34.0
Cash for purchases (60 × £0.50)	(30.0)
Closing balance	82.0

Statement of financial position as at end of day 3

	£
Cash balance	82.0
Inventories of unsold goods	–
Total assets	82.0
Equity	82.0

2.6 Conversation

(a) The income statement reveals the changes in wealth arising as a result of trading operations. It shows the increase in wealth (revenue) during the period, the decrease in wealth (expenses) in order to generate revenue and the resulting net increase (profit) or decrease (loss) in wealth for the period. While most businesses hold some of their wealth in the form of cash, wealth is also held in other forms, such as non-current assets, receivables and so on.

(b) To be included in a statement of financial position as an asset, a resource must provide potential economic benefits. These benefits may arise from selling the asset in the market, but they may also arise from its use – for example, in production.

There are other conditions that must be met in order for an item to be included in the statement of financial position. These are:
- the business must control the asset; and
- the asset must be measurable in monetary terms with a reasonable degree of certainty.

(c) The accounting equation is:
$$\text{Assets} = \text{Equity} + \text{Liabilities}$$

(d) Non-current assets are assets that do not meet the criteria for current assets. They are normally held for the long-term operations of the business. Some non-current assets may be immovable (for example, property) but others are not (for example, motor vans).

(e) Goodwill may or may not have an indefinite life – it will depend on the nature of the goodwill. There are no hard and fast rules that can be applied. Where this asset has a finite life, it should be amortised. Where it is considered to have an indefinite life, it should not be amortised but should be tested annually for impairment.

2.7 Crafty Engineering

(a)

Statement of financial position as at 30 June last year

	£000
ASSETS	
Non-current assets	
Property, plant and equipment	
Property	320
Equipment and tools	207
Motor vehicles	38
	565
Current assets	
Inventories	153
Trade receivables	185
	338
Total assets	903
EQUITY AND LIABILITIES	
Equity (which is the missing figure)	441
Non-current liabilities	
Long-term borrowings (loan from Industrial Finance Company)	260
Current liabilities	
Trade payables	86
Short-term borrowings	116
	202
Total equity and liabilities	903

(b) The statement of financial position reveals a large investment in non-current assets. It represents more than 60% of the total investment in assets (565/903). The nature of the business may require a heavy investment in non-current assets. The current assets exceed the current liabilities by a large amount (approximately 1.7 times). Hence, there is no obvious sign of a liquidity problem. However, the statement of financial position reveals that the business has no cash balance and is therefore dependent on the continuing support of short-term borrowing to meet maturing obligations. When considering the long-term financing of the business, we can see that about 37% (that is, 260/(260 + 441)) of total long-term finance is supplied by borrowings and about 63% (that is, 441/(260 + 441)) by the owners. This level of long-term borrowing seems high but not excessive. However, we need to know more about the ability of the business to service the borrowing (that is, make interest payments and repayments of the amount borrowed) before a full assessment can be made.

Chapter 3

3.1 Comments

(a) Equity does increase as a result of the owners introducing more cash into the business, but it will also increase as a result of introducing other assets (for example, a motor car) and by the business generating revenue by trading. Similarly, equity decreases not only as a result of withdrawals of cash by owners but also by withdrawals of other assets (for example, inventories for the owners' personal use) and through trading expenses being incurred. Generally speaking, equity will alter more as a result of trading activities than for any other reason.

(b) An accrued expense is not one that relates to next year. It is one that needs to be matched with the revenue of the reporting period under review, but that has yet to be met in terms of cash payment. As such, it will appear on the statement of financial position as a current liability.

(c) The purpose of depreciation is not to provide for asset replacement. It is an attempt to allocate, in a systematic way, the cost, or fair value, of the asset (less any residual value) over its useful life. Depreciation provides a measure of the amount of a non-current asset that has been consumed during a period. This amount is then charged as an expense for the period. Depreciation is a book entry (the outlay of cash occurs when the asset is purchased) and does not normally entail setting aside a separate amount of cash for asset replacement. Even if this were done, there would be no guarantee that sufficient funds would be available at the end of the asset's life for its replacement. Factors such as inflation and technological change may mean that the replacement cost is higher than the original cost of the asset.

(d) In the short term, the current value of a non-current asset may exceed its original cost. However, nearly all non-current assets wear out over time through being used to generate wealth. This will be the case for buildings. Thus, some measure of depreciation is needed to reflect the fact that the asset is being consumed. Some businesses revalue their buildings upwards where the current value is significantly higher than the original cost. Where this occurs, the depreciation charge should be based on the revalued amount, which will lead to higher depreciation charges.

3.3 Business owner

Making a profit, while experiencing a downward movement in cash, may arise for various reasons. These include the following:

- the purchase for cash during the period of assets (for example, motor cars and inventories) which were not all consumed during the period and are, therefore, not having as great an effect on expenses as they are on cash;
- the payment of an outstanding liability (for example, borrowings), which will have an effect on cash but not on expenses in the income statement;
- the withdrawal of cash by the owners from the equity invested, which will not affect the expenses in the income statement; and
- the generation of revenue on credit where the cash has yet to be received. This will increase the sales revenue for the period but will not have a beneficial effect on the cash balance until a later period.

3.4 Missing values

(a) Rent payable – expense for period £9,000
(b) Rates and insurance – expense for period £6,000
(c) General expenses – paid in period £7,000
(d) Interest (on borrowings) payable – prepaid £500
(e) Salaries – paid in period £6,000
(f) Rent receivable – received during period £3,000

3.7 WW Associates

Income statement for the year ended 31 December 2017

	£
Sales revenue (211,000 + 42,000)	253,000
Cost of goods sold (127,000 + 25,000)	(152,000)
Gross profit	101,000
Rent (20,000)	(20,000)
Rates (400 + 1,500)	(1,900)
Wages (−1,700 + 23,800 + 860)	(22,960)
Electricity (2,700)	(2,700)
Machinery depreciation (9,360)	(9,360)
Loss on disposal of the old machinery (13,000 − 3,900 − 9,000)	(100)
Van expenses (17,500)	(17,500)
Profit for the year	26,480

The loss on disposal of the old machinery is the carrying amount (cost less depreciation) less the disposal proceeds. Since the machinery had only been owned for one year, with a depreciation rate of 30%, the depreciation to date is £3,900 (that is, £13,000 × 30%). The effective disposal proceeds were £9,000 because, as a result of trading it in, the business saved £9,000 on the new asset.

The depreciation expense for 2017 is based on the cost less accumulated depreciation of the assets owned at the end of 2017.

Statement of financial position as at 31 December 2017

	£
ASSETS	
Machinery (25,300 + 6,000 + 9,000 − 13,000 + 3,900 − 9,360)	21,840*
Inventories (12,200 + 143,000 + 12,000 − 12,700 − 25,000)	15,200
Trade receivables (21,300 + 211,000 − 198,000)	34,300
Cash at bank (overdraft) (8,300 − 23,000 − 25,000 − 2,000 − 6,000 − 23,800 − 2,700 − 12,000 + 42,000 + 198,000 − 156,000 − 17,500)	(19,700)
Prepaid expenses (400 − 400 + 5,000 + 500)	5,500
Total assets	57,140
EQUITY AND LIABILITIES	
Equity (owner's capital) (48,900 − 23,000 + 26,480)	52,380
Trade payables (16,900 + 143,000 − 156,000)	3,900
Accrued expenses (1,700 − 1,700 + 860)	860
Total equity and liabilities	57,140
* Cost less accumulated depreciation at 31 December 2016	25,300
Carrying amount of machine disposed of (£13,000 − £3,900)	(9,100)
Cost of new machine	15,000
Depreciation for 2017 (£31,200 × 30%)	(9,360)
Carrying amount (written-down value) of machine at 31 December 2017	21,840

The statement of financial position could now be rewritten in a more stylish form as follows:

Statement of financial position as at 31 December 2017

	£
ASSETS	
Non-current assets	
Property, plant and equipment	
Machinery at cost less depreciation	21,840
Current assets	
Inventories	15,200
Trade receivables	34,300
Prepaid expenses	5,500
	55,000
Total assets	76,840
EQUITY AND LIABILITIES	
Equity	52,380
Current liabilities	
Trade payables	3,900
Accrued expenses	860
Borrowings – bank overdraft	19,700
	24,460
Total equity and liabilities	76,840

3.8 Nikov and Co.

An examination of the income statements for the two years reveals a number of interesting points, which include:

- An increase in sales revenue and gross profit of 9.9% in 2018.
- The gross profit expressed as a percentage of sales revenue remaining at 70%.
- An increase in salaries of 7.2%.
- An increase in selling and distribution costs of 31.2%.
- An increase in bad debts of 392.5%.
- A decline in profit for the year of 39.3%.
- A decline in the profit for the year as a percentage of sales revenue from 13.3% to 7.4%.

Thus, the business has enjoyed an increase in sales revenue and gross profits, but this has failed to translate to an increase in profit for the year because of the significant rise in overheads. The increase in selling costs during 2018 suggests that the increase in sales revenue was achieved by greater marketing effort, and the huge increase in bad debts suggests that the increase in sales revenue may be attributable to selling to less creditworthy customers or to a weak debt-collection policy. There appears to have been a change of policy in 2018 towards sales, and this has not been successful overall as the profit for the year has shown a dramatic decline.

Chapter 4

4.1 Comment

Limited companies cannot set a limit on the amount of debts they will meet. They must meet their debts up to the limit of their assets, just as private individuals must. Reserves are part of the shareholders' claim against the assets of the company. These assets may, or may not, include cash. Dividends are normally paid in the form of cash but the legal ability of a company to pay dividends is not related to the amount of cash that it holds.

Preference shares do not carry a guaranteed dividend. They simply guarantee that the preference shareholders have a right to the first slice of any dividend that is paid. Shares of many public companies can be bought and sold by investors through the Stock Exchange. These transactions, however, has no direct effect on the company. The company is issuing no new shares. It is simply existing ('second-hand') shares that are being transferred between investors.

4.2 Comments

(a) The first part of the quote is incorrect. Bonus shares should not, of themselves, increase the value of shareholders' wealth. The total amount of shareholders' equity will not change as bonus shares are created through a transfer from reserves to ordinary share capital. Bonus shares, reflecting the amount of the transfer, are then distributed to shareholders in proportion to their existing shareholdings. Each shareholder's stake in the company will be unaffected by this transaction.

(b) This statement is incorrect. Shares can be issued at any price, provided that it is not below their nominal value. Once a company has been trading profitably for a period, its shares will not be worth the same as when the company was first formed (the nominal value). In these circumstances, issuing shares at above their nominal value would not only be legal, but essential to preserve the wealth of the existing shareholders in relation to any new shareholders.

(c) This statement is incorrect. Legally, the company is limited to making a maximum dividend based on the amount of its revenue reserves. These reserves reflect accumulated after-tax profits, or realised gains, remaining after previous dividend payments or trading losses. From a legal viewpoint, cash is not an issue when determining the maximum dividend. It would be perfectly legal for a company without cash to borrow the funds needed to pay a dividend. Whether such action would be commercially prudent is another question.

(d) This statement is partly incorrect. Companies do indeed have to pay tax on their profits. Depending on their financial circumstances, shareholders may also have to pay tax on their dividends.

4.4 Iqbal Ltd

Year	Maximum dividend £	
2014	0	No profit exists out of which to pay a dividend.
2015	0	There remains a cumulative loss of £7,000. Since the revaluation represents a gain that has not been realised, it cannot be used to justify a dividend.
2016	13,000	The cumulative net realised gains are derived as (−£15,000 + £8,000 + £15,000 + £5,000).
2017	14,000	The realised profits and gains for the year.
2018	22,000	The realised profits and gains for the year.

4.6 Pear Limited

Income statement for the year ended 30 September 2018

	£000
Revenue (1,456 + 18)	1,474
Cost of sales	(768)
Gross profit	706
Salaries	(220)
Depreciation (249 + 12)	(261)
Other operating costs (131 + (2% × 200) + 2)	(137)
Operating profit	88
Interest payable (15 + 15)	(30)
Profit before taxation	58
Taxation (58 × 30%)	(17)
Profit for the year	41

Statement of financial position as at 30 September 2018

	£000
ASSETS	
Non-current assets	
Property, plant and equipment	
Cost (1,570 + 30)	1,600
Depreciation (690 + 12)	(702)
	898
Current assets	
Inventories	207
Trade receivables (182 + 18 − 4)	196
Cash at bank	21
	424
Total assets	1,322
EQUITY AND LIABILITIES	
Equity	
Share capital	300
Share premium account	300
Retained earnings (104 + 41 − 25)	120
	720
Non-current liabilities	
Borrowings – 10% loan (repayable 2020)	300
Current liabilities	
Trade payables	88
Other payables (20 + 30 + 15 + 2)	67
Taxation	17
Dividend approved	25
Borrowings – bank overdraft	105
	302
Total equity and liabilities	1,322

4.7 Chips Limited

Income statement for the year ended 30 June 2018

	£000
Revenue (1,850 − 16)	1,834
Cost of sales (1,040 + 23)	(1,063)
Gross profit	771
Depreciation (220 (−2 − 5 + 8) + (94 × 20%))	(240)
Other operating costs	(375)
Operating profit	156
Interest payable (35 + 35)	(70)
Profit before taxation	86
Taxation (86 × 30%)	(26)
Profit for the year	60

Statement of financial position as at 30 June 2018

ASSETS

	Cost £000	Depreciation £000	£000
Non-current assets			
Property, plant and equipment			
Buildings	800	(112)	688
Plant and equipment	650	(367)	283
Motor vehicles (102 − 8);(53 − 5 + 19)	94	(67)	27
	1,544	(546)	998
Current assets			
Inventories			950
Trade receivables (420 − 16)			404
Cash at bank (16 + 2)			18
			1,372
Total assets			2,370

EQUITY AND LIABILITIES

	£000
Equity	
Ordinary shares of £1, fully paid	800
Reserves at beginning of the year	248
Retained profit for year	60
	1,108
Non-current liabilities	
Borrowings – secured 10% loan notes	700
Current liabilities	
Trade payables (361 + 23)	384
Other payables (117 + 35)	152
Taxation	26
	562
Total equity and liabilities	2,370

Chapter 5

5.1 Accountants' judgement

The quotation probably overstates the case. It is true that choice has been removed in some areas, but there is still plenty of scope for accountants to make choices and to exercise judgement. Many decisions involving the valuation of assets and liabilities and the treatment of unusual items can involve difficult judgements. We have also seen that some accounting standards require judgements to be made (for example, those dealing with inventories and valuation).

Occasionally, accountants have been criticised for not wishing to exercise judgement. The former chair of the IASB, for example, has stated that accountants often prefer further clarification of certain standards from the IASB to that of exercising judgement.

5.2 Information volume

Apart from increases in accounting regulation, financial reports have increased because of:

- increasing demands by influential user groups, such as shareholders and financial analysts, for financial information relating to the company;
- the increasing sophistication of influential user groups, such as financial analysts, to deal with financial information;
- the increasing complexity of business operations requiring greater explanation; and
- increasing recognition of the need for greater accountability towards certain user groups (such as employees and community groups) requiring the need for additional reports, such as environmental reports and social reports.

5.5 I. Ching (Booksellers) plc

Statement of comprehensive income for the year ended 31 May 2018

	£000
Revenue	943
Cost of sales	(460)
Gross profit	483
Distribution expenses	(110)
Administrative expenses	(212)
Other expenses	(25)
Operating profit	136
Finance charges	(40)
Profit before tax	96
Taxation	(24)
Profit for the year	72
Other comprehensive income	
Revaluation of property, plant and equipment	20
Foreign currency translation differences for foreign operations	(15)
Tax on other comprehensive income	(1)
Other comprehensive income for the year, net of tax	4
Total comprehensive income for the year	76

5.6 Manet plc

Statement of changes in equity for the year ended 31 May 2018

	Share capital £m	Share premium £m	Revaluation reserve £m	Translation reserve £m	Retained earnings £m	Total £m
Balance as at 1 June 2017	250	50	120	15	380	815
Changes in equity for the year						
Profit for the year (see Note 1)					160	160
Other comprehensive income for the year (see Note 2)			30	(5)		25
Dividends (see Note 3)	-	-	-	-	(80)	(80)
Balance at 31 May 2018	250	50	150	10	460	920

Notes:
1 Profit for the year is transferred to retained earnings.
2 The effect of each component of comprehensive income on each component of shareholder equity must be shown. The revaluation gain and loss on exchange translation are each transferred to a specific reserve.
3 Dividends have been shown in the statement rather than in the notes. Either approach is acceptable.

5.7 Accounting regulation

The following points might be made concerning accounting regulation and accounting measurement:

For:

- It seems reasonable that companies, particularly given their limited liability, should be required to account to their members and other. Furthermore, rules should prescribe how this should be done – including how particular items should be measured. It also seems sensible that these rules should try to establish some uniformity of practice. Investors could be misled if identical items appeared in the financial statements of two different companies but had been measured in different ways.
- Companies would find it difficult to attract finance, credit and possibly employees, without publishing information about their financial health. An important measure of financial performance is profit, and investors often wish to make judgements concerning relative performance within an industry sector. Without clear benchmarks by which to judge performance, investors may not invest in a company.

Against:

- It may be argued that companies should decide whether or not they can survive and prosper without publishing information about themselves. If they can, so much the better, as, by not doing so, substantial costs can be avoided. If a company needs to provide financial information so as to attract finance and so on, then it should make the decision as to how much information is required and what forms of measurement should be used.
- Not all company managements view matters in the same way. Allowing companies to select their own approaches to financial reporting enables them to reflect their particular personalities. Thus, a conservative management may adopt conservative accounting policies, such as writing off research and development expenditure quickly. A more risk-oriented management, on the other hand, may adopt less conservative accounting policies, such as writing off research and development expenditure over several years. The choices made concerning accounting policies may give investors an insight to the risk attitudes of the management team.

Chapter 6

6.1 Three businesses

A plc operates a supermarket chain. The grocery business is highly competitive and to generate high sales volumes it is usually necessary to accept low operating profit margins. Thus, we can see that the operating profit margin of A plc is the lowest of the three businesses. The inventories' turnover period of supermarket chains also tends to be quite low. They are often very efficient in managing inventories and most supermarket chains have invested heavily in inventories control and logistical systems. The average settlement period for receivables is very low as most sales are for cash. A low inventories turnover period and a low average settlement period for receivables usually mean that the investment in current assets is low. Hence, the current ratio (current assets/current liabilities) is also low.

B plc is the holiday tour operator. We can see that the sales to capital employed ratio is the highest of the three businesses. This is because tour operators do not usually require a large investment of capital: they do not need a large asset base in order to conduct their operations. The inventories turnover period ratio does not apply to B plc. It is a service business that does not hold inventories for resale. We can see that the average settlement period for receivables is low. This may be because customers are invoiced near to the holiday date for any amounts outstanding and must pay before going on holiday. The lack of inventories held and low average settlement period for receivables lead to a very low current ratio.

C plc is the food manufacturing business. We can see that the sales to capital employed ratio is the lowest of the three businesses. This is because manufacturers tend to invest heavily in both current and non-current assets. The inventories turnover period is the highest of the three businesses. Three different kinds of inventories – raw materials, work in progress and finished goods – are held by manufacturers. The average receivables settlement period is also the highest of the three businesses. Manufacturers tend to sell to other businesses rather than to the public and their customers will normally demand credit. At least a one-month credit period for customers is fairly common for manufacturing businesses, although customers may receive a discount for prompt payment. The relatively high investment in inventories and receivables usually results in a high current ratio.

6.2 Amsterdam Ltd and Berlin Ltd

The ratios show that the average settlement period for trade receivables for Amsterdam Ltd is three times that for Berlin Ltd. Berlin Ltd is therefore much quicker in collecting amounts outstanding from customers. However, there is not much difference between the two businesses in the time taken to pay trade payables.

It is interesting to compare the difference in the trade receivables and payables settlement periods for each business. As Amsterdam Ltd allows an average of 63 days' credit to its customers, yet pays suppliers within 50 days, it will require greater investment in working capital than Berlin Ltd, which allows an average of only 21 days to its customers but takes 45 days to pay its suppliers.

Amsterdam Ltd has a much higher gross profit margin than Berlin Ltd. However, the operating profit margin for the two businesses is identical. This suggests that Amsterdam Ltd has much higher overheads (as a percentage of sales revenue) than Berlin Ltd. The average inventories turnover period for Amsterdam Ltd is more than twice that of Berlin Ltd. This may be due to the fact that Amsterdam Ltd maintains a wider range of inventories in an attempt to meet customer requirements. The evidence therefore suggests that Amsterdam Ltd is the one that prides itself on customer service. The higher average settlement period for trade receivables is consistent with a more relaxed attitude to credit collection (thereby maintaining customer goodwill). The high overheads are consistent with incurring the additional costs of satisfying customers' requirements. Amsterdam Ltd's high inventories levels are consistent with maintaining a wide range of inventories, with the aim of satisfying a range of customer needs.

Berlin Ltd has the characteristics of a more price-competitive business. Its gross profit margin is much lower than that of Amsterdam Ltd, that is, a much lower gross profit for each £1 of sales revenue. However, overheads have been kept low, the effect being that the operating profit margin is the same as Amsterdam Ltd's. The low average inventories turnover period and average settlement period for trade receivables are consistent with a business seeking to minimise current asset investment, thereby reducing costs.

6.5 Harridges Ltd
(a)

	Year before last	Last year
ROCE	$\dfrac{310}{1{,}600} = 19.4\%$	$\dfrac{350}{1{,}700} = 20.6\%$
ROSF	$\dfrac{155}{1{,}100} = 14.1\%$	$\dfrac{175}{1{,}200} = 14.6\%$
Gross profit margin	$\dfrac{1{,}040}{2{,}600} = 40\%$	$\dfrac{1{,}150}{3{,}500} = 32.9\%$
Operating profit margin	$\dfrac{310}{2{,}600} = 11.9\%$	$\dfrac{350}{3{,}500} = 10\%$
Current ratio	$\dfrac{735}{400} = 1.8\%$	$\dfrac{660}{485} = 1.4$

	Year before last	Last year
Acid test ratio	$\dfrac{485}{400} = 1.2\%$	$\dfrac{260}{485} = 0.5$
Trade receivables settlement period	$\dfrac{105}{2{,}600} \times 365 = 15$ days	$\dfrac{145}{3{,}500} \times 365 = 15$ days
Trade payables settlement period	$\dfrac{300}{1{,}560^*} \times 365 = 70$ days	$\dfrac{375}{2{,}350^*} \times 365 = 58$ days
Inventories turnover period	$\dfrac{250}{1{,}560} \times 365 = 58$ days	$\dfrac{400}{2{,}350} \times 365 = 62$ days
Gearing ratio	$\dfrac{500}{1{,}600} = 31.3\%$	$\dfrac{500}{1{,}700} = 29.4\%$

* Used because the credit purchases figure is not available.

(b) There has been a considerable decline in the gross profit margin during last year. This fact, combined with the increase in sales revenue by more than one-third, suggests that a price-cutting policy has been adopted in an attempt to stimulate sales. The resulting increase in sales revenue, however, has led to only a small improvement in ROCE and ROSF.

Despite a large cut in the gross profit margin, the operating profit margin has fallen by less than 2 per cent. This suggests that overheads have been tightly controlled during last year. Certainly, overheads have not risen in proportion to sales revenue.

The current ratio has fallen and the acid test ratio has fallen by more than half. Even though liquidity ratios are lower in retailing than in manufacturing, the liquidity of the business should now be a cause for concern. However, this may be a passing problem. The business is investing heavily in non-current assets and is relying on internal funds to finance this growth. When this investment ends, the liquidity position may improve quickly.

The trade receivables period has remained unchanged over the two years, and there has been no significant change in the inventories turnover period during last year. The gearing ratio seems quite low and provides no cause for concern given the profitability of the business.

Overall, the business appears to be financially sound. Although there has been rapid growth during last year, there is no real cause for alarm provided the liquidity of the business can soon be improved. In the absence of information concerning share price, it is not possible to say whether an investment should be made.

Chapter 7

7.1 Strengthening the independence of external auditors

Auditor independence may be strengthened in various ways. They include:

- preventing, or restricting, auditing firms from undertaking non-audit work for a client company;
- rotating external auditors on a regular basis (say, every five or ten years);
- rotating the audit partner responsible for overseeing the audit (rather than the audit firm) on a regular basis;
- requiring peer group assessment (where another audit firm reviews the work that has been done for a client company). This type of assessment may be carried out every three years or so;
- establishing audit committees, which monitor and review the work carried out by the audit firm; and
- preventing an audit firm from undertaking an audit where the audit fee would represent a large proportion (say 10 per cent or more) of the total annual fees generated by the audit firm.

7.2 Non-executive directors

The following criteria may be used to evaluate the performance of a non-executive director:

- willingness to spend time in understanding the business and in acquiring additional skills to improve effectiveness;

- contribution made to board discussions on key issues such as strategy development;
- effectiveness in challenging proposals made by identifying key weaknesses and assumptions;
- independence of mind and ability to resist undue pressure from other directors;
- perseverance in following up unresolved issues and in defending positions taken; and
- ability to work as part of a team, when required, and to establish effective relations with key individuals, including other board members.

This is not an exhaustive list.

7.4 Institutional shareholders

The benefits that may accrue from close ties with institutional shareholders are as follows:

- It provides the board of directors with the opportunity to explain the future direction of the company, which may lead to a better understanding of board proposals and decisions that have been made. This may, in turn, make institutional shareholders more willing to offer support during difficult times.
- It may encourage institutional shareholders to take a long-term view. If the board can provide a clear vision and strategy for the company, the shareholders may become less concerned with any short-term setbacks and become more concerned with achieving long-term goals.
- It can impose an external discipline on the board. The directors will be subjected to considerable scrutiny when meeting institutional shareholders. They will have to justify their decisions and be prepared to answer tough questions. This can, however, improve the quality of decisions made.
- It can provide valuable feedback on board proposals. Institutional investors may be sounded out on particular ideas that are under review. Their views can then be taken into account when making a final decision.
- It can help in future funding. Where institutional shareholders have good relations with the board and have confidence in the future direction of the company, they are more likely to be sympathetic to requests for additional funding.

There are various problems that can arise from close links with institutional shareholders. For example, there is a risk that certain commercially sensitive information provided to them will not be treated in confidence. There is also a risk in upsetting small shareholders, who may feel that large institutional shareholders are given undue influence over decisions. Finally, there is a problem in determining what are the acceptable limits to the discussions and information that is offered.